"This is a marvelous and creative collection of essays designed to honor Michael Casey for his pivotal contributions to monastic thinking in our time. The essays help us to know Michael's thought better in two different ways. Some engage him directly and dialogue with him. Others take their inspiration from themes that he himself has opened up and explored. So many of us are grateful for Michael, and I am grateful for this book which does him honor."

> —Abbot Jeremy Driscoll, OSB
> Mount Angel Abbey

"This book exceeded my expectations. I expected to cherish Michael Casey, but I found this book to quicken my own 'love of learning and desire for God.'"

> —Mary Margaret Funk, OSB

"This volume is a ringing testimony to the return to the sources of Benedictine monasticism stimulated by the renewal of Vatican II, and also to the remarkable contribution to that effort by Australia, which provides over half the authors for this collection. No one will question the expression of gratitude to Michael Casey, who has been at the heart of this movement both worldwide and locally. With these essays readers will be able to catch up on research of recent years and also to share the excitement of new investigations. The book is clear evidence that the renewal in Benedictine studies is far from over."

> —Fr. Jerome Kodell, OSB
> Subiaco Abbey, Arkansas

"Through the years, monastic men and women have been treated to the writings of Father Michael Casey. With an intellectual undercurrent, he has been able to communicate to us some of the important spiritual and pastoral elements of life under the Rule of Saint Benedict in a manner that is consistently inviting, useful, and inspiring. That same spirit pervades the series of articles that rightly honor his contribution to monastic literature these recent decades."

> —Abbot Primate Gregory Polan, OSB
> Sant'Anselmo, Rome

CISTERCIAN STUDIES SERIES: NUMBER TWO HUNDRED SIXTY-NINE

A Not-So-Unexciting Life

Essays on Benedictine History and Spirituality
In Honor of Michael Casey, OCSO

Edited by Carmel Posa, SGS

α

Cistercian Publications
www.cistercianpublications.org

LITURGICAL PRESS
Collegeville, Minnesota
www.litpress.org

A Cistercian Publications title published by Liturgical Press

Cistercian Publications
Editorial Offices
161 Grosvenor Street
Athens, Ohio 54701
www.cistercianpublications.org

1   2   3   4   5   6   7   8   9

Library of Congress Cataloging-in-Publication Data

Names: Casey, Michael, 1942– honouree. | Posa, Carmel, editor.
Title: A not so unexciting life : essays on Benedictine history and
    spirituality in honor of Michael Casey, OCSO / edited by Carmel
    Posa, SGS.
Description: Collegeville, Minnesota : Cistercian Publications, 2017. |
    Series: Cistercian studies series ; number two hundred sixty-nine |
    Includes bibliographical references.
Identifiers: LCCN 2017015326 (print) | LCCN 2017034419 (ebook) | ISBN
    9780879070526 (ebook) | ISBN 9780879072698
Subjects: LCSH: Benedictines—Spiritual life. | Monastic and religious life.
    | Benedict, Saint, Abbot of Monte Cassino. Regula.
Classification: LCC BX3003 (ebook) | LCC BX3003 .N68 2017 (print) |
    DDC 271/.1—dc23
LC record available at https://lccn.loc.gov/2017015326

Contents

Abbreviations

ABR	*American Benedictine Review*
ASOC	*Analecta Sacri Ordinis Cisterciensis*
CCCM	Corpus Christianorum, Continuatio Mediaevalis
CCSL	Corpus Christianorum Series Latina
CF	Cistercian Fathers series
Conf	Cassian's *Conferences*
CS	Cistercian Studies Series
CSEL	Corpus Scriptorum Ecclestiasticorum Latinorum
CSQ	*Cistercian Studies Quarterly*
GCS	*Griechischen Christlichen Schriftsteller*
ICEL	International Commission for English in the Liturgy
MGH	*Monumenta Germaniae Historiae*
PL	Patrologia Latina, ed. J.-P. Migne
RB	Rule of Saint Benedict
RBen	*Revue Bénédictine*
RBS	*Regulae Benedicti Studia*
SBOp	Sancti Bernardi Opera, Editiones Cistercienses, Rome
SCh	Sources Chrêtiennes, Éditiones du Cerf, Paris
SRM	*Scriptores rerum Merovingicarum*
TJ	*Tjurunga: An Australasian Benedictine Review*

Introduction

Michael Casey's book, provocatively titled *An Unexciting Life: Reflections on Benedictine Spirituality*,[1] is a gathering of talks and articles that Michael had published earlier in various journals. In many ways, it represents a broad sweep of Michael's extraordinary contribution to monastic history and spirituality over the past forty or so years. Michael explains the nuance of his use of *unexciting*, employing his inimitable and playful talent as a wordsmith: "Exterior dullness is a condition for inner excitement. To describe this happy state I coined the phrase 'creative monotony.'"[2]

This Festschrift to honor Michael's unstinting service to the Cistercian and Benedictine world in particular, and the Christian community in general, deliberately reverses the title he gave to his volume of collected essays so as to read *A Not-So-Unexciting Life*. As his former abbot notes in the biography to follow, Michael's own life can "hardly be described as 'an unexciting life.'" Indeed, I hope that what is offered here imitates a little of his own passion and depth of scholarship in the areas of monastic history and spirituality so as to excite in the reader the deep "love of learning and desire for God" that marks Michael's own life.

Contributors to this collection, both monastic and non-monastic, span the globe and include Michael's colleagues, those inspired and influenced by his wisdom, and those with whom

[1] Michael Casey, *An Unexciting Life: Reflections on Benedictine Spirituality* (Petersham, MA: St Bede's Publications, 2005).
[2] Casey, *An Unexciting Life*, 14.

he has developed deep personal and professional friendships over many years. The authors were not assigned any specific theme on which to focus, and there was no specific organizational plan for the volume. Nevertheless, many chapters have emerged that voice Michael's method of communicating the fruits of his communal life, his prayer and study—that of "existential hermeneutics"—where experience comes to the fore and profoundly resonates with the reader because, as Michael himself insists, "it is just common sense."[3]

There are also chapters that demonstrate Michael's solid academic adherence to "firsthand contact with the texts of tradition," as well as his careful analysis of context, "watching history bring to the surface elements of the tradition that were partially concealed even from those who were its expositors," and, finally, what he calls the obvious third step in the process: "seeing ourselves as continuators" of tradition, bringing forth the old in order to both understand and help shape the present and the future.[4]

Many of the contributors clearly indicate that Michael's work has influenced their own thinking; they draw from his extensive body of work in formulating their own reflections and deepening their research. Others have taken up his focus on monastic history, while some have chosen to concentrate on their own specialty without there being any apparent connection to Michael's investigations, yet they honor him in their attention to text and context.

Although the resulting structure of the volume was not intended, it falls neatly into four clearly defined areas: the initial chapters take us into the primacy of the Word in monastic spirituality, exploring topics that include *lectio divina*, hospitality, community, and ritual. These chapters have a distinctly experiential focus. In this regard, Benedict's Rule is

---

[3] Casey, *An Unexciting Life*, viii.
[4] Casey, *An Unexciting Life*, viii.

renowned for its overall balanced approach to the spiritual life. Helen Lombard presents this distinctive wisdom through three aspects of work that are discernible in the Rule: the work of seeking God, the work of cenobitic living, and the work of hospitality and service. She challenges the reader to consider this "balanced lifestyle" in terms of its transformative end through her provocative questioning of our deepest desires.

The characteristically monastic practice of reading, *lectio divina*, draws us into a desire to question all aspects of our life and toward the God who draws us ever deeper into mystery. Without questions we live a truly "unexciting life," and the God of mystery eludes us, and we are led into a stagnant humanity incapable of moving beyond ourselves into the inexpressible delight of God. Manuela Scheiba revitalizes this concept of questioning in the practice of *lectio divina*, placing the activity of the questioning reader at the center of the Rule of Saint Benedict and drawing us away from dangerous ideological positions that are likely to stifle the authentic experience of mystery.

Experience of the Word in liturgy and *lectio divina* shapes our monastic lives. Over a lifetime it forms us into words spoken by the Word itself. Both David Barry and Mary Collins draw on their experience of the Word in order to lay bare the profound way in which the Word works at shaping monastic life. David reveals an intimate glimpse into his long monastic journey with the Word. His own "personal statement of understanding" weaves its way through this account of a lifetime of "humbly welcoming the Word." In the context of Generativity, Mary shares her experience of the place ritual plays as monastic communities face difficult journeys into the future, journeys of continuity and of termination.

The second section of the volume pays homage to Michael's achievement in historical study and engagement with the Rule of Saint Benedict, particularly in terms of its relevance to the spiritual life today. In this volume monastic history and spirituality are approached through a broad lens. Brendan Thomas's essay, for instance, takes the lives and writings of Saint Benedict of Nursia and Saint Francis of Assisi in order to lead the reader into a fascinating journey that parallels their characters, motives, and visions with those of Pope Benedict XVI and Pope Francis. It seems that wholeness in our world today can only be achieved through a combination of both approaches to the spiritual life.

Michael's scholarly journey began with his own engagement with the works of Bernard of Clairvaux. His contribution to this field of study, in both translation and commentary, has been outstanding. Bernard's intimate encounter with the love of God in his commentary on the Song of Songs is the focus of Constant Mews's exploration of Bernard's "pursuit of ecstacy" and its influence on Richard of Saint Victor's more systematic approach to this highly experiential spirituality. Constant masterfully draws the reader, not just into the rise of scholastic theology of the time, but also into the dazzling array of sources from which Bernard and Richard drew in order to formulate a language that was capable of speaking about their longing for God.

The role of the abbot in the Rule of Saint Benedict presents a model of leadership that clearly indicates Benedict's own experiential struggle with coming to terms with the humanity of those desiring to travel along the spiritual road. The hard lessons of community living softened Benedict's understanding of leadership considerably from chapter 2 through to his writing of chapter 64 of his little Rule. Elias Dietz's study, which also pays homage to Michael's work on Saint Bernard, takes us back to the beginning of Bernard's life as a young abbot. Here he uncovers a zealous, yet perhaps naïve, Bernard, who also learns the hard lessons of experience as he struggles to understand the meaning of monastic leadership.

The realities that one faces as the leader of a monastic community can be overwhelming and can leave one feeling totally inadequate for the task. These struggles and demands of leadership are beautifully and humbly set forth in Aelred of Rievaulx's *Pastoral Prayer*. Bernardo Bonowitz artfully weaves the model of Benedict himself through Aelred's struggle with his own sense of unworthiness and his deep and abiding love for the community. It is, in the end, an unwavering trust in God's grace and mercy, indeed, trust in the presence of the Holy Spirit, that enables monastic leaders to be sustained in their vocation.

Though the impact of women in monastic history is often downplayed, particularly in textbooks on monastic history, even to this day, Michael has himself explored this field through his study of the mystical writings of Beatrice of Nazareth. Terrence Kardong and Elizabeth Freeman add further to the recovery of women's significance in monastic history. Terrence engages the reader by making a sustained and entertaining argument for the feminine authorship of the seventh-century Rule of Walbert. Elizabeth's study of extant manuscripts of the Rule of Saint Benedict focuses on the medieval English nuns of Wintney Priory, an "unexceptional and poor nunnery." Here she shows the reader a remarkable and continuous desire to engage with the wisdom of feminized versions of Benedict's little Rule, a desire that sustained the tradition of their spiritual and liturgical lives over several centuries.

Ecumenical dialogue continues to be emphasized within the monastic endeavor of the modern world and particularly as it moves into the future. The English church has always held fast to its monastic roots, particularly in its forms of prayer and worship, throughout its long and sometimes turbulent history. Austin Cooper traces this influence throughout the centuries since the Reformation through to the nineteenth-century Romantic movement. He gives a taste of the prayers, poems, hymns, and writings of many English writers from George Herbert to John Henry Newman. This vibrant and continuous tradition led to the development of a unique Anglican spirituality built on the sure foundation of the Benedictine legacy. This tradition remains alive and flourishing in the church today.

One of Michael's enduring legacies to the monastic world is his contribution to understanding the spirituality of the Rule of Saint Benedict. His most recent publications focus on particular chapters of the Rule, drawing from each verse wisdom for living the Christian life deeply even in the most ordinary and mundane of circumstances. Both Katharine Massam and Margaret Malone also engage the study of the Rule of Saint Benedict in their contributions to this volume, yet in very different ways. Katharine uncovers the paradox inherent in Benedict's cloister: a physical and defining space for contemplative encounter, yet also "a liminal boundary" reflecting monastic identity beyond itself with its values of hospitality, reconciliation, and discipleship. Margaret focuses on the monastic spirituality of tranquility of heart as expressed throughout Benedict's Rule. The phrase *aequo animo*—with a quiet mind—aptly sums up this spirituality. In dialogue with the Quaker tradition of stillness, she explores the Rule's pervasive insistence that calming the restless heart is both essential in one who desires encounter with God and also the resultant gift from that encounter.

The third section of the book delves into new directions and the future of monastic life in our changing and often resistant world. The perceived crisis of religious life during our times is only too obvious. Bernhard Eckerstorfer discusses what he terms the "transitory nature of monastic life today." In a challenging overview, he dares us to draw our focus away from the negative aspects of this position, so as to question the "normative status" of the past in relation to our reenvisioning of the future of monastic life with its powerful message of hope for the broken lives of people today.

Columba Stewart offers a fascinating and personal analysis of the study of monasticism through the ages and its profound influence on the developing charism of monasticism. In this postmodern era of uncertainty and individualism, with its correspondingly deep hunger for authenticity and communion, he identifies a unique "monastic moment" whereby the "natural role" of monastics is "as guardians of memory and sustainers of community."

Finally, we are given a glimpse into the eclectic personality of Michael himself. The transcript of Francisco Rafael de Pascual's interview with Michael and Bishop Graeme Rutherford's afterword tribute stamp a more personal note on the Michael we are honoring in this volume.

I am particularly grateful to *The New Norcia Institute for Benedictine Studies*, which has been the context out of which this Festschrift has come to fruition, and for the support and encouragement I have received from Jill O'Brien, SGS, whose advice has been invaluable as I have gathered and edited each chapter. Finally, we are all grateful to Michael Casey, who with his open and direct Australian style and wit has been for many of us a generous spiritual and inspirational wisdom figure, mentor, director, and guide, as well as friend and colleague.

May God lead us all together to everlasting life.

Carmel M. Posa, SGS

Chapter 1

Michael
A Short Biography

David Tomlins, OCSO

Michael Casey is not an uncommon name in Australia. The one being honored by this collection was
born in Ringwood, Melbourne, on June 27, 1942.
A large shopping mall graces the spot today. Michael was the
youngest of the seven children of Richard Casey and Mary
(née McConville). His first published book, *Athirst for God:
Spiritual Desire in Bernard of Clairvaux's Sermons on the Song of
Songs* (1988), was dedicated to his parents. His siblings—Mary,
Patrick, John, Anne, Richard, and Robert (Br. Julian, FMS)—attracted the dedication for a subsequent volume, *Toward God:
The Ancient Wisdom of Western Prayer* (1996).

The Cistercians of Mount St. Joseph Abbey, Roscrea, in
County Tipperary, Ireland, had made a foundation at Tarrawarra, Yarra Glen, Australia, in November 1954. Michael's
mother made early contact with Fr. Cronan Sherry, the first
superior. Subsequently, she received a personal invitation
from him to the blessing of the Abbey church by the legend-
ary Archbishop Daniel Mannix on September 8, 1957. There
was standing room only, and Mary, brandishing her invitation,
contrived to find a seat within close proximity to the archbishop. Michael, probably in short pants (as Fr. Malachy Mara
delighted in portraying his juniors), and his father stood for
the duration. Despite not being very devoutly focused on that

1

occasion, Michael, fresh from school, entered the community a little over two years later on February 2, 1960. At his clothing as a novice, he was given the religious name of Br. Aloysius, successfully reverting to Michael after the Second Vatican Council. He was Solemnly Professed on March 17, 1965. Archbishop (later Cardinal) James Knox ordained him to the priesthood in St. Patrick's Cathedral in Melbourne on June 15, 1968.

Between 1960 and 1968 Michael received his basic philosophy and theology education in the Tarrawarra community. From 1971 to 1973 he was at Katholieke Universiteit te Leuven, Belgium, where he earned both an MA and an STL. He continued with doctoral studies at the Melbourne College of Divinity, 1977–1980. He reworked his thesis on spiritual desire in Saint Bernard's Sermons on the Song of Songs into his first book, referred to above.

Michael has been involved in the formation programs at Tarrawarra in a variety of capacities. He has taught Scripture, philosophy, and monastic studies since 1969. He was appointed both dean of studies and master of the junior professed in 1998, and he held the position of vocation director from 1998 to 2012. In addition, he served the community as prior between 1988 and 2003.

The Australian and New Zealand Benedictine Union, a free association of communities following the Rule of Saint Benedict, was formed in 1970 in response to a general suggestion of the Second Vatican Council. Michael has enriched the Union in many ways. He has been a regular contributor to the Union's journal, *Tjurunga: An Australasian Benedictine Review,* and served as editor between 1996 and 2012. He has lectured extensively in the communities of the Union. Sister Helen Lombard, whom he described in his dedication to her in *Strangers to the City: Reflections on the Beliefs and Values of the Rule of St. Benedict* (2005) as "Sister of the Good Samaritan, and A Lover of the Rule," was midwife to a course on the Rule originally designed, in 1980, for the Sisters of the Good Samaritan of the Order of Saint Benedict. Subsequently, all the communities of the Union took it up, and, decades later, in response to international requests, it appeared as *Introducing Benedict's Rule: A Programme of Formation* (2006).

Like all other Orders and Congregations in the Church, the Cistercians, following Vatican II, had to rewrite their *Constitutions*. After a period of experimentation, this task was undertaken during the 1980s. Michael was recruited to the team and entrusted with this important and delicate work. As Dom Bernard Johnson, OCSO, later explained, "It became increasingly evident that one single person would have to coordinate the valuable work already done and add to it this unity of vision. The Consilium Generale of 1983 decided this person should be Fr. Michael Casey of the Abbey of Tarrawarra. Fr. Michael, with his unlimited talents and energy together with a charm of language (even when translated officially into Latin), became the author of Project III. This text would serve as the working document for the General Chapter of 1984, the Holyoke Chapter."

In May 1983 Michael was with the Order's Law Commission at the monastery of Laval in France for the initial work. In November of the same year he was in Rome writing the document. He was again with the Law Commission in January 1984 at the Abbey of Scourmont, Belgium. In May of that year he attended the Abbots' General Chapter at Holyoke, Massachusetts, in the United States. In April 1985 he similarly participated at the Abbesses' General Chapter at Escorial, Spain, as they worked with the text. Then he was at the joint Chapter of the Abbots and Abbesses in Rome in November 1987 when the two branches of the Order put the finishing touches to the *Constitutions* to be submitted to the Vatican for approval. Pentecost 1990 at last saw their promulgation.

Michael's scholarship has had a strong focus on the Rule of Saint Benedict. He has published a series of pastorally oriented studies on particular texts in the Rule: *The Road to Eternal Life*

(2011), a verse-by-verse commentary on the Prologue; *Seventy-Four Tools for Good Living* (2014), mining chapter 4 of the Rule; *A Guide to Living in the Truth: St. Benedict's Teaching on Humility* (2001), exploring the practical wisdom of chapter 7; *The Art of Winning Souls: Pastoral Care of Novices* (2012), an overview of aspects of monastic formation, obviously connecting with chapter 58. Others treat more thematically of Benedictine beliefs, values, and practices: *An Unexciting Life: Reflections on Benedictine Spirituality* (2005); *Sacred Reading: The Ancient Art of Lectio Divina* (1996); and *Strangers to the City: Reflections on the Beliefs and Values of the Rule of Saint Benedict* (2005). Two deal with the broader monastic tradition of contemplative prayer: *The Ancient Wisdom of Western Prayer* (1996) and *The Undivided Heart: The Western Monastic Approach to Contemplation* (1994).

"Brethren who don't go very far," one translation of the heading for chapter 51 of the Rule, is definitely not descriptive of Michael, whose frequent-flyer points are a source of envy! Equipped with such rich insights into the Rule, he has been much sought after by Cistercians and Benedictines for lecture series and retreats. He has shared the fruits of his labors in over sixty Cistercian and forty Benedictine communities in forty countries on six continents. Both formators and those in formation have called on him to run workshops. These began with inter-congregational programs in Victoria in 1975, and have been mounted regularly for the Asian-Pacific communities of the Cistercian Order and in many other parts of the world; since 2000, he has lectured annually at the Monastic Formators' Programme in Rome and Assisi.

Michael has also had a scholarly focus on the primitive documents of the Cistercian Order and the writings of the authors of the Order's golden age, such as Bernard of Clairvaux, Aelred of Rievaulx, Lutgarde, and Beatrice of Nazareth. On at least three occasions—1983, 1990, and 1998—he has lectured at the International Medieval Congress at Kalamazoo in the

United States, delivering the keynote plenary address in 1990. The ninth centenaries of the birth of Saint Bernard of Clairvaux (1090) and the foundation of "the New Monastery of Citeaux, the Mother of us all" (1098) both resulted in busy, productive years. To celebrate Saint Bernard's birthday, between February and July 1990 Michael did a lecture tour of twenty-three Cistercian monasteries in the Philippines, Korea, Japan, the United States, Canada, France, Scotland, Ireland, England, and Indonesia. In June of that year he had lectured at the International Bernardine Congress in Lyon, France. He was back in Rome in September of that year to deliver a paper at another International Bernardine Congress attended by the members of the general chapters of both the Cistercians of the Strict Observance (OCSO or Trappist) and the Order of Cistercians (OCist).

These few pages give a limited but significant view onto what could hardly be described as an unexciting life. Michael has published in excess of a hundred articles, forewords, booklets, contributions to collective works, and book reviews, in over thirty journals. He has been translated into at least German, Spanish, Dutch, Polish, Korean, and Chinese. He has also been involved over many years with the editorial board of the *Cistercian Studies Quarterly*. The monastic world owes him a huge debt of gratitude. The question poses itself: Does he have time to clean his teeth?

Chapter 2

Benedict's Balanced Lifestyle:
Is This Your Life? [1]

Helen Lombard, SGS

We all have some concept of balance in the form of scales, where two sides with opposing forces are counterbalancing one another. Once when I was talking to an Irish priest he said, "You know the definition of a balanced Irishman? It's a pint of Guinness in each hand!" This is one concept of balance, where you think about getting two opposites equal so that the object is in equilibrium.

I do not think Saint Benedict is concerned about that kind of balance at all. Yet we often act out of that concept. We have to have that perfect balance between community and work, prayer and activity, and so forth, as if it all hangs together because we have opposites counterbalancing one another. What Benedict is actually on about is quite a different concept of balance. It is balance as integration of the whole. An example of this is the ballet dancer. When she is on her toes at that perfect point of balance, all parts of her body are knitting together and her focus is on the whole. She has to deal with the reality of what she has, and what she is, in order to bring all this to some

[1] This is the edited text of a series of talks given at Lourdes Hill Convent, Hawthorne, in Queensland, and Mount St. Benedict Centre, Pennant Hills, New South Wales, in Australia, 1997. Helen died in 2000, so as editor, I have taken the liberty of inserting updated references to some of her quotations. CP

point of balance. All the parts have to be integrated and held together, and all parts are not equal like the two pints of Guinness! They are all different and varied, but somehow they all have to become knitted together. And if one limb is not strong, there is no point in thinking that she will get perfect balance by cutting it off. It has to be accepted and held there in interaction with all the other parts. That is Benedict's concept of balance: all parts integrating to come together into a whole. This sort of balance embraces complexity. To bring things together to a point of simplicity is not achieved by denying complexity.

I think we have to be absolutely real about this. It would be lovely in an ideal life with no tensions and strains and pressures, where things are simple and therefore in balance. We cannot wait for a moment when life is less complex, and in Benedict this is eminently obvious. Monastic life, indeed human life, is a very complex, varied life, and no element can be rejected or suppressed; neither can we pretend that these complexities are not there. Times, seasons, personalities, the pressure of extra work, sickness, a wave of unexpected visitors—all these make life complex, yet it can have a coherence.

So balance is an integration of the whole that embraces complexity and is dynamic. Balance is a continuing project, a continuing challenge, and you never really get it all together perfectly. It is never achieved once and for all. If you look at the ballet dancer, when she is on that point of perfect balance, twirling around, all parts of her body are in some sort of dynamic movement with one another. If one part were not, she would just fall over. Balance is not any sort of static moment. It is dynamic, and you have to continue to work at it to hold it in place.

In this sense of dynamism I thought of another image, that of the surfboard rider. He is on a moving wave, and he cannot wait for the wave to stop to hold his balance. If he gets into calm water, he has lost his whole identity as a surfboard rider. So too, you have to ride the wave of life and adjust your position all the time as you go. In the Rule, Benedict is like a surfboard rider, riding the wave. He is continually adjusting and indicating where you could adjust, aware of the reality of the wave he is riding. And that is how he wants us to live this Benedictine way of life.

Lifestyle

Benedict is not simply concerned with practices that lead to God; he is concerned primarily with a *way of life* that leads to God. The practices and way of life are very different. You could tick off two or three practices like daily *examen*, or half-an-hour's meditation, or other such practices; however, Benedict is not on about this idea. Rather, he is focused on an entire lifestyle, a *conversatio*. As Gregory the Great says, the big issue is that we live life whole,[2] and Benedict is talking about *how* we live life whole. What integration of elements makes life whole? There is a *way* that leads to life, that leads us to see good days (see RB Prol.15). His Rule is wisdom literature that is setting out a map by which we might organize and integrate our life so that it has a quality of wholeness about it. I like to talk about Benedictine balance as involving the integration of three essential elements:

> The first: ***the work of seeking God***
> The second: ***the work of cenobitic living***
> The third: ***the work of hospitality and service***

In a Benedictine life, or a life that draws from Benedictine spirituality, there are lots of other elements, lots of other personal practices, but if we are not working at these three primary elements, then we are not really living a Benedictine life. The work of Benedictine living means working at seeking God, at

---

[2] See Gregory the Great, *On Ezekiel* 1.11.6.

cenobitic living, and at hospitality and service. The wholeness of life involves all these elements working together in a dynamic relationship, as on the wave, although they may not all be necessarily equal. We are not talking about equality; we are talking about a relationship of elements. And I would say to those of us who have professed this way of life that this is the commitment we have taken on. If anyone asks, "What is your work?" we very often immediately give the answer to another question: "What do you do?" The one point I would make is that the three of these elements above are work, and work involving not drudgery but a sense of purpose and a direction of energy. All three have to be worked at. We are professed with energy and commitment into these three areas of life, and into integrating them with one another.

The Work of Seeking God

Joan Chittister once said, "Seeking God is the universal human quest. It is common to all cultures. It is the fundamental human project. . . . It is common to all human beings, necessary to all human endeavor, central to all human effort and ultimate to all human activity."[3] The Benedictine way of life is "a way of life intentionally organized to pursue the human quest for God."[4] For the cenobite everything is incidental to "the life pursuit of mystery among us."[5] Note the words "intentionally organized." What Benedict does achieve in his Rule is an intentional organization of life.

This work of seeking God touches on that deep desire we all feel for life in another dimension. Benedict's opening question taps into this desire: "Which of you desires life and longs to see

---

[3] Joan Chittister, *The Fire in These Ashes: A Spirituality of Contemporary Religious Life* (Leominster, Herefordshire: Gracewing, 2001), 46.

[4] Chittister, *The Fire*, 46.

[5] Chittister, *The Fire*, 46.

good days?" (RB Prol.15). There is life at a richer dimension that is possible for us. I am reminded of an example of a friend of mine who went snorkeling for the first time on Australia's Great Barrier Reef. She said she just could not believe that she had been walking around this earth all this time while just a few centimeters below the surface was this whole other world that she had never seen. I think this richer dimension is not simply about eternal life, out there somewhere when we die. It is about this other dimension of life now. Which of you desires life? Where is the one who is longing for this dimension of life?

In *Night Letters*, Robert Dessaix wrote, "I have known ever since I could know anything that I did not come from where I was."[6] Here is such a simple statement: "I did not come from where I was." For Dessaix, there was something other to be sought, elusive, yet longing to be desired. He talks about a search for what he calls *motherland* and says, "Ahead I sensed there was a journey to some wonderful promised land. Again though, I did not know where it was, but there was something ahead and something before."[7]

That same invitation is in the book of Deuteronomy: *that you may enter the land Yahweh promised you and make it your own* (Deut 8:1). There is a land promised *now*! Enter it; make it your own! I think this is the underlying question of the gospel of the Good Samaritan (Luke 10:25-37). We often look at the answer, but what about the question? "Master, what must I do to gain eternal life?" That, to me, is the fundamental question that comes through the gospel: "What must I do to gain eternal life?" In chapter 72 of his Rule, Benedict replies to this question with "This is the good zeal that leads to eternal life" (RB 72.3).

This question about eternal life drew people to Christ and made them ask, *Master, where do you live?* (John 1:38), and he replied, *Come and see* (John 1:39). For me this text has a

---

[6] Robert Dessaix, *Night Letters: A Novel* (Sydney: Picador, 1999), 91.
[7] Dessaix, *Night Letters*, 91.

slightly richer dimension. I briefly knew Catherine LaCugna, the American theologian who wrote *God for Us*, a work on the Trinity.[8] I attended one of her summer schools; it was there that we *really* met each other. You know how you meet some people, very briefly, and it ends up being a *real* meeting. Catherine died in 1997, aged forty-four. Although she lived a short life, it was a life lived at another dimension. I was really quite moved when I heard of her death, and I wondered why. I had only met her briefly, but it had something to do with the sense of that question, "Master, where do you live?" She lived at a level that really attracted me.

I think we have often experienced this reaction with people, and I think that was the same issue for the apostles with Christ when they asked, "Master, where do you live?" What Benedict asks is, "Which of you desires life and longs to see good days?" The work of seeking God is based on that fundamental desire we all have—where I am now is not where I came from; where I am going is still a mystery—it is a desire to put on the snorkel and explore this other dimension.

Benedict tells us that the answer is only found in Christ and that this experience of Christ is possible now, not just in the future. We need to organize a way of life that makes it possible to enjoy its richness now. This idea is absolutely rooted in Scripture, as is all of Benedict's Rule. We all know Christ's prayer: *Father, this is my prayer, that they may be with me where I am* (John 16:22); the Pauline texts are full of this call to oneness with Christ based firmly in the paschal mystery. For Benedict, Christ is the paschal Christ. He writes in terms of the resurrection's having happened, in terms of that mystery being *the* mystery that opens up to us the possibility of entering into Christ now.

In Paul's letter to the Romans, he asks that just as Christ has been raised, we too might walk in newness of life (Rom 6:4). In

[8] See Catherine Mowry LaCugna, *God for Us: The Trinity and Christian Life* (New York: HarperSanFranscisco, 1991).

our baptism, we have been buried with Christ, we have died like him, so that just as Christ was raised by the Father's power from the dead, we too might live and move in a new kind of existence. And in the letter to the Colossians Paul states, *Your true life now is hidden with Christ in God* (Col 3:3). Therefore we are to seek the things that are above, where Christ is. It is this dimension that is now opened up to us: *Our homeland is now in heaven* (Phil 3:20). So for Benedict, obviously, if you want to live this life to the full, the call is to enter into Christ. It is not a place. It is to enter into the person of Christ, put on Christ, enter into the consciousness of Christ, so that *the mystery that is at work in him may be at work in us* (Col 1:27).

For Benedict this desire, which is fundamental to all human persons, is all very well, but vague longings are not enough. They are the stirrings and the groanings of the Spirit in us, but they are only the beginning point. It is from here that one must start: "Get up, gird yourself, and do something" (see RB Prol.21). "Let us hasten to act now," says Benedict, "that we may enjoy the fruits of this life" (see RB Prol.43-44). The Rule really sets out a way of life—structures and practices—that discipline us and form us so that we put on Christ more and more.

A Buddhist-Christian Intermonastic Dialogue took place at Gethsemani Abbey in 1997. The Dalai Lama was there as part of the Buddhist group. At one of the sharing sessions, he said, "You ask me if I am a monk, if I am truly seeking God. It is the wrong question. Ask me rather, 'What are my structures? What are my practices?'" Now I think a Benedictine way of life geared to the seeking of God is one "intentionally organized to pursue the quest." It is all about intentional organization, and so it provides structures and practices that support the life. Some of these structures and practices are essential, and we do not have to start setting them up ourselves. There can be lots of other aspects to our life, but if these essential elements are not there, we are not really taking Benedict seriously. What are these essential practices and structures?

Living within the Rhythm of the Liturgical Year

Benedictine spirituality is a liturgical spirituality, but it is about more than just celebrating feasts. The liturgy is certainly the structure within which the Rule is written. It shows things as beginning in terms of Lent and Easter (see RB 49 and RB 8, 10, 15, 41, 48); Benedict adjusts them according to Easter, not according to May, June, July, or August; Easter and Lent are key points within the structure of the Rule, as is Sunday (see RB 11, 12, 13, 14, 15, 18, 38, and 48). He defines a rhythm that one can slip into by means of this liturgical life.

For the community and for individuals, the liturgy is the underpinning structure of life, and of course it is the structure of the church's year. The point is that we become what we celebrate. So the liturgical year leads us to experience something, to become something, that is, to be transformed.

The *Constitutions of the Sisters of the Good Samaritan of the Order of St. Benedict* talks about living within the rhythm of the liturgical year, "allowing ourselves to be shaped by the mystery of Christ as it is celebrated in the recurring seasons." This means that Christ's mysteries become our mysteries. We put on Christ, and, on a contemplative level, we enter the consciousness of Christ. What is at work in his life is at work in ours. As Julian of Norwich says, "Let each one feel in herself what is in Christ Jesus."[9] One begins actually to feel as Christ feels, to respond as Christ responds, to act as Christ acts, and so we begin to be Gospel people. We begin to be transformed as we participate in the mysteries.

For a Benedictine this transformation in Christ over a lifetime is the path of contemplation. Contemplation is seeing with the eyes of Christ and feeling with the heart of Christ. Injustice becomes something we have to deal with because

---

[9] Julian of Norwich, *Showings*, Short text, chap. 10, trans. Edmund Colledge and James Walsh (New York: Paulist Press, 1978), 142.

we are feeling as Christ feels, as Julian says. Mary Collins articulates this magnificently when she says, "If we live within this rhythm it becomes a contemplative participation in the mystery of Christ."[10]

The structure is there within the life. Is this your life? Is this rhythm your rhythm of life? How aware are we of the rhythm of the liturgical year? What practices do we take up to really participate? For example, let's look at our celebration of the feast of Pentecost: To what degree do I participate? Am I moved by the readings? Did I go through the texts? Did I think about the prayers at first and second Vespers for the feast? What place did Sunday hold in my celebration of the feast? Did I spend time quietly with the readings of the day? When I celebrated with the community, the parish, or wherever, had I already pondered the word so that when I heard it within the assembly, it really did do something to me? Did it touch me? This structure, to live within the rhythm of the liturgical year, is basic to Benedictine life. Now I want to look at two other practices that are also part of Benedictine life.

The Practice of Lectio Divina

The practice of *lectio divina* is again basic. It is through *lectio divina* that our life is Benedictine. If Benedictine life is anything, it is the life of the book. What is put on your coffin when you die? What is the symbol of your life? What do you most treasure or carry around with you? Someone once asked me, "What will you be remembered for, Helen? Holding a coffee pot or the book, the Bible?"

Benedictine spirituality is a spirituality of the heart, and for the Benedictine, the heart has to be open to be shaped by the Word, to listen to the Word, to be touched by the Word,

---

[10] Mary Collins, *Contemplative Participation:* Sacrosanctum Concilium: *Twenty-Five Years Later* (Collegeville, MN: Liturgical Press, 1990), 83.

to be formed by the Word. *Lectio divina* opens up to us the possibility of participating much more deeply in the rhythm of our liturgical life and so becoming much more part of the mystery we celebrate.

A series of carvings on the north door of the medieval cathedral at Chartres shows a range of human activity—plowing, hunting, sewing, cooking, etc.—and in the middle of it all is a series with a woman seated with a book, depicting the contemplative life.[11] It is as much part of the rhythm of ordinary life as feeding the pigs or peeling the potatoes. There are about six carvings in the series, and I want to use them as a mode of approaching *lectio divina*, our reflective reading.

plate 1

The first in the series (plate 1) is the hardest, and probably the most important. The issue is to be disengaged, to cease other activities. This disengagement is so that one might be engaged at another level; one might open oneself to the possibility of reflective thinking on a deeper level. This is sacred or holy leisure, which is essential to a Benedictine life. Part of work is to ensure that we have leisure: leisure to take up the book and to read and reflect with it. We become disengaged in order that we might really move to a new quality of presence to ourselves and to life. This is very different from the idea of leisure as escapism, which we can also need at times. However, disengagement for *lectio* means to stop, to return to the self.

The first woman in the series has no frown on her face; she has a hint of a smile. The wonderful thing also is that she has a hand on the book. Something is going to help her. She does not have to do it all on her own. There is a way into this contemplation. Augustine's words could have been addressed to the woman as she sat there: "Warned by these writings that I must return to myself, I entered under your guidance the innermost places of my being."[12] There are times in our lives when we hear that admonition to stop and return to ourselves, but with the Word for guidance. The reading goes on: "Late have I loved you, Beauty so ancient and so new, late have I loved you! Lo, you were within, but I outside, seeking there for you, and upon the shapely things you have made I rushed headlong, I, misshapen. You were with me, but I was not with you."[13]

This return to the self is the return to really touching the presence of the Word within. To come to this point of disengagement, you need to come as you are. You do not put on a religious persona. As Augustine says, "See, I do not hide my wounds."[14] So it is a real presence of the real self that one brings to contemplation. Dom John Chapman, in his *Spiritual Letters*, wrote, "Pray as you can, and do not try to pray as you can't."[15] I think of all the images in the Gospel of people coming to Christ: they come as they are. That is the only way into the Word. There is no religiousness that has to be put on, no holy thoughts.

We have now moved into the *lectio* phase, where the woman in the sculptures, first and simply, opens the book (plate 2).

---

[12] Augustine, *The Confessions* 7.10.16, trans. Maria Boulding (New York: New York City Press, 1997), 172.

[13] Augustine, *Confessions* 10.27.38, 262.

[14] Augustine, *Confessions* 10.28.39, 262.

[15] John Chapman, *Spiritual Letters* (London: Burns and Oates, 1935), 109.

This very deliberate opening of the book says everything about the Word of God in Scripture. Second, she reads (plate 3). You can tell by her face that she is engaged in the reading, that she is present to it. She reads, and then she closes the book. She moves into the *meditatio* phase (plate 4). The book is now on her lap. Meditation for Benedict was simply taking the Word of God to the heart, chewing it over, ruminating on it, carrying it, letting the word speak, and asking oneself, "What word strikes me?" This

plate 2

plate 3

plate 4

plate 5

is meditation. It is not my own holy thoughts. It is the word touching my heart and forming me in Christ. In chapter 4 of the Rule, on the tools for good works, Benedict links reading to *meditatio* and *oratio* (prayer). He says, first, that you "listen intently to holy reading"; then the very next tool is that you "give yourself frequently to prayer" (RB 4.55-56). One is linked with the other.

Next, with the book still there, the woman is teaching (plate 5). So action and prayer/contemplation go together. She acts. I would like to suggest another word to describe this action—*operatio*. She becomes operative out of what she has heard. She teaches. I am reminded at this point of the story of Benedict in his cave. Here he thought he would get away from everything, yet all the shepherds came to him and he had to teach. And then he had to go down to the monastery; he could not stay in the cave; he did not end his life up there. The sculptors of the women contemplating on the north door of the Gothic cathedral at Chartres understood this.

In the last sculpture the woman is caught up into God in some way (plate 6—this is a heavily damaged sculpture). This is the *contemplatio*. Now she is simply and really present to the mystery of God. And I assume that she then goes back to peeling the potatoes, doing the farmwork, and all the rest that life demands of her.

During a conference in Melbourne, Australia, on Aboriginal reconciliation in 1997, Sir Ronald Wilson spoke about his report on the Stolen Generation: "I sat, I listened, I was moved and grieved by what I heard, and I was changed; and now I cannot do other than live out of my new convictions."[16] This was the impact of the word on him. "I sat, I listened." He was caught up in compunction, which means the heart is pierced. He did not say that, but he did say he was moved and grieved, which is the same thing. He was changed, and now—this is the action—he cannot do other than live out of his convictions.

plate 6

The practice of *lectio divina* is vital to a Benedictine life. There is a whole integration in all of this. It is not a prayer apart from life, and it is linked intimately to how we enter into that rhythm of the liturgical year.

The Practice of Keeping Vigil

The practice of keeping vigil is part of our *conversatio*. Chapter 8 of the Rule of Saint Benedict, "The Divine Office at Night," comes right after those huge, all-embracing chapters about our interior life. It is the opening of the Liturgical Code. Terrence Kardong comments that this Night Office is based very much

---

[16] Cited in Margaret Malone, "How Women's Experience of Monastic Life Can Speak to Hungers for Community Today," in *One Heart, One Soul: Many Communities*, ed. Mary Forman (Collegeville, MN: St. John's University Press, 2009), 128.

on the early Christian practice of keeping vigil on great feasts. He goes on to say, "It can be said that Vigils is the office most characteristic of monks."[17] People go to Tarrawarra, the Cistercian abbey in Victoria, for retreat, and often the first thing they say to you is, "Yes, I got up every morning at four o'clock for Vigils." The other Offices are common to the whole church— they were said in the cathedrals—but not Vigils.

I'm not going to comment on the Office of Vigils itself, but on what that Office actually symbolizes: our heart's being awake so that we can enter into the mystery, being awake when Christ comes. Why do monastics get up early? To keep watch for the coming of the Lord. Why do we celebrate the Easter Vigil? To keep watch so that we are there and awake for the participation in the mystery, as it says in the psalm: *As those who watch long for dawn, so my heart longs for you, O God* (Ps 130:6). It is something to do with this intent of the heart, an intent unto God, a desire for God. Our heart has to keep vigil, to keep watch, so that we are open for that coming, whenever and however it happens.

In Israel I once saw a wonderful tapestry that was placed before a scroll of the Torah. It had the following words on it: "The heart of man is the lamp before the Lord." The heart of a human person is the lamp before the Lord. So it is the heart that has to be alive, to be alight. And there was also another verse on the scroll: "My spirit within me keeps vigil before thee." So the spirit is to be there, keeping vigil.

This idea of keeping watch is present in the parable of the ten virgins (Matt 25:1-13), and it is very much a part of the celibate life. Vigiling is present in the story of the agony in the garden: Christ says, *Could you not keep watch one hour with me?* (Matt 26:40). It is also there, actively, in the wise and busy steward. Who is the one who is going to be awake when the

---

[17] Terrence Kardong, *Benedict's Rule: A Translation and Commentary* (Collegeville, MN: Liturgical Press, 1996), 169.

Master returns (Mark 13:35)? Who is the one responsible enough to give people their measure of food in due season? It is the one who is awake, who is waiting for the Master's return. And so Christ would say, "Stay awake, keep watch, be alert." All of those admonitions are part of the call to us to keep vigil.

The question is, where do I keep vigil in my life? Where is the space in my life for keeping vigil, for watching, for waiting, for being open? Where am I like the ten virgins? Is my lamp alight? Is my heart alight? We may not be getting up for Office at four o'clock, but what the practice of keeping vigil symbolizes is very much a part of Benedictine life. Why did Benedict put this structure in the Rule? It was not just that he liked rising early in the morning! It symbolized a whole stance. It was part and parcel of *conversatio*.

The Rhythm of the Liturgical Hours

The last structure I want to talk about is the rhythm of the liturgical hours. This structure again is given. It is the most characteristic structure for Benedictines and is simply assumed by them. When Benedict is talking about how the work for the day will be organized, he says that you go out from Prime and do what needs to be done (RB 48.3). He does not even bother to say that first you have to say Prime; that is assumed. You are living within a structure that is already there. And then when he talks about the people on a long journey—they are out, they are busy—nevertheless, he says that you have to stop somewhere in the middle of this activity and celebrate the appropriate liturgical hour (RB 50.3).

For Benedict there are constant adjustments—"as necessity demands"—to live within this liturgical rhythm. The hours do not supply the rhythm. They are a rhythm that fits into the whole rhythm of life itself. The whole of life is to be made holy. This is why the American Benedictines wrote a document in 1976 on their way of life and called it *Of Time Made Holy*. Is the rhythm of the liturgical hours a rhythm in my life? Not just

Morning Prayer, but the other hours as well? Is Evening Prayer there? Compline? The Midday hours? This work of seeking God involves our *conversatio*. It is about structures and practices that reflect the work to which we have committed ourselves, if we are serious about it. There will be other practices that are personal, part of our own makeup, but unless those four basic practices are there, we are not truly opening ourselves to the possibility that Benedict puts before us. In all this, we are left with a real question in our own lives: What are my structures and what are my practices? These will reveal whether I am really working at seeking God.

The Work of Cenobitic Living

The work of cenobitic living is the realization that we have to work at, and that we profess to work at, living together in community. Obviously Benedict has written his Rule for cenobites. These are the people who profess to live together in community, to share the common life. The word *cenobite* comes from the Greek *koinos bios*, meaning common life. The foundational text for this concept is Acts 4:32: *The whole group of believers was united heart and soul. None of them claimed for their own use anything that they had, and everything they had was owned in common.* That "owned in common" is what I am talking about—the common life. Benedict wrote his Rule for the strongest sort of monastics: the cenobites (see RB 1.13). They were different because they chose to live in community. They chose it; they desired to do it. What this is saying at a Gospel level is applicable to whatever for us is the community with which we share a common life—family, partner, friend. To whom am I committed in some way through common life? With whom do I share life in common? Am I really living a common life?

Michael Casey once made the comment that Benedictine life was "uncompromisingly cenobitic," and this is the commitment we undertake over a lifetime. There are different periods of life when we might be living singly, of course, but my concern is about what my commitment is to the whole of life, not three years or some short period living alone. Community is not just a place where we live and touch down. It is something we work at the whole of our life.

I think it is a challenge to acknowledge cenobitic living as a primary work of our life. We could ask, why have we chosen this? We are people who have chosen to live together "under a Rule and a superior." There is a way of life, and a person who leads us and adjusts that way of life, a person who is aware of the situations that are calling for that way of life to be measured out to different people. Placid Spearritt, OSB, a former abbot of New Norcia in Western Australia, was once asked what qualities he needed most as abbot. He said that the qualities were compassion and adaptability, to make the Rule not just lived but livable.

The question is this: Why is cenobitic living so foundational or basic to Benedictine life? Why is it such a good and something we desire? When we take up the Rule, we find that we are described as those who hold nothing dearer than Christ (RB 5.2). Equally we describe ourselves as those who hold nothing dearer than cenobitic living, and the ultimate punishment in the Rule is exclusion from the community.

For Benedict life together in community is not there just as a mutual support society. Rather, it is the primary place where we learn to live the Gospel. It is the privileged place, though not necessarily the most comfortable. It is, first of all, where we become disciples, where we learn discipleship. It is where God most closely and actively shapes us and forms us as Gospel people. So if we avoid the commitments of living with one another in community—the presence this requires, the relationships—if we live together coldly, in community but apart, we are taking ourselves outside this sphere of God's activity. We cannot learn to live the Gospel alone in safe, secure, and splendid isolation, or aside from real engagement with other people. Benedict calls the community "the school for the Lord's service" (RB Prol.45), because it is, first of all, where we learn to live the Gospel, and often in ways we would have neither desired nor imagined possible. I think this can be said also for family life, where one is similarly fashioned and shaped, learning to respond as Christ responds.

For Benedict, the community, the cenobium, is a workshop where we are given tools to use. Chapter 4 of the Rule describes this workshop; here we find that all the tools are Gospel tools. We are meant to be workers who take up the tools of our craft and exercise them within the workshop that is the cenobium. Here we have the tools of the spiritual craft: do not be jealous, do not be habitually quarrelsome; if you have a quarrel, make peace before sundown; do not return evil for evil; do not abandon love; speak the truth, both in your heart and in your mouth, etc. The conclusion of RB 4 is significant: "These, then, are the tools of the spiritual craft. If we have wielded them ceaselessly day and night, and returned them on the Judgment Day, we will receive that reward from the Lord which was promised: *What eye has not seen nor ear heard. . . .* The workshop where we should work hard at all these things is the monastic enclosure [life in the community] and stability in the community" (RB 4.75-78). So the way of life is uncompromisingly cenobitic. Community living is part of my work; it takes time, energy, and commitment, and it is where first of all I learn discipleship.

In chapters 71 and 72, Benedict goes on to talk about the good zeal we should have for all of this work. If you look at the words *zeal* or *zealot*, they refer to someone who burns with enthusiasm—real enthusiasm. Because I understand just what possibility this way of life has for fashioning me into Christ and for enabling me to "put on Christ"—thinking with the mind, and feeling with the heart of Christ, acting with the hands of Christ—how is it possible that I would choose any other way? Have we this passion, this *zeal*, for living in community? Obviously this also has relevance in the married state and for family life.

The Josephite Sisters in Australia once published a book called *Mary MacKillop's Sisters*.[18] The life stories told within the book are not just about why these women chose to come to religious life. They are about why they chose to stay. These are both very significant questions: Why did they choose to make a commitment to one another in community, and why did they choose to continue it? I think Benedict also has something to say to us in relation to these questions. The answer is tied up with the concept of what we mean by mutuality in community.

Chapters 71 and 72 of the Rule have to be read together. RB 71 is headed "That They Obey One Another" and begins, "The blessing of obedience is not only something that every-one ought to show the abbot, but that the brothers should also show one another. They know that they will go to God by this path of obedience" (RB 71.1-2). We need to be mindful that the underlying question coming from our desire for God is, "What must I do to gain eternal life?" And here in chapter 71 of the Rule is the answer: "They go to God by this path of obeying one another." Benedict continues, "Therefore, except for an order of the abbot or the prior appointed by him, which we permit no private command to override, all juniors must obey the seniors with every mark of loving attention" (RB 71.3-4). Ranking in a Benedictine community has first to do with the time the members come into the community. Then, because one is wiser in monastic life than another, that person becomes a senior, a wise elder, from whom a younger one can learn and find a model for his or her behavior. Benedict is thinking of this mutual obedience within a community where some are wiser than others and some are newer than others. Whether you are a priest or non-ordained, it does not matter. A priest could well be junior to an old monk who has been in the monastery for years. Whether you are slave or free does not matter. Of

[18] Anne Henderson, *Mary MacKillop's Sisters: A Life Unveiled* (Sydney: HarperCollins, 1997).

course, this was all contrary to the accepted categorizations in Benedict's society. So when you are in a community, you have some wiser than others, some older, some with different gifts in monastic life, and you practice obedience one to another.

In chapter 72, "Of the Good Zeal That Monks Ought to Have," Benedict goes on to say, "Just as there is an evil and bitter zeal that separates one from God and leads to hell, so too there is a good zeal that separates one from evil and leads to God and eternal life" (RB 72.1-2). And then he follows with the answer for the one who truly seeks life and wants to see good days:

> Thus monks should practice this good zeal with the most fervent love. *Let them strive to be the first to honor one another.* They should bear each other's weaknesses of both body and character with the utmost patience. They must compete with one another in obedience. No one should pursue what he judges advantageous to himself but rather what benefits others. They must show selfless love to one another. Let them fear God out of love. They should love their abbot with sincere and humble charity. Let them prefer absolutely nothing to Christ, and may he lead us all together to life everlasting. (RB 72.3-12)

Living mutually in the Benedictine way of life does not presume equality or perfect reciprocity, yet we often look for this. It is not a mutual support society, where all are equally strong, equally virtuous. In a letter to a nun from Saint Mary of Troyes, Bernard of Clairvaux had a wonderful, pithy answer to her desire to leave the community: "If you are one of the foolish [virgins], the convent [community] is necessary to you; if you are of the wise, you are necessary to the convent [community]."[19]

---

[19] Bernard of Clairvaux, *Letter LII. 2*, retrieved from http://www.ccel.org/ccel/bernard/letters.lvi.html. Accessed July 13, 2016.

Benedictine life is a journey, but a journey that is like a marathon. It is a society with people who are at all stages of this journey. Chapters 71 and 72 are really important in relationship to one another because chapter 71 shows that the cenobium is a discipleship of equals, yet not everyone is equally advanced or at the same place on the road to that discipleship. It is a huge claim that if we love one another in mutuality, we will have the path that will take us to God and eternal life.

Probably one of the favorite images in Benedictine and all monastic literature is the washing of the feet. Christ lived this out in his own cenobitic community of disciples, where he shared the common life (see John 13). These disciples were the ones closest to him, those with whom he lived and traveled day after day, ate and slept on the road, and with them he shared the whole mystery of life and where it was leading, the agony of what might and did happen.

Christ exercised obedience toward the members of his community through washing their feet. He, the most virtuous, was washing the feet of the others, who did not come anywhere near him in virtue. And Peter understood this: he knew there was something special in Christ. To see Christ washing his feet was something he found hard to come to grips with. And Christ, of course, pointed out the lesson: *The one who is greatest must be your servant.* And the consequence of this was, *Just as I have washed your feet, so you must learn to wash one another's feet* (John 13:15).

I think those words open up a huge level of mystery. Benedict also talks about a way of life where we are required to wash one another's feet: "It is love that drives these people to progress toward eternal life" (RB 5.10). As Saint Basil would say, if you do not live in community, "whose feet then will you wash?"[20] Where will you start off on this exercise? A person becomes most Christlike, and is most formed in Christ, in this cenobitic living and in the washing of one another's feet in community, in obeying one another, revering one another, giving way to one another, thinking of the other before one thinks of oneself.

So cenobitic living is the primary place where we work with the tools of the Gospel, where we learn to be Gospel people. It asks different things at different times, and I think we need to be very concrete about this. Where am I at the moment? What community is *my* cenobitic community now? And what does it mean for me really to work at this and give energy to this community? What does it mean to give some priority to it in my life? What does it mean to be present to this community and to allow myself to be really shaped by it in ways I could not have predicted? Living community is real work, real monastic work, real Benedictine work.

Michael Casey talks about the demands of social living. He has said that to live socially with one another is a Benedictine virtue—even to live civilly with one another. Rembert Weakland once said that in the church at large, with all the polarization that is going on, civility is the thing that is most missing. Further to this, Sir William Deane once said in a speech concerning indigenous and nonindigenous relationships, "If we only learn to talk quietly with one another, honestly with one another, openly with one another . . . we will arrive."

To live socially is a primary witness to Benedictine living. Then community does not become just a space I fill, a space where I bed down, a launching pad for good works. Here together we learn to live the Gospel over a lifetime; great stamina is required for it, and a real mutual love and commitment. Benedict says, "Let us with God's help turn to arranging a way of life for that most vigorous kind of monk, the cenobite" (RB 1.13). He does not underestimate that this is going to take real stamina, as it is for those who are most vigorous. Yet in the end we pray, "May he lead us all together to life everlasting" (RB 72.12). We are not going to escape from this community. We are all going to be there when we get to heaven. So we had better do something about it now! The communion of saints stretches across the grave.

Within community, and in the common life that we share, the call is still individual. We often say that we progress with the support of many brethren, but we are called as individuals, not as a community. Benedict addresses us as individuals at the beginning of his Rule: *Where is the one who longs for life?* (RB Prol.15). The baptismal call is an individual call, and all through Scripture we have that calling of individuals. There is a whole sense of calling right through our lives, but why we have been called is a continuing mystery to us.

There are various ways home, and we do not all run the way of God's commandments in the same way. Within community, the support we offer one another is really to accept the individual nature of the journey of the one with whom I live most closely. More than this, as Benedict says, you reverence it, you honor it, and above all you do not try to draw the map for the other person, or to conform that person's journey to your own map. That is the support we need to find within cenobitic living with one another. We are all called, but the journey is very individual, even within that common framework of structures and practices. So we have to allow one another's journeys to take place and to be there steadfastly for one another.

Let me return to Dessaix's *Night Letters*. In the book Dessaix is diagnosed with AIDS and goes to see his partner, Peter. There is a most poignant moment when he tells Peter his news. Peter just sits for a while, and then he says, "I will be there for you, right through it all."[21] This is the quality of support that the

---

[21] Dessaix, *Night Letters*, 11.

individual requires of many brethren within community—"I will be there for you, right through it all." This is the necessary level of our lifetime commitment to one another.

So do we really grasp what the work of cenobitic living is about? Do we give time to it? Do we give effort to it? Do we become Gospel people? What am I hearing through this? What is it saying to me? Is this my life? That was the question we began with.

The Work of Hospitality and Service

The third work of Benedictine life is the work of hospitality and service. In reading the Rule of Saint Benedict we can be surprised that it is so geared to activity. People often think of monastic living as being away from the world, and they go to a monastery to experience peace. I hope one does experience this peace, but Benedictine communities themselves are very different places. The life is geared to activity, but more than that, it is geared to active Gospel living. It is full of activity, of people responding to needs and serving the good of the community. When the Rule talks about all the officials in the monastery, it is mostly about what they do.

The early verses of the Prologue set the tone: "Look, the Lord in his devotion to us shows us the way to life. Therefore, let us belt our waist with the faith that leads to the performance of good works" (RB Prol.20-21). You put your belt on when you are going to do something or when you go out on a journey. Faith leads to doing things, as Benedict says: "Let us set out on his path with the Gospel as our guide" (RB Prol.21). And what is to be the end of all this sort of actively living the Gospel, this way that transforms us into Christ? Benedict tells us, "But as we progress in the monastic life and in faith, our hearts will swell with the unspeakable sweetness of love, enabling us to race along the way of God's commandments" (RB Prol.49).

We are to be more active than ever. In the end we are racing along the way of God's commandments, and this *is* living the Gospel. We do not more or less retire from it and become more advanced in some sort of personal closeness with God that absorbs us. Our ability to become active implementers of the Gospel values, Gospel principles, should increase as we progress in the way of life.

As Benedict shows us, there are always needs to be met within the community, and this applies also to the total world community, church community, and family community. So you have people who do things to help meet those needs: the cellarer, the doorkeeper, those working in the field, those collecting the tools and cleaning them, those giving out the clothing or the money, etc. All these people perform tasks that help meet needs. And there are particular people to be served. There are people who arrive unexpectedly, those to be fed, to be housed and washed, with a roof put over their heads, and the sick with their particular needs. All of these needs have to be responded to within the community, according to the gifts of the individual involved and the assignment of tasks made by the abbot. This is the context within which Benedict understands the work of hospitality and service being carried out. It challenges us all, wherever we live, and certainly within our church.

In chapter 53 of the Rule, "The Reception of Guests," we read, "All guests who arrive should be received as Christ, for he himself will say, *I was a stranger and you took me in.* Proper respect should be shown *to all, especially fellow monks and pilgrims*" (RB 53.1-2). This whole chapter leaves us with questions: Who is receiving whom? Am I receiving Christ in the guest? Am I receiving someone to whom I am going to give a gift, or am I receiving a gift? In verse 14 we read, "God, we have received [*suscepimus*] your mercy." The word used here is related to the *Suscipe*, which is sung at profession, when we pray, "*Receive me,*

Christ, *as you have promised"* (RB 58.21). As Christ has received us, so we receive guests. This is related to the Pauline phrase, *Receive one another as Christ has received you to the honor of God* (Rom 15:7). I do not know if there is any answer to the question "Who is receiving whom?" It is perhaps a mutual reception. There is an exchange of gifts, and this is why we are glad when the guest comes. Christ is visiting us.

Hospitality is not just about guests. It is a dimension of the whole of life, and I would say the same about service, which is absolutely vital to Benedictine life. In talking about service, Benedict says, "Each person is endowed with a special gift" (RB 40.1). This is where you start. There is no hierarchy; each one has a special gift. In the Rule, Benedict talks about the weekly kitchen servers. He starts with such a bald statement: "The brothers should serve one another" (RB 35.1). In one sense, you do not have to go further than that. Benedict continues, "Therefore no one may be excused from this kitchen duty except for illness or occupation with an essential task. For thus is merit increased and love built up" (RB 35.1-2). We serve one another just as Christ does in washing the feet of his disciples. Yet, realistically, Benedict adds, "Let help be provided for the weak so that they do not lose heart. But let all have help according to the size of the community or the circumstances of the place. If the community is rather large the cellarer should be excused from the kitchen. As we have said, those occupied with essential tasks should also be excused. But the others should serve one another in love" (RB 35.3-6).

Further, again in chapter 71 and then chapter 72, Benedict writes that monastics should honor one another and should give way to one another and serve one another in love. It is the "one another" I would like to emphasize. The one should serve the other; each has a special gift of his or her own to give. In the Office of Readings for the feast of the Ascension, we read from Ephesians 4:7-13, which reveals Benedict's source for this precept:

Each one of us has been given a special gift, in proportion to what Christ has given. As the Scripture says, "When he went up to the very heights he took many captives with him; he gave gifts to his people." Now what does "he went up" mean? It means that first he came down—that is, down to the lower depths of the earth. So he who came down is the same one who went up, above and beyond the heavens, to fill the whole universe with his presence. It was he who "gave gifts to his people"; he appointed some to be apostles, others to be prophets, others to be evangelists, others to be pastors and teachers. He did this to prepare all God's people for the work of Christian service, to build up the body of Christ. And so we shall all come together to that oneness in our faith and in our knowledge of the Son of God; we shall become mature, reaching to the very height of Christ's full stature.

Benedict is writing out of this same church. Who is serving whom? It is mutual again. All have gifts; all serve one another so that we make a unity in the work of service.

When we look at this aspect of service, the word *ministry* might have some dangers. At one stage it was argued from Canon Law that the only ministers were ordained ministers such as priests or deacons, or those who had been initiated into some sort of ministry such as acolytes. It is dangerous to get into the mentality of believing that one person has a gift of ministering while another does not, or that some have a lesser gift than ministry. Ministry can have this implication. However, that is not the way ministry in community works for Benedict.

The church environment that was Benedict's is not the same as ours today. It is very difficult to get that sense of mutuality. The person who comes most to mind to me in this regard is Jean Vanier of the L'Arche community. He really lives knowing that he receives as much as he gives, and I think this is an incredible witness to what Benedict is talking about.

Conclusion

In the end this work of hospitality and service is integrated into the whole way of life. In other words, we are back to that idea of intentional organization. How do I really work at those three elements at different periods of my life, in different ways, to make sure that I am being true to Benedict's concept of balance? Is this my life? Have I really seized the possibilities that Benedict offers? At the moment, at what point am I in this work of integrating these three elements—the work of seeking God, the work of cenobitic living, and the work of hospitality and service—into a rich life, a demanding life, sometimes exhilarating, sometimes sheer plod? A life that answers my deepest desires.

Chapter 3

The Exciting Life of Being a Questioner

Manuela Scheiba, OSB

I Need This Book!

During his talk at the Thirty-Seventh Congress on German Language Literature in Klagenfurt, Austria, in July 2013, the Viennese writer and actor Joachim Meyerhoff presented a story about a shoplifter in a bookstore.[1] In the story a detective caught the thief and arrested him. The shoplifter, a young man, cried out, "But I need this book!" The detective, however, continued to hold him down. Yet the shoplifter shouted, tugged, and moaned sorrowfully. Suddenly something incomprehensible happened: the detective dashed the book energetically to the boy's chest, telling him to just take it and go. The young man had to bear the weight of the book smashed against the center of his body, that is to say his heart—as if the book were essentially inscribed on his interior.

During the discussion following Meyerhoff's talk, participants of the literature congress asked themselves whether people today would still steal books. Some people expressed their doubts, suggesting that perhaps thirty years ago things

---

[1] See Joachim Meyerhoff, *Ich brauche das Buch,* Tagen der deutschsprachigen Literatur 2013, archiv.bachmannpreis.orf.at/bachmannpreis .eu/de/texte/4390/index.html, acc. Aug. 4, 2015.

had been different. Back then, a book still contained treasures that one can find everywhere today—broadcast by mass media and on the internet. Is this story of the twenty-two-year-old shoplifter desperate for a book only a chapter in the lost history of humankind and our recorded cultural achievements? What is striking in the story is that the young thief had no sense of guilt! While listening to Meyerhoff's episode, people became witnesses to a young man's unquenchable thirst for life, a thirst that made him become a seeker to the point of even resorting to shoplifting. Obviously the young man did not wish to stay clean and untouched by life's messiness. Along with all the other things that make life possible, he thought that he needed this particular book, and this belief led him to break away from the normal dynamics of life.[2]

And what about us? The Rule of Saint Benedict puts an emphasis on the fact that monastic life is a way of life "with the Gospel for our guide" (RB Prol.21).[3] Moreover, monastic life is pervaded by Sacred Scripture, which is read alone and in community,[4] a book that is made omnipresent in the monastery through reading aloud, listening, meditating, memorizing, practicing, acting it out, and living it. In order to be able to accomplish this, Benedict's Rule also suggests further readings, such as "book[s] of the holy catholic Fathers, the *Conferences* of the Fathers, their *Institutes* and their *Lives* . . . [and] also the Rule of our holy father Basil" (RB 73.4-5).

Following a thought-provoking wordplay (which is difficult to reproduce in English), monastic life is, in a sense, a "refined or select life"—"select" in the sense of the German

[2] See Christoph Schulte, "Fikus und Ferse—der Preis des Lebens," *Christ in der Gegenwart* 65, no. 30 (2013): 331–32.
[3] Unless otherwise noted, the Rule of Saint Benedict is quoted from *RB 1980: The Rule of St. Benedict in Latin and English with Notes*, ed. Timothy Fry (Collegeville, MN: Liturgical Press, 1981).
[4] See for example, RB 8–20; 38; 42; 48–49; 53; 58; 73.

word *erlesen*, with its double and implied meanings. First, it can mean something that is not ordinary but cost-intensive and precious. For example, the adjective *erlesen* is used in the German translation of Isaiah 25:6 in relation to expensive, best, finest aged wines, wines of choice quality. So monastic life is *erlesen* in the sense that it is not an ordinary life; it requires lots of effort, labor, trouble; it costs a lot. Monastic life is precious because it is a gift from God and because its outcome—mature, spiritual people who live in closeness to God, who encourage other Christians, etc.—can also be precious. Second, *erlesen* can mean to gain information and insights through reading. In relation to defining monastic life, the wordplay indicates that authentic monastic life requires reading in order to be continually nourished and deepened. There can be no authentic monastic life without reading. The result of the wordplay in German is that monastic life is like a choice wine or select food, but it also implies reading in order to be deepened, to be continually refined, as in the process of refining sugar.

Do we, whether we are Benedictine monastics or not, still experience a real passion for a book, for reading, for the old and ever new practice of *lectio divina*?[5] And when we read, what is our key motivation? Are we just curious and obedient to what is in vogue, to what advertising campaigns and the bestseller charts plug? Are we simply looking for information, knowledge, or entertainment? Do we try to escape from reality by being immersed in a book? Or are we reading to receive nourishment, edification, and strength in order to approach our life, ourselves, and the people around us as they really are?

---

[5] See the many books and articles by Michael Casey on this topic, e.g., "Seven Principles of *Lectio Divina*," TJ 12 (1976): 69–74; "From the Silence of God to the God of Silence: The Experience of Progress in 'Lectio Divina,'" TJ 43 (1992): 3–24; "The Practice of *Lectio Divina*," CSQ 31 (1996): 459–76; and *Sacred Reading: The Ancient Art of* Lectio Divina (Liguori, MO: Triumph Book, 1995).

Are we reading in the midst of life's fundamental questions, seeking orientation, searching for an answer?

Saint Benedict asks a crucial question at the beginning of his Rule: "Is there anyone here who yearns for life and desires to see good days?" (RB Prol.15, see Ps 33 [34]:13). Today, there are large shelves in bookshops packed with advice and self-help books that promise to help people cope with life's problems and questions. Can we trust all the books we read?

John Cassian, an important inspiration and source of Benedict's Rule, wrote his famous book of the *Conferences* intentionally in a dialogue form to offer spiritual guidance to people in the Latin West who were seeking God.[6] Cassian's idea in writing these *Conferences* was that when there is no spiritual father and guide at hand, a spirit-filled experienced elder can enter the room of those who are asking for advice through the spiritual reading of the *Conferences* themselves. Cassian, who powerfully influenced the medieval monastic and mystical tradition, writes in his preface to *Conferences* 18–24 that he arranged the discourses of the best of the fathers with such care that their teaching would suit people who were living different monastic ways of life. Thus monastics and spiritual seekers of all times who are interested in the wisdom of experienced elders can receive "the very authors of the conferences into their cells, along with the books of the conferences, and as if [they] were speaking with them by way of daily questions and answers, they will not seek out by their own devices the hard and almost unknown path in this region."[7]

---

[6] The twenty-four Conferences are reminiscences of Cassian's interviews with the Desert Fathers—written some twenty years after leaving Egypt. See John Cassian, *Collationes*, Latin text with French trans., *Jean Cassien: Conférences*, ed. Eugène Pichery, 3 vols., SCh 42 *bis*, 54, 64 (Paris; Les Éditions du Cerf, 1955, 1958, 1959); *John Cassian, The Conferences*, trans. Boniface Ramsey (New York: Paulist Press, 1997).

[7] Conf 18. Preface (Ramsey, *John Cassian*, 627).

Father, Tell Me a Word: How Can I Be Saved?

Many anecdotes about the Desert Fathers tell about people seeking God. These people approached one of the ascetic fathers, whom they considered spirit-bearers,[8] with an urgent, existential question: "Say a word for me," or "How can I be saved?" or "Tell me what I must do."[9] Questions that are presented, that grow, that make people stop and repeat them: such questions are a real gift in the life of every human person, of every community, in every society. And the spiritual father often answered with a quotation from Sacred Scripture.

Often children can teach us how we can discover the world and ourselves by the hundreds of questions they ask continuously. They ask insistently, and yet, at the same time, they are patient with regard to the possible answer they may receive. Essentially there is no answer that would truly satisfy a real and valued question. This type of question is far from simply coming from any self-serving motives, or any insensitive, banal curiosity. There are questions in human life that are like a door that must be kept open, a door that invites people to set out for the fullness of life.[10] We should not become frightened in the face of the greatness and the challenge of these types of questions, which forever leave their mark on our lives.

In 1903, the Bohemian-Austrian poet and novelist Rainer Maria Rilke (1875–1926) wrote to a young poet, "Have patience with everything that remains unsolved in your heart. Try to love the questions themselves, like locked rooms and like books written in a foreign language. Do not now look for the answers.

---

[8] See, for example, Tim Vivian, *Saint Macarius, the Spiritbearer: Coptic Texts Relating to Saint Macarius the Great* (Crestwood, NY: St. Vladimir's Seminary Press, 2004).

[9] See Kees Waaijman, *Spirituality: Forms, Foundations, Methods* (Dudley, MA: Peeters, 2002), 269.

[10] See Johanna Domek, *Befreiungen. 24 meditative Fragen der Bibel* (Münsterschwarzach: Vier Türme, 2004), 7–11.

They cannot now be given to you because you could not live them. It is a question of experiencing everything. At present you need to live the question. Perhaps you will gradually, without even noticing it, find yourself experiencing the answer, some distant day."[11] Questions and answers imply contact, an encounter, a relationship, a dialogue. One puts oneself into the questions by the way one asks the question. And one allows oneself to be asked the question also. All this reveals much about a person and his or her ability to live honestly with others and to live sincerely with God.[12]

The Lutheran pastor and protagonist in the Protestant resistance movement against German fascism, Dietrich Bonhoeffer (1906–1945), asked, "Who am I?" in a letter to his friend, Eberhard Bethge. This letter was written only a few months before Bonhoeffer's arrest and imprisonment by the Nazi regime in the concentration camp at Flossenbürg.

> Who am I? They often tell me,
> I step out from my cell,
> composed, contented and sure,
> like a lord from his manor.
>
> Who am I? They often tell me,
> I speak with my jailers,
> frankly, familiar and firm,
> as though I was in command.
>
> Who am I? They also tell me,
> I bear the days of hardship,
> unconcerned, amused and proud,
> like one who usually wins.

[11] Rainer Maria Rilke, *Letters to a Young Poet* (San Rafael, CA: W. W. Norton & Company, 1993), 35.
[12] See Domek, *Befreiungen*, 16.

Am I really what others tell me?
Or am I only what I myself know of me?
Troubled, homesick, ill, like a bird in a cage,
gasping for breath, as though being strangled,
hungering for colours, for flowers, for songs of birds,
thirsting for kind words, for human company,
quivering with anger at despotism and petty insults,
anxiously waiting for great events,
helplessly worrying about friends far away,
empty and tired of praying, of thinking, of working,
exhausted and ready to bid farewell to it all.

Who am I? This or the other?
Am I then, this today and the other tomorrow?
Am I both at the same time? In public, a hypocrite
and by myself, a contemptible, whining weakling?
Or am I to myself, like a beaten army,
flying in disorder from a victory already won?

Who am I? Lonely questions mock me.
Who I really am, you know me, I am yours, O God![13]

The Piety of Thought

Reflecting on technology and education, the German philosopher Martin Heidegger (1889–1976) wrote, "Questioning is the piety of thought."[14] It is impossible to protect ourselves

---

[13] Edwin Robertson, ed., *The Prison Poems of Dietrich Bonhoeffer: A New Translation with Commentary* (Guildford, Surrey, UK: Eagle, 1998), 38.

[14] Martin Heidegger's essay of 1954, "The Question Concerning Technology," closes with the words, "The closer we come to the danger, the more brightly do the ways into the saving power begin to shine and the more questioning we become. For questioning is the piety of thought" (cited in David F. Krell, ed., *Basic Writings: Martin Heidegger: From Being and Time (1927) to The Task of Thinking (1964)* [New York: Harper Collins, 1993], 341). According to Heidegger, questioning is not merely permissible; it is essentially necessary when seeking the truth.

or other people from life as it really is, with its good and bad experiences. We cannot spare ourselves or others from life's difficulties, from experiences of injustice, failure, and sin. We are called, rather, to help each other, even by means of the questions we ask in order to discover the right way to live,[15] the different tasks and challenges involved in this way, and the deepest questions and desires that lie at the heart of every human being.

Generally people are more willing to follow somebody's train of thought when they are asked questions instead of being simply assailed by words.[16] There are key moments in our lives when someone presents us with questions and is confident in our capacity to answer them.[17] The Swedish diplomat, economist, author, and second secretary-general of the United Nations, Dag Hammarskjöld (1905–1961), wrote in his diary, "I don't know Who—or what—put the question, I don't know when it was put. I don't even remember answering. But at some moment I did answer Yes to Someone—or Something— and from that hour I was certain that existence is meaningful and that, therefore, my life, in self-surrender, had a goal."[18]

---

[15] This corresponds to some degree to the famous maieutic method of the ancient Greek philosopher Socrates: a series of questions is asked not only to draw individual answers but also to encourage fundamental insight into the issue at hand. The art of posing such questions can be properly understood as analogous to the work of a midwife (μαια, *maia*). People foster life in this way. See also Domek, *Befreiungen*, 29.

[16] See Domek, *Befreiungen*, 123.

[17] For example, we might remember the ritual for being admitted to the monastic community as it is still—with some modifications—practiced in many monasteries today. The postulant stands, kneels, or prostrates in the chapter room in the midst of the gathered community and is called by the superior with the crucial question, "What do you want?" See also Gotthard Fuchs, "Am Ariadnefaden der Antwort," *Christ in der Gegenwart* 64, no. 50 (2012): 563.

[18] Dag Hammarskjöld, *Markings*, trans. Leif Sjöberg (New York: Ballantine Books, 1964), 205.

When Saint John the apostle went to the tomb where his crucified Lord had been buried, he bent over and looked in, and here he turned into a living question that shouted without words, *What does all this mean?* (see John 20:3-8). The apostle, however, found only a humble answer: strips of linen lying on the ground. Saint John was able to live with such an answer as he allowed himself to be touched by what he saw, and he dared to propose a possible answer. And we? Do we still have questions, or are we already done with everything? Are we willing to bear and to live with unresolved questions?

Lectio Divina and Human Questioning

Lectio divina is a privileged space where monastics and seekers of all times can discover questioning as "the piety of thought." The practice of *lectio divina* is not only an invitation to resist any fashion or ideology. It also challenges us to resist our own fears and our own laziness. Giving in to fear and indolence often results in focusing on merely minor, insignificant, and unessential issues. *Lectio*, however, challenges people to fight their own fears and laziness. Indeed, it challenges them to address their real and essential issues.

A *homo religiosus* must be a reading person—reading, because human literature expresses, not least, the fundamental questions arising from all of humanity. This is especially true with regard to Sacred Scripture, the book of books, the Word of God. In a letter written from prison to his brother-in-law Rüdiger Schleicher, on April 8, 1936, Dietrich Bonhoeffer affirms that one must read the Bible differently from other books, "because in the Bible, there God speaks to us":

> First of all I will confess quite simply—I believe that the Bible alone is the answer to all our questions, and that we need only to ask repeatedly and a little humbly, in order to receive this answer. One cannot simply

read the Bible, like other books. One must be prepared really to enquire of it. Only thus will it reveal itself. Only if we expect from it the ultimate answer, shall we receive it. That is because in the Bible God speaks to us. And one cannot simply think about God in one's own strength, one has to enquire of him. Only if we seek him, will he answer us. Of course it is also possible to read the Bible like any other book, that is to say from the point of view of textual criticism, etc.; there is nothing to be said against that. Only that that is not the method which will reveal to us the heart of the Bible, but only the surface, just as we do not grasp the words of someone we love by taking them to bits, but by simply receiving them, so that for days they go on lingering in our minds, simply because they are the words of a person we love; and just as these words reveal more and more of the person who said them as we go on, like Mary, "pondering them in our heart," so it will be with the words of the Bible. Only if we will venture to enter into the words of the Bible, as though in them this God were speaking to us who loves us and does not will to leave us alon[e] with our questions, only so shall we learn to rejoice in the Bible.[19]

Haven't You Read . . . ?

Sacred Scripture has many scenes featuring readers and their subsequent discussions. They shed light on the significance and the effect of God's word on human life in their own time and also for us today.[20] "Haven't you read . . . ?" This is a frequently asked question by Jesus in the gospel according

---

[19] Eric Metaxas, *Bonhoeffer: Pastor, Martyr, Prophet, Spy; A Righteous Gentile vs. the Third Reich* (Nashville, TN: Thomas Nelson, 2010), 136.

[20] See for what follows Elmar Salmann, "Die Magie des Lesens," *Erbe und Auftrag* 83, no. 2 (2007): 127–36, 128.

to Matthew.[21] It indicates the crucial conflict between Jesus and the Pharisees: the interpretation of the Divine Law. How must one read, receive, expound, and live the normative words of God? What do *we* read in this law? What light does the text of the Scriptures shed on our life today? Reading and existence, that is, reception of the word and the life of every human person, are closely connected in Sacred Scripture as well as in human life in our times. Right at the beginning of his public life and mission, Jesus emerged as a reader of God's word in the synagogue of Nazareth (Luke 4:16-30). The Word himself read the words of the Divine Law. And in this reading, Jesus announced and accepted the law of his own life. By this reading, he recognized and revealed himself and his very own vocation, the meaning of his life.

"Haven't you read?" Reading has consequences. When we read the Scriptures, when we practice *lectio divina*, the chosen text can be transformed into a face that gazes at us, a Lord who captures us. The text we read may turn into a metaphor that makes us understand its message and urges us to apply it and its challenge to our own lives. While we are reading, the text can turn into a kind of spectacle that urges us to take our part in it. In Benedict's Rule, Sacred Scripture is presented as a speaking and acting person.[22] Thus Benedict brings the Word of God before us in terms of a personal address, of something—or, better—*someone* who is alive. Through Sacred Scripture, through the mouth of prophets and apostles, it is God,

[21] See Matt 12:3-5; 19:4; 21:16; 22:31; 24:15; see also Mark 12:10.

[22] With regard to Sacred Scripture, Benedict uses expressions in which Scripture shouts (*clamat*, RB 7.1), says (*dicit/dicens*, RB Prol.8; RB 7.1, 19, 21, 25, 33, 36-37, 38, 41, 45), shows (*ostendat*, RB 7.41), orders (*praecepit*, RB 7.25), exhorts (*hortans*, RB 7.45), indicates (*monstrans*, RB 7.57), arouses (*excitante*, RB Prol.8), etc. See Sigismund Pawlowsky, *Die biblischen Grundlagen der Regula Benedicti* (Vienna: Herder Verlag, 1965), 34–37, 42–43; Michaela Puzicha, *Die Heilige Schrift in der Regel Benedikts, Weisungen der Väter 7* (Beuron: Beuroner Kunstverlag, 2009), 88–89.

it is Christ himself who is addressing and taking hold of us. *Lectio divina* is a vital encounter, and that is why it won't leave us unaffected. As in any real encounter, there is a power that may change our approach to life, to other people, to God, and to ourselves. We probably feel urged to change our way of evaluating things or judging other people. Thus *lectio divina* may have a liberating effect on our life as a whole and on our vision of it and the world in which we live. *Lectio* has the power to regenerate a strength in us that captures us, an energy that enlarges our hearts and encourages us to come out of our shell and to give ourselves joyfully to life.[23]

Questions in Sacred Scripture

In practicing *lectio divina* (reading, meditating on, praying the Bible), we will discover Jesus himself as a human being who asks questions. In an interesting article, Theo Paul points out that in the four gospels together, Jesus asks more than three hundred questions.[24] These questions cover the gamut of human emotions, and Jesus' desperate cry on the cross to God is his last existential question in the gospel according to Mark.

Most of Jesus' questions occur during his instructing colloquia and his disputations with Scribes and Pharisees. In the Sermon on the Mount, Jesus asks seventeen questions, which are mainly of a rhetorical nature. These questions involve the people listening to Jesus in his time, and they also involve us as readers of the Bible now. We feel invited to reflect on the topic of Jesus' teaching from the point of view of our own experience today. Thus these questions press us to take up a position. Moreover, Jesus' questions are often somewhat unmasking, particularly

[23] See RB Prol.48-49; RB 5.16; 2 Cor 9:7; Salmann, *Die Magie*, 132–33.

[24] For what follows in this passage: Theo Paul, "Die Fragen Jesu," *Christ in der Gegenwart* 63, no. 47 (2011): 537–38. Even if we eliminate parallel texts of the Synoptic Gospels, two hundred questions remain.

when Jesus defends the poor and the weak. Let us consider, for example, the case of the healing of the crippled woman on the Sabbath, which is presented in the gospel according to Luke. Jesus addresses the synagogue leader and the people: *You hypocrites!* He continues, *Doesn't each of you on the Sabbath untie your ox or donkey from the stall and lead it out to give it water? Then should not this woman, a daughter of Abraham, whom Satan has kept bound for eighteen long years, be set free on the Sabbath day from what bound her?* (Luke 13:15-16). Here we as readers are challenged to let Jesus' question be addressed to us in our own context.

In the gospel according to Mark, half of Jesus' questions are directed to his disciples. It is a characteristic feature of this gospel that Jesus—more often than in other gospels—turns toward them and other people who are asking for help so that they may be healed, and also addresses them directly. Only after this does he heal them. Mark presents the Lord as someone who is totally present, close, and full of care for people who suffer as they did in his time and continue to do so today. In spite of his power to heal, Jesus seeks first of all a dialogue with the person in front of him. Men and women are healed already when Jesus turns to them, through the attention he pays them and through his caring presence.

Jesus' angry questions show the Lord as one who is touched and wounded by the resistance and hardness of the heart of his disciples as well as that of the Pharisees. We may think of the disputes with the teachers of the law and Pharisees. Consider the following text from Matthew's gospel: *You blind fools! Which is greater: the gold, or the temple that makes the gold sacred? You blind men! Which is greater: the gift, or the altar that makes the gift sacred? You snakes! You brood of vipers! How will you escape being condemned to hell?* (Matt 23:17, 19, 33). This Jesus, a man who is sad, angry, and suffering because of a given situation yet at the same time determined not to give in to these feelings, encourages us so that we also do not give in to the difficulties, problems, or unanswered questions that we face today.

In the gospel according to John, compared to the Synoptic Gospels, Jesus asks very few questions. It contains about fifty questions. In contrast, his insecure and somewhat dull-witted and sluggish listeners, who are often similar to us, ask many more questions.[25]

In the account of Jesus' healing the man born blind we encounter seventeen questions.[26] At the end of this incident, the healed man provides the crucial answer to this question from Jesus: *Do you believe in the Son of Man?* The man born blind replies, *Lord, I believe* (John 9:35, 38). And we? What is our answer when the Lord asks us this question during our *lectio divina*?

The instruction and reasoning of Jesus in John's gospel are developed through the numerous questions of the Jews, the teachers of the Law, and the disciples. In this way, the evangelist lays the foundation and prepares for the drama of the cross. The questions reveal how difficult it is for the people to renounce their own way of thinking and to open themselves to the Spirit and the truth. This openness is also an essential precondition for *lectio divina* in the monastery as well as in a parish or at home.

Reading the Gospel of John, we discover how the Samaritan woman—just by her questions to Jesus and the answers she also gives—is preparing the reader, in a particular way, for the revelation of Jesus' true identity.[27] Is there enough space for God to reveal himself given the way we practice *lectio divina*?

John's gospel contains a meaningful contrast between the theological depth of the Lord's discourses, on the one hand, and, on the other, his very personal questions when he turns to individuals. Some examples are as follows: In the case of the man at the pool of Bethesda: *When Jesus saw him lying there and learned that he had been in this condition for a long time, he asked*

25 See John 1:19-28; 6:22-59; 7:25-52.
26 See John 9:1-41.
27 See John 4:11-15.

him, *"Do you want to get well?"* (John 5:6). With the woman caught in adultery: *Jesus straightened up and asked her, "Woman, where are they? Has no one condemned you?"* (John 8:10). In response to Philip's query about seeing the Father, Jesus answered: *Don't you know me, Philip, even after I have been among you such a long time? Anyone who has seen me has seen the Father. How can you say, "Show us the Father"? Don't you believe that I am in the Father, and that the Father is in me?* (John 14:9-10). And finally, at the empty tomb: *Jesus asked Mary Magdalene, "Woman, why are you crying? Who is it you are looking for?"* (John 20:15). We may also think of the rousing dialogue at the end of this gospel:

> *When they had finished eating, Jesus said to Simon Peter, "Simon son of John, do you love me more than these?"*
>
> *"Yes, Lord,"* he said, *"you know that I love you."*
>
> *Jesus said, "Feed my lambs."*
>
> *Again Jesus said, "Simon son of John, do you love me?"*
>
> *He answered, "Yes, Lord, you know that I love you."*
>
> *Jesus said, "Take care of my sheep."*
>
> *The third time he said to him, "Simon son of John, do you love me?"*
>
> *Peter was hurt because Jesus asked him the third time, "Do you love me?"* He said, *"Lord, you know all things; you know that I love you."*
>
> *Jesus said, "Feed my sheep."* (John 21:15-17)

These questions are addressed to us also. They are the kind of questions that resist any of our efforts to give our answers too quickly or in a superficial way. The questions of the Lord are intended to touch our heart. They don't spare us from compunction.[28] We will succeed in avoiding these questions only up

---

[28] See, for example, Michael Casey, "Spiritual Desire in the Gospel Homilies of St. Gregory the Great," CSQ 16 (1981): 297–314.

to the point that Christ has not really touched us yet, until his caring glance has not changed us in some way. In this regard let us particularly recall the dialogue between Jesus and the rich man: *As Jesus started on his way, a man ran up to him and fell on his knees before him. "Good teacher," he asked, "what must I do to inherit eternal life?" "Why do you call me good?" Jesus answered. "No one is good—except God alone. . . ." Jesus looked at him and loved him. "One thing you lack," he said. "Go, sell everything you have and give to the poor, and you will have treasure in heaven. Then come, follow me"* (Mark 10:17-21).

Questions asked by Jesus himself—even if they sound rough and challenging—are always situated in the context of the great promise of God's saving presence.[29] Essentially, many of Jesus' questions are variations of what he said to Martha: *Jesus said to her, "I am the resurrection and the life. The one who believes in me will live, even though he dies; and whoever lives by believing in me will never die. Do you believe this?"* (John 11:25-26).

The Power of Questions

Your faith healed you (Mark 5:34; 10:52). There is a power, a dynamic that operates in these words. There is something that we experience when we consider the questions of the Lord as if they were questions addressed to us also.

Often the questions of Jesus are not easy to stomach. They confront us with our weakness and our narrowness, with our scepticism and our poor faith. The questions of Jesus addressed to us during *lectio divina* challenge us and help us to recognize that we are men and women who are full of questions. Fol-

---

[29] See, for example, Mark 5:39: *Jesus went into the house of Jairus, the synagogue leader, and said to them, "Why all this commotion and wailing? The child is not dead but asleep"*; and John 2:4: *At the wedding which took place at Cana, Jesus replied, "Woman, why do you involve me? My hour has not yet come."*

lowing the gospel accounts, we are not only enriched by the contents of the discourses of Jesus but also learn a good deal of his rhetoric. We are not only confronted with the challenge of the commandments but also learn mindfulness and openness to the needs, worries, and afflictions of the people we encounter on our way.

To live the practice of *lectio divina* implies posing questions to oneself and being open to the questions asked by others—and *the* Other, who is God. To remain a questioner seems to be a fundamental Christian attitude. It includes critically scrutinizing the ecclesiastical, socio-political, and economic positions and events of our time and simultaneously indicating our readiness to enter into a true dialogue.[30] As persons who dare to ask questions, we actively involve others in a dialogue. We show our interest in the other, and we show how much we care for the other. We listen and let others truly express themselves.

Internalizing and Updating the Questions of Jesus

Benedictine monastics and all people who are familiar with the practice of *lectio divina* need to make Jesus' questions to the people in the gospels their own. We must ask these questions ourselves and so care for our neighbor just as Jesus did. These are the members of our community, family, or parish group, our companions at school and our colleagues at work, and participants in all other encounters that we have. People nourished by *lectio divina* will even learn to ask similar questions of Jesus: "What do you want me to do for you?" "Why do you cry?" etc. Being men and women who ask questions implies the ability to remain open to people from other generations

[30] See, for example, the question of Jesus in Matt 15:3: *Jesus replied to the Pharisees and teachers of the law, "And why do you break the command of God for the sake of your tradition?"*

and other cultural and religious backgrounds.[31] People who practice *lectio divina* feel the need to go exploring and involve others in this activity of caring.[32]

And finally, the questions of Jesus in the gospel will become questions that all readers will ask themselves. Below is a series of these questions from various scriptural texts for use in *lectio divina*:

> Do I want to get well like the invalid lying near the pool called Bethesda? (John 5:6)
>
> Who am I, what is my name—is it perhaps "Legion," like that of the impure spirit that tortured the demon-possessed man in the region of the Gerasenes? Am I unbearable to others? (Mark 5:9)
>
> Do I really believe—as the two blind men did—that Jesus can help me? (Matt 9:28)
>
> Why do I look at the speck of sawdust in my brother's eye and pay no attention to the plank in my own eye? (Matt 7:3) Why am I continuously judging others?
>
> Who do I say Jesus is? (Matt 16:15)
>
> What am I usually arguing about with others on life's road? About who is the greatest among us? (Mark 9:33)
>
> Am I envious because God is generous to others, to the last who will be first? (Matt 20:15-16)
>
> Do I really love Jesus? (John 21:15-17)

Even the cry of Jesus on the cross—*My God, my God, why have you forsaken me?* (John 21:15)—may be part of readers' internalization and actualization of the questions of Jesus in their own lives.

---

[31] See Luke 24:17: Jesus asked the two men on the road to Emmaus, *What are you discussing together as you walk along?*

[32] See Mark 4:30: *Again Jesus said, "What shall we say the kingdom of God is like, or what parable shall we use to describe it?"*

Questions in the Rule of Saint Benedict

Benedict uses rhetorical questions especially in the Rule's Prologue, the Epilogue, and chapter 7. Here he addresses his readers or listeners by *you* or *we* in a very personal way, saying, for example, "Listen carefully, my son" (RB Prol.1), "What, dear brothers, is more delightful?" (RB Prol.19), "brothers, let us listen well" (RB Prol.24), "Brothers, now that we have asked the Lord" (RB Prol.39), "Brothers, divine Scripture calls to us" (RB 7.1), "brothers, if we want to reach the highest summit of humility" (RB 7.5), and "as for us . . . being so slothful" (RB 73.7).[33]

The rhetorical questions in RB 73 are closely connected with Benedict's invitation to listen to God's word in Sacred Scripture, being respectful of its living and concrete explanations given by the patristic and monastic fathers.[34] Benedict asks: "What page, what passage of the inspired books of the Old and New Testaments is not the truest of guides for human life? What book of the holy catholic Fathers does not resoundingly summon us along the true way to reach the Creator?" (RB 73.3-4), and, "Then there are the *Conferences* of the Fathers and their *Institutes* and *Lives*, along with the Rule of our holy father Basil. What else are they for monks who live upright and obedient

[33] Benedict's personal tone in RB 73 led the translators of *RB 1980* to translate RB 73.8 by putting the phrase into an interrogative form that reads, "Are you hastening toward your heavenly home? Then with Christ's help, keep this little rule that we have written for beginners." Terrence Kardong's translation, however, is closer to the original Latin text: "Therefore, if you long to attain the heavenly homeland, with Christ's assistance carry out this modest Rule for beginners that we have sketched out" (Terrence G. Kardong, *Benedict's Rule: A Translation and Commentary* [Collegeville, MN: Liturgical Press, 1996], 603).

[34] The same principle is mentioned in RB 9.8: "Besides the inspired books of the Old and New Testaments, the works read at Vigils should include explanations of Scripture by reputable and orthodox catholic Fathers."

lives but tools of virtue?" (RB 73.5-6).[35] This ardent invitation, which is like a personal legacy at the end of the Rule, has already been present and explicit at its beginning in the Prologue: "What, dear brothers, is more delightful than this voice of the Lord calling to us?" (RB Prol.19).

Through a word or a phrase from the Scriptures it is God himself who is addressing the reader or listener of the Rule, as the Prologue emphasizes:

> Let us get up then, at long last, for the Scriptures rouse us when they say: *It is high time for us to arise from sleep* (Rom 13:11). Let us open our eyes to the light that comes from God, and our ears to the voice from heaven that every day calls out this charge: *If you hear his voice today, do not harden your hearts* (Ps 94 [95]:8). And again: *You that have ears to hear, listen to what the Spirit says to the churches* (Rev 2:7). And what does he say? *Come and listen to me, sons; I will teach you the fear of the Lord* (Ps 33 [34]:12). (RB Prol.8-12)

The invitation in the Prologue continues and culminates in another question: "Seeking his workman in a multitude of people, the Lord calls out to him and lifts his voice again: *Is there anyone here who yearns for life and desires to see good days?* (Ps 33 [34]:13)" (RB Prol.14-15).

Along with other biblical texts, quotations from the psalms are a medium of special importance when addressing and asking questions to the reader or listener of the Rule. For instance, Prologue 23 invites people in the following way: "But let us ask the Lord with the Prophet: *Who will dwell in your tent, Lord; who will find rest upon your holy mountain?* (Ps 14 [15]:1)." Outside the Prologue, in chapter 2, God addresses and admonishes

[35] I am here following the translation by Kardong, as *RB 1980* did not maintain the interrogative form of these verses. See Kardong, *Commentary*, 603.

a superior who is failing in the required twofold teaching, by word and example, with a question quoted from a psalm: *"How is it that you repeat my just commands and mouth my covenant when you hate discipline and toss my words behind you* (Ps 49 [50]:16-17)?" (RB 2.14).

To priests who want to join the monastic community the Rule vividly points out that regardless of their priestly ordination they "have to observe the full discipline of the rule without any mitigation" (RB 60.2-3). Emphasizing the crucial relevance of this basic requirement, the priests are addressed by the question that Jesus asked Judas in the hour of his betrayal: *"Friend, what have you come for* (Matt 26:50)?" (RB 60.3).

After having been seriously reminded that "divine Scripture calls to us, saying, *Whoever exalts himself shall be humbled, and whoever humbles himself shall be exalted* (Luke 14:11; 18:14)" (RB 7.1), a monastic may address God with these words from the psalms: "But what *if my thoughts are not humble? What if I rise up in pride? Then you will refuse me as a mother does a weaned child*" (RB 7.4, referring to Ps 130 [131]:2).[36] Here we can see a clear example of what in our time Pope Benedict XVI explained when he was addressing representatives from the world of culture on September 12, 2008, at the Collège des Bernardins in Paris: "We . . . are brought into conversation with God by the word of God. The God who speaks in the Bible teaches us how to speak with him ourselves. Particularly in the book of Psalms, he gives us the words with which we can address him, with which we can bring our life, with all its high points and low points, into conversation with him, so that life itself thereby becomes a movement towards him."[37] This is also what

---

[36] I am quoting here from Kardong's translation, which is closer to the Latin original than *RB 1980*. See Kardong, *Commentary*, 132.

[37] See http://w2.vatican.va/content/benedict-xvi/en/speeches /2008/september/documents/hf_ben-xvi_spe_20080912_parigi-cultura .html; acc. August 1, 2015.

Saint Benedict offers in his Rule, and, simultaneously, this is the context for the many questions in the Rule.

Particularly in the Prologue and in chapter 7, Benedict involves the reader in a dialogue that takes place between God and himself or herself through verses from the psalms or other biblical books[38] quoted in these texts.[39] Benedict is following the Christocentric interpretation of the Psalter, and of Sacred Scripture in general, which was common in patristic theology and Christology.[40] The Fathers heard the voice of Christ in the psalms.[41] They regarded the psalms as speaking about Christ

---

[38] In RB Prol.37 Saint Benedict addresses the reader not by a verse from the psalms but by words from Saint Paul's letter to the Romans, asking, *Do you not know that the patience of God is leading you to repent?* (Rom 2:4).

[39] See Aquinata Böckmann, "Zum Prolog der Regel Benedikts V. RB Prolog 23-35," *Erbe und Auftrag* 79 (2003): 389–407, here 391, 394; for further reading, see Manuela Scheiba, "The Transforming Power of Sacred Scripture in the Rule of Saint Benedict," ABR 64, no. 4 (2013): 384–403.

[40] See Michaela Puzicha, "Das Buch der Psalmen im Kontext der Benediktusregel," *Bibel und Liturgie* 77, no. 3 (2004): 182–92; Christian Schütz, "Christus—der Herr in der Benediktusregel," *Lebendiges Kloster. Festschrift für Abt Georg Holzherr*, ed. Magnus Löhrer and Markus Steiner (Fribourg: Paulusverlag Freiburg Schweiz, 1997), 125–45.

[41] See for example Michael Fiedrowicz, *Psalmus vox totius Christi. Studien zu Augustins "Enarrationes in Psalmos"* (Freiburg: Herder, 1997), 145–47. With regard to Psalm 33 (34):12-16, quoted in RB Prol.12–18, *RB 1980* points out that this psalm "is understood to mean that Christ is calling out and inviting men. This supposes that the 'Lord' of the psalm is Christ, and that the psalm is prayed to him as God. This view, which is frequent in the RB, is often found in the early Church. . . . This usage derives from the conviction that Christ is the fulfillment of the Old Testament: since the title *Kyrios* is conferred upon him, the *Kyrios* of the Old Testament can be understood as Christ already present. This view was propagated by Origen, in whose exegesis Christ is discovered speaking through the Old Testament under the veil of symbols. His exegesis was particularly influential in monastic circles, where the practice of praying to Christ was very common" (see Fry, *RB 1980*, 159n).

or as addressed to him, or they understood that Christ was *in* them, speaking to them through the words of the psalm.[42]

Lectio Divina as an Alternation between Questions and Answers

A significant number of the questions in the Rule concern an invitation to listen to God's voice, that is, to Christ's voice in Sacred Scripture. A crucial point when practicing *lectio divina* is the discovery of Christ and of ourselves as persons who are essentially questioners. It is important to pose questions while practicing *lectio*, to consent to being asked questions, and to ask God questions through the words presented in the Scriptures in front of us. We are invited into a lively interchange of questions and answers, into a dialogue that is close to the biblical words that we read, and we are thereby nourished by this dialogue. Benedictine monastics, as well as all Christians, are invited to live and breathe in Sacred Scripture, to live the Bible, and to express the internalized biblical words in our own lives.

Experiencing a Book

A few years ago, people who were absorbed in a book while traveling by train were interviewed and asked, "What does a book mean to you and to your life as a whole?"[43] Among the many answers were statements such as, "A book is like a vacation, like an island, like an adventure." We too could ask ourselves from time to time: "What does this or that book mean to me? What is the role of Sacred Scripture in my life? Did any book,

---

[42] See Balthasar Fischer, "Le Christ dans les Psaumes. La devotion aux Psaumes dans l'Église des Martyrs," *La Maison-Dieu* 27 (1951): 86–113; François Vandenbroucke, *Les Psaumes, le Christ et Nous*, 2d ed. (Louvain: Centre Liturgique, Abbaye du Mont César, 1965).

[43] See Albert Schmidt, "Lesen in einem Zug. Streiflichter von unterwegs," *Erbe und Auftrag* 87, no. 3 (2011): 290–92.

did any passage of the Bible leave its mark on me, a wound, anything that really affected and changed my life? Is there any metaphor that might express what *lectio divina* provokes in my life?"

The Austrian-Hungarian writer Franz Kafka (1883–1924) made a remarkable statement in a letter (written on January 27, 1904) to his childhood friend, the art historian Oskar Pollak:

> If the book we are reading does not wake us, as with a fist hammering on our skull, why then do we read it? So that it will make us happy? . . . We should be happy if we had no books, and such books as make us happy we could, if need be, write ourselves. But what we must have are those books that come upon us like ill fortune and distress us deeply, like the death of one we love better than ourselves, like suicide. A book must be an ice-axe to break the sea frozen inside us.[44]

This ardent, provoking statement makes me think how enriching it could be in the life of monastic communities, parish groups, families, etc., if we, the readers, questioners, and God seekers of today, would share from time to time our experiences with books and/or with *lectio divina*.

Still today, books, biblical passages, phrases, or single words operate in the lives of people. Still today, Christians and monastics practicing *lectio divina* can experience what is written in the letter to the Hebrews: *For the Word of God is alive and active. Sharper than any double-edged sword, it penetrates even to dividing soul and spirit, joints and marrow; it judges the thoughts and attitudes of the heart* (Heb 4:12).

---

[44] George Steiner, "To Civilize Our Gentlemen," in *Language and Silence: Essays on Language, Literature and the Inhuman* (New York: Open Road, 1986), 67; "Ich glaube, man sollte überhaupt nur solche Bücher lesen, die einen beißen und stechen. Wenn das Buch, das wir lesen, uns nicht mit einem Faustschlag auf den Schädel weckt, wozu lesen wir dann das Buch? . . . Ein Buch muß die Axt sein für das gefrorene Meer in uns," in *Franz Kafka: Briefe 1902–1924*, ed. Max Brod (Frankfurt am Main: Fischer Taschenbuch Verlag, 1958), 27–28.

Conclusion

For many people, the word *God* is a kind of exclamation mark, a definitive answer to any question. Essentially, this simplistic and truncated conception might be—perhaps unconsciously—an attempt to choke the probing questions of human life in general: the continuing search for God.[45] A sincere, authentic practice of *lectio divina*, however, leads the reader to the mysterious experience that confirms that any "god of answers" consistently, and in an indomitable way, gives rise to another "god of questions." Literature, and in particular Sacred Scripture, is part of the great pharmacy for humanity. Anybody who enters into the text has questions.[46] A true question is a space where God dwells. Christians, monastics, and spiritual seekers of all times and places should be prayerful when entering these sacred, mysterious spaces, which are overwhelming and indefinable. These spaces are lacking definitions, terms, words. True, essential, and existential questions cannot be put into linguistic forms that people can leave behind and forget after having been given an answer. There are questions in human life that should not be damaged by any answer. The point is not to overcome our questions and make them disappear by our own responses. Questions are more than vehicles used in order to arrive as quickly as possible at an answer or a solution. We should, rather, remain and dwell in our questions, embracing them and bearing with them. These questions should be allowed to act in our life, in the "workshop," where we are to operate "the tools of the spiritual craft" (RB 4.78, 75), be that inside or outside a monastic lifestyle, as well as in the "interior workshop," where our thoughts rise.

As long as we live in this world, we will face the truth that God dwells in the question and not merely in the answer. We should be thankful during our time of *lectio divina* that there

---

[45] See Gottfried Bachl, *Gott bewegt* (Würzburg: Echter, 2012), 21.
[46] See Schulte, "Fikus," 331–32.

still remains a reality that is worth questioning, that is worth time and effort, and for which it is perhaps worth maintaining a kind of "intellectual siege" of our own.[47] Any true literary *opus* never claims fully to explain either our existence or the world as a whole. However, reading a good book helps us to express our questions, to set signposts for ourselves and others. It encourages us to open up new paths on our way through this world. The spiritual practice of *lectio divina* will lead us sometimes to stand on the edge of an abyss and at other times to reach marvelous vantage points. There are ups and downs in our spiritual life, as there are in human life in general. Is *lectio divina* supposed to offer a consolation at all costs?[48] At times the reader will in fact get into the rain of interrogation marks.[49] It can be profitable, however, to stay in that rain, remembering the cleansing and enlightening waters of baptism,[50] and allow oneself to feel torn away, beyond ourselves and toward that which is unquestionable—where our questions will become silent in the face of the answer—God's very self.[51]

---

[47] See Bachl, *Gott bewegt*, 22.

[48] See Schulte, "Fikus," 331–32.

[49] See Bachl, *Gott bewegt*, 27.

[50] For the baptismal background of RB see, e.g., Pedro Max Alexander, "Le rinunzie battesimali nella 'Regula Benedicti,'" in *Santificazione nelle tradizioni Benedettina e Metodista: Testi di una conferenza ecumenica mondiale*, ed. Cavazzutti Rossi, Libri Gabrielli (Febe: Negarine, 1998), 191–214; Fernando Rivas, "Aspectos bautismales de la Regla Benedictina," *Cuadernos Monásticos* 30 (1995): 492–511; Michaela Puzicha, "Leitworte altkirchlicher Taufspiritualität im Prolog der Benediktusregel," *Monastische Informationen* 98 (1998): 19–24.

[51] This seems to be what Benedict's Rule is promising with the invitation "Let us set out on this way, with the Gospel for our guide, that we may deserve to see him *who has called us to his kingdom*" (RB Prol.21).

Chapter 4

Welcoming the Word—
Then and Now

David Barry, OSB

Goal of Cenobitic Monastic Life

Called by you, our Father,
    following the example of your Son made man,
    inspired and directed and indwelt by your Spirit,
we monks seek to help one another
to create,
to preserve,
or to restore—by prayer (liturgical and personal, active and
        contemplative)—
a climate, an atmosphere, an ambience
of interior and exterior peace and openness
in which your WORD may be heard, listened to, relished,
        ruminated on, celebrated,
    meditated, enjoyed, digested, "belched forth," kept in
        one's heart and pondered
    reverently, received, conceived, perceived as living
        and effective,
        sharp, penetrating and dividing soul and spirit,
        judging the thoughts and affections of the heart,
        condemning, acquitting,

fathomed and plumbed and found too deep for thought
 and word,
returned to daily and started from afresh—
 your WORD in all its manifestations and expressions—
in the created universe, in your providential guidance
 of history,
 especially that of your people,
in Sacred Scripture, in tradition, in persons and events
 and relationships,
especially those proper to each one of us,
and *above all in Jesus our Lord*, and all that is his—his life,
 work, teaching, suffering,
death and resurrection, body and blood, Spirit given,
 church—
bearing fruit in hearts and lives continually transformed
in the likeness of our Creator, our Redeemer, our Sanctifying
 Lover.

This personal "statement of understanding" of the goal of
the cenobitic monastic life was formulated during a twenty-
five-day *Heart of Life Institute* lived at the Redemptorist Monastery in North Perth, Western Australia (WA), which began
a few days before New Year 1982. The *Institute* consisted of a
quiet, reflective lead-in day, a fifteen-day silent directed retreat,
then a rest day followed by a seven-day workshop reflecting
on the retreat and a final debriefing day. I made the retreat
with over thirty others, mainly women religious and a few
men religious, both priests and brothers, in the lead-up to my
silver jubilee of monastic profession on March 12, 1982.

   The team of directors was led by Fr. Frank Andersen, MSC,
a gifted musician and composer of contemporary hymns and
Scripture songs. The team consisted of another Missionary of
the Sacred Heart priest, a Christian brother, and two women
religious, one a Dominican sister and the other a Marist sister,
all of them experienced spiritual directors. The carefully

thought-out package came out of a spirituality program that included formation in spiritual direction developed by the MSCs at their *Heart of Life Institute* in Melbourne, Victoria; this was the first time that it had been presented in Western Australia.

After a quiet introductory day that involved a good deal of rest (the retreat was being made by many who might otherwise have been enjoying a couple of weeks' annual holiday after a busy year of service in schools, hospitals, aged-care homes, or parishes), of prayer for the Lord's blessing on directors and retreatants, and of allocation of the latter to one or another director after preferences had been canvassed, the retreat began. It was my first experience of a directed retreat, and I had requested the Dominican sister as my director-cum-prayer companion.

On the first evening a Scripture reading from Hosea 6:3 was suggested for all the retreatants in a general session. The approach was heavily and refreshingly scriptural. The only books we were encouraged to read were the Breviary and the Bible. As is normal with directed retreats, the director did a lot of listening and the directee most of the speaking. At the initial interview on the first day, further Scripture readings were suggested for the time between then and the following day's interview, and that was the procedure adopted for each day. Every day culminated in a specially and carefully prepared celebration of the Eucharist. Either the first reading or the gospel reading was dramatized, the homily or commentary was well crafted and well delivered, and the weekday celebrations lasted the best part of an hour, with periods of silence for quiet, reflective prayer and much prayerful singing. A very prayerful Second Rite of Reconciliation was held one evening after the evening meal, and the communal foot-washing on one of the last nights was a deeply moving experience for all of us retreatants. By that stage a rest day was very much appreciated and enjoyed, most of us going together to the coastal resort of Yanchep for a picnic day. There followed seven days of retreatlike workshopping of the retreat experience itself in the groups formed by those having the same director.

It was on day five of the retreat that my spiritual director, Sr. Diana Woods, OP, suggested that I write my own psalm, along the lines of Ps 88 (89), after having first prayed over that psalm and the second Servant Song (Isa 49:1-6). Vocation is a strong theme of both readings. After pondering them for some time and writing the suggested psalm, I felt inspired to write the "statement of understanding" placed at the beginning of this essay, which is the basis of the title of this chapter: "Welcoming the Word—Then and Now."

Rereading the above statement after more than thirty years prompts me to reflect on some of the more significant instances of "welcoming the Word" in my childhood, adolescence, teen years, and monastic life that preceded its writing and that have occurred since. My hope in adopting this approach is that it may serve to prompt fellow monastics and believers to recall their own significant encounters with the Word and nudge them in the direction of a renewed response in hope, faith, and love.

Apart from the first six months of 1941, my primary schooling took place as a boarder in a country boarding-plus-day school conducted by the Lochinvar Sisters of St. Joseph at Aberdeen, New South Wales (NSW). The sisters encouraged boys and girls to think about a vocation to the priesthood or religious life. We were kept supplied with vocational literature from several orders and congregations. At the age of ten, I was strongly attracted to the Missionaries of the Sacred Heart and eager to transfer to their Apostolic School at Douglas Park, NSW. My mother thought I was a trifle young. By the time I was twelve, I was fairly sure I wanted to be a Benedictine, even though I had not met a Benedictine monk, and the only monastery of theirs in Australia at that time was in faraway Western Australia, on the other side of the continent. Some of the reading that fostered this attraction were two books of

Fr. M. Raymond, OCSO: *Three Religious Rebels: The Forefathers of the Trappists (The Saga of Cîteaux: First Epoch)* and *The Family That Overtook Christ: The Saga of Cîteaux; Second Epoch.*[1] Two of Mary Fabyan Windeatt's 1940s series of juvenile hagiography that struck many chords in me were *Lad of Lima: The Story of Blessed Martin de Porres* and *Hero of the Hills: The Story of St Benedict.*[2] In hindsight I can recognize this reading as one of the ways in which the seeds of a monastic vocation were being sown and watered in me. However, there were obstacles and hurdles, both interior and exterior, to negotiate.

When it came time for secondary (or high) school, I was again a full-time boarder at St. Joseph's College, Hunters Hill, in Sydney, an all-boys boarders' school conducted by the Marist brothers. Adolescence was working its changes, and by the time I was fourteen, I found the idea of becoming a monk less attractive. The school retreat for all of us boarders was held during the Easter Triduum, and in my second or third year it was another book of Fr. M. Raymond, OCSO, *The Man Who Got Even with God—The Life of an American Trappist*, that kept alive the flickering flame of a monastic vocation.[3] I suppose I could identify with some of the spiritual struggles that John Hanning Green went through before and after joining the Trappists of Gethsemani Abbey, Kentucky, USA. Without being fully aware or able to articulate the experience, I could see some of Green's struggles exemplified in a few of the nearly thirty Marist brothers on the staff at the college, men who did

---

[1] M. Raymond, *Three Religious Rebels: Forefathers of the Trappists (The Saga of Cîteaux: First Epoch)* (New York: P. J. Kenedy, 1944), and *The Family That Overtook Christ: The Saga of Cîteaux: Second Epoch* (Dublin: Clonmore and Reynolds, 1944).

[2] Mary Fabyan Windeatt, *Lad of Lima: The Story of Blessed Martin de Porres* (New York: Sheed and Ward, 1942); and *Hero of the Hills: The Story of St. Benedict* (New York: Sheed and Ward, 1943).

[3] M. Raymond, *The Man Who Got Even with God—The Life of an American Trappist* (Dublin: Clonmore and Reynolds, 1946).

not seem happy in their religious vocation. I witnessed, along with our whole division of over a hundred boys, one very distressing display of uncontrolled anger and physical abuse by a fully grown man of a boy of thirteen, which left me deeply shocked, saddened, puzzled, and angry. On the other hand, I also saw daily examples of great generosity and dedication among the brothers that helped to counterbalance the negative effects of that instance of abuse.

Among the dreams I had in adolescence was that of joining the Royal Australian Navy as a cadet-midshipman at the age of fifteen. Partly because of color blindness, I failed the entrance medical examination. A few months later I left school, before the end of the first term of my fourth year of the five-year high school course, not because I had to, but because I wanted to and was allowed to. I regretted the decision within a week but was too proud to admit to what seemed like a huge mistake. I enjoyed and endured two years as an apprentice bricklayer, during which time I regularly attended Sunday Mass, but I squandered a good portion of my leisure time in less-than-edifying reading. In the next two years (May 1953 to March 1955), I was employed on a million-acre cattle station in the remote north of Western Australia, about as far away from home as I could get without actually leaving the country. Sunday Mass attendance was out of the question, the nearest town being over a hundred miles away, and (given the rudimentary roads in the Kimberley at that time) several hours away by any motor vehicle.[4]

I had with me Fr. Stedman's *My Sunday Missal*, and I would sometimes go off by myself on a Sunday and walk along the dry riverbed below the homestead, reading the Mass texts for the day and some of the devotional prayers in the *Missal*. I became increasingly unhappy with myself, with my life, with

[4] "The Kimberley" is the regional name for the far northern region of Western Australia.

my lack of purpose; the dormant desire at least to attempt the monastic life resurfaced.

Early in 1955, I summoned all my courage and wrote to the only Benedictine monastery I knew of in Australia, that is, New Norcia.[5] As I was living and working in the far north of Western Australia, and some of the station workers were from the south of Western Australia, I became familiar with the name Subiaco, a suburb of Perth. I knew from my school study of church history that Subiaco was associated with Saint Benedict, and not having the resources to make sure of the monastery's address, I wrote to the Rev. Father Superior, New Norcia Monastery, Subiaco, WA. What was then the PMG (Postmaster General's Department, now Australia Post) delivered the letter to the right place, and an answer was sent to me at my father's address in Maitland, NSW.

When eventually I received the anxiously awaited letter, with its "you may come and try your vocation here" response, I gave a fortnight's notice and prepared to return to Maitland to say good-bye to family and friends before leaving for New Norcia. In that fortnight, the biggest flood in Maitland's history occurred, early in March 1955. I arrived home via Alice Springs, where I had spent two days waiting for the Darwin-Adelaide plane, and a night in Adelaide before taking a flight coming from Perth en route to Sydney that was landing in Adelaide to refuel. It was still in the days of pre-jet travel, and flying was still not all that common.

Once back in a devastated Maitland, I spent several weeks helping to get our house back into livable shape (it had been half-submerged in over eight feet of water). Maitland's Pro-Cathedral had had four feet of water, but it was back in service for Holy Week. For the first time I attended the Offices of Tenebrae on Wednesday evening for Holy Thursday and Thursday

---

[5] New Norcia is located about eighty miles north of Perth.

evening for Good Friday, little realizing that that year was the last for the unrevised form of the liturgy, which included a feature much loved by schoolboys when they were required to attend Tenebrae: the *fragor et strepitus*, "a crashing and loud noise" after the concluding prayer of the Office. I cannot say that there was anything memorable as a spiritual experience in my attendance at Tenebrae that year.

But there certainly was in the weeklong parish mission given by the Redemptorists a few weeks after Easter. It provided a strong moment of awareness of the shabbiness of my inner state and the resistance to God's call that I was capable of, and yet there was a deep desire for things to be otherwise, and a first movement in the direction of the lifelong conversion process I came to recognize as part of my Christian and then monastic vocation. Without then being able to grasp what was going on, it seems to me now that the Word was being welcomed and resisted from day to day, from moment to moment. I was keen to leave behind all compromise and enter the monastery, where I would have the example and support of men who were fully dedicated to God. Meantime, once able to move back into our house, I got a job as a navvy on the railways at Maitland, where the flood had done significant damage to the extensive rail system and workers were in demand. After several weeks of unpaid employment, I needed to top up my dwindling funds as I waited to receive the final go-ahead from New Norcia.

Leaving for New Norcia, June 24, 1955: with me were Frank Sheed's translation of *The Confessions of Saint Augustine*,[6] purchased at a general bookseller's in Sydney; from the same bookseller a non-Catholic edition of *The Imitation of Christ*, which did not have book 4, *About the Blessed Sacrament*; and the 1954 edition of the *Saint Andrew Daily Missal*, which I had bought from the religious bookstall at the Pro-Cathedral during

---

[6] *The Confessions of Saint Augustine*, trans. Frank J. Sheed (London: Sheed and Ward, 1942).

the parish mission the previous month. On my way to New Norcia, when I was about to board the *Duntroon*, an interstate coastal passenger ship, and depart Sydney for Fremantle in Western Australia, my brother Jim gave me a copy of *Waters of Silence (Waters of Siloe)* by Thomas Merton, OCSO.[7] Merton was quite unknown to me at the time. In the slightly less than two days of sea travel between Sydney and Melbourne, I devoured the Merton book and learned for the first time that the Cistercians had indeed arrived in Australia and were newly settled at Tarrawarra, Yarra Glen, which is not that far from Melbourne. For a few hours I was strongly tempted to abandon my West Australian plans and head off to knock on the door at Tarrawarra seeking admission but then thought better of it. I would probably have lasted a few weeks at the most in what was their then austere monastic regimen.

In New Norcia: Reading Dom Columba Marmion's *Christ the Ideal of the Monk* was my first in-depth exposure to the person, life, and teaching of Christ himself and to the riches of a theological and devotional reading of Scripture by way of *lectio divina*. Not that we then used the term *lectio divina* or practiced it as a "method"—that had to wait until the renewal of all aspects of the church's life, including monastic life, promoted by Vatican Council II! What we had was "spiritual reading" and, initially, Jesuit-style meditation. As a postulant I joined the monastery's five novices for their daily half-hour meditation in the oratory at five o'clock after a period of manual work; the book in use was *Practical Meditations for Every Day in the Year on the Life of Our Lord Jesus Christ: Chiefly for the Use of Religious.*[8] The book being read for the ten minutes of

---

[7] Thomas Merton, *The Waters of Silence* (London: Hollis and Carter, 1950).

[8] *Practical Meditations for Every Day in the Year on the Life of Our Lord Jesus Christ: Chiefly for the Use of Religious,* by a Father of the Society of Jesus (London: Burns, Oates, 1868).

community pre-Compline reading in the monastery oratory, where we celebrated all the daily Offices and weekday Conventual Mass, was Alfonso Rodriguez's *On Christian Perfection.*[9] This last work, incidentally, gave me my first exposure to the lives and sayings of the Desert Fathers, some of which, being still a teenager, I found uproariously funny—*gravitas* was a word I had not yet met.

In my six months as a postulant I attended some of the novitiate classes and also diligently (and to my secret delight) resumed the study of Latin (I had not looked at it since leaving school at fifteen), taking two classes each day, one with Bell's *Latin Grammar*, the other working on the hymns and other texts from the *Breviarium Monasticum*. Toward the end of that time, it was thought by the monastic superiors that I might benefit from joining the clerics (junior monks studying for the priesthood) for a fortnight's holiday before entering the novitiate several weeks later at the end of February 1956. At Dongara, a coastal town forty miles south of Geraldton and some 190 miles northwest of New Norcia, the community had a holiday house. It was patronized for a fortnight at a time, in turn, by the Benedictine Missionary Sisters of New Norcia, the junior monks and lay brothers, some senior monks, the diocesan priests of the Abbey Nullius (for a week), the Aboriginal girls of St. Joseph's Hostel, and then the Aboriginal boys of St. Mary's Hostel from New Norcia.

So it was that while on my first holiday at Dongara in early January 1956 I had one of those mind- and heart-expanding experiences of "welcoming the Word." I knew from my reading of Abbot Marmion, and from his life by Dom Raymond Thibaut,[10] how important in his life of prayer and work were the writings of Saint Paul. Monsignor Ronald Knox's new English

---

[9] Alfonso Rodriguez, *Christian Perfection* (New York: P. O'Shea, 1878).
[10] Raymond Thibaut, *Abbot Columba Marmion: A Master of the Spiritual Life, 1858–1923* (London: Sands, 1942).

translation was in use for our refectory reading at the time, and I had with me the Knox version of the New Testament. Television had not arrived in Western Australia, and access to radio transmission was subject to many kinds of interference, so apart from playing billiards, snooker, or cards, there was little other than reading to occupy the evening leisure time before retiring. On one of those sultry January nights in that part of Western Australia, when it was a struggle to read and, at the same time, keep the numerous insects out of the room and away from the forty-watt lamp powered by our own thirty-two-volt generator (it was some years before we joined the town power supply and later the state electricity grid), I began reading the Letter to the Ephesians.

And for the first time, on reading the first chapter, I seemed to get an insight into what Dom Marmion was on about, with his teaching on the divine plan of salvation centered on Christ, our adoption as God's children, our predestination to holiness through love, and the revelation of the mystery of God's purpose to "recapitulate all things under Christ as head" and to unite Jews and Gentiles as the one body of Christ. I welcomed the Word that evening in an altogether unaccustomed way. And the Letter to the Ephesians has retained a very special place in my prayer life ever since. I shall refer to it again later in this essay.

In the years before Vatican II, the junior monks in New Norcia had restricted access to the monastery library. Our studies for the priesthood were very much in the "safe textbook" style, with an occasional window being briefly opened by our philosophy lecturer, recently returned from philosophical studies at Sant'Anselmo in Rome, who often departed from the text of Josephus Gredt's *Elementa Philosophiae Aristotelico-Thomisticae* (partly because we were still struggling with Latin). In theology we used, and followed very closely, Adolphe Tanquerey's *Synopsis Theologiae Dogmaticae* (29th edition, 1959) and Eduard Genicot's *Institutiones Theologiae Moralis* (16th edition,

1946). We did experience some of the trickle-down effects of Pius XII's 1943 encyclical on Scripture, *Divino afflante Spiritu,* through Alexander Jones's *Unless Some Man Show Me,*[11] Charles Hauret's *Beginnings: Genesis and Modern Science,*[12] and Bruce Vawter's *A Path Through Genesis.*[13] These, and *A Catholic Commentary on Holy Scripture,*[14] helped prepare me for Vatican II's Constitution on Divine Revelation, *Dei Verbum.*

Nothing, however, had prepared me for a vernacular liturgy. Our community had a strong tradition of liturgical celebration, with extensive use of polyphony at Mass on major feasts and Gregorian chant at daily Conventual Mass and Vespers, but not of liturgical studies. Our monks were generally content to follow changes introduced by Rome: the Revised Easter Vigil (1951), and then the reform of the whole of the Holy Week Liturgy, promulgated in 1955 and introduced during my novitiate in time for Holy Week 1956. The simplification of the rubrics for Mass and Office promulgated in 1960 was well received, but there was no hint of a change in language, as far as I remember. Talk about that possibility was left to people in faraway Europe and North America. As a novice and young monk, I looked forward happily to living with a Latin liturgy for the rest of my life, and so set about learning by heart many of the psalms and also Scripture passages that appeared regularly in the Office and Mass. I found that the repeated use of the *orationes* and *collectae,* especially those of the temporal cycle, made them relatively easy to commit to the storehouse of memory. These memorized biblical passages and prayers became treasures

---

[11] Alexander Jones, *Unless Some Man Show Me* (London: Sheed and Ward, 1951).

[12] Charles Hauret, *Beginnings: Genesis and Modern Science* (Dubuque: Priory Press, 1955).

[13] Bruce Vawter, *A Path Through Genesis* (London: Sheed and Ward, 1960).

[14] *A Catholic Commentary on Holy Scripture* (London: Thomas Nelson, 1951).

on which to draw in time of personal prayer and for prayer moments during other occupations.

My horizons were greatly enlarged and my fairly rigid approach to monastic observance and other areas of Church life challenged when, a few weeks after ordination to the priesthood, I left for Rome to spend two years studying for the licence in theology at the International Benedictine College of Sant'Anselmo. I arrived there in mid-October 1963, during the second session of Vatican II. The end of that session saw the promulgation of *Sacrosanctum Concilium*, the Constitution on the Sacred Liturgy. I had as lecturer for Dogma I the dynamic young Swiss monk, Fr. Magnus Löhrer, and as Dogma II lecturer the Romanized-German *Rector Magnificus*, Fr. Augustinus (later Cardinal) Mayer. It was something of a culture shock for me to see and hear the response/reaction of the hundred or more students, Benedictines from the five continents, some Cistercians, and others (notably the Somaschi—Clerics Regular of Somasca, whose student house was nearby) to news about the council proceedings delivered by each of the lecturers—scraping of shoes on the floor, banging of desks, expressing approval or disapproval.

The lectures were still in Latin, and I became very familiar with the names of Sanctus Thomas, Sanctus Augustinus, and Carolus Rahner as we plunged into *De Deo Uni-trino*, which I found very stimulating after Tanquerey's *De Deo Uno* and *De Deo Trino*. There were enlightening lectures on ecclesiology and ecumenism (at the time a new word and new world for me) from Fr. Gerard Békés, a monk of Pannonhalma, exiled in Rome following the Communist takeover of Hungary in 1949; on the Eastern Churches from Fr. Emmanuel Lanne of Chevetogne in Belgium; and a much-needed catch-up course in general and special methodology from Fr. Kassius Hallinger of Münsterschwarzach (I had done all my studies in New Norcia without learning how to prepare a bibliography, to reference quotations, or to write footnotes!). The Pontifical Liturgical

Institute, located at Sant'Anselmo, was still in its infancy, and only a little senior to it was the Monastic Institute, in which I attended minor courses with its president, Fr. Basil Steidle of Beuron, and Fr. Raphael Schulte of Gerleve, who was also the supervisor of my licentiate *thesina*, on the Eucharist and Christian life according to Saint Cyprian (which I only managed to complete, with much encouragement from Fr. Raphael, a few years after returning to Australia).

This is not the place to recall all the places of religious, cultural, and historical interest that I was able to visit during my two years of study in Rome. At that time, intercontinental travel for most people was still by sea; jet plane travel was progressively introduced from the early to mid-1960s, and it almost completely replaced travel by sea. For Australian monks studying in Europe, the summer holidays were usually an opportunity to visit monasteries in other countries, to broaden our experience of living "according to the Rule of Saint Benedict." Over the course of two summers in Europe I was able to visit monasteries in England, France, Spain, Germany, Belgium, and, of course, Italy.

I mentioned earlier an experience of "welcoming the Word" in the Letter to the Ephesians. I was fortunate to have that experience deepened while at Sant'Anselmo through one of the notable Jesuit Scripture scholars of that period. Fr. Maximilian Zerwick gave conferences on two separate "Days of Recollection" to the student body at Sant'Anselmo: on the first day, in Advent 1963 (December 1), expounding the first chapter of Ephesians and, on the second day (May 16, 1964), chapter 4:1-16 in a way that made a great impression on me.[15] I have become

[15] Maximilian Zerwick and Stanislaus Lyonnet were two Jesuit professors at the Pontifical Biblical Institute in Rome who had been suspended by the Holy Office from lecturing in the New Testament in the time of Pope Saint John XXIII, under pressure from one of the Roman university's biblical studies staff. While restricted to lecturing on bib-

increasingly convinced that having a real grasp of the first three chapters of Ephesians (which might be summed up as "this is the great mystery in which we believe") is most helpful in order to appreciate and embrace the remaining three chapters ("In the light of what we believe, this is how we strive to live"). It was not surprising to find that, among the early responses to *Dei Verbum*, Vatican II's Constitution on Divine Revelation, there should be a German series published in English translation by Sheed and Ward with the series title The New Testament for Spiritual Reading (1968–1971) and that Zerwick should have been the author of the volume on Ephesians. Other memorable spiritual conferences for the monks at Sant'Anselmo in my time were given by Abbot Christopher Butler, abbot of Downside and, as abbot president of the English Benedictine Congregation, one of the council fathers; by Abbot Isidoro Tell of Praglia; by the rector, Fr. Augustine Mayer; and by the student master, Fr. Conrad Louis of St. Meinrad.

During my time in Rome, I became increasingly aware of gaps in my secondary education that had not been attended to and that could perhaps be addressed. Without my going into all the details, a year or so after returning to my monastery, I was allowed (I wouldn't quite say encouraged!) to begin

---

lical Greek, Zerwick managed to enthuse many students with zeal for New Testament studies. He was well known for his *Graecitas Biblica* (*Biblical Greek: Illustrated by Examples*, trans. Joseph Smith [Rome: Pontifical Biblical Institute, 1963]) and his earlier *Analysis philologica novi testamenti graeci* (Rome: Pontifical Biblical Institute, 1960), translated as *A Grammatical Analysis of the Greek New Testament*, trans. and ed. Mary Grosvenor (Rome: Pontifical Biblical Institute, vol. 1, 1974; vol. 2, 1979). For an account of the attack on the Biblical Institute, see Joseph A. Fitzmyer, "A Recent Roman Scriptural Controversy," *Theological Studies* 22, no. 3 (1961): 426–44; Joseph A. Komonchak, "The Struggle for the Council during the Preparation of Vatican II (1960–1962)," in *History of Vatican II*, ed. Giuseppe Alberigo, English version ed. Joseph A. Komonchak (Maryknoll, NY: Orbis Books, 1996), 1:280–81.

tertiary studies as an external student with the University of Western Australia, majoring in classics (Latin and Greek). After achieving the pass BA degree, I was able to go on to do the honors course in classics, studies that have stood me in good stead since that time in pursuing the study of Scripture and the fathers and other languages.

Early in my spiritual awakening and before I entered the monastery, I had had some slight contact with the writings of Saint Teresa of Jesus. (At that time non-Carmelites in general knew her as Saint Teresa of Avila, but that was to change under instructions from Pope Saint John Paul II. With all due respect to the Polish pope, "Teresa of Avila" still comes more naturally to some of us.) In reading something attributed to her about the importance of "mental prayer," I understood that she was convinced that if one was faithful to the regular practice of mental prayer, it was most unlikely that one would fall into mortal sin, or remain in it should one have that misfortune. One would either give up prayer or give up sin. That understanding made a deep impression on me, and since not only holiness but also salvation depended on avoiding mortal sin, mental prayer of some kind, however imperfect, has remained a nonnegotiable practice for me.

There are other insights gained from Saint Teresa's life and writings that have stood me in good stead over the years, as have also those gained from the life and writings of her partner in the reform of the Carmelite Order, Saint John of the Cross. Having over the years acquired a good working knowledge of Spanish, I used to spend a few sessions each week reading aloud Saint Teresa or Saint John to our last Spanish abbot, Dom Gregory Gomez, when he was in his late eighties (he retired in 1971 and died at ninety-one as a result of a road accident in 1995). He himself grew up in the province of Burgos and would comment that sometimes in hearing Saint Teresa he was reminded of the women of his village conversing and exchang-

ing views on a range of topics to do with home and church
and country and prayer. And sometimes after a particularly
insightful passage from Teresa or John, he would exclaim, "The
monks need to hear this!" I now look back on all these contacts
with the saints and teachers of Christian life as occasions on
which I was being graced to "welcome the Word."

Our annual retreats, especially since Vatican II, became
more and more scripturally and liturgically oriented, bringing a deeper exposure to the Word. The only monastic retreat
master we had in the 1960s and 1970s was in 1968, when we
had the superior of the Sylvestrine-Benedictine monastery at
Arcadia, New South Wales, Fr. Simon Tonini, OSB (later abbot
general of the Sylvestrines). The year 1980 witnessed a major
event for our community. To celebrate the sesquimillennium
of Saint Benedict's birth, after much careful planning and a
lot of hard work on the part of the monks and staff, a five-day
symposium on contemporary spirituality was held in New
Norcia. The Australian Scripture scholar, Fr. Francis Molony,
SDB, was one of our two speakers, the other being the English
Benedictine nun Dame Maria Boulding, of Stanbrook Abbey.
Fr. Molony spoke on discipleship as portrayed in the gospel of
Saint Mark; Dame Maria spoke from her thirty years' experience of monastic life and significant involvement with theologians of the English Benedictine Congregation, her theme
being the Word of the cross and of the resurrection in Jesus'
life and mission, and monastic life as a sharing in that Word
of cross and resurrection.

The matter and delivery were of a very high standard, and
the participation of the hundred or so attending, mainly women
religious but a sprinkling of religious and secular priests as
well as laypeople and Benedictine oblates, further stimulated
the speakers to excel. Dame Maria developed material from
her book *Marked for Life: Prayer in the Easter Christ*, and two
years after the symposium she published another book, *The*

Coming of God.[16] I have used this last book many times when giving weekend or weeklong retreats here in New Norcia and elsewhere, and in providing spiritual direction and accompaniment to individuals in the past thirty years. I have said on numerous occasions that it is the only book I wish I had written. I think we are now indebted to Conception Abbey, Missouri, for keeping *The Coming of God* in print. The central chapter of the book is chapter 5, "Listening to the Word," in which the writer expounds a deeply contemplative Christology. Jesus, the Word Incarnate, in his human mind listens to the Father's Word to him throughout his life and obeys, even unto death on the cross. And he obeys still, but now it is the Word of resurrection. And because he listened and obeyed, we too as his members can listen to that Word and be brought into conformity with him in his obedience. One of the most perceptive and, to me at least, moving passages in the book is in that chapter:

> Between the simplest believer and the highest mystic the same communion of faith [communication of faith by the way others pray and read the Good News and live] holds. The great Christian mystics are not some in-group with access to special mysteries; they are baptized men and women who have fed on the same vital word, and allowed the Easter Christ to take them the whole way. The communication of faith is not only horizontal, between contemporaries; it spans generations. The minds and lives of Christians all down the ages, the minds of the saints and mystics and of the humble, heroic, unknown believers of every age and place, have been formed and fertilized by the same seed of the word.[17]

[16] Maria Boulding, *Marked for Life: Prayer in the Easter Christ* (London: SPCK, 1979), and *The Coming of God* (London: SPCK, 1982).
[17] Boulding, *The Coming of God*, 78. American editions since 2000, 80.

Before I leave Maria Boulding, I should say that her 1980 visit to New Norcia came at a time of painful personal and vocational crisis for me, arising from strong differences of opinion within our community about how to implement the fostering of emotional maturity encouraged by Vatican II in article 18 of *Perfectae Caritatis* (Decree on the Up-to-Date Renewal of Religious Life). I will be ever grateful to Dame Maria for listening to my rather anguished outpouring of emotional turmoil and for her few steadying words, "Let it wash around you. Cling to Christ."

New Norcia monastery is perhaps the most isolated Benedictine house in the world, as our nearest neighboring monastery in the Benedictine family is the Cistercian Abbey of Tarrawarra in Victoria, which is about three thousand miles to our east. We are not on a well-trodden pilgrim path taking in a number of monasteries, and so we do not have many monastic visitors. Since the late 1960s the Australasian Benedictine Union has been a valuable means of mutual support for women's and men's Benedictine communities in Australia and New Zealand. Besides encouraging writing on scriptural, liturgical, and monastic spirituality and history among its members for publication in *Tjurunga*, the Union's journal, it has also held symposia on monastic themes, usually in either Sydney or Melbourne, and for a number of years the annual general meeting of superiors to discuss Benedictine Union matters has included a Benedictine studies day open to the public.

The existence of the Union has also encouraged the sharing of overseas speakers and retreat givers among member communities. Thus, in 1980, Dame Maria Boulding, after her time in New Norcia, spoke at another sesquimillennium symposium held at St. Benedict's Monastery, Arcadia, New South Wales, and was able to visit communities of the Good Samaritan Sisters of the Order of St. Benedict in South Australia, Victoria, New South Wales, and Queensland, before going on to visit Japan and the United States on her way back to England. In 1981 New Norcia invited Fr. Michael Casey, OCSO, of Tarrawarra, Victoria, to bring us up to date with the more recent study on the Rule of Benedict, which he did in a slightly abbreviated presentation of Benedictine studies, a program he prepared with his confrere Fr. David Tomlins, OCSO (later abbot of Tarrawarra), and the Good Samaritan Sisters at Belgrave, especially Sr. Helen Lombard, SGS (later congregational leader of the Good Sams, as they are affectionately known in Australia). It was on the same extended visit to New Norcia that Michael also led the community retreat, with some of his hallmark deeply scriptural-monastic spirituality and culture. During that retreat I really heard for the first time James 1:21: *Humbly welcome the Word which has been planted in you and can save your souls* (New Jerusalem Bible translation), which is the basis of the title of this chapter.

It may not be necessary, but it is important, I think, to acknowledge here my own indebtedness to Fr. Michael for his personal encouragement in our meetings and correspondence and for the writings with which he has done honor to the monastic order and Australian monasticism and benefited many of its members, both Cistercian and Benedictine. To mention some of his books that have helped me on my monastic journey: *Towards God*; *The Art of Sacred Reading*; *Strangers to the City*; *Truthful Living*; *The Road to Eternal Life*.[18] Three articles that Michael gave me as offprints have been particularly valuable: "Spiritual Desire in the Gospel Homilies of Saint Gregory the Great,"[19] "Mindfulness of God in the Monastic Tradition,"[20] and

---

[18] Michael Casey, *Towards God: The Western Tradition of Contemplation* (Blackburn, Victoria: Dove, 1995); *The Art of Sacred Reading* (North Blackburn, Victoria: CollinsDove, 1995); *Strangers to the City* (Brewster, MA: Paraclete Press, 2005); *Truthful Living* (Petersham, MA: Saint Bede's Publications, 1999); *The Road to Eternal Life: Reflections on the Prologue of Benedict's Rule* (Mulgrave, Victoria: John Garratt, 2011).

[19] CSQ 16, no. 4 (1981): 297–314.

[20] CSQ 17, no. 2 (1982): 111–26.

"Intentio Cordis."[21] Two of his recent books are on my list of books to read: *Seventy-Four Tools for Good Living* and *The Art of Winning Souls.*[22]

To give an idea of the emphasis we have laid on sourcing up-to-date scriptural, monastic, and liturgical teaching for our community, I mention in a footnote the names of our retreat directors since 1981, by country of origin.[23]

---

[21] RBS 6/7 (1981): 105–20.

[22] Michael Casey, *Tools for Good Living: Reflection on the Fourth Chapter of Benedict's Rule* (Collegeville, MN: Liturgical Press, 2014), and *The Art of Winning Souls: Pastoral Care for Novices* (Collegeville, MN: Liturgical Press, 2012).

[23] From England in 1983 came Fr. Placid Spearritt, of Ampleforth Abbey (he returned to New Norcia at the end of 1983 for a fourteen-year stint as prior administrator, followed by eleven years as abbot before his sudden death in 2008), and from the same country and monastery Fr. Henry Wansborough in 2008, and Abbot Timothy Wright in 2011; from Turvey Abbey, UK, we had Olivetan Sr. Zoe Davis in 1996.

From Glenstal in Ireland, Fr. Simon Sleeman in 2003.

From the United States, Fr. Joel Rippinger of Marmion Abbey, Illinois, in 1984; Dom Bernard Johnson, the Trappist abbot of Conyers in Georgia, in 1992; Fr. Columba Stewart, of Saint John's, Collegeville, Minnesota, came for the first time in 1993 and again in 2009 (very helpful with his deep knowledge of Cassian, Evagrius, and Origen), and also from Collegeville, Fr. Kevin Seasoltz in 2000; from Christ in the Desert, New Mexico, Prior Philip Lawrence in 1995; from St. Meinrad's, Indiana, Fr. Columba Kelly in 1999 and Fr. Eugene Hensell in 2004; from Subiaco Abbey, Arkansas, Abbot Jerome Kodell in 2010; Sr. Shawn Carruth of Mount St. Benedict Monastery in Crookston, Minnesota, in 2013.

From South Africa, Bishop Fulgence Leroy, OSB, of Pietersburg (the former Abbey *Nullius* is now called Polokwane) in 1990.

Australian monastics: from the Cistercian Abbey at Tarrawarra, Victoria, Fr. Michael Casey in 1981 and again in 2001; Fr. Stephen List in 1986, and Fr. David Tomlins in 1987; from the Sylvestrine-Benedictine monastery at Arcadia, NSW, Fr. Edward Doran in 1989; Fr. Michael Kelly (currently abbot general of the Sylvestrines) in 1991; Fr. David Orr in 1998, and Fr. Bernard McGrath in 2007; from the Good Samaritan Sisters of the Order of St. Benedict, Sr. Margaret Malone in 2002.

In 2015, Fr. Luigi Gioia, OSB, an Italian-born and international Olivetan-Benedictine monk, at present lecturing in theology at Sant'Anselmo and deeply immersed in Saint Augustine's *The Trinity*, was our retreat director. Fr. Luigi's enlightened appreciation of Saint Augustine confirmed and fueled my own. Augustine certainly stretches me intellectually, and it would be presumptuous of me to think that I can remain at, or even reach the heights of, his speculation in *The Trinity*, his study of time in book 11 of *Confessions*, his meditations on the incarnation in the *Homilies on the Gospel of John*, and his anti-Arian and anti-Pelagian writings. But I do find my soul resonating with his when he speaks of the power of the Word in such words as in book 10.6 of the *Confessions*: "It is with no doubtful knowledge, Lord, but with utter certainty that I love You. *You have stricken my heart with Your Word*, and I have loved You."[24]

In fact, the first ten books of the *Confessions* can be viewed as a prolonged meditation on the Word with which "you have stricken my heart," bringing Augustine through a winding path of self-discovery and self-acceptance to obedient humility and conversion, acceptance of Christ as the Mediator, and a burning love responding to infinite Love. The final three books, which start out as a reflection on the book of Genesis, are shot

---

Australian diocesan and religious bishops and priests: in 1985, before he was appointed the first bishop of Broken Bay, NSW, we had the then-Australian expert on John Cassian, Fr. David Walker; the Carmelite Fr. Peter Slattery in 1988; the Discalced Carmelite Fr. Greg Burke in 1994; the bishop of Geraldton, Western Australia, Justin Bianchini in 1997; Oblate of Mary Immaculate Fr. Austin Cooper in 2006; the retired auxiliary bishop of Sydney, Geoffrey Robinson, in 2012. Two Australian Jesuits: Fr. Andrew Hamilton (on the Sayings of the Desert Fathers) in 2005, and Fr. Joseph Sobb, SJ (a model of the contemplative Scripture scholar), in 2014. All of those listed above provided many "strong moments" of listening to and welcoming the Word.

[24] Augustine, *Confessions* 10.6; trans. Sheed, 170. Emphasis mine.

through with prayer and with prayers in response to the Word on which he is reflecting. He confesses not in order to inform God but to stir himself and his readers to love. Book 11 begins:

> But, Lord, since You are in eternity, are You unaware of what I am saying to You? Or do you see in time what takes place in time? But if You do see, why am I giving You an account of all these things? Not, obviously, that You should learn them from me; but I excite my own love for You and the love of those who read what I write, that we all may say: *The Lord is great, and exceedingly to be praised.*[25] Thus we are laying bare our love for You in confessing to you our wretchedness and Your mercies towards us: that You may free us wholly as You have already freed us in part, so that we may cease to be miserable in ourselves and come to happiness in You.[26]

I hope I may be forgiven for quoting at some length my homily on Trinity Sunday 2015:

> On a somewhat personal note, in the year 2000 I read for the first time the new English translation of St. Augustine's *The Trinity* and I'm now reading it for the sixth time. In his introduction, the translator, Fr. Edmund Hill, OP, has some helpful things to say about the work, and also why it is comparatively unknown outside the circle of professional theologians. He writes, "The central point was missed entirely . . . [by medieval theologians, including even Saint Thomas], and that is that Augustine is proposing the quest for, or the exploration of, the mystery of the Trinity as a

---

[25] This is the verse with which the first line of the *Confessions* (bk 1.1) begins, Ps 144 (145):3. See Ps 47 (48):1.

[26] Sheed, *Confessions*, 208.

complete program for the Christian spiritual life, a program of conversion and renewal and discovery of self in God and God in self. Thus it has come about that the *doctrine* of the Trinity has been effectively detached from the wider movements of Christian spirituality and devotion in the West, and the *mystery* has come to be regarded as a curious kind of intellectual luxury for theological highbrows, a subject on which not many priests are eager to preach sermons, nor congregations to listen to them."[27]

And a bit later Fr. Hill writes, "[Augustine] presents his quest for God the Trinity as both an all-absorbing personal preoccupation, and a kind of plan for the spiritual life of any Christian. We are all urged to join in the quest, not just by Augustine, but by the Spirit of God in the Scriptures. Three times, at key points in his work, he quotes Psalm 105:3-4: *Let their hearts rejoice who seek the Lord; seek the Lord and be strengthened; seek his face always* [more familiar to some of us in the Grail translation: *let the hearts that seek the Lord rejoice. Consider the Lord and his strength; constantly seek his face* (Ps 104:3-4)]. It is a summons addressed in the plural to all who fear the Lord. . . . [Augustine's] quest [is] a magnificent, a most successful failure."[28]

I find in Augustine an inspiring teacher and a fellow seeker, well ahead of me in the "school for the Lord's service" (RB Prol.45), who points me time and again to the inspired Word and to the incarnate Word. He drew life, insight, and energy from the one and the other and shared his ever-active desire for

[27] Edmund Hill, Introduction 5, in Saint Augustine, *The Trinity*, trans. Edmund Hill, ed. John E. Rotelle, The Works of Saint Augustine: A Translation for the 21st Century, part 1, vol. 5 (New York: New City Press, 1991), 19 (emphasis mine).
[28] Hill, Introduction 10, p. 21.

knowledge and wisdom with his congregation and those who, sharing his faith, have read and studied his writings down to the present day.

In the process of writing this essay, I have been reminded many times of the privilege that is mine as a Benedictine monk to be several times each day, day in day out, exposed in the choral celebration of the *Opus Dei* to the words of the psalms and other books of Sacred Scripture, and to reflections on these by writers and teachers of the various ages of the church—sub-apostolic, patristic, medieval, renaissance, modern. Saint Benedict seems to have thought that the psalms and other passages of Scripture learned by heart would provide readily available material for the "frequent prayer" he expected his monks to practice: "To devote oneself frequently to prayer" (RB 4.56). I suspect that he thought that the daily use of Psalm 50 (51), the *Miserere*, would help the monk in the practice of the next two instruments of good works: "Daily in prayer to confess to God with tears and groaning one's past evils," and "to make amends for those evils in the future" (RB 4.57-58).

This "frequent prayer" and "prayer with tears," sustained by long daily periods of *lectio divina* (see, for example, RB 48.4, 5, 10, 13, 14, 22; 49.4) may at times flame out in Cassian's *oratio ignita*, "fiery prayer,"[29] both in solitary prayer and in community praying of the Divine Office. While *The Cloud of Unknowing* promotes the use of "a sharp dart of longing love" (chaps. 6, 12) or "a naked intent unto God for himself" (chaps. 3, 7, 24) or "a meek stirring of love" (chaps. 7, 16, 49, 50) frequently repeated during the time set aside for prayer, it can be useful to remember Saint Bernard's sober words that, for most of us most of the time, the intense experience of God's presence and

[29] See *Jean Cassian: Conférences* 9.26, ed. Eugène Pichry, SCh 54 (Paris: Les Éditions du Cerf, 1958), 51.

love will be a matter of *rara hora et parva mora*, "infrequent and not long-lasting."[30]

Benedictine writers like Dom Prosper Guéranger, Madame Cécile Bruyère, and Dom Columba Marmion,[31] in discussing the need for and usefulness of methods in learning and practicing mental prayer, are happy to leave monks and nuns to the method of the Church's liturgy. In reply to a hypothetical question expressing fear of "leaving the Christian soul to go at haphazard, and to pray as it were at random," Madame Bruyère writes, "our answer in the first place is that all the children of the Church have the science of their Mother in the sacred liturgy, which contains the most perfect method of prayer, the most traditional, the best ordered, the most simple, and the one which leaves the greatest scope to the liberty of the Holy Spirit."[32]

I find myself close to finishing this chapter on January 1, 2016, the Solemnity of the Most Holy Mother of God. It is relevant, then, to state briefly something about my own approach to the Mother of Jesus, the Word Incarnate. Early in my monastic life I was influenced by someone whose devotion to Mary was strongly colored by his association with the Legion of Mary and who encouraged the kind of devotion to Mary preached and taught so powerfully by Saint Louis Grignon de Montfort, particularly in his work variously known as *True Devotion to Mary* or *True Devotion to the Blessed Virgin*. I entered into the practice with gusto but found after some time that it did not sit quite right with me. I don't recall how long this

[30] SCh 23.15; SBOp 1:148. I have the late Abbot Placid Spearritt to thank for encouraging me to persevere with reading *The Cloud of Unknowing*, and to read it in the Middle English.

[31] Columba Marmion, *Christ the Ideal of the Monk*, trans. by a nun of Tyburn Convent (London: Sands & Co., 1926). See chap. 15 ("Monastic Prayer"), esp. 354–58.

[32] Cécile Bruyère, *The Spiritual Life and Prayer: According to Holy Scripture and Monastic Tradition*, trans. the Benedictines of Stanbrook (London: Art and Book Company, 1900), 124, chap. 9.

state of unease lasted, but I was relieved when I chanced across an example of humble spirituality and enlightened spiritual direction in Dom Marmion's letters of direction.[33] I was able to accept that the New Testament and the liturgy were providing me with ample material to nourish a thoroughly Catholic and monastic devotion to "oure Lady Seint[e] Mary[e]" (as *The Cloud of Unknowing*, once in chapter 4 and twice in chapter 15, calls her in the lovely Middle English with its erratic spelling!).

One pithy saying of Saint Louis Grignon that I have treasured down the years is, "When we say Mary, she says God." And I deeply appreciate Vatican II's *Lumen gentium* (Constitution on the Church), chapter 8, "The Role of the Blessed Virgin Mary, Mother of God, in the Mystery of Christ and the Church." Eschewing downplaying the role of Mary in the mystery of Christ and the Church (minimalism) and overemphasizing it (maximalism), the Council, in speaking of Mary, took the middle path that does full justice to the primacy of Christ her Son and to Mary's divinely appointed role in God's plan for our salvation. In the infancy narrative of his gospel, Saint Luke shows Mary as the model of the contemplative, receiving the Word of God through the angel Gabriel. Augustine and others were careful to emphasize that Mary received the Word in her heart by faith before conceiving the Word in her womb—in both instances "welcoming the Word" in a way that continues

---

[33] Raymond Thibaut, *Union with God according to the Letters of Direction of Dom Marmion*, trans. Mother Mary St. Thomas (London: Sands & Co., 1935), 201–2, n. 3. There Marmion wrote, "For *certain souls*, drawn to it by grace, this devotion is doubtless fruitful and sanctifying. . . . As for myself, I have tried it, but it rather had the effect of giving me distractions. . . . In practice, I do not use it for myself, I go to God through Jesus, and Mary helps me to know her Son and to go to him. As for others who have an attraction for it, I encourage them, for this devotion was propagated by a Saint, and it seems to us exaggerated perhaps because we are not yet at the diapason of holiness."

to inspire and sustain her fellow disciples, who, as brothers and sisters of her Son, are her children.

On looking over this chapter, I can understand why some readers might conclude that I have perhaps something of the *dilettante* about me. Since reading Thibaut's life of Dom Marmion sixty years ago, I have endeavored to keep in mind how that holy Irish monk, when teaching at the monastery of Mont-César, which he helped found in Louvain (it is now Kaisersberg, in Leuven), encouraged his students to approach all their ecclesiastical studies as "love seeking knowledge in order to love the more."[34] It has become steadily clearer to me that Marmion's injunction is simply another way of saying, *Humbly welcome the Word which has been planted in you and can save your souls* (Jas 1:15), and of embracing the riches contained in Romans 15:4, *And all these things which were written so long ago were written so that we, learning perseverance and the encouragement which the scriptures give, should have hope,* and of praying with Paul in the next two verses, *Now the God of perseverance and encouragement give you all the same purpose, following the example of Christ Jesus, so that you may together give glory to the God and Father of our Lord Jesus Christ with one heart.* And finally, picking up the third important theological word in verse 4, *hope,* the splendid prayer at the end of that section, in verse 1, *May the God of hope fill you with all joy and peace in your faith, so that in the power of the Holy Spirit you may be rich in hope.*[35]

[34] Marmion, *Christ the Ideal of the Monk,* 350.

[35] All Scripture quotations in this paragraph are from *The New Jerusalem Bible* (London: Darton, Longman & Todd, 1985).

Chapter 5

Ritualizing Endings for the Sake of New Beginnings

Mary Collins, OSB

Michael Casey devoted a chapter to "Generativity" in his 2005 essay collection *Strangers to the City*.[1] He speaks there at some length about the intergenerational monastic work of mentoring and nurturing, the task of fostering newer members to "full adult maturity." At the beginning stages, he observes, the senior monastics accept the younger monastic colleague as an "apprentice" in learning the monastic life. The mentoring relationship eventually comes to an end when the maturing monastic finds his own way forward, first becoming "productive," then exercising some creativity in the tasks with which he has been charged, and then becoming an actor in the "recycling succession of moments" that maintain the subculture of the place for each new generation.

Monastic *conversatio* involves more than simple mentoring, however, according to Casey. It requires nurturing. Intergenerational engagement in the daily life of a monastic community means learning together what continued fidelity to the monastic profession demands in real life. Certainly the newcomer

---

[1] Michael Casey, "Generativity," in *Strangers to the City: Reflections on the Beliefs and Values of the Rule of Saint Benedict* (Brewster, MA: Paraclete Press, 2005), 124–41.

learns to temper a beginner's zeal for learning the "rules," on the one hand, and, on the other hand, to let go of the assumption that "good enough" will satisfy. But that is only the start of lifelong learning. Saint Benedict's chapter 72 on the good zeal of the monks reminds us—if the commentators on the Rule are to be believed—that the beloved abbot required his own lifelong learning in order to come to the fullness of his vision. What was the outcome for Benedict of Nursia of a lifetime living the wisdom of the Prologue and the other seventy-one chapters of the Rule of Benedict? It is nothing less than love and mercy in our dealings with one another—"supporting with the greatest patience one another's weakness of body or behavior" and "pursuing what [she or he] judges better for someone else"—beyond the self (RB 72.7).

Casey's positive essay on intergenerational *conversatio* may well depict the reality of a vital monastic culture of the equatorial South, especially of the Asian-Pacific world and also of the African continent. In these places there is much mentoring and nurturing to be done. For example, Benedictine houses of women in Korea report scores of candidates for monastic profession each year; the numbers are similar in the Philippines. So also in both East and West Africa. In men's monasteries in both these regions the numbers are fewer but still proportionately substantial in both Cistercian and Benedictine houses. Unfortunately the steady increase in new candidates for monastic profession is no longer true in the North American church, nor in fact in the North Atlantic region. In places where monasteries once flourished, few or none come to receive the gift. Casey writes, in sum, "The continuance of the monastic charism is one of the prime functions of a monastic community; that is why when there is no one to receive the gift, communities often lose vitality to the point of seeming dead."[2]

---

[2] Casey, "Generativity," 133.

In this essay on monastic generativity, I intend to address the real complexity of "seeming dead" in monasteries that have few or none to receive the gift. I begin with an extended reflection on what might be further said about the apparent dying of monasticism in the North Atlantic Church at the onset of the twenty-first century. Here the focus will be on monasteries of Benedictine women primarily in North America, specifically on steps taken within the Federation of St. Scholastica to address its present and its future, both positively and realistically. Next I will look at a set of case studies in which ritualizing endings and new beginnings to mark the dissolution of a particular monastery has been an uncommon act of vitality, a strange form of generativity. Handing on the monastic charism seems to elude our human control, yet that is because it always has been and will be a mysterious work of God.

The challenge of welcoming and mentoring new members confronts monastic life in the entire North Atlantic region, both in Western Europe and in North America. The once famous English monastery of contemplative nuns at Stanbrook Abbey recently made a difficult decision about their present and their future, despite objections from many of their public. They knew numbers were steadily declining, and new candidates for profession were few. The abbey, established in eighteenth-century England, sent into exile in France, and then returned in the nineteenth century, had been a powerhouse for creative and learned Benedictine nuns for more than a century. Yet like every other place in the North Atlantic region, it was vulnerable to the times. While the news media focused on the disposition of their Victorian buildings designed by the famous architect August Pugin, the real danger was to the household of Benedictine nuns themselves. They took a celebrated risk—an expression of their vitality—to relocate and to build a smaller monastic compound, a twenty-first-century "green" building. There they are living into their unknown future.

On the British Isle of Wight the Benedictine abbey of Quarr, founded earlier from the French Abbey of Solesmes and heir to the early nineteenth-century restoration of European Benedictine life, has been placed under an administrator. The dozen monks wonder and await their future. Unfortunately these two stories of dealing with decline are not exceptional cases but simply illustrations of what is occurring. Because I am a professed Benedictine sister in the US Midwest, I will focus briefly on what I know best, speaking on the varied strategies being explored for a hopeful future for monasteries without new members. Only then will I consider the role of ritualizing at the time of endings and new beginnings for those for whom options have run out.

There are solid reasons for the decline in newer vocations beyond the control of monastic houses themselves.[3] Monasteries tend to be local, drawing their membership and making their impact primarily where they reside.[4] They implant themselves from the beginning as evangelizing communities, living the life of the Gospel according to the Rule and under a local abbot. Most of the Midwestern monasteries founded 150 to 175 years ago were in rural communities, the place where most German and Irish immigrants made their new homes on the land. Some entrants were escaping military conscription, others famine and its aftermath; all were hoping for better lives. Most of these immigrants were carrying with them the European Catholic faith of their forebears and were eager to hand it on to their children.

---

[3] See Kathleen Sprows Cummings, Fadica Report, "Understanding U.S. Catholic Sisters Today," December 2015, https://www.scribd.com/document/292793672/Understanding-U-S-Catholic-Sisters-Today, for a comparison of entrance rates at the outset of the twentieth and twenty-first centuries. The mid-twentieth-century numbers are the anomaly.

[4] See Joel Rippinger, "Transmitting a Common Core for Monasticism: A Survival Kit for the Future," ABR 66, no. 4 (2015): 367–68, for his discussion on "Locality."

Farm families were large: three daughters, even three sons, making monastic profession from a single family was not an uncommon reality in the Midwest abbeys and monasteries throughout most of those early decades. Rural life, farming, and the size of rural families have all changed dramatically. Just as significantly, the missionary work of evangelizing and catechizing the settled Midwestern families is completed. The great granddaughters and grandsons of the original settlers, still living in rural communities but many fewer in number, still come within the orbit of the monastery but now as bene-factors or as local college students earning double degrees in business administration and pastoral ministry, to the delight of their parents. The increasing scarcity of ordained priests means that the rural church, already flourishing under the lay-led leadership of the parental generation, will continue the work of maintaining the faith begun earlier by once-large numbers of Benedictine sisters and monks.

This does not mean no new people in the Midwest are wait-ing to be evangelized and catechized, but they are not living close by our monasteries or joining us. New generations of immigrants are seldom drawn to small Midwestern towns that are now being depopulated. Vietnamese, Mexican, and Central Americans are living and worshiping in urban and suburban ethnic enclaves of the Midwest, often in churches borrowed from earlier immigrant populations. Some young people are generous in their impulse to aid their own immigrant commu-nities as men and women religious. But their lives are often a difficult fit within the established monastic communities founded in an earlier century. The residual German and Irish cultures of the North American monasteries are European and so foreign to them. Language difference is only the surface chal-lenge. Most features of monastic culture itself are also alien in the postmodern American society into which they were born. Who will aspire to be the next generation of monastics, if we are to continue to be intergenerational monastic communities?

Midwestern American monastic leaders have been reflecting deeply on this dilemma; it is the agenda of countless discussions. Terrence Kardong, editor of the *American Benedictine Review* and an opinion maker among American monastics, has judged that simply trying harder to recruit is useless. Doing the same kind of recruiting now as in the past has already been found wanting. He argues that it is not time to give up on the monastic life but rather to devote ourselves to living with integrity the commitment we ourselves have made.[5] Dare we believe this? Can it be fruitful, or is it irresponsible, to leave the future of Midwestern monastic life to God and to let go of our impulse to intergenerational generativity? Kardong's is virtually a solitary voice at this time. Most opinion makers are not yet ready to abandon all efforts to interpret and to shape their futures through renewed strategies for newer membership.

Another voice speaking about the present lack of new membership is that of Sandra Marie Schneiders, an Immaculate Heart of Mary sister from the upper Midwest, who had earlier written a three-volume history and spirituality of religious life, earning her credentials as a reliable observer of past, present, and future. More recently she caught people's attention through an address in 2014 to CORI, the Conference of Religious of Ireland, where she recommended that women's communities simply accept their present situation as an opportunity.[6] Like other aging North Atlantic sisters, the Irish are dealing with smaller numbers and fewer new members, whether as an outcome of the scandal of their sisters' involvement in the earlier abuse of young women or because of general decline in commitment to

---

[5] Terrence Kardong, "Hope without Illusions: Coping with the Vocation Crisis," address to the 2013 biennial meeting of North American Association of Oblate Directors. Retrieved from naabod.org/Hope-without-Illusions-Kardong.pdf, acc. July 12, 2016.

[6] Sandra Marie Schneiders, "The Ongoing Challenge of Renewal in Contemporary Religious Life," www.cori.ie/sandra-schneiders-paper-delivered-at-cori-conference-25th-april-2014, acc. Dec. 31, 2015.

the Church. This is now the "new normal" says Schneiders, and communities must move on to fulfill their mission to evangelize and catechize, to spread the Gospel of Mercy with what they have. Some of what Schneiders had to say resonated in the United States with members of the active religious orders, the population similar to the one she was actually addressing in Ireland. Some Benedictines, too, began to try on the concept of the new normal. What might have resonated?

Monastic women in the United States, like apostolic sisters, are living healthy lives well into their nineties. Some laywomen who have pursued careers and raised families have found themselves at age fifty wondering what to do with the rest of their equally long lives. Might they be interested and encouraged to enter monastic life? Professionally educated and already multi-competent, they are looking for new challenges. Sometimes the challenge is to live their faith more deeply.

Michael Casey's account of generativity in an intergenerational monastic community would have to take on a new shape in the setting of this "new normal." Yet the process of generativity would focus on the same reality. How might a community nurture mature adults into an embrace of the monastic charism? How should they be introduced to the culture of the ever-changing local monastic community and the works of the monastery? How, in short order, to make them productive in good works and evoke their creativity as monastic people as they begin life in an aging community admittedly suspicious of too much change? While they may be late starters in the monastic journey, Schneiders suggests that once communities embrace the "new normal," healthy newcomers at age seventy can be mentored for creative community leadership in a variety of offices, and they can exercise these roles often into their eighties. A generative community of the middle-aged, upper-middle-aged, and mature-old-aged is possible. There has never been retirement from commitment to the monastic way of life, no matter at what age it begins.

Not everyone is ready to accept a future for their monasteries by wagering on Schneiders's "new normal." Alternate approaches can be found among communities that are struggling with the challenges of depleted membership. Some have wondered about forming new relationships with oblates, a group growing in large numbers as candidates for monastic profession decrease. But this is problematic. "Oblation is a different vocation than monastic profession—not lesser but different," Julia Upton observes in a recent report of her study of North American oblates.[7] Yet when a community of twenty members finds itself with more than one hundred oblates, it may see in them the promise of a possible future for the monastery. Will something like a "new monasticism" flourish as an older generation that learned to "hold fast" now learns to "let go"?

Meanwhile existential situations need to be addressed, specifically the difficult situation of monasteries that seem "dead." In her address to a Federation of St. Scholastica chapter at the end of her twelve years of service, Benedictine sister Esther Fangman spoke of the challenges of her pastoral service to the twenty-plus federated monasteries to which she had ministered.[8] Fangman reflected on troubled monasteries in a federation whose houses were loosely knit because most of them had been founded as daughter houses of monasteries themselves founded almost a century earlier. She noted telltale signs that a monastic chapter needed to begin early planning for what she called "restructuring." It was not numbers alone that concerned her. The real issue, as she saw it, was adequate leadership in the monasteries. When leaders no longer had energy or the competence suited to the role of prioress, when

---

[7] Julia Upton, "Benedictine Oblates, Profile and Analysis: Glorifying God by Their Lives," ABR 66, no. 4 (2015): 373–90, here 389.

[8] Esther Fangman, "Listening Turns the Soul to God," *Benedictines* 63, no. 2 (2010): 7–16.

monastic communities no longer had vitality, she judged it was time for the communities to think about restructuring.

Until recently the obvious solution to an internal problem had been to ask authorities to designate an administrator to give the monastic community time to discern their situation. The assumption was that the monastery's troubles were temporary and that time under good appointed leadership would lead to an election. But if that could not be assumed, what other options existed? Fangman noted that communities had a history of opening their doors to individual monastics looking for a new monastic home when that need arose. But it did not necessarily speak to a situation where the entire community wanted or needed something more.

The times called for new alternatives when whole communities were under stress. Fangman and her federation council dared to meet the challenge. With good planning, new ideas and new possibilities could be explored. For example, what would it take for a dying community to stay in place, with members living out their years in their own monastery under the canonical protection of a more secure monastery? Working with particular cases and lawyers, canonical and civil, they discovered how and under what conditions this and other solutions could be undertaken.

Alternately, what would it take for a whole community to make its transition to another monastery precisely as a group? Could a smaller, tightly knit monastic community unanimously choose to let itself be absorbed by a house that showed promise of competent leadership, vitality, and so longevity? The canonical suppression of a monastery when it no longer had members was possible, and such suppression had been done.

Some aging communities with no expectation of new members, but with suitable leadership and adequate financial resources, had already addressed their immediate futures by building smaller monastery facilities more suited to their present and projected needs. In North America many nineteenth-century and even mid-twentieth-century buildings existed that had housed both the monastic community and facilities for its ministries under a single large roof. Some chapters made arrangements for the sale of their older property to local schools, colleges, and universities, or even to social service agencies. Monastic communities that were able to follow the route of rebuilding took pride in their new sites and twenty-first-century monasteries.

Nevertheless, Fangman's larger point in addressing the question "what next for troubled monasteries?" was her focus on the impact on individual monastics of such an identity shift or identity loss. It is axiomatic that most people face major change with difficulty. What happens to a whole group that has solved its problem but whose individual members are nevertheless dealing with irreparable personal loss?[9] This question had been mine since the 1980s, when I led a special federation visitation requested by a single, isolated community facing a major internal problem. With only the familiar road map of naming an administrator and postponing an election, and early in the business of dealing with dying communities, it was easy for everyone to accept the importance of buying time for the community to prepare for a future election, but not of planning for dissolution and the inevitable scattering of its members.

What does any of this have to do with Michael Casey's reflection on "Generativity" with which I began this essay? At least this: it looks at the reality of monastic life today in the twenty-first-century United States when continued effort to invite new members into our monasteries fails to produce results. What can be done when there are no next-generation newcomers ready to accept the gift of the monastic charism? What happens to individual members when the dissolution of a monastery seems inevitable, for reasons beyond anyone's control?

The first monastery closing I was present for came after two earlier interventions by federation-designated leaders. A special

[9] Fangman, "Listening," 11.

canonical visitation led to the judgment that the small community was seriously divided after two earlier close elections. No third election would heal the breach, for sides had been drawn. Healing would have to precede any future discernment of leadership. A recently retired prioress from a nearby community accepted the role of administrator, with a specific three-year plan of pastoral care. At the end of that time the community would return to formal discernment. However, within eighteen to twenty months it was clear that dissolution was inevitable. The chapter voted to close. Each sister was personally advised about her canonical situation. She could arrange for transfer to another Benedictine house or, since the monastery in which she had professed stability would no longer exist, she could freely leave monastic life.

Most upper-middle-aged and older sisters chose to take up residence in other Benedictine houses of their federation. The monasteries were profoundly welcoming to the women, who were simultaneously relieved and troubled. Some went alone to their new homes; most departed in twos and threes. Those who left religious life, primarily younger women, were taken in by friends or families of origin until they could establish themselves. Their departures were arranged over a period of many months, based on the reciprocal readiness of the sister and those who would host her.

There were no closing rituals, no recognition of the major rupture the group was facing. This was unfortunate, since as Benedictine monastics, the group members enjoyed what the late Catherine Bell called "ritual mastery." In her study *Ritual Theory, Ritual Practice* she wrote of a "ritualized social body," that is, a corporate body with the ability to "deploy in wider social contexts the schemes internalized in the ritual social environment."[10] Over years of daily liturgical life and the daily

---

[10] Catherine Bell, *Ritual Theory, Ritual Practice* (New York: Oxford University Press, 1992), 107.

social rituals of monastic life, these women were indeed a social body that had come to possess a "cultural sense of ritual." Yet this resource was not on anyone's mind as the sisters coped with "practical" matters. Because ritualization of the dissolution was not pursued, the group simply scattered without addressing the rupture of relationships.

It was more than a decade later, under Esther Fangman's guidance, that another troubled Benedictine community had time to plan their future together. In the process, they contacted three neighboring monasteries to see whether a group move would be possible and under what conditions. With extended visiting among members of the monasteries and after continuing discernment, this monastic community found a fit for itself in a larger group with a comparable monastic culture. One member chose to depart from religious life during the process, but ten were ready to make the major shift in their identity. To make the move they had to arrange for buyers of the property, empty their quarters, transport belongings and furnishings, and attend to myriad details. Then, by mutual agreement, it was time to plan the ritual dimension of the move away from their monastic home and into a welcoming host monastery. Relationships required attention.

Both the receiving and the moving monastic communities enjoyed what Bell called "ritual mastery." I personally had the privilege of speaking with them about what the transition required of them and what my own receiving monastery required. The work of ritually negotiating old and new relationships would take place in our monastic chapel and in the refectory. Only at the end of a two-day process was the canonical decree dissolving the small monastery officially proclaimed. With the dissolution, their incorporation within a new community was completed. But some ritual work had to be done first.

The ritual process, mutually arranged, began on a Saturday at evening prayer. After the reading of the Sunday gospel, the prioress of the incoming group exercised her final act of authority by addressing the whole gathering. Then the receiving prioress went to join her at the ambo, to negotiate their new relationship. The departing prioress simply handed over her copy of the Rule of Saint Benedict to their new prioress. In this simple but clear symbolic action she ceded her authority to another. As she took her place within the gathered assembly of sisters, the receiving prioress concluded the Office of the day.

In a second step that same evening, the members of both communities moved to the monastic refectory for storytelling. Members of the incoming community, each in turn, told aspects of the monastic living that had formed them over more than fifty years and had led them to this moment. Anger, humor, sadness, bewilderment, laughter, joy, and delight blended together in the telling. The receiving community listened carefully. There was much that remained to be said at the end of more than an hour. But the storytelling in a moment of vulnerability was an invitation to the welcoming community to follow up with one-on-one conversations with their new sisters. The action had publicly authorized the establishing of new relationships of friendship, vulnerability, and even intimacy, a process filled with pain, joy, and an awareness of loss that would endure in the weeks, months, and years ahead.

Sunday morning the blending communities celebrated a festive Eucharist. At the presentation of the gifts, the liturgists had expanded the ritual of table setting with the song "We Come to Your Feast."[11] Each of the verses in turn called forward a dancer carrying one of the furnishings for the table: the cloth, the bread, the wine, a bowl of incense. Last in the procession, a senior member of the incoming community moved forward as the assembly sang a newly written verse. She bore a tray carrying the rolled-up profession scrolls of each sister. She placed them on the altar table, where they would remain throughout

[11] J. Michael Joncas, "We Come to Your Feast" (Chicago: GIA Publications, 1994).

the Eucharist, at the end of which the prioress would remove them to be deposited in the monastery archive. The act was a corporate reenactment of what each sister had done individually at the time of her original profession. The Rule of Saint Benedict states clearly that the original profession documents are to be maintained in the community archives (RB 58.29). Moving them was a symbolic act whose meaning everyone present knew. New relationships were being sealed. At the close of the Sunday Eucharist liturgy, a festive meal was served in the refectory where the storytelling had taken place the evening before.

One thing remained to complete the transition process. In the Sunday evening prayer, Fangman, as the federation president, read the formal juridical decree declaring that the monastery that had long been their home was dissolved—because it now had no members. Their transition, which had begun months earlier with a vote of the receiving chapter to accept the group as full members, needed ecclesiastical confirmation. And so it was done. Again it was a time of great joy mixed with great sadness. The work of deepening the new relationships, ritually enacted over the two days, would be done as time unfolded. But it was clear what they intended. Now one body, they would slowly become "one mind, one heart."

The placement of the ritual acts within the Liturgy of the Hours and the eucharistic liturgy signaled a common frame of meaning for the two blending monastic communities. What was being done was an extended religious act, symbolic in its performance in an explicitly Catholic setting. Trinitarian presence, sacramental and real, was invoked and celebrated. The two prioresses, each of whom was understood to "hold the place of Christ in the monastery" (RB 2.2), had symbolically enacted a new relationship, one becoming less in the world's eyes while retaining "the full stature of Christ" in her act of handing over the authority she had held. The storytelling narrated a journey that passed through multiple dyings to new life in a new monastic house. The profession reenactment at the eucharistic table joined the spiritual sacrifice of the ten monastic women with the sacrifice of the altar, promising them new strength for continuing the journey. The juridical declaration dissolving their cherished monastery was the larger church's blessing on their ending and new beginning.

The particular schemes of ritualizing needed no explanation for those participating in them. They had been conceived mutually in response to the question, "What do we need to do to attend to relationships being severed and being formed?" As ritual theorist Bell had observed, the "deployment of familiar schemes" both structured the shared experience of the two blending assemblies and simultaneously reinforced the world shaped by the acts. The ritual mastery common to each body sealed the fit or coherence between the purpose of the ritual makers and their shared environment. The fit was both enacted and experienced as redemptive for those being empowered by the symbolic ritual process.[12] They were acting with the shared belief that the presence and power of God was among them and with them now and in all the days ahead.

If this ritualization of an end and a new beginning of publicly professed monastic relationships was straightforward, a second monastery closing whose ritualization I also guided was different and more difficult. The second monastery was closing at the direction of a different Midwestern federation to which it belonged because efforts at discernment about a new beginning had failed. Put simply, the eight members had no trust in the discernment process because of successive failures in making group decisions. An outside administrator had been charged not with preparations for a future election but with supervising the closing of the monastery, vacating and selling the property, and assisting members making their personal

---

[12] Bell, *Ritual Theory*, 115.

plans for finding a welcoming home in another monastic house or arranging for departure from religious life.

At the invitation of two prioresses, I had twice led earlier community retreats in this community. I was aware of the dysfunction to be contended with, primarily through confidential conversations with each of the members. Some of the dysfunction could well have been attributed to the youth of its founding sisters in the years following the Second Vatican Council in the 1960s. They were zealous for the good works of ministry. They did not realize the work to be done in building up a communal monastic enterprise. An intergenerational monastic community might well have been generative in its mentoring and nurturing of its young and in its transmission of its evolving monastic charism. But there was no turning back the clock to make up for the absence of a cohort of wise elders living among them from the start. They only slowly realized that the long-standing individualism tolerated in their early years meant that they had no future together. My final summons was to assist this group of fifty- and sixty-year-old monastic women in dissolving their bonds with dignity and grace. We were working with not much other than the assumption that whatever accumulated ritual mastery they enjoyed would make up for what was lacking in good memories of a richly shared life.[13]

Where to begin? Over the course of a day I had individual conversations with each sister. My questions: "What part of this life have been good for you spiritually? What will you most miss? Have you found and been accepted by another monastery where you can live peacefully?" Not surprisingly, most answered with affirmation of the ministries each had pursued. Fewer replies reflected monastic practices and relationships formed in the daily common life. I retired that night wondering

---

[13] Bell, *Ritual Theory*, 107.

whether and how the diffusion might be celebrated ritually. In my restlessness, a stray line from a long-forgotten poem by Gerard Manley Hopkins began to take shape: *give beauty back to God, beauty's self and beauty's giver.* I rose before dawn to begin my search. The monastic library was already partially packed in boxes. But I found in an anthology of Catholic poetry what needed to be retrieved and pondered, Hopkins's *The Leaden Echo and the Golden Echo.*[14]

We had an early morning gathering scheduled. How might we ritualize the end of their monastic life together? We looked at Hopkins's poem, which begins with a question that was also our question:

> *How to keep—is there any . . .*
>   *catch or key to keep*
> *Back beauty, keep it, beauty . . .*
>   *from vanishing away?*

The leaden echo sounds in reply, banishing any hope:

> *O there's none; no no no no there's none:*
> *Be beginning to despair, to despair,*
> *Despair, ...*

Yet the leaden echo is not the last word. What the sisters had named as good and life-giving despite decades of difficulties was substantial, more than something to despair. It was, and it was good. The poet had attuned his ear and ours to the "golden echo."

> *Spare!*
> *There is one, yes I have one . . .*

---

[14] Gerard Manley Hopkins, "The Leaden Echo and the Golden Echo," in *Immortal Diamond: The Spiritual Vision of Gerard Manley Hopkins* (New York: Doubleday Image, 1995), 105–10.

One. Yes I can tell such a key, I do know such a place . . .
Give beauty back, beauty, beauty, beauty, back to God, beauty's
self and beauty's giver.

Here we found our common refrain for the ritual they would
enact as they prayed together in the monastery chapel one last
time. Each of the members had memories of great beauty—
fragments given them in their shared monastic life—for which
she wished to give thanks publicly.

The eldest among them, remembering the more than forty
women who had been part of the community over its five
decades, wanted to recognize the blessing of their presence,
whether they had left earlier or had died. So our ritual began
with a quasi-roll call of all the members of the now vanishing
monastery. Each name invoked was followed by a brief silence
for remembering. Then the eldest placed an earlier photo of
some part of the group on the altar table, returning the once
beloved community now to God's care. In another moment,
the youngest member chose the framed declaration long ago
handed to the founding members on that day when the local
bishop had come to bless their beginning. She read it aloud.
A bittersweet phrase resonated in the chapel quiet: this was a
monastery being established "in perpetuity." The declaration
too was placed on the altar table, beauty being returned to
God too soon.

A member who had worked with the monastery's oblates
spoke of the joy they had brought into her life and into the
monastery. She had a roster of their names. It was added to the
items being gathered on the altar. As each item was brought
forward, Hopkins's golden echo was sounded quietly together:
"Give beauty back, beauty, beauty, beauty, back to God,
beauty's self and beauty's giver." And so it continued until
many of the memories of beauty in plain sight around them
were named and symbolized through each member's gesture
of restoration to God's keeping.

The last thing set aside by the monastic women had been named as beloved by each of them: the forty acres of land on which the monastery sat, some wooded and some landscaped yard. The chapel windows looked out on the grounds in three directions. Each sister took her place at a window. Then the members of the dissolving monastery, with hands raised in blessing and voices joined, prayed that those who would next reside in this place would experience its goodness and beauty as they had, and give thanks to God.

Before the group broke up it was time for mutual blessing, a risk I had ventured as my contribution to the ritual. First the administrator among them was blessed and thanked; she had no lengthy history of their shared failures. Next came a sister ready to depart in the morning, back to the founding monastery. The initial approaches for blessing were awkward since not much trust or mutual affection had been expressed among them in recent months, even years. Without a model to follow but responding to a word of invitation, they slowly approached her and each other in turn: hands on shoulders, arms around shoulders, hand on a sister's head, and even embraces. Then it was time to go. The table was laid in the refectory, and a final meal prepared by the administrator was to be shared.

The end of generativity and nurturing among the community had already been sealed earlier when the chapter voted against the admission of a newcomer to monastic profession without speaking clearly to the others of their reasons. Discernment had failed. Observance of chapter 72 of the Rule of Saint Benedict had been bypassed for all practical purposes. Bearing one another's weaknesses had been trumped by steady preference of what was better for oneself (RB 72.7). Despite this fatal flaw, the group had possessed and had used the ritual mastery they had as a resource for severing the bonds that had tied them to the place and to one another. Good memories, even those tainted with a dose of self-interest, were set out in a final communal act as matters to be returned to God, the giver of all beauty. And returning the beauty was enough. Freed from relationships of the past set out in symbols, and perhaps learning from that past, they were freed to start again. Four returned to the founding community from which they had come. Two went elsewhere. One of these had been traumatized by a painful experience years earlier and needed a third new home to begin monastic life again. The youngest sister, who had not come from the founding community, also chose a new beginning. A third sister turned to the care of an aging parent, avoiding indefinitely a decision about either beginning anew or departing permanently.

This ritualizing of relationships begun and relationships ended has by no means become standard practice in houses undergoing restructuring or dissolution in North America. Thus a monastery almost 175 years old dissolved recently under the direction of its federation after years with an outside administrator. It had been the original motherhouse for most North American Benedictine monasteries. Its remaining members were mostly elderly women, sisters who had lived together much more than half a century. But new life was not coming, and they were scattering, moving to different host monasteries. While they too enjoyed a measure of ritual mastery from years of monastic living, it was not used to close down relationships that had caused them so much pain as well as moments of affirmation. Each simply left when departure plans could be arranged.

The sample of those who did ritualize the beginning and ending of relationship is too small to test in any formal way. However, I am ready to suggest, on the basis of the four samples, that taking the time to plan and to invest community members in such rituals has a positive effect on the well-being of those who took part in the restructuring and in the dissolution rituals. I share Bell's answer to the question "How is it that *ritual* activities are seen or judged to be the appropriate thing to do?" Why choose ritualization strategies over other ways of acting in a given situation?[15]

Making the choice for ritual acts is most effective, in her judgment, first when the relationships of power being negotiated are based on indirect claims of power in the situation. Second, the operative power can and must be made socially redemptive in order to be personally redemptive. In short, the original act of monastic profession is an act of faith, an act of trust in the community that is believed to mediate the power and presence of God. The power relationship is understood as a covenant, with God calling and the monastics responding with their lives. How can anyone simply set it aside? Not easily, without self-doubt or even guilt, unless the setting aside or renegotiating of relationship is done publicly and as an act of prayer, drawing on the familiar schemes of the already socialized body. Done with the blessing of the church and of the monastics themselves, the changes being made are also acts of faith.

So we return to the question of generativity as Michael Casey set it out for students of the monastic life. What we have considered here is less than the ideal intergenerational transmission of the monastic charism. Yet it is what has been and might yet be done when the handing on of the charism is no longer possible. It is my contention, after viewing these and other monastery closings over the last quarter century, that what might seem dead still contains a reserve of vitality. This vitality courses through the network of lifelong relationships that still warrant attention. To attend to them in public ritual action is to free those who share them to begin life again, trusting in the living God.

[15] Bell, *Ritual Theory*, 115.

Chapter 6

Benedict and Francis
Two Popes and Two Saints in Conversation

Brendan Thomas, OSB

S t. Peter's Square is one of the great theaters of the world, and its most spectacular production is the presentation of a new pope after a conclave. Twice I have had the opportunity to be present in the Piazza, first for the election of Pope Benedict (2005) and then for Pope Francis (2013). I have never experienced such a collective sense of anticipation and joy. Even before the name of the new pope is announced there is a rapturous response to the very fact of an election. The band of the Swiss Guards stops playing, the curtains part, and we hear the words, *annuncio vobis gaudium magnum: habemus papam.*

Perhaps it was no surprise that Joseph Ratzinger took the name *Benedict*. He was partly thinking of the "prophet of peace," Benedict XV, who steered the Church through the chaos of the First World War. But he was also inspired by "the extraordinary figure of the great 'Patriarch of western monasticism,' Saint Benedict of Norcia," whom he saw as a reference point for the unity of Europe and "a powerful call to the irrefutable Christian roots of European culture and civilisation."[1]

When Jorge Bergoglio appeared on that same balcony, he was more of an unknown entity: no one around me seemed to recognize his name. Indeed, he himself said that evening

[1] Pope Benedict XVI, *General Audience*, April 27, 2005.

that he had come "from the end of the world" to be with the people of Rome as their bishop. The first surprise of this man of many surprises was that he would take the name Francis. Strangely, the moment the name of the new pope was announced a phrase came into my head from G. K. Chesterton's biography of Francis of Assisi: "What Saint Benedict had stored, Saint Francis scattered."[2] For me this was a beautiful intuition of what might lie ahead. It is a phrase that has stayed with me and has helped me reflect on both the continuities and the discontinuities between the two popes, in light of the saints who inspired them, the two "Sons of Umbria," Saint Benedict and Saint Francis.

I would like to reflect on the priorities of these two popes in relation to their holy patrons. For a pope, a name is not just a name but a program. Benedict, Patron of Europe, and Francis, the Poor Man of Assisi, are two men who have shaped the hearts and minds of thousands of people, the former with his Rule, the latter with his life and spirit. But what program do these two saints represent, and what vision of life and faith do they offer?

What Benedict Stored . . .

Before his election, Cardinal Ratzinger had drawn on the writings of Arnold Toynbee and his analysis of the rise and fall of great civilizations.[3] Toynbee's thesis was that civilizations collapse primarily from internal decline rather than external assault: "Civilisations die from suicide, not by murder."[4] How,

---

[2] Gilbert K. Chesterton, *St. Francis of Assisi* (London: Hodder & Stoughton, 1923), 112.

[3] Arnold Toynbee, *A Study of History*, 12 vols. (London: Oxford University Press, 1934–1961).

[4] Although this phrase is much quoted, Toynbee never used these exact words, but rather, referring to Edward Gibbon's view of the decline of the Roman Empire, he said, "I think it really began to decline in

then, are great civilizations kept alive? The answer is to be found in "creative minorities," small groups whose energies and talents can revitalize society and who, because of their passion and vision, are able to exercise an influence beyond their numbers. Cardinal Ratzinger's program for the Church seemed to borrow this idea of "creative minorities." He seemed to envision a church that was smaller yet more vital, a church more sure of its own identity, more cohesive and focused than it currently was.

After the turbulent changes in the world of the mid-twentieth century, and after the unsteadiness in the Church following the Second Vatican Council, Ratzinger wanted to steady the boat with a surer and clearer teaching. As cardinal, he had promoted the Catechism of the Catholic Church, and as pope, he has left perhaps the greatest teaching legacy of any of his predecessors, like a modern church father. He was also concerned to promote a holiness and faithfulness in the Church that would shine out in the midst of decay. The Church would be a mustard seed in a decaying society, an image that he frequently saw as appropriate to the wintertime of the faith.[5] He saw the energy and vitality of creative minorities in the Church as necessary to revitalize culture and society.[6]

---

the fifth century before Christ. It died, not by murder, but by suicide" (Arnold Joseph Toynbee, *Civilisation on Trial* [Oxford: Oxford University Press, 1948], 200).

[5] In his 1996 interview with Peter Seewald, he said, "Maybe we are facing a new and different kind of epoch in the church's history, where Christianity will again be characterized more by the mustard seed, where it will exist in small, seemingly insignificant groups that nonetheless live an intense struggle against evil and bring good into the world—that let God in" (Joseph Cardinal Ratzinger, *Salt of the Earth* [San Francisco: Ignatius Press, 1996], 16).

[6] "We do not know what the future of Europe will be. Here we must agree with Toynbee, that the fate of a society always depends on its creative minorities. Christian believers should look upon themselves as

It is easy to see Pope Benedict's appeal to the so-called Benedictine Centuries, where monasteries responded to the collapse of the Roman Empire by storing up and shoring up Western culture. This was the "storing" referred to in Chesterton's phrase: not so much the work of an individual saint, but of the whole Western monastic movement that Benedict inspired (Benedictine and, later, Cistercian). As Kenneth Clark put it in his landmark BBC television series of 1969, *Civilisation*: "monks kept civilisation alive," Christian monasticism saved European culture, and we got through "by the skin of our teeth." When for five hundred years practically no layperson could read or write, monasticism was the agent of rebirth. "By the year 1000, the year in which many timid people had feared that the world would come to an end, the long dominance of the barbarians was over, and Western Europe was prepared for its first great age of civilisation."[7]

Around the first feast of Saint Benedict after the papal election, the pope spoke of the saint as founding a fraternal community on the primacy of the love of Christ. He added, "Amid the ashes of the Roman Empire, Benedict, seeking first of all the kingdom of God, sowed, perhaps even without realizing it, the seed of a new civilisation which would develop, integrating Christian values with classical heritage."[8]

just such a creative minority, helping Europe to reclaim what is best in its heritage and thereby to place itself at the service of all humankind" (Joseph Ratzinger and Marcello Pera, *Without Roots: The West, Relativism, Christianity, Islam* [New York: Basic Books, 2006], 79). See also his interview on Vatican Radio, reported in *Zenit* on November 25, 2004.

[7] Kenneth Clark, *Civilisation* (London: John Murray Publishers, 1969), 31. The book accompanied the television series *Civilisation* of the same year.

[8] Pope Benedict XVI, "Angelus Address," July 10, 2005 (https://w2.vatican.va/content/benedict-xvi/en/angelus/2005.index.html, acc. Jan. 27, 2017).

Saint Benedict is a symbol of new birth in the midst of chaos. For me, one of the most moving and symbolic monastic sites is Nero's Villa, Subiaco, Italy. Most people pass it by as they head up to the Sacro Speco, the "Holy Cave" where Benedict retreated to be alone with God. Yet it was in the ruins of Nero's Villa that Benedict established one of these creative Christian communities, his first monastery dedicated to Saint Clement. There he offered order and stability so that the dynamic of love could be creative. And it was creative: soon Benedict had founded twelve monasteries in the Subiaco valley, and as history progressed monasteries would be founded in tens, hundreds, and thousands. Pope Benedict's project of renewal for the Church was founded on the creativity of the monastic centuries, for which Saint Benedict is the inspiration.

The pope noted that the saint had not founded a missionary order; rather, he had set up communities with the sole objective of its members' seeking God. Renewal, he said, comes through the creative dynamic of holiness, of people who have learned to direct their gaze toward God: "Benedict . . . indicated to his followers that the fundamental, and even more, the sole objective of existence is the search for God: *Quaerere Deum*. He knew, however, that when the believer enters into a profound relationship with God he cannot be content with living in a mediocre way, with a minimalist ethic and superficial religiosity."[9]

Just the day before Pope John Paul II died, Cardinal Ratzinger had been at Subiaco, delivering a lecture precisely on this theme, Europe's crisis of culture. He began his lecture by saying, "We live in a moment of great danger and of great opportunity for man and for the world, a moment which also is one of great responsibility for all of us." He went on to explain his Benedictine vision, that what the Church needed most at that moment of history was holiness, "a true pastoral

---

[9] Pope Benedict XVI, "Angelus Address."

imperative in our time." Not, he said, the negative testimony of Christians "who speak about God and live against him," but the witness of "men who, through an enlightened and lived faith, render God credible in this world." He concluded his Subiaco lecture with these words:

> Only through men who have been touched by God, can God come near to men. We need men like Benedict of Norcia, who at a time of dissipation and decadence, plunged into the most profound solitude, succeeding, after all the purifications he had to suffer, to ascend again to the light, to return and to found Montecasino, the city on the mountain that, with so many ruins, gathered together the forces from which a new world was formed.
>
> In this way Benedict, like Abraham, became the father of many nations. The recommendations to his monks presented at the end of his "Rule" are guidelines that show us also the way that leads on high, beyond the crisis and the ruins.[10]

Saint Benedict and his brothers witnessed to a love of God, but also to God's love for the individual. Putting "nothing before the love of God," they were to show "unfeigned and humble love" to their abbot and the "pure love of brothers" to their fellow monks (see RB 72). The saint reminded his men to honor the old and the sick, the poor and the pilgrim, and

---

[10] Cardinal Joseph Ratzinger, "On Europe's Crisis of Culture," Subiaco, April 1, 2005 (http://www.catholiceducation.org/en/culture/catholic-contributions/cardinal-ratzinger-on-europes-crisis-of-culture.html, acc. Jan. 27, 2017). There are echoes here of Alasdair MacIntyre's book, *After Virtue*, in which he spoke of waiting "for another—doubtless very different—St. Benedict." This new Benedict would help construct "local forms of community within which civility and the intellectual and moral life can be sustained through the new dark ages" (Alasdair MacIntyre, *After Virtue* [London: Duckworth, 1981], 263).

to find something to love in the young. He taught them the importance of *humanitas*. The monks' gaze toward God allowed them to understand true humanity.

The vision of renewal proposed by the shy scholar-pope, Benedict, could appear rather inward looking. But in his estimation, the Church cannot have an impact on the world unless it is faithful, true, and holy. So the teacher-pope worked to reinforce the Church's sense of its identity and purpose. He urged that Christian communities should be creative witnesses to a different reality, the love of God revealed in Christ. He realized, along with Paul VI, that what were most needed were witnesses rather than teachers,[11] or, to use the language of his predecessor, Pope John Paul II, "heralds of the Gospel who are experts in humanity."[12] For Saint Benedict the way to be the "light on the hilltop" at Monte Cassino was to go first into the darkness of the cave at Subiaco, to "live with oneself"—to grow in understanding of oneself before God—before any work of transformation could be confidently undertaken.[13] There is a time for storing.

---

[11] "Modern man listens more willingly to witnesses than to teachers. And if he does listen to teachers, it is because they are witnesses" (Paul VI, *Evangelii Nuntiandi, Apostolic Exhortation on Evangelisation in the Modern World*, 1976, 41 (http://w2.vatican.va/content/paul-vi/en/apost_exhortations/documents/hf_p-vi_exh_19751208_evangelii-nuntiandi.html, acc. Jan. 27, 2017).

[12] "We need heralds of the Gospel who are experts in humanity, who know the depths of the human heart, who can share the joys and hopes, the agonies and distress of people today, but at the same time contemplatives who have fallen in love with God. For this we need new saints. The great evangelizers of Europe were those saints" (Pope John Paul II, *Address to the Council of the European Episcopal Conference*, October 11, 1985, no. 13, *L'Osservatore Romano*, English edition, 21).

[13] Gregory the Great, *Dialogues* II.1.3, in *Gregory the Great: The Life of Saint Benedict*, trans. Adalbert de Vogüé (Petersham, MA: St. Bede's Publications, 1993), 10.

. . . Francis Scattered

At the first opportunity, the day after his election, Pope Francis explained his choice of name. As the voting reached the required two-thirds majority and there was the customary applause, Cardinal Hummes turned and hugged his friend and said, "Do not forget the poor." Pope Francis later commented,

And that word stuck here [tapping his forehead]; the poor, the poor. Then, right away, thinking of the poor, I thought of Francis of Assisi. Then I thought of war. . . . And so the name came to my heart: Francis of Assisi. For me he is the man of poverty, the man of peace, the man who loves and safeguards creation. . . . He is the man who gives us this spirit of peace, the poor man. . . . Oh, how I wish for a Church that is poor and for the poor![14]

While Nero's Villa represents a new, mustard-seed beginning for the church in the life of Benedict, a ruined chapel on the hillside below Assisi signals both the decline of one era and the birth of a new one. The irony should not be lost on us that it was in the ruins of a Benedictine church, San Damiano in Assisi, that Francis received the call from Christ on the cross to "Rebuild my church."

Tides of creativity come and go, and Benedictine life was no longer a vital force in the Church. Through wealth, power, and human encumbrances, its strength had been sapped, and it was no longer an effective transformer of society. The monasteries that had once kept civilization alive now seemed too distant and self-satisfied, inward looking and detached from the life of the world.

---

[14] Pope Francis, *Address to the Representatives of the Communications Media*, March 16, 2013 (http://w2.vatican.va/content/francesco/en /speeches/2013/march/documents/papa-francesco_20130316 _rappresentanti-media.html, acc. Jan. 27, 2017).

Arnold Toynbee speaks of how a "creative minority" can
cease to be creative, while degenerating into a merely "dominant minority." It becomes a proud worshiper of its old self
rather than an energetic force. The majority continues to obey,
but it no longer merits obedience. He argues that "creative
minorities" deteriorate because of worship of their former self,
by which they become proud and fail adequately to address
new challenges. Perhaps there is something in that.

Francis recognized this disconnect with the world outside
and knew that it was not enough for the Word of God to be
stored securely within monastic walls; it needed to go out, and
to be lived out, with new vigor. Saint Benedict had fled the city;
Saint Francis saw it was time to embrace it.

It is easy to see the Saint of Assisi in Pope Francis. This is a
pope of action, who bounds among the people and is moving
swiftly and fearlessly in the direction of a church reform that
Pope Benedict was unable to implement. He is a man who has
also spent some twenty years as a street-and-slum bishop and
has a natural empathy for those on the margins. Whereas Pope
Benedict seemed happiest alone with his books in the solitude
of the Apostolic Palace, Pope Francis felt the need to be down
on the ground among the people, staying at the Santa Martha
Guesthouse for his own psychological good. He loves "the smell
of the sheep." He is a gifted preacher like his predecessor, but
with a natural ability to translate Christ's teaching into action
through concrete gestures. The Word must go out. "What Saint
Benedict had stored Saint Francis scattered. What had been stored
into the barns like grain was scattered over the world like seed."[15]

Frequently Pope Francis has spoken of a missionary church.
In his first solo encyclical, *Evangelii Gaudium*, he elaborated a
vision of a Church governed by "a missionary impulse capable
of transforming everything, so that the Church's customs, ways

[15] Chesterton, *St. Francis*, 112.

of doing things, times and schedules, language and structures can be suitably channelled for the evangelisation of today's world rather than for her self-preservation."[16] Under Francis the Church has moved into a different mode. He presents a vision of a Church of open doors; the Church as a "field hospital" reaching out to others, healing, preaching, evangelizing; a Church with a mission to the margins. He is the "Pope of the Peripheries." We can imagine him in the fields of Assisi, joyously working with Francis and his band of brothers. The fact that the pope is "from the ends of the earth," is key, because he sees that the center must serve the margins. Pope Francis has put the Church on Franciscan mission alert. The impulse is always outward, and with it he offers a critique of power being stored at the center. He has constantly criticized aspects of the Church that are inward looking and self-serving. He exhorted the Brazilian bishops, "Today, we need a Church capable of walking at people's side, of doing more than simply listening to them; a Church which accompanies them on their journey."[17]

There is no doubt that Pope Francis appreciates his patron at many levels: "He's great because he is everything. He is a man who wants to do things, wants to build, he founded an order and its rules, he is an itinerant and a missionary, a poet and a prophet, he is mystical. He found evil in himself and rooted it out. He loved nature, animals, the blade of grass on the lawn and the birds flying in the sky. But above all he loved people,

[16] Pope Francis, *Evangelii Gaudium* 27, November 2013 (http://w2 .vatican.va/content/francesco/en/apost-exhortations/documents /papa-francesco-esortazione-ap_20131124_evangelii-gaudium.html, acc. Jan. 28, 2017).

[17] Pope Francis, *Address to the Bishops of Brazil*, Saturday, July 28, 2013 (w2.vatican.va/content/francesco/en/speeches/2013/july/documents /papa-francesco_20130727_gmg-episcopato-brasile.html, acc. Jan. 28, 2017).

children, old people, women. He is the most shining example of . . . agape, love."[18]

Benedict and Francis: Some Contrasts

With the general framework set, it seems useful to draw out a few further contrasts between the Benedictine and the Franciscan popes.

1. Stability and Itinerancy

Saint Benedict probably wrote his Rule at Monte Cassino, a place of strategic importance that looks down on a major thoroughfare between the north and south of Italy. One of the leaders that Gregory the Great records visiting the abbot was King Totila of the Goths, the man who sacked Rome (the Gothic wars raged from 535 to 553).[19] We know only too well in our day how invasion and war leads to refugees and the displacement of peoples. What greater teaching could Benedict offer a world in turmoil than the importance of stability?

"'Give me but one firm spot on which to stand, and I will move the earth' said Archimedes."[20] Benedict established firm places of commitment and community, strongholds where peace would be prized, where wounded souls could find healing, where people could learn the art of living together in concord and cherish mutual love.

It is more than likely that Benedict's community would have been a very mixed community, one that had within it all

---

[18] Pope Francis, "A Dialogue with Eugenio Scalfari," *La Repubblica*, October 1, 2013.

[19] Gregory the Great, *Dialogues* II.14 and 15.

[20] A remark of Archimedes quoted by Pappus of Alexandria, *Collection or Synagoge*, book 8, ca. AD 340, in *The Oxford Dictionary of Quotations*, 2nd ed. (London: Oxford University Press, 1953), 14.

the different levels of society and different ethnicities. The rich and the poor, learned and illiterate, Romans and Goths, the young and the old, were challenged to live in love despite their differences and the inevitable tensions, to find peace among the thorns of difficulties. The monastery was the workshop of human relationships.

One of the most important things that monks could offer in the Middle Ages was to live out their vow of stability. Monasteries became fixed places on the medieval landscape. People came to settle near the monasteries, so that, over many generations, towns and cities were built up around them. In a time of great chaos their decision to stay rooted shaped an entire culture. No wonder Benedict's monks began each day crying out to the Lord as a Rock who saves (RB 9). Nothing was more important than to be anchored in God.

The needs of Saint Francis's day were different. He would sail through the villages, such as Poggio Bustone, endearing himself to the people with the cheery greeting *Buon giorno, buona gente!* [21] (Good morning, good people!) There is a plaque in the town recording Francis's instruction to his first seven companions: "Go, dearest brothers, two by two into the various parts of the world announcing peace to the people." The saint's model was Jesus on the move: itinerant, preaching, with nowhere to lay his head.

Saint Benedict preached at Monte Cassino, but Saint Francis made preaching his wholehearted mission: to town and city folk, to the pope, to the animals, and to the birds. He used poetry and word-pictures, gestures and song to get his message home. At Greccio in 1223 he brought the Christmas gospel to life with a living ox and an ass. When he traveled to Egypt he preached to a Muslim sultan with the idea of making peace.

---

[21] Many Italians seem to prize Pope Francis's simple greeting from the balcony, *Buona sera* (Good evening).

I wonder where we would find Saint Benedict in the parable of the Good Samaritan. I am sure the good man would not pass by the wounded on the road, but he didn't think monks should roam about. I sometimes think of Benedict as the one doing the caring at the inn. The innkeeper is perhaps a bit neglected in our usual telling of that parable, but he was charged with the ongoing care of this man left battered and bruised on the roadside and brought him back to life. Benedict's communities were inns of hospitality, places of refuge, places of order, but above all places where wounded souls could go and find healing, where wounds could be bandaged and oil and wine poured on them—places where the weak would not be left behind.

But Francis was out there on the road, searching out the wounded, embracing those whom the Church had seemingly ignored.

2. Pragmatism and Idealism

In his Testament of 1226 Francis declared that God personally revealed to him that he should live according to the form of the Holy Gospel. Nothing less than this was to be his Rule of life, and Christ was the only model he needed. When the cardinal protector tried to persuade Francis to accept the wise guidance of the earlier monastic rules, he stubbornly responded, "My brothers! My brothers! God has called me by the way of simplicity and humility. . . . Therefore I do not want you to mention to me any Rule—whether of Saint Augustine, or of Saint Bernard or of Saint Benedict, or any other form of life except the one that the Lord in his mercy has shown and given to me. And the Lord told me what he wanted: he wanted me to be a new kind of fool in this world. God did not wish to lead us by any other way than this."[22] Yet as his merry band

---

[22] *The Mirror of Perfection*, 68, in *Francis of Assisi: Early Documents*, vol. 3, *The Prophets*, trans. Regis J. Armstrong, J. A. Wayne Hellman, and William J. Short (New York: New City Press, 2001), 314.

of followers increased from a few dozen to an order of five thousand in his lifetime, it became clear that Francis would have to provide some organizational structure and guidance if the Order was to grow prudently and survive the charismatic inspiration of one man.

This was the beginning of much heartache for Francis, for his own friars rejected his first Rule (the Primitive Rule of 1221). Finally a rule was approved by Honorius III (Regula Bullata of 1223) with an emphasis on poverty, loyalty to the Roman church, and preaching. Yet Francis was not happy with the compromises that he was forced to make. His friars demanded something more "observable." Yet another draft was brought back to him for revision, omitting some key gospel passages that defined his mission, and his real anger and frustration came to the fore: "Who are these people? They have snatched out of my hands my religion and that of the brothers. . . . I'll show them what is my will."[23]

The truth is that the Order was falling apart. The emphasis on poverty was the cause of great tension, and it hindered the development of studies and pastoral activity. It was one thing to be a poor friar, "naked to follow the naked Christ" (to use Saint Jerome's phrase). But their priests: Should they be trained, should they study, should they have books or buy chalices? Would even the possession of a psalter distract a friar from ministering to the poor? Different views on poverty within the Order eventually led it to fall apart with recriminations.

The crux of the issue is that Francis seems to have been a hopeless romantic and visionary. He was not satisfied with anything less than a radical living of the Gospel. He had one model: Christ himself. He had one rule: the Gospel. He saw no need to write another.

---

[23] *Assisi Compilation* II, 44, in *Francis of Assisi: Early Documents*, vol. 2, *The Founder*, trans. Regis J. Armstrong, J. A. Wayne Hellman, and William J. Short (New York: New City Press, 2000), 146.

Someone once said that a martyr is "someone who lives with a saint." Not everyone is able to measure up to, or live with, a man of such clear vision as Francis: an idealist who found it difficult to temper his principles to human needs.

Saint Benedict, on the other hand, was a pragmatist and knew how to carry people with him. He challenged the strong but would not let the weak fall behind: *"Do not scour the rusty pot. . . . Do not crush the bruised reed. . . .* Give the strong something to aim for; do not let the weak fall behind" (RB 64). Rightly his biographer, Pope Gregory the Great, saw discretion as the hallmark of his Rule. Benedict himself calls it "the mother of virtues." He says, "Drawing on this and other examples of discretion, the mother of virtues, he must so arrange everything that the strong have something to yearn for and the weak nothing to run from" (RB 64.19).

Benedict claims, in effect, that his Rule will not take his men to the heights, calling it "a little Rule for beginners" (RB 73.8). But we must make a beginning, and the first step must always be from where we are. We mustn't allow the best to become the enemy of the good. We mustn't be paralyzed because we cannot attain perfection. It is better to do something than do nothing. Michael Casey has likened the Rule to buildings in earthquake zones: anything that is too rigid will collapse; flexibility is the key. He has also pointed out that Benedict is far from being the perfect legislator.[24] But this imperfection allows him to reveal a measure of humanity. The content of the Rule suggests that Benedict is comfortable with the fact that in real life there is a gap between what the rules say and what actually happens. But Francis struggled to see it.

[24] "Far from being a blueprint issuing from the far-seeing mind of a genius the Rule is, perhaps, better understood as a working document, progressively nuanced on the basis of a lifetime's experience" (Michael Casey, *"Quod Experimento Didicimus*: The Heuristic Wisdom of Saint Benedict," TJ 48 [1995]: 3–22).

3. *Individual and Communal Poverty*

The difference between ideals and reality is evident in the approach of the two saints to poverty. Both were certainly influenced by their historical contexts. Living in the dying days of the Roman Empire, Benedict was not the only one to leave the city and head off into the countryside. Urban life was in decline, society became more rural, and feudal institutions developed among the landed aristocracy. Francis, on the other hand, lived in a changing world where cities were growing and a shift was being made to a market economy. The new wealthy merchant class pursued money as a primary goal and indicator of status. Francis's father, Pietro di Bernardone, was part of this new moneyed class, a cloth merchant, importing luxury fabrics (his trading visits to France may have earned the young Giovanni de Bernardone the nickname *Francesco*, "Frenchy").

Yet in a momentous decision Francis gave his belongings to the poor. He made a famous naked protest at the beginning of his ministry and proclaimed his love for a new mistress, Lady Poverty, the "fairest bride in the whole world."[25] Dispossession became the chosen path of Francis's discipleship of Christ.

[25] This image, portrayed in a fresco by Giotto in the Lower Basilica of Assisi, was perhaps inspired by one of the richest texts of the early Franciscan movement, *Sacrum Commercium*, or *The Sacred Exchange between Saint Francis and Lady Poverty*, which became an important self-expression of the Franciscan ideal. It tells how Francis sought out the poor, despised, and hated Lady Poverty and made her his bride. The theme is perhaps drawn from a story that Thomas of Celano later relates of the young Francis saying to his friends, "I will take a bride more noble and more beautiful than you have ever seen, and she will surpass the rest in beauty and excel all others in wisdom," though the Bride represented there is not Holy Poverty, but the order to which Francis is wedded. See *The Life of Francis by Thomas of Celano, The First Book*, III.7, and *The Sacred Exchange* in *Francis of Assisi: Early Documents*, vol. 1, *The Saint*, trans. Regis J. Armstrong, J. A. Wayne Hellman, and William J. Short (New York: New City Press, 2000), 188, 534–35.

Later, Francis described the following ideal for his brotherhood in his Testament: "Those who wished to embrace the life gave the poor everything they had and contented themselves with a tunic patched inside and out, and a belt and some underclothes. And we did not wish for anything more."[26] Francis, who saw a similarity between money and feces, forbade his friars to touch money: "I firmly command all the brothers that they in no way receive coins of money, either personally or through an intermediary."[27]

Saint Benedict was equally uncompromising about private ownership. At his clothing a monk must give away his possessions and recognize that whatever he may have for his personal use is the common property of the community (RB 58). But his teaching is more practical than is that of Francis in allowing a monk what is deemed necessary. Needs were to be provided for good, well-fitting clothing and a knife, tablet, and stylus (RB 55.19). In fact Saint Benedict never uses the word *poverty*, or rather only once, where poverty is mentioned as the exception, where difficult times may force monks to work in the field: poverty is thus the exception, not the norm (RB 48.7). Poverty was not an end in itself, and Benedictines do not traditionally take a vow of poverty.

Abbot Cuthbert Butler of Downside argued that if the religious life was the imitation of Christ and religious poverty is the imitation of Christ's poverty, then we may talk of the different kinds of poverty in the different phases of Christ's life. There was the poverty of Jesus in his three years of public ministry, where the *Son of Man has nowhere to lay his head* (Luke 9:58), which led to the poverty of the cross, but there was also the humble simplicity of Nazareth. There was the ideal given to the rich young man

---

[26] Francis of Assisi, *The Testament, 16,* in *Francis of Assisi: Early Documents,* vol. 1, *The Saint,* 125.

[27] Francis of Assisi, *The Later Rule, IV,* in *Francis of Assisi: Early Documents,* vol. 1, *The Saint,* 102.

(Mark 10:17-22), but there was also the ideal of common owner-ship of the first Jerusalem Community (Acts 2:44-45; 4:32-34).[28]

So Butler argued that Calvary was the ideal of Franciscan poverty—the "highest poverty"—and Nazareth the type of Benedictine poverty. Benedictine poverty is not the poverty of the beggar but the poverty of the simple workman, the carpen-ter, the artisan: simplicity and frugality rather than want. Ben-edict insists on stewardship, responsibility, care of goods, and well-fitting clothes. Benedict's monks gave their old clothes to the poor; Francis's friars wore them. Of course some monas-teries did become very rich over time, and that would become a grave problem. The Franciscan problem, on the other hand, was the Poverello's uncompromising stance on poverty (a con-viction reinforced by Clare). Over time his Order tore itself apart over his strictures. Francis also had his external critics: wealthy clerics and landowning monasteries would certainly have been uncomfortable with his radical teaching, but so were other mendicant orders. As Franciscans and Dominicans began to attend universities, their theologians had heated debates. Thomas Aquinas countered that love, not poverty, was the measure of perfection. The Franciscans responded by sim-ply forbidding their members to read Thomas's writings! A modern critique suggests that those who voluntarily embraced this Franciscan practice of poverty may have done the real poor very little good at all and may even have worsened their plight rather than alleviating it, as Francis's begging friars came into direct competition with real impoverished beggars.[29]

---

[28] Cuthbert Butler, *Benedictine Monachism* (London: Longmans, Green & Co., 1919), 146–60.

[29] "Francis's extreme love of poverty, pursued for the sake of his own spiritual progress . . . potentially made the lives of those suffering from involuntary poverty even more difficult" (Kenneth Baxter Wolf, *The Poverty of Riches: St. Francis of Assisi Reconsidered* [Oxford: Oxford University Press, 2003], 4).

While Pope Francis has eschewed the papal apartments and limousine (giving a new meaning to the phrase "Papal Fiat"), it is, I think, unfair to contrast his personal life with that of Pope Benedict, who seemed to display a respect for tradition rather than a love of personal opulence. Perhaps there is a parallel with monks living in relative personal poverty while residing in great baroque edifices. The sign value is certainly missing. Pope Francis is concerned with the sign we give. But his critics have leveled the charge of "pauperism" at him, a charge that he has explicitly repudiated while yet fully insisting on the gospel message of not serving two masters, God and wealth. He has stated, "The Gospel does not condemn the rich but idolatry of wealth, that idolatry that renders [us] insensitive to the cries of the poor."[30]

While it seems absurd to us that Francis of Assisi would not let his friars touch money, we can hear an echo of his concern in the pope's criticism of unchecked capitalism.[31] There does seem to be something a little unnatural about the world of usury and the accumulation of massive debts. There does seem something unreal about the way markets behave, where the swings of stocks and shares can affect the lives of ordinary people. There does seem to be something inhuman in the activities of loan sharks who disregard the dignity of other human beings.

Neither Umbrian saint could have foreseen the world of modern economics, but Saint Benedict would pay special care to the poor knocking on the door, while Saint Francis would be going out to live among them.

[30] Pope Francis, interview in *La Stampa*, January 11, 2015.

[31] "We have created new idols. The worship of the golden calf of old has found a new and heartless image in the cult of money and the dictatorship of an economy which is faceless and lacking any truly humane goal" (Pope Francis, *Address to Ambassadors*, May 16, 2013 [http://w2 .vatican.va/content/francesco/en/speeches/2013/may/documents /papa-francesco_20130516_nuovi-ambasciatori.html, acc. Jan. 27, 2017]).

4. Culture, Nature, and Art

It would seem easy to contrast Saint Benedict and Saint Francis as a "Man of Culture" against a "Man of Nature." While Francis had little interest in books and learning, Benedict promoted reading (we might think of his insistence that monks take a book in Lent and read it from beginning to end—no flicking through or dipping into [RB 49]). Francis preferred people to books and the land to libraries. Benedict's monks seemed to go out into the fields only through force of circumstance; Francis and his band were men of the open air. Benedict is a man of the cloister, but Francis's cloister is the world.

Yet we might note some paradoxes that challenge this broad characterization. First, the Franciscans grew in numbers precisely because they were present at the universities that were developing in the cities, while the Benedictines often remained detached from these new seats of learning.

Likewise a case can be made for the Benedictine attachment to the land. In a television program for the BBC in the 1980s, Prince Charles went to Subiaco, not Assisi, and declared that Benedict, not Francis, should be considered patron saint of the environment precisely because the Benedictines (particularly the Cistercians) showed themselves to be true stewards and cultivators of the land, transforming but not exploiting the terrain. Perhaps the prince considered Francis more a Dr. Dolittle than a true steward of the environment. Nothing, however, can expunge the popular image of Francis as the "Saint of the Bird-Bath," nor should it, and Pope Francis's encyclical on the environment, *Laudato Sì*, rightly takes its title from the first words of his patron's Canticle of Creatures: "All praise be yours, my Lord, through all that you have made."[32]

---

[32] Pope Francis, *Laudato Sì* 1, May 24, 2015 (w2.vatican.va/content /francesco/en/encyclicals/documents/papa-francesco_20150524 _enciclica-laudato-si.html, acc. Jan. 27, 2017).

Saint Benedict encouraged the craftsman in his monastery as long as human pride did not get in the way, and Benedictine monasteries are often places of beauty in their buildings and decoration. We might expect Francis's contribution to art to be rather more modest. Yet the impact of his teaching on the development of Western art can hardly be exaggerated. Andrew Graham-Dixon has argued that the Franciscans didn't just provide a background chapter to the Renaissance but were a fundamental part of it:

> The rise of Franciscanism marked a sea-change in attitudes, and in that sea-change may be found the origins of many of the most distinctive impulses of Renaissance art. The notion that an enhanced realism, an enhanced psychological penetration or an enhanced persuasiveness might be desirable in art—all these Renaissance articles of faith can demonstrably be shown to have been prefigured in the imperatives of Franciscan piety. Franciscanism was a credo which unleashed the imagination of artists, because it encouraged a certain independence of vision, an independence which has become deeply ingrained in the Western art tradition itself. It is sometimes thought that the Christian religion and the ambition for a Renaissance were forces pulling against one another. As the role of Franciscan ideas in accelerating artistic change demonstrates, religion was one of the great driving forces behind Renaissance art—not the brakes, so to speak, but the motor.[33]

It is indeed a paradox that Francis, who insisted on being buried among the graves of the poor on the Colle dell'inferno (Hill of hell) in Assisi, should find his tomb encased in one of the finest treasures of Western art, a double basilica that

---

[33] Andrew Graham-Dixon, *Renaissance* (London: BBC Books, 1999), 24.

counts Cimabue and Giotto as its artists. But why implicate Francis in the artistic movement that followed him? Precisely because his spiritual sensibility brought new feeling into the expression of faith.

Saint Benedict's image of Christ would have been shaped by those majestic Pantocrators glimpsed in the Roman basilicas of his day: Christ, sitting on a jewel-encrusted throne, majestic, all-powerful, portrayed as an emperor and as a teacher. At a time when the Arian Goths were threatening Italy and denying the divinity of Christ, Benedict affirmed his faith in Christ, the Lord and King, and had but one aim, to serve him.

In contrast, Francis felt no need to defend the divinity of Christ but sought to remind the world that God had become small in Christ. His living crib at Greccio—"a new Bethlehem"—was intended to bring home the humility of the incarnation in the littleness of the Child. Francis rehumanized Christ and returned him to the poor.

Art shifts in emphasis from the elegant yet rigid Byzantine style to a new naturalism. Now it is no longer the magi who come in procession to the enthroned Christ Child, but poor shepherds who bring their lambs to a baby in his crib. Christ is shown not at his most powerful but his most vulnerable—in the crib and on the cross, in the humility of the incarnation and the charity of the passion. Artists captured this new feeling. Perhaps it is not insignificant that Francis's first revelation at San Damiano was prompted by a work of art, for imagery would be at the heart of Franciscan preaching. So too, Francis would be among the first to write in vernacular Italian. As Christ had made himself humble, so must the language of the preacher be in order to reach his hearer.

Benedict is a man of tradition; Francis a man of innovation. Benedict's is the objective spirituality of the Scriptures, the liturgy, and the patristic age; for Francis it is subjective, full of natural human sentiment and devotion, easily understood by all. Perhaps we could also add that Benedict is paternal; Francis is more maternal.[34] For Benedict, Christ is always Lord and King—he never uses the personal name, Jesus. But Francis was "always with Jesus; Jesus in his heart, Jesus in his mouth, Jesus in his ears, Jesus in his eyes, Jesus in his hands, he bore Jesus always in his whole body."[35] We can hardly imagine Benedict "licking his lips" as did Francis as he said the name Jesus.

As for the two popes, can we in their homilies detect affinities of style and spiritual sensibility with their patrons? Pope Benedict is a man of deep culture, rooted in the church fathers, a lover of art and music and tradition, who sees the beauty of the faith as a key to bringing people to Christ. He could be called the "theologian's preacher," who wants to raise people up to God. Pope Francis shows little concern for music and art (for example, he does not attend public concerts), yet he preaches no less effectively and often more forcefully than Pope Benedict, with vivid, concrete imagery. He could be called the "people's preacher" (he has been described as "the world's parish priest"), who reminds them of the beauty of Christ's actions, which make God present in the world. So perhaps we could extend those words to these popes: Benedict is a man of the cloister, but Francis's cloister is the world.

5. The Horizontal and the Vertical

We do not choose the moment of our death, but how frequently the manner of a person's death reveals something of his or her whole life. The same can surely be said of these two

---

[34] For example, Benedict begins his Rule, "Listen carefully, my son, to the master's instructions. . . . This is advice from a father who loves you" (RB Prol.1), while Francis in his Rule for Hermits says of his hermit friars, "Let two who are 'mothers' keep the life of Martha and the 'two sons' the life of Mary" ("A Rule for Hermitages," in *Francis of Assisi: Early Documents*, vol. 1, *The Saint*, 61).

[35] Thomas of Celano, *The Life of Francis, The Second Book*, IX, in *Francis of Assisi: Early Documents*, vol. 2, *The Founder*, 283.

saints. The whole of Benedict's life seems to have been marked by an upward movement. Born in Norcia, a walled town surrounded on all sides by mountains, the young boy must surely have looked up for inspiration. In the surrounding heights lived hermits from whom he could have imbibed the monastic tradition, but there too is the most beautiful landscape of the Piano Grande of Castelluccio (so beautiful in fact that Franco Zeffirelli used it as the setting for much of his film about Francis, *Brother Sun and Sister Moon*, 1972). So the life of Benedict could be characterized by a yearning, an upward movement that would end on a commanding mountain: Monte Cassino.

Francis in contrast makes a downward move, from the city of Assisi on the hillside to live in the valley below, at Rivotoro (where he spent the happiest time of his life among the lepers) and the Portiuncula (the place that he made his base and where he died). Perhaps the life of Francis is marked by this descent following the path of God, who made his own descent in Christ in the "humility of the incarnation," to live among his people. As he approached his death, Francis instructed his companions: "When you see that I have come to the end, put me out naked on the ground . . . and once I am dead allow me to lie there for as long as it takes to walk a leisurely mile."[36] Francis is portrayed as dying alone, naked, on the earth: the horizontal. Benedict, in contrast, died in the Oratory of Monte Cassino, surrounded by his brethren: "He strengthened himself for his departure by receiving the Body and Blood of the Lord. While the hands of his disciples held up his weak limbs, he stood with his hands raised to heaven and breathed his last breath amidst words of prayer."[37] Benedict is portrayed dying standing upright, in perfect communion with his brethren and with God: the vertical.

[36] Thomas of Celano, *The Remembrance of the Desire of a Soul*, chap. 163, in *Francis of Assisi: Early Documents*, vol. 2, *The Founder*, 388.

[37] Gregory the Great, *The Dialogues* II.37.3, in Vogüé, *Gregory the Great*, 174.

Reading the life of Francis, one gets the sense that he was a man of great ideals, but they came to set him apart from those who were once his joyous companions. He was weak, blind, and frail. Benedict, on the other hand, may not have demonstrated the same radical sanctity but would die at peace with his brethren. It is a perfect image of communion. He could only receive the Body of Christ because his brothers were around him to hold him and support him. Benedict could not go it alone.

Benedict and Francis Together

It is notable that the oldest image of Saint Francis is not to be found in Assisi but at the Sacro Speco of Subiaco. Without a halo or stigmata, and referring simply to "Brother Francis," not "Saint Francis," it was possibly painted while he was still alive, but certainly before his canonization. There is a delightful tradition that Francis made a journey to Subiaco and turned Benedict's ascetical thorns into roses. Francis honors Benedict with a pilgrimage; Benedict's monks show their respect for Francis by painting his image in a chapel close to Benedict's cave. To this day, the Franciscans (who traditionally do not own property) pay a symbolic rent of a basket of fish to the Benedictines in Assisi for the Church of the Portiuncula. The Benedictines in their turn are happy to reciprocate with a gift of olive oil.

"Everyone has his own gift from God, one this, and another that," says Saint Benedict, citing Saint Paul (RB 40; 1 Cor 7:7). The Church grows and is enriched through difference and complementarity. Popes and saints, men and women, come with their own personal qualities and character traits that inevitably highlight different aspects of the Christian mystery. The Church grows and is enriched through diversity and complementarity. Pope Benedict remarked that "Catholicism . . . has always been considered the religion of the great 'et . . . et': not of great forms of exclusivism but of synthesis. The exact meaning of

'catholic' is 'synthesis.'"[38] He was talking about having to make a choice between two alternatives, playing football and attending eucharistic adoration, but it might equally apply to saints. For me, it is not a question of "better" or "worse." The Church is a thick soup enriched by both Benedictines and Franciscans, and equally by two popes with very different styles and qualities. It is a church of "both . . . and."

Fr. Michael Casey's scholarship and insight into the monastic tradition has contributed immensely to the work of formation in our monastic communities. He has been a great supporter of the Monastic Formators' Program from its inception, regularly teaching the almost thirty Benedictine and Cistercian men and women who gather each year from all over the world. The final few weeks of the program are spent in Assisi, and I always feel that although rooted with great delight in our own Benedictine tradition, the whole group is enriched and renewed through its meeting with Francis and Clare. We all go away as sons and daughters of Saint Benedict, certainly, but with a Franciscan spring in our step, sowing and scattering as we go.

[38] Meeting of Pope Benedict XVI with the Clergy of the Dioceses of Belluno-Feltre and Treviso, Auronzo di Cadore, July 24, 2007.

Chapter 7

Magistra Humilitas
Young Bernard's Hardest Lesson

Elias Dietz, OCSO

In the first book of the *Vita prima* (VP1), paragraphs 27–29, William of Saint-Thierry describes a serious crisis in the life of the young abbot Bernard.[1] The foundation of Clairvaux took place in 1115, and Bernard was already abbot, but if the chronology of VP1 is accurate, he had not yet been ordained or received the bishop's blessing as abbot. In any case, as William points out in the story that leads into the account of this crisis, the community was still preoccupied with basic material needs and not yet in a position to expand, as it did in 1118 when it founded Trois Fontaines. So a likely time frame for this episode is 1116 or 1117.

In sharp contrast to the admiring portrait of his subject painted thus far in VP1, William is uncompromising in his description of Bernard's immaturity and of the tensions that developed between the young abbot and his community. Because hagiographers rarely engage in such penetrating and critical assessments of their subjects, this account has a ring of authenticity. The timing of the account reinforces this impres-

[1] *Vita prima* 1.27–29; CCCM 89B:54–56, ll. 771–841; PL 185:243–44. Subsequent references to this passage will give only the line number in the CCCM edition. An English translation of this passage will be found in an appendix at the end of this article. The episode can be situated in the earliest days at Clairvaux, when Bernard was in his mid-twenties.

sion: Bernard's earliest works date to a period just subsequent to it (1118–1120), and the central theme of these writings is precisely what Bernard learned from this crisis, namely, humility.[2] This passage, then, would seem to be a privileged window on Bernard as a young abbot learning the hardest and most important lesson of his life.

But how transparent is this window? To what degree can we expect William's account to correspond with historical fact? According to historians like Adriaan Bredero, readers of VP1 should expect to find a seriously distorted presentation of the events of Bernard's life, since the sole purpose of the work is to turn Bernard into a legend and to make a case for his sainthood.[3] Jean Lerclercq, who largely accepted Bredero's conclusions, adds a psychological perspective, suggesting that much of what William says about Bernard is a projection of his own experience.[4] Alternatively, Leclercq suspects that William is proposing Bernard and the early community of Clairvaux as examples of his own ideals of monastic reform.[5] According to these approaches, the passage in question would be a mirror instead of a window.

Not all scholars, though, have accepted these extreme attitudes toward VP.[6] Most would concur with Michael Casey

---

[2] Christopher Holdsworth dates *De gradibus* to 1118/1119 and *De laudibus beatae Mariae* to 1119/1120; see his article "The Early Writings of Bernard of Clairvaux," *Cîteaux* 45 (1994): 21–61.

[3] See especially Adriaan Bredero, "Études sur la Vita Prima de S. Bernard," ASOC 17 (1961): 3–72, 215–60; 18 (1962): 3–59; and *Bernard of Clairvaux: Between Cult and History* (Grand Rapids, MI: Eerdmans, 1993). For an overview of Bredero's work, see W. Eugene Goodrich, "The Reliability of the *Vita Prima Sancti Bernardi*," CSQ 21 (1986): 213–27.

[4] Jean Leclercq, *Nouveau visage de Bernard de Clairvaux: Approches psycho-historiques* (Paris: Cerf, 1976), 27.

[5] Leclercq, *Nouveau visage*, 20.

[6] In addition to the article mentioned above in n. 2, see W. Eugene Goodrich, "The Reliability of the *Vita Prima Sancti Bernardi*: The Image

that it is important to take into account the nature of hagiography, to appreciate the intentions of the authors, to seek out parallel sources of information, especially from Bernard's own writings, and perhaps even to make intuitive leaps in interpreting VP.[7] To date, the most significant contribution along these lines is the work of Ferruccio Gastaldelli, who focused mostly on Bernard's early life as presented in Geoffrey of Auxerre's *Fragmenta* and in William of Saint-Thierry's VP1.[8] Although his judgment on the historical veracity of the various episodes recorded in these works is carefully nuanced and circumscribed, Gastaldelli nevertheless considers these writings to be valuable sources of information when it comes to ascertaining Bernard's character.

Another contribution worth mentioning here is Jacques Paul's article on the beginnings of Clairvaux, which is in fact a penetrating analysis of William's intentions in book 1 of VP1.[9] Paul remains extremely circumspect with regard to the historical value of the account, which, as he says, freely mixes "the true, the probable, and the incredible."[10] According to Paul, what stands out most in William's description of early

of Bernard in Book I of the *Vita prima* and His Own Letters; A Comparison," ASOC 43 (1987): 153–80.

[7] Michael Casey, "Toward a Methodology for the *Vita prima*: Translating the First Life into Biography," *Bernardus Magister*, CS 135 (Spencer, MA: Cistercian Publications, 1992), 69–70.

[8] Ferruccio Gastaldelli, "I primi vent'anni di san Bernardo," ASOC 43 (1987): 11–148; "Le più antiche testimonianze biografiche su san Bernardo. Studio storico-critico sui 'Fragmenta Gaufridi,'" ASOC 45 (1969): 3–80. Both articles are reprinted in Ferruccio Gastaldelli, *Studi su san Bernardo e Goffredo di Auxerre* (Florence: SISMEL-Galluzzo, 2001).

[9] Jacques Paul, "Les débuts de Clairvaux: Histoire et Théologie," *Vies et légendes de saint Bernard de Clairvaux: Création, diffusion, réception (XIIe–XXe Siècles), Actes des Rencontres de Dijon, 7–8 juin 1991*, ed. Patrick Arabeyre, Jacques Berlioz, and Philippe Poirrier (Brecht: Cîteaux, commentarii cistercienses, 1993), 19–35.

[10] Paul, "Les débuts," 23.

Clairvaux are his usual areas of strength, namely, theology and spirituality. The question, then, is less to what extent William conveys the facts than to what extent his theology and spirituality coincide with the mentality of the founders of Clairvaux. The main purpose of the present article is to engage in a close reading of William's description of Bernard's crisis as a young abbot. As a striking text by a profound and accomplished theologian and spiritual writer, it amply rewards such a reading. At the same time, this passage is an interesting testing ground for the various views of VP1 just mentioned. There can be no doubt that William provides his readers with a well-defined character portrait of young Bernard. Once that portrait is in clearer focus, the question will be to what degree it depicts Clairvaux's Bernard and to what degree William's.

Two preliminary notes are needed before delving into the text. First, it is important to keep in mind that the differences between redactions A and B of VP1 do not come into play for the passage in question.[11] The Corpus Christianorum, Continuatio Mediaevalis edition used here contains redaction A, but readers who refer to Migne (PL 185), where versions A and B are sometimes intermingled, will find essentially the same text. Second, nearly the entire passage is the work of William alone. Geoffrey of Auxerre's *Fragmenta*, provided ahead of time for William's use, contain only the following brief allusion to this crisis:

> Nevertheless, he was still troubled in his thoughts, considering the ideas that came to mind to be of no import and worthless. Because of his humility, no doubt, he supposed that all the others were pondering matters deeper and more divinely inspired. Thus, afraid to speak, he held back in silence what he considered to

[11] For a list of the variants between the A and B redactions, see Bredero, "Études sur la Vita Prima," ASOC 17 (1961): 27–60.

be of little worth. But then one night there stood by him, as it were, a wonderfully bright apparition of a young boy, telling him to speak with great confidence whatever came to mind, because it would not be he who spoke, but the Spirit of the Father in him.[12]

Apart from the night vision, which William retains with little change, there is a striking difference between his full account of the episode and Geoffrey's short note. Whereas Geoffrey describes a minor crisis attributable to Bernard's humility, William has Bernard learning humility as a result of a major crisis.

A Close Reading of *Vita Prima* 1.28–29

This episode is framed by stories involving members of Bernard's immediate family. In the story that leads into it (the end of VP1 27), his brother Gerard, the cellarer of the community, comes to Bernard in a panic, faced with a lack of supplies and money at the onset of winter. Assuring Gerard that there is no need for worry, Bernard ascertains what sum of money is needed and, turning to God in fervent prayer, soon receives sufficient funds from a visiting benefactor. Next comes the story of Bernard's crisis. It is followed by a few lines about the arrival of his father, Tesciline, to join the community, and then by the dramatic story of the visit and conversion of his sister, Humbeline. This framing is clearly William's work: the *Fragmenta* place the episode with Gerard later in the sequence of events and contain no mention of Tesciline's entrance or Humbeline's visit.

Transitioning from the story about Gerard to the story of the crisis, William deftly turns Bernard's miraculous fund-raising into a problem. He notes that "sensible men" (*viri prudentes*) in

---

[12] Translated from *Fragmenta Gaufridi*, CCCM 89B:280–81, ll. 214–21.

the community thought Bernard too delicate to be involved in the material concerns of the house and arranged to keep him out of such matters. Bernard is clearly not to be numbered among these sensible men of the house. Even though his family plays a large role in the immediate context, these *viri prudentes* are not necessarily his brothers or relatives. Version A of VP1 makes it clear that the founding group included "his brothers, along with other religious men," a detail omitted in version B.[13]

The shift in tone away from a predominantly admiring presentation of Bernard is especially noticeable in William's choice of vocabulary: it was on account of his "fragility" or "delicacy of soul" (*teneritudo mentis*) that Bernard needed to be spared temporal concerns. William frequently uses *tener* and related words when speaking of novices or beginners. Ironically, in VP1 20, he notes that Bernard will later on exhort the novices, "sparing their fragility" (*parcens teneritudini eorum*). The founding group had concerns about Bernard from the very start. His appointment was made "to their amazement, since they were mature and strong men both in religion and life experience." They were afraid for him, as much for his "delicate, youthful age" (*pro tenioris aetate iuuentutis*) as for his "physical frailty and little experience in external affairs" (VP1 25). William is making it clear that Bernard the young abbot still has unfinished business from his novitiate, a point to which he will soon return. Nonetheless, the founders of Clairvaux gladly recognize Bernard as their legitimately appointed abbot and consult him on spiritual concerns (*de interioribus conscientiis suis et causa animarum suarum*). A little further on, William also returns to the nature of these consultations.

At the outset of paragraph 28, William repeats the pattern of raising Bernard up as an exceptional human being and then

---

[13] VP 25, CCCM 89B:52; l. 710; for the differences between versions A and B here, see Bredero, "Études sur la Vita Prima," ASOC 17 (1961): 34.

undermining the reader's expectations. The comparison with Moses is almost breathtaking in its implications about the depth of Bernard's spiritual life and his nearness to God. To compare a living person—much less a young, inexperienced one—to Moses is a bold choice of image. But then William lets the Exodus account, as he knew it in the Vulgate, play a trick on the reader. Just as Moses came down from the mountain with horns sprouting from his forehead (*facies eius cornuta*), just so frightful did the exceptionally gifted Bernard become to his monks. It is unfortunate that translators of the VP1 tend to render this passage according to their modern Bible, restoring the original Hebrew meaning, namely, that Moses' face emitted light.[14] But William quotes the Vulgate and indicates by this image that Bernard was becoming something of a monster.

The essential tensions of the story are already in place. There is a certain aura around Bernard, but his exceptional gifts are

---

[14] Geoffrey Webb and Adrian Walker have: "his face seemed to send forth beams of radiance" (*St. Bernard of Clairvaux: The Story of His Life as Recorded in the* Vita Prima Bernardi *by Certain of His Contemporaries, William of St. Thierry, Arnold of Bonnevaux, Geoffrey and Philip of Clairvaux, and Odo of Deuil* [Westminster, MD: Newman, 1960], 47). Martinus Cawley adjusts the Vulgate meaning somewhat: "and his face appeared gleaming with hornlike rays from his colloquy with the Lord" (Bernard of Clairvaux, *Early Biographies*, vol. 1 [Lafayette, OR: Guadalupe Translations, 1990], 37). Pauline Matarasso has: "his face was so bright from his converse with the Lord that they fled in terror" (*The Cistercian World: Monastic Writings of the Twelfth Century* [London: Penguin, 1993], 27–28). François Guizot takes an approach similar to Cawley's: "par l'effet de sa conversation avec le Seigneur, sa face partit [*sic*; parut] armée de rayons et si terrible que le peuple fuyait devant lui" (*Vie de saint Bernard* [Clermont-Ferrand: Paléo, 2004], 50). Hilary Costello's recent translation is also close to Cawley's: "His face was beaming with horns of light and was so awesome that the people fled away from him" (*The First Life of Bernard of Clairvaux*, CF 76 [Collegeville, MN: Cistercian Publications, 2015), 31. An exception is Ivan Gobry: "de ce colloque avec le Seigneur, son visage apparaissait comme surmonté de cornes, et pour cela terrible" (*Vie de Saint Bernard* [Paris: François-Xavier de Guibert, 1997], 70).

distancing him from a community that is supposed to be benefiting from them. Bernard appears to be an uncommonly holy man but at the same time shows signs of still being a common novice. William now raises the tension around this latter theme by recalling Bernard's time in "the wilderness of Cîteaux," that is, his short novitiate there. At first sight, William's vocabulary may appear to show admiration for his young subject, who enjoyed "lofty contemplation in silence," seemed to have attained the heights of heaven, and therefore possessed a kind of "superhuman purity." But the fact that these attributes frighten everyone away undermines their usual positive meaning. William seems to be applying to Bernard observations he makes elsewhere about the ambiguities of novice fervor:

> Indeed this is what usually happens to beginners; spiritual carelessness envelops their frail and unwary souls and prevents them from attaining the goal of perfection. At the slightest taste of the new sweets of contemplation and its sweeter experiences they immediately suppose that they have passed beyond all need of contending with the vices of flesh and spirit. They dream of nothing but the charms of the virtues, which are naturally delightful; and they take no trouble to possess the virtues truly and securely, disdaining the need to practice them. Trusting in the sweetness they have tasted (which comes rather from God who shows mercy than from him who wills or him who runs), they pay no heed to serious dangers arising from their side and preying upon them from within.[15]

The dangers become even more serious in the case of a novice who is also an abbot. William continues to increase the tension in the story by introducing another defect in his

---

[15] William of Saint-Thierry, *Exposition on the Song of Songs* 6.69, CF 6 (Kalamazoo, MI: Cistercian Publications, 1970), 56–57.

subject veiled in apparently complimentary language. Bernard, he writes, "spoke to men the language of angels." A little later Bernard becomes troubled when he finds out that his fellow monks are not angels. His "angelic kind of purity" makes him blind to "the common condition of human weakness." This evocation of angels recalls a theme that comes up frequently in William's writings and even more frequently in Bernard's, namely, the discernment of spirits. The Scripture passage that almost invariably accompanies this theme is 2 Corinthians 11:14: *Satan transforms himself into an angel of light.* For William to qualify Bernard as angelic in this context becomes extremely ambiguous. Ambiguity turns to irony at a key point in the unfolding of the crisis, when the young abbot becomes disconnected from his community: "all contact was lost between his light and their darkness."

William seems to be hinting that the little monster with horns risks becoming a devil disguised as an angel of light. As for the monks, they have no angelic illusions about themselves and continue to confide their very human struggles to their abbot. These confessions are to be understood not in the sacramental sense but as the everyday confessions described in the *Ecclesiastica officia* (chap. 70) or as the revelation of thoughts to the abbot recommended in the fifth step of humility (RB 4.44-48). These sensible monks not only receive a strained hearing but also are taken aback by the "newness of what they heard," novelty usually being an undesirable thing in the monastic context. Worse yet, Bernard seems to be leading people where the angel of darkness usually leads them, laying out for his monks "a seedbed of despair." It is a serious charge against an abbot, especially in the light of the Rule of Saint Benedict, where monks are exhorted "never to despair of the mercy of God" (RB 4.74).

Related to the angel of light/angel of darkness theme is the notion that Bernard was not keeping his place. Like the Moses image, the allusion to John 6:61 (*his words seemed hard*) evokes a parting of the ways between the leader and the led. Even though this is not the only instance in which William's choice of Scripture text is excessively strong,[16] the reference suggests that Bernard was usurping the place of Christ. A similar insinuation occurs just before the dénouement of the crisis, where the monks are said to have "blamed everything on their weakness in the sight of the man of God [i.e., Bernard], inasmuch as no living man can be justified in the sight of God,"[17] an uncomfortable juxtaposition, to say the least.

The next sentence marks the turning point in the story and is the key to William's understanding of the young abbot's development: "Thus it came about that the dutiful humility of the disciples became the tutor of the teacher" (*Vnde factum est ut fieret magistra magistri pia humilitas discipulorum*). With its play on the feminine and masculine forms *magistra* and *magister*, it is impossible to give a satisfactory rendering of this beautiful formula in English. Moreover, the adjective *pia* can take on a range of meanings: dutiful, filial, loving, upright, kind, gracious, etc., nearly all of which have their place here. The adverbial use of this same word to describe the monks as "sensible men of duty" (*pie prudentes*) earlier in the text may help orient the translator's choice. All along, the community has, in fact, been dutifully bearing with its young abbot.

The most important thing to notice in this sentence is that Bernard does not resolve the crisis on his own. He needs to be taught. And the teacher here is the persistent, gentle, and yet forceful effect of the other monks' humility. To already-mentioned rifts between Bernard and his disciples now has to be added that they were humble and he was not. The young abbot begins to see the discrepancies. His *zelus* (vehemence) evokes the bitter zeal of RB 72.1, especially since it is zeal *against*

---

[16] Another example is VP1 Prol., ll. 50–51, citing 1 John 1:1, *quae . . . vidimus, et audivimus, et manus nostrae contrectaverunt.*

[17] VP1 29; ll. 809–11.

brothers who are humble and submissive (*adversus fratres humiles et subiectos*). Whereas before it seemed that they were incapable of understanding his lofty wisdom, he notices now that they have been using his every hint (literally *nod*) to humble themselves further. William depicts Bernard becoming suspicious of himself, again using vocabulary from the Rule, which instructs the abbot "to be wary of his own frailty" (RB 64.13: *Suamque fragilitatem semper suspectus sit*).

Once self-knowledge has made this breech, the insights begin to flood in. Bernard now sees that his bitter zeal was misplaced, that his brothers did not deserve such severity, and, most important, that he expected of them a degree of perfection he did not possess. In other words, he sees that his sense of superiority prevented him from experiencing empathy and compassion. Conversely, he begins to recognize the worth of his fellow monks and even wonders if they would not be better off without his thus-far ineffectual help. The precocious young abbot begins to pull in his horns and to recognize that there are other sources of light within the community, in spite of the fact it contains no angels.

At this point William integrates into the story Geoffrey's brief note in the *Fragmenta*, retaining the vocabulary but reversing the meaning. Whereas Geoffrey attributes Bernard's withdrawal into silence to his innate humility, William depicts him as reduced to silence by the harrowing lesson in humility he has just undergone. William is also more emphatic about the intensity of Bernard's turmoil and the depth of his withdrawal: he is "extremely upset and saddened," experiences "a great upheaval of mind and much heartache," and therefore retreats to his "inner self," in the "solitude of his heart and in the secrecy of silence." The now speechless Bernard is sufficiently reduced to a state of passive receptivity that grace can begin its work in him.

The divine intervention takes the form of a night vision, the general outline of which William adopts from Geoffrey's story about the boy who appears and speaks to Bernard, along with a few significant changes worth noting. In William's version the boy instructs Bernard "with great authority," as if to put him in his place and to redress the unbalanced authority that brought on his crisis. Also, after saying that the Spirit will speak through him (an allusion to Matt 10:20 also present in the *Fragmenta*), the boy in William's account adds that the Spirit will prompt Bernard "with an abundance of meanings when he comments on the Scriptures," a gift William mentions often throughout VP1.[18] But most significant of all here is William's added note that the Spirit "increased his 'understanding of the needy and the poor' [Ps 40:2], that is, of the penitent sinner in search of pardon." By the intervention of grace, Bernard becomes more understanding and more compassionate.

As a kind of coda to the entire episode, William summarizes what Bernard learned and mentions the arrival of his father at Clairvaux, where he spent his final days—all in one sentence. This closing reference to Bernard's family functions as an inclusion, since it was an episode with his brother Gerard that introduced the passage. Moreover, by placing the arrival of the father here—a detail not given in Geoffrey's *Fragmenta*—William intimates the change in Bernard as a kind of homecoming, from which point forward he is capable of being a father to his community. Most significant of all is the way William sums up the transformation in Bernard: he has "learned to live among men and to engage in and put up with things human." Each word here carries a great deal of weight. He has learned (*cum didicisset*), he now lives like a human (as opposed to an angel) among other human beings, and he now accepts common human realities both as an active agent in them and a tolerant recipient of them (*humana agere et tolerare*). As if to underscore these words, William restates them with even greater

[18] See for instance VP 23.671; 24.690–98; 58.1497–1500.

clarity a little later in the work, noting that Bernard "learned and became accustomed to being a man among men."[19]

A Window on Bernard or a Mirror Image of William?

William wrote VP1 at over twenty-five years' remove from the events. He had Geoffrey's notes to stimulate his memory and to orient his work, but, as a comparison of the *Fragmenta* and VP1 for this passage shows, William rearranged the material for his own purposes and added a great deal of his own material. It is significant that Geoffrey, who could have only second- or thirdhand information for this period, nonetheless knew something about this crisis. William, on the other hand, had more direct sources of information from his contact with Bernard and other monks during the foundation's early years. His reversal of the meaning of Geoffrey's material along with the tensions between this passage and the rest of VP1 are signs that this story has an authentic core. One could argue that by narrating the episode with such sophistication William is saying indirectly that the crisis was quite severe.

Gastaldelli, moreover, finds significant parallels between William's character portrait of Bernard and personality traits mentioned by Geoffrey of Auxerre and Berengar of Poitiers, this latter being a sharp critic of Bernard.[20] In all three cases, the descriptors used are not typical of the hagiographical genre. The main characteristics in question are a constitutional shyness coupled with keen intelligence, which results in a tendency toward withdrawal and introspection, along with a desire for affirmation that manifests itself in a strong competitive bent. Gastaldelli concludes:

[19] VP1 38.1067–72.
[20] See the section titled "Il carattere del giovane Bernardo," *I primi vent'anni*, 13–18.

Bernard therefore seems to be an introverted boy with
a slightly negative tendency (isolation), which could
impede the harmonious devolvement of his personality and make him anti-social. But he also has positive
characteristics that stand out especially in the very
gifted boy that he was, like introspection and competitiveness, which, as they matured during his adolescence, transformed the timid and introverted boy into
a brilliant and extremely charming young man.[21]

From this point of view, there were several tensions in Bernard
that inevitably came into play as he transitioned from the novitiate to the abbatial office at a rather young age.

Even if one agrees in general with scholars like Bredero that
William tends to turn his subject into a legend, the episode
studied here resists such sweeping views. In fact, when Bredero
does deal with this passage, he misunderstands it entirely and
fails to notice William's ambiguous use of the Moses image.[22]
Moreover, in spite of William's overall gentle handling of the
young abbot's crisis, it is not fair to claim that his purpose here
is to defend Bernard from criticism.[23] In this instance the close
reading that Bredero calls for actually shows William engaging
in a penetrating, critical evaluation of his subject.[24]

Leclercq's characterization of this text, which also suffers
from a fundamental misunderstanding, is worth citing:

The passage in William's book 1 on Bernard, which,
for being rare in this kind of text has most interested
biographers, is the one describing a long and painful
interior crisis that brings the young abbot from intran-
sigence to moderation. Engaging early on in excessive

---

[21] Gastaldelli, *I primi vent'anni*, 17.
[22] Bredero, *Bernard of Clairvaux*, 135–36.
[23] Bredero, *Bernard of Clairvaux*, 87.
[24] Bredero, *Bernard of Clairvaux*, 87.

austerity, he became sick. He was then tormented by
sadness and trouble. Oddly enough, it had to be someone who is not a monk (although it is true that he was
a canon regular), William of Champeaux, bishop of
Châlons, to come teach this monk, this abbot, who was
to become a theologian of Christian and monastic life,
a correct spirituality.[25]

As Gastaldelli points out, Leclercq here conflates several
crises.[26] In the first, Bernard comes to terms with his excessively
demanding approach through self-knowledge and undergoes
a transformation in silent withdrawal (VP1 27–29). The second
crisis has to do with Bernard's chronic ill health and William
of Champeaux's intervention to secure him a time of recovery
(VP1 31–33). In the third a more moderate Bernard, trying un-
successfully to temper his monks' excessively penitential diet,
welcomes an intervention on the part of William of Champeaux
in favor of greater balance. When Leclercq does focus clearly
on the first of these episodes, he concludes, "One is led to think
that William here describes his own crisis over what to think
and what to say, which he then applies to Bernard."[27] This re-
ductive reading takes into account only one aspect of a complex
crisis. Moreover, it is unreasonable to charge William—who did
not become abbot right out of the novitiate—with projecting
his own experience on Bernard. In any case, if William was
trying to read himself into Bernard's story, it is unlikely he
would have been so uncomplimentary.

The authenticity of the episode in question receives its
most serious challenge when VP1 is considered as a forum

[25] Translated from Leclercq, *Nouveau visage*, 27.

[26] Ferruccio Gastaldelli, "'Optimus Praedicator.' L'opera oratoria
di san Bernardo," *Studi su san Bernardo e Goffredo di Auxerre*, ASOC 51
(1995): 135–37; this article was reprinted in Ferruccio Gastaldelli, *Studi
su san Bernardo e Goffredo di Auxerre* (Florence: SISMEL-Galluzzo, 2001).

[27] Translated from Leclercq, *Nouveau visage*, 30.

for William's own spiritual teaching. As seen in a text from his *Exposition on the Song of Songs* (6.69) cited earlier, there are parallels between this description of unbalanced novice fervor and William's description of Bernard as a young abbot. Was it that Bernard's actual behavior reminded William of his habitual characterization of novices, or that William forces young Bernard into his own preconceived patterns? Another aspect of William's spiritual teaching to keep in mind here is his overall view of the importance of Clairvaux for the church of his times. As Jacques Paul so perceptively points out, William wants to impress upon his readers that the foundation of Clairvaux was a spiritual enterprise referring back to the New Testament.[28] More precisely, he presents the monks of Clairvaux, who chose to go from a life of prosperity and honor in the world to a monastic life of poverty and hard work, "as imitators of the Son of God in his incarnation and abasement."[29] As William says in his description of the "golden age of Clairvaux," the monks, "considering that they lived not for themselves but for Christ and the brothers, counted as nothing whatever they lacked."[30] He even notes that "in the simplicity and humility of the buildings the valley spoke without words of the simplicity and humility of the poor men of Christ who lived there."[31] In other words, with his emphasis on the kenotic character of the whole enterprise at Clairvaux, William places its mystical foundations even earlier in time than the apostolic community at Jerusalem.[32] The question then needs to be asked whether this story of Bernard's abasement is part of William's view of the spiritual significance of Clairvaux or an actual incident in the young abbot's life.

[28] Paul, "Les débuts," 24.
[29] Paul, "Les débuts," 24.
[30] VP1 35.992–94.
[31] VP1 35.997–99.
[32] Paul, "Les débuts," 29.

On the other hand, it is in Bernard's writings that we find the most compelling articulation of this conception of the monastic life as an imitation of and a sharing in the kenosis of Christ. Perhaps William is using a method similar to the one he claims Bernard used when interpreting the Scriptures with the Scriptures; William is interpreting Bernard and the life of his community with Bernard's fundamental teachings on humility. More particularly, the crisis as described in VP1 corresponds to the three degrees of truth in Bernard's treatise *The Steps of Humility and Pride*: self-knowledge, compassion, and contemplation. Granted, they are presented in reverse order, because Bernard's impressively angelic and contemplative novitiate was not yet grounded in knowledge of common human nature and knowledge of self. So in addition to wondering whether William shapes this crisis according to his own spiritual doctrine, it has to be asked whether he is not patterning it on Bernard's own teaching.

Conclusion

This analysis of William's project in writing VP1 serves to underscore the fact that it is a carefully composed literary work. The reader should not look for history where historiography is not intended, nor dismiss as fiction every artful element of the narration. Because of the abundance of firsthand sources available to him, William deserves a careful listening, no matter how he chooses to present his materials. His general tendency may be to idealize his subject, but in cases like the text studied here, he reveals some of Bernard's fundamental complexities and internal tensions. The resulting portrayal is consistent with the character traits mentioned by contemporaries and noticeable in Bernard's own works.[33] A close reading of this

---

[33] Jean Leclercq rightly points out Bernard's various prologues as particularly good sources in this regard; see "Les prologues de S. Bernard

crisis episode brings to light certain of William's strategies that may be found at work elsewhere in VP1: his artful ordering of events, as in the method of inclusion used here; the way he transforms material from the *Fragmenta* to serve his own purposes; the subtle use of ambivalence to turn an apparent miracle (meeting Gerard's request for funds) into a problem (the monks' decision to keep Bernard out of temporal matters); his ambiguous use of biblical images and citations simultaneously to reveal Bernard's gifts and defects; and perhaps his use of Bernard's own doctrine in shaping his narrative. The text of the VP1 is neither a transparent window on Bernard nor a mirror image of its author, William. But like a stained-glass window, the closer you get to it the more you can see through it.

☙

Appendix

From the *Vita prima*, book 1, by William of Saint-Thierry[34]

27. [. . . Because Bernard counted solely on divine intervention for the foundation's material needs], sensible men, realizing that the hand of God was with him, avoided burdening with concern for outward things the delicacy of soul of one who had so recently emerged from the delights of paradise. As far as possible they arranged among themselves to take care of such matters, consulting him only with regard to their interior lives and the needs of their souls.

28. In this situation, however, the same thing nearly happened to them as what we read happened to the Israelites long ago with regard to Moses. After spending a long time with the Lord on Mount Sinai and having emerged from the dense cloud

---

et sa psychologie d'auteur," in *Recueil d'études sur saint Bernard et ses écrits* (Rome: Edizioni di Storia e Letteratura, 1969), 3:13–31.
   [34] Translated from CCCM 89B; VP 1.27–30.770–846, pp. 54–56, ll. 770–846.

and come down to the people from his conversation with the Lord, Moses "appeared to have horns" [Exod 34:29], and his face was so frightful that the people fled from him. For that holy man [Bernard], having emerged from the presence of the Lord, which he had enjoyed for some time in the wilderness of Cîteaux and from the heights of the most lofty contemplation in silence, seemed to bring with him from heaven into the midst of men a kind of miracle of superhuman purity that he had acquired from God. He frightened away from himself nearly all the men he had come to guide and among whom he had come to live.

When he had occasion to talk to them on spiritual matters and for the upbuilding of their souls, he spoke to men in the language of the angels and was hardly understood at all. In particular, when the topic was human conduct, speaking to them from the abundance of his heart, he proposed such high standards and demanded of them such perfection that his "words seemed hard" [John 6:61], so much so that they did not understand what was being said to them.

Moreover, when he listened to them individually as they confessed to him, accusing themselves of the various fantasies [*illusionibus*] of common human thoughts, which no man living in the flesh can entirely avoid, it was especially then that all contact was lost between his light and their darkness. In other words, he found to be men those whom up until then he had considered to be angels. For he enjoyed to a great extent an angelic kind of purity, and, judging on the basis of the singular grace he had long before received from God, he ingenuously underestimated the common condition of human weakness. He either found it unthinkable that a religious could fall into temptations or impure thoughts of this kind, or he no longer considered such a man to be a religious if he did fall.

29. But these truly religious and sensible men of duty were in awe of what Bernard said to them in his preaching and in confession, including things they could not grasp, even if they

were taken aback by the newness of what they heard. It got to the point that he seemed to be laying out for them a seedbed of despair. They, however, as blessed Job once said, thought it reprehensible "to contradict the sayings of a holy man" [Job 6:10] and, instead of exonerating themselves, blamed everything on their weakness in the sight of the man of God, inasmuch as "no living man can be justified in the sight of God" [Ps 142:2].

Thus it came about that the dutiful humility of the disciples became the tutor of the teacher. For when those who were being accused were humbled at a mere hint from their accuser, the spiritual teacher became wary of his own vehemence toward humble, submissive brothers. This was so much the case that, when he did not know what to say, he now rather blamed himself and lamented the fact that he could not remain silent. He feared not so much that he was going over the heads of these men as that he was speaking to them more severely than they deserved, that he was harming the interior life of his hearers, and that he was rigorously exacting perfection from simple brothers, whereas he had not yet reached such perfection in himself.

He began to think that what they meditated on in silence was far better and more appropriate for their salvation than what they might hear from him, that they worked out their salvation more dutifully and effectively on their own than by following his example, and that they were more likely to be confused by his preaching than to derive any benefit from it.

He became extremely upset and saddened by this state of affairs, and various thoughts arose in his heart. After a great upheaval of mind and much heartache, he decided to withdraw from all external matters into his inner self, and there to remain in the solitude of his heart and in the secrecy of silence, waiting upon the Lord, until he somehow in his mercy revealed his will for him in this matter.

And the mercy of God did not delay in providing timely help. Indeed, a few days later, he saw in a night vision a boy with a heavenly aura standing near him and instructing him with great authority to speak confidently whatever came to mind when he opened his mouth, because "it would not be he who spoke, but the Holy Spirit that would speak through him" [Matt 10:20]. From then on the Holy Spirit spoke more clearly in him and through him, making his word more powerful and prompting him with an abundance of meanings when he commented on the Scriptures. The Spirit also made him more gracious and persuasive before his hearers and increased his "understanding of the needy and the poor" [Ps 40:2], that is, of the penitent sinner in search of pardon.

30. And when he had already for some time learned to live among men and to engage in and put up with things human, and when he was beginning to enjoy the fruits of his conversion in the midst of his brothers, and along with them, his father also, who alone had remained at home, came to his sons and joined up with them. Having spent some time there, he died at a good old age.

Chapter 8

Bernard of Clairvaux and Richard of Saint-Victor on the Pursuit of Ecstasy and the Development of a Mystical Theology

Constant J. Mews

Michael Casey has made a powerful contribution to demonstrating the centrality of the theme of desire for God in the writing of Bernard of Clairvaux (1090–1153) and thus his central role in shaping Christian mystical theology.[1] In this paper, written to honor someone who has

---

[1] Michael Casey, *Athirst for God: Spiritual Desire in Bernard of Clairvaux's Sermons on the Song of Songs*, CS 77 (Kalamazoo, MI: Cistercian Publications, 1988). Two guides to the broader tradition of medieval commentary on the Song of Songs are those of E. Ann Matter, *The Voice of My Beloved: The Song of Songs in Western Medieval Christianity* (Philadelphia: University of Pennsylvania Press, 1990), and Ann W. Astell, *The Song of Songs in the Middle Ages* (Ithaca: Cornell University Press, 1990). See also Denys Turner, *Eros and Allegory: Medieval Exegesis of the Song of Songs*, CS 156 (Kalamazoo, MI: Cistercian Publications, 1995), more relevant to the later medieval period, when the theology of Dionysius the Areopagite became important. For translations of excerpts of patristic and medieval commentaries on the entire text of the Song, see Richard A. Norris Jr., ed., *The Song of Songs: Interpreted by Early Christian and Medieval Commentators* (Grand Rapids, MI: Eerdmans, 2003). The works of Bernard of Clairvaux will be cited from SBOp, ed. Jean Leclercq, Charles H. Talbot, and Henri M. Rochais, 9 vols. (Rome: Editiones Cistercienses,

himself contributed powerfully to renewing understanding of Bernard's achievement, I wish to consider not only what made Bernard's reading of the Song of Songs so important but also his influence on Richard of Saint-Victor (d. 1173), who transposed many of Bernard's concerns with the role of experience in spiritual life into a more theological systematic framework. Over the next three centuries, both Bernard and Richard played key roles in shaping medieval reflection on the spiritual life. Dante would assign them both a special role in Paradise, describing Richard as a flaming soul, "whose contemplations made him more than a man," and Bernard as one filled with interior joy: "His eyes, his cheeks, were filled with the divine / joy of the blest, his attitude that every tender-hearted father knows."[2] While the speech that Dante assigns to Bernard in the *Paradiso* is imagined rather than historically authentic, it serves to remind us of the creative inspiration that Bernard exerted on medieval culture, not just for his reflection on love, but also for his hinting at future ecstasy in the world to come. Bernard was first of all a preacher, known for his criticism of one of the great schoolmen of his day, Peter Abelard (1079–1142). Richard, an Augustinian canon active in Paris just as Peter Lombard was asserting himself as the dominant voice of scholastic theology, drew on Bernard's teaching about experience but transformed it into a more systematic body of doctrine, relevant to those outside as well as within a monastic milieu.

1957–1998). Translations in this paper are generally my own, although reference is sometimes made to other translations.

[2] Dante, *Paradiso* X.132 (*che a considerar fu più che viro*); *Paradiso* XXXI.61–63 (*Diffuso era per li occhi e per le gene / di benigna letizia, in atto pio / quale a tenero padre si convene*); Dante, *The Divine Comedy*, vol. 3, trans. Mark Musa (London: Penguin, 1984), 123, 367. On Dante's interpretation of Bernard, see Steven Botteril, *Dante and the Mystical Tradition: Bernard of Clairvaux in the Commedia* (Cambridge: Cambridge University Press, 1994).

One way of evaluating the contributions of both Bernard and Richard is to compare their responses to a single verse of the Song of Songs (2:5), translated into English in the Jerusalem Bible as *I am wounded with love*. Bernard and Richard were aware of two versions of this verse, one from the Vetus Latina, derived from the Septuagint, and widely repeated by Augustine and other Latin church fathers: *Vulnerata caritate ego sum* (I am wounded by love). The other was that of Jerome, who replaced the more theologically precise *caritas* with the more passionate *quia amore langueo* (because I languish in love). Both translations communicate something of how love wounds the soul and drives its longing for ecstatic union with the beloved.[3] Bernard and Richard drew not only on this scriptural legacy, as interpreted by Augustine, but also on an older theological tradition, that of the Greek fathers, mediated in part by Origen's homilies and commentary on the Song of Songs, known in the West through their translation into Latin by Rufinus.[4] Richard of Saint-Victor, I suggest, expanded Bernard's highly personal reading of the Song of Songs, developing it into a theological system that set great value on a concept that Bernard valued highly, that of experience.

Patristic Tradition on the Song of Songs

Before observing how both Bernard and Richard respond to the Song of Songs, we should consider the Latin patristic tradition to which they were responding and its foundations in

---

[3] This translation is that of the Jerusalem Bible, rendered in the Vulgate, Song 2:5: *fulcite me floribus stipate me malis quia amore langueo.*

[4] On Origen's reading of the Song, see Matter, *The Voice of My Beloved*, 25–31. I have already hinted at some of the themes in this paper in Constant J. Mews, "Intoxication and the Song of Songs: Bernard of Clairvaux and the Rediscovery of Origen in the Twelfth Century," in *The Medieval Book of Pleasure*, ed. Piroska Nagy and Naama Cohen (Turnhout: Brepols, 2017).

Greek thought, indeed in the New Testament itself. Early Christian commentators understood the core image of the Song, that of the lover seeking out her beloved, as elucidating a central theme of John's gospel, namely, the longing of the soul for the Lord. They were building on the implicit allusion to the Song in the Gospel of John of how faithful women, above all Mary Magdalene, sought out the body of the Lord, only to discover that the one she was seeking had now risen. The standard early Christian exegesis of the Song, exemplified by Hippolytus of Rome and Cyprian of Carthage, was to interpret the bride as the church, just as Jews had interpreted it as Israel in her longing for God.[5]

An important inflection to this reading, however, was given by Origen, who, following a precedent set by Philo, related the bride not just to the church but to the soul as well: *Ecclesia vel anima*.[6] Origen sought to connect Greek philosophical reflection (above all Platonic) about love to Jewish understanding of the Song, to show how Scripture could make sense to those shaped by the philosophical culture of Alexandria, while countering heretical gnostic interpretations of the Gospel in purely individual terms, as being about interior enlightenment. He believed that the Song of Songs could help unlock the typological

---

[5] The continuity of this ecclesiological reading is emphasized by Karl Shuve (University of Virginia), who was kind enough to share with me a draft of his monograph, *The Song of Songs and the Fashioning of Identity in Early Latin Christianity* (Oxford: Oxford University Press, 2016).

[6] For the translation by Rufinus, see Origen, *Commentarium in Canticum Canticorum*, ed. W. A. Baehrens, GCS 33 (Leipzig: J. C. Hinrichs, 1925), 61–241, and *Homélies sur le Cantique des Cantiques*, ed. Olivier Rousseau, SCh 37*bis* (Paris: Cerf, 1966), 46–49 (on the manuscript transmission). The brief *Expositio sancti Hieronimi presbiteri in libro Cantici canticorum* is a summary of Aponius, a late fifth-century follower of Origen, ed. B. de Vregille and L. Neyrand, CCSL 19 (Turnhout: Brepols, 1986), 315–90. For the phrase *Ecclesia uel anima*, see Origen, *Commentarium in Canticum Canticorum* 2, 3, ed. Baehrens, 61, 167, 185, 190, 292.

and literary framework that underpinned the theme, evident in all the gospels, of the longing of the soul for the Lord. Thus Origen interpreted "being wounded by love" as about the soul being wounded by Christ, as if he were an arrow that wounds the soul.[7] While Origen had no truck with a purely sexualized reading of the Song, he was fully aware of the different ways in which Scripture uses different words for love, such as (to use the translation of Rufinus) *amor* (the normal term for love in erotic literature), *dilectio* (not a common classical word), and *caritas*.[8]

Origen's reading of the Song would influence Ambrose of Milan, who frequently alluded to the Song in his ascetic writings, integrating it into his theology. Ambrose frequently repeated Origen's phrase, *Ecclesia vel anima*, but tended to explain the bride in the Song (such as 2:5, *Vulnerata caritate*) first of all as *Ecclesia*.[9] He interpreted her longing as best exemplified in virginal ascetics, preferring to distinguish *caritas* and *dilectio* from the more worldly *amor*.[10] He thus tended to interpret the bride as more about the church than the individual soul.

Compared to Ambrose, Augustine is much more selective in his quotation of the Song.[11] Not only does he never employ the

---

[7] Origen, *In Psalmos XXXVI–XXXVIII homiliae IX*, ed. E. Prinzivalli, H. Crouzel, L. Brésard, SCh 411 (Paris: Cerf, 1995), 134.

[8] Origen, *Commentarium*, Prol., ed. Baehrens, 68: *Et in his ergo et in aliis pluribus locis invenies Scripturam divinam refugisse amoris vocabulum et caritatis dilectionis que posuisse.* See also 69 and 72.

[9] Ambrose, *De Isaac vel anima* 4.30, ed. C. Schenkl, CSEL 32.1 (Vienna: Tempsky, 1897), 661: *et ideo ecclesia, quae diligit Christum, uulnerata est caritatis.* Cf. Ambrose, *De Isaac* 1.2, 642: *descendit itaque ad sapientiae fontem uel ecclesia uel anima, ut totum uas inpleret suum et hauriret purae sapientiae disciplinas, quas haurire Iudaei de fonte profluo noluerunt.*

[10] Thus Ambrose interprets John 21:17 (*diligis me?*) as indicating a higher form of love than *amor*: *Expositio evangelii secundum Lucam* X.176, ed. M. Adriaen, CCSL 14 (Turnhout: Brepols, 1957), 397.

[11] F. B. A. Asiedu, "The Song of Songs and the Ascent of the Soul: Ambrose, Augustine, and the Language of Mysticism," *Vigiliae Christianae* 55, no. 3 (2001): 299–317.

phrase *Ecclesia vel anima*, but he avoids such intensely personal verses as the verse about kissing on the mouth (1:1: *Osculetur me osculo oris sui*) or the injunction to eat, drink, and get drunk (5:1: *Comedite amici, bibite et inebriamini*). Among the verses of the Song that he does quote are 2:4-5. Thus in the *City of God* he explains 2:4 (*ordinavit in me caritatem*) as a comment by the bride, in the person of the church, saying that for most people, *caritas*, that is, *dilectio* and *amor*, is disordered: "with order disturbed, the sons of God have neglected God and have loved the daughters of man."[12] In his commentary on the Psalms, he explains 2:5, about being "wounded by love" (*Vulnerata caritate*), in a relatively banal way: "For he who has what he loves, loves and does not mourn. But who loves and does not yet have what he loves, must mourn in sorrow, hence what the bride of Christ says in the Song in the person of the Church: since I am wounded by love."[13]

While Augustine frequently refers in his commentary on the Psalms to the experience of *excessus mentis* or ecstasy as a mode of knowledge, experienced by Saint Paul and other saints, he never describes it as part of his own experience. In his *Confessions* Augustine relates how at Ostia he once shared with his mother brief reflection on the way no bodily pleasure could compare with the happiness of the life of the saints, yet he emphasizes that this was a passing moment: "with a sigh

[12] Augustine, *De civitate Dei* 15.22, ed. W. Mountain, CCSL 48 (Turnhout: Brepols, 1955), 488: *unde mihi uidetur, quod definitio breuis et uera uirtutis ordo est amoris; propter quod in sancto cantico canticorum cantat sponsa christi, ciuitas dei: ordinate in me caritatem. Huius igitur caritatis, hoc est dilectionis et amoris, ordine perturbato deum filii dei neglexerunt et filias hominum dilexerunt.*

[13] Augustine, *Enarrationes in Psalmos*, Ps 37.5, ed. E. Dekkers and J. Fraipont, CCSL 38 (Turnhout: Brepols, 1956), 386: *nam ille et amat et non dolet, qui habet quod amat; qui autem amat, ut dixi, et nondum habet quod amat, necesse est ut in dolore gemat. Inde illud in persona ecclesiae sponsa Christi in cantico canticorum: quoniam uulnerata caritate ego sum.*

. . . we returned to the sound of our own speech."[14] In his later writings, Augustine emphasized that humans are so weighed down by the stain of original sin that any vision of ecstasy is passing and imperfect because of their condition. He is not excited by the Song of Songs and can only express regret that the experience of ecstasy was an achievement of the saints but is not for us here and now. Augustine's caution toward the Song of Songs may be related to his concern about the enthusiasm of Pelagius and his followers about reading that text as offering an optimistic vision of human potential.

By the late fourth century, the reputation of Origen as an exegete of Scripture was becoming tarnished by a wave of criticism (in which both Augustine and Jerome participated) of what was seen as his excessive optimism about the nature of humanity and its capacity for salvation.[15] This in turn led to Jerome's breaking his friendship with Rufinus, signaling a new current of hostility toward certain (although not all) writings of Origen. Yet while the Greek originals would largely disappear in the East, Latin ascetics like Cassian, trained in the desert and familiar with the translations of Rufinus, maintained familiarity with those texts, even if they would never gain wide circulation until the twelfth century.[16] Cassian preserved a monastic tradition that insisted on the value of ascetic effort against Augustine's increasing emphasis on dependence on grace and sense that no one could come close to being divine.

---

[14] Augustine, *Confessionum* 9.10, ed. L. Verheijen, CCSL 27 (Turnhout: Brepols, 1981), 147–48: *attingimus eam modice toto ictu cordis; et suspirauimus et reliquimus ibi religatas primitias spiritus et remeauimus ad strepitum oris nostri, ubi uerbum et incipitur et finitur.*

[15] On the controversy and connections between Pelagius and Origen, see Elizabeth Clark, *The Origenist Controversy: The Cultural Construction of an Early Christian Debate* (Princeton, NJ: Princeton University Press, 1992).

[16] On the textual transmission of Origen's writings in the Latin West and the transformation that took place in the twelfth century, see Jean Leclercq, "Origène au XIIe siècle," *Irénikon* 21 (1951): 425–39.

Only the opening of Gregory the Great's commentary on the Song of Songs survives. Nonetheless, it is important for showing how the tradition of Origen and Cassian could be formulated in a way that was fully orthodox, interpreting its words about love (*amor*) in a moral context, as about the longing of the soul: "Hence in this book, written about the Song of Songs, words of physical love are placed so that a soul cooled through words of habit may be aroused through words of the love that is below to the love that is above."[17] Gregory was much more open than Augustine to explaining how the bride could voice the sentiments of the soul as well as of the church. Whereas Cassian had expounded a fourfold theory of the meaning of Scripture, defining Jerusalem, for example, as historically a city, allegorically the church, anagogically the heavenly Jerusalem, and tropologically the soul, Gregory held that there were just three layers to the meaning of Scripture, of which the highest he saw as the moral sense, to do with the soul.[18] While Bede remained loyal to a fourfold theory, Gregory's threefold way of looking at Scripture gained a wide following in the twelfth century in being adopted by both Hugh of Saint-Victor and Bernard of Clairvaux.[19] Gregory the Great

---

[17] Gregory the Great, *Expositio in Canticum Canticorum* 3, ed. Pierre-Patrick Verbraken, CCSL 144 (Turnhout: Brepols, 1963), 4: *Hinc est enim, quod in hoc libro, qui in canticis canticorum conscriptus est, amoris quasi corporei uerba ponuntur: ut a torpore suo anima per sermones suae consuetudinis refricata recalescat et per uerba amoris, qui infra est, excitetur ad amorem, qui supra est.*

[18] Cassian, *Collationes* 14.8, ed. Michael Petschenig, CSEL 13 (Vienna: Tempsky, 1886), 405: *igitur praedictae quattuor figurae in unum ita, si uolumus, confluunt, ut una atque eadem Hierusalem quadrifarie possit intellegi: secundum historiam ciuitas Iudaeorum, secundum allegoriam ecclesia Christi, secundum anagogen ciuitas dei illa caelestis, quae est mater omnium nostrum, secundum tropologiam anima hominis, quae frequenter hoc nomine aut increpatur aut laudatur a domino.*

[19] Bede repeats Cassian's fourfold formulation but places the anagogical sense after the moral sense, implying that it was superior, in *De tabernaculo* 1, ed. David Hurst, CCSL 119A (Turnhout: Brepols, 1969),

expounded this exegetical approach most influentially in his *Moralia in Job*, a text that had previously been commented on by Julian of Eclanum, a follower of Pelagius and a married bishop of the fifth century.[20] In doing so, Gregory provided an inspiration for reading the Song in a moral (or we might say psychological) perspective that others would develop, most importantly, Bernard of Clairvaux.

Augustine's caution toward the Song of Songs remained influential in the early medieval period, not least through Bede's commentary on the Song, in which Bede included significant extracts from the commentary of Julian of Eclanum in order to dispute its argument. Bede followed Augustine in condemning the way Julian interpreted the Song as praising sexual love.[21]

25, and *De schematibus et tropibus* 2, ed. Calvin B. Kendall, CCSL 123A (Turnhout: Brepols, 1975), 166, 168, 169. On these two models, see Henri de Lubac, *Exégèse médiévale: les quatre sens de l'Écriture*, 4 vols. (Paris: Aubier, 1959–1964), 1:139–69; trans. Mark Sebanc (vol. 1) and Edward M. Macierowski (vols. 2–3) as *Medieval Exegesis: The Four Senses of Scripture* (Grand Rapids, MI: Eerdmans, 1998, 2000, 2009). De Lubac comments on this division in *Exégèse médiévale*, 1:139–69, esp. 158 and 201–2 (on the popularity of the threefold model and its use by Origen).

[20] Gregory the Great, *Moralia in Job, Ep Ad Leandrum*, ed. Marc Adriaen, CCSL 143 (Turnhout: Brepols, 1979), 4: *Sciendum uero est, quod quaedam historica expositione transcurrimus et per allegoriam quaedam typica inuestigatione perscrutamur, quaedam per sola allegoricae moralitatis instrumenta discutimus, nonnulla autem per cuncta simul sollicitius exquirentes tripliciter indagamus.* See Julian of Eclanum, *Expositio in Job*, ed. L. De Coninck, CCSL 88 (Turnhout: Brepols, 1977), 3–109. See Origen, *In Genesim homiliae* 2.6, trans. Rufini, ed. W. A. Baehrens, GCS 29 (Leipzig: J. C. Hinrich, 1920), 36; *In Leviticum homiliae* 5.5, trans. Rufini, ed. Baehrens, 344; cf. Ambrose, *Expositio evangelii secundum Lucam* 3.20, ed. Marc Adriaen, CCSL 14 (Turnhout: Brepols, 1957), 86. This passage of Gregory's letter to Leander, prefacing the book of Job, is translated as *Registrum* 5.53a by John R. C. Martyn, *The Letters of Gregory the Great* (Toronto: Pontifical Institute of Mediaeval Studies, 2004), 382.

[21] The surviving fragments of Julian's *Commentarius in Canticum canticorum* are edited from Bede by Lucas De Coninck, CCSL 88, 398–401;

In a monastic environment, Julian's attention to a historical reading of the Song (which did not exclude it from having an allegorical and moral meaning) was viewed as a distraction from its spiritual meaning, which for Bede was ultimately about longing for the heavenly Jerusalem.

Bernard of Clairvaux, the Song of Songs, and Loving God

Bernard of Clairvaux was first of all a preacher rather than a systematic theologian. The Cistercian monasticism to which he was attracted reacted against an impersonal hierarchical style of traditional monasticism. He appreciated its concern to recover a more personal, intimate spirituality, connecting back to the spirit of the Desert Fathers. While Bernard avoided the term *theologia*, he was profoundly steeped in the fathers, not just in Augustine (whose doctrinal authority was dominant for schoolmen like Anselm of Laon), but also in the writings of Gregory the Great and Origen. In the process, he subtly transformed monastic spirituality without ever challenging the views of the fathers in the manner of Peter Abelard.[22] The notion to which he persistently returned in all his writings is that of *experientia*. As he explained when introducing the

---

see 398: *Dicit [Julian] eundem quamdiu nihil de genitalitatis uoluptate desiderat, quasi ad solius animi moueri arbitrium, et in actibus suis habere iucunditatem, ut perturbationis immunem, ita etiam libertate gaudentem.* Most of Julian's other writings are only known from excerpts, such as through Augustine, *Contra duas epistolas Pelagianorum* 1.15.31, ed. Carolus F. Vrba and Joseph Zycha, CSEL 60 (Vienna: Tempsky, 1913), 448: *Ad hoc respondemus* [i.e. Julian] *motum genitalium, id est ipsam uirilitatem sine qua non potest esse commixtio, a deo dicimus institutam, ut nihil haberet pudendum.* (To this we reply that movement of the genitals, namely, virility itself, without which there cannot be intercourse, is instituted by God.)

[22] The literature comparing Bernard and Abelard is extensive. For a recent survey, see Constant J. Mews, "Bernard of Clairvaux and Peter Abelard," in *A Companion to Bernard of Clairvaux*, ed. Brian Patrick McGuire (Leiden: Brill, 2011), 133–68.

Song of Songs to his readers, this was first of all "the book of experience. Turn to yourselves and let each person listen to his conscience on those things which must be said."[23] Bernard gave primacy to learning from experience, not simply formulated in the teaching of the schools.

Before Bernard embarked on his project of creating a sermon on each verse of the Song (covering only its first two chapters, roughly as much as what Origen had covered in his commentary), he composed ca. 1130 a treatise about loving God (*De diligendo Deo*), a topic never attempted by any previous writer. Bernard drew on the imagery of the Song of Songs to postulate that there were four stages in loving God, the first stage of love (*amor*) being that of one loving oneself for one's own sake.[24] The second stage of love he saw as another form of self-interested love, when one loves God for one's own sake.[25] For Bernard, the third stage introduced a transition out of the ego, as one loved God for his sake; only in a fourth stage does one love oneself for the sake of God.[26] The formula, elegant in its simplicity, skillfully wove together Augustine's sense of the selfishness of human behavior, before the advent of grace, with a more optimistic sense that the human soul was capable of becoming less selfish through its encounter with the visitation of grace, becoming like the lover in the Song. Bernard never acknowledges any explicit debt to the sources by which he is influenced. Nonetheless the theme of loving another person for that person's sake rather than out of selfish desire was a core theme of the ethical thought of Peter Abelard, in his case

[23] Bernard of Clairvaux, *Sermones super Cantica Canticorum* 3.1; SBOp 1:14: *Hodie legimus in libro experientiae. Convertimini ad vos ipsos, et attendat unusquisque conscientiam suam super his quae dicenda sunt.*

[24] Bernard, *De diligendo Deo* 23; SBOp 3:138.

[25] Bernard, *De diligendo Deo* 26; SBOp 3:140.

[26] Bernard, *De diligendo Deo* 27–28; SBOp 3:142–43.

argued from Cicero's definition of friendship and influenced by his discussions with Heloise.[27]

Bernard sees the Bride as embodying the true church, who goes through these stages in seeking out her beloved, the Word of God, embodied in Christ. He argues that love is a universal obligation, known to natural law.[28] Bernard is quite traditional in claiming that Christians have a supreme advantage over others in being able to embrace Christ: "They easily love more who understand themselves to be loved more; one given less loves less. Neither the Jew nor the pagan is incited by such goads of love as the church experiences when it says, 'I am wounded by love.'"[29] Yet Bernard is equally at home in speaking about love in a personal sense. When delivering a sermon on Song 2:5, *quia amore langueo*, he has no hesitation in interpreting the verse as being about the weakness of desire in the soul rather than of the church.[30] The innovative quality of his writing lies in his sensuous imagery: "By the newness of flowers and fruits, the beauty of the field breathing the sweetest odor, the Father delights in the Son, innovating all things."[31] Augustine understood the divine Trinity to be sharing in mutual love, as the Holy Spirit proceeded from both the Father and Son. Christians could participate in that ecstasy only insofar as they shared the

[27] On this theme, see Constant J. Mews, "Abelard, Heloise, and Discussion of Love in the Twelfth-Century Schools," in *Rethinking Peter Abelard: A Collection of Critical Essays*, ed. Babette S. Hellemans (Leiden: Brill, 2014), 11–36.

[28] Bernard, *De diligendo Deo* 6; SBOp 3:123.

[29] Bernard, *De diligendo Deo* 7, SBOp 3:124: *Iudaeus sane, sive paganus, nequaquam talibus aculeis incitatur amoris, quales Ecclesia experitur, quae ait: vulnerata caritate ego sum, et rursum: fulcite me floribus, stipate me malis, quia amore langueo.*

[30] Bernard, *Sermones in Cantica* 28:13; SBOp 1:201: *Vel sic: Sol iustitiae decoloravit me Christus, cuius amore langueo. Languor iste coloris quaedam exterminatio est, et defectus in desiderio animae.*

[31] Bernard, *De diligendo Deo* 9; SBOp 3:126.

life of Christ, and then most fully only at the end of time, after the Last Judgment and the resurrection of the dead, when true beatitude would be attained.

Bernard modified Augustine's sharply drawn contrast between worldly *amor* and spiritual *caritas*, fully attainable only in the life to come, by considering how selfish *amor* can evolve into selfless *dilectio* and *caritas*. He deployed his skills in satire to explain that much love, like that of a man's lust for a beautiful wife or for material wealth, is in fact self-interest.[32] Bernard combined Augustine's awareness of sin with the moral teaching of Cassian and Gregory the Great, filtered through his reading of Origen, who encouraged him to see how *amor*, *dilectio*, and *caritas* might all be connected. Bernard gave particular attention to the concept of *experientia* as a way of developing one's understanding of God. Yet although he was profuse in expressions of love toward his friends within his letters, he never explored the theory of friendship in the manner of his English disciple, Aelred of Rievaulx, in *On Spiritual Friendship*.

Bernard presented the fourth stage of love, that of loving oneself for the sake of God, as not fully complete until after the resurrection of the dead. Thus he interprets the injunction of the Song (5:1), *Eat, friends, and drink, dearest ones; let us be inebriated* (*comedite, amici, bibite et inebriamini, carissimi*), as an ecstasy that may begin in this world but is not complete until the world to come: "Eat before death, drink after death, and be inebriated after the resurrection."[33] He closes the treatise by drawing on a vision of eternal lovers: "And this fourth stage of love is possessed from this when God is solely and supremely loved, because we do not love ourselves except for him, so that he is the reward for lovers, the eternal reward of

---

[32] Bernard, *De diligendo Deo* 18; SBOp 3:134.

[33] Bernard, *De diligendo Deo* 33; SBOp 3:147: *Comedite ante mortem, bibite post mortem, inebriamini post resurrectionem.*

lovers for eternity."[34] Bernard suggested that ecstasy in the life to come could be compared to that of eternal lovers—imagery that would appeal to a generation fascinated by ideals of love.

The Abbey of Saint-Victor

While Bernard used homilies on the Song of Songs to deliver his more personal, experiential account of Christian teaching, he was not a systematic theologian. His many admirers keenly sought to collect as many *Sententie* as they could, comparable to the *sententie* of theologians like Anselm of Laon (d. 1117) and William of Champeaux (d. 1121). Their message was more moral, however, than doctrinal.[35] Even though Bernard had been befriended and ordained an abbot in 1115 by the most famous teacher of the early twelfth-century schools, William of Champeaux (from whom he certainly absorbed his animus against Abelard), his style of exposition was more suited to the monastic cloister than to urban schools. Before meeting Bernard, William had decided in 1111 to give up his position as a secular master at the cathedral school of Notre-Dame by establishing a community of canons regular at a disused abbey, dedicated to Saint-Victor, on the left bank of Paris.[36] After 1115,

---

[34] Bernard, *De diligendo Deo* 33; SBOp 3:147: *ut sit ipse praemium amantium se, praemium aeternum amantium in aeternum.*

[35] Bernard of Clairvaux, *Sententiae*, SBOp 6.2, 7–255; *Bernard of Clairvaux, The Parables and The Sentences: Parables*, ed. Maureen M. O'Brien, CF 55 (Kalamazoo, MI: Cistercian Publications, 2000), with translations by Michael Casey, Francis R. Swietek, and John R. Sommerfeldt.

[36] On the foundation of Saint Victor, see Constant J. Mews, "William of Champeaux, the Foundation of St. Victor (Easter 1111) and the Chronology of Abelard's Early Career," in *Arts du langage et théologie aux confins des XIe et XIIe siècle*, ed. I. Rosier-Catach (Turnhout: Brepols, 2011), 83–104; and "Memories of William of Champeaux: The Necrology and the Early Years of Saint-Victor," in *Legitur in necrologio victorino. Studien zum Nekrolog von Sankt Viktor*, ed. Anette Löffler and Björn Geberd, Instrumenta Historica 7 (Münster: Aschendorff Verlag, 2015), 71–97.

perhaps because of suspicions about the sincerity of his conversion to the religious life, William decided to become closer to the monks of Clairvaux than to the canons of Saint-Victor and took a monastic habit in the last week of his life. After the cut and thrust of the schools (in which Abelard was becoming increasingly dominant), William preferred the more isolated atmosphere of a reformed monastic life to that of an urban school.

Nonetheless, around 1115, the arrival at Saint-Victor of a young scholar from Saxony, Hugh (d. 1141), transformed the fortunes of that abbey. Hugh would shine in his ability to present expositions of Christian doctrine that emulated the method of Anselm of Laon and William of Champeaux in their systematic framework but sought to transpose monastic contemplative ideals into the way of life of a canon regular. Whereas the Rule of Saint Benedict insisted on detachment from the world, the Rule of Augustine modeled the way of life of its canons on the example of the early Christians in Jerusalem, combining action and contemplation. In 1127 Hugh wrote to Bernard of Clairvaux, asking him for his views on a number of contentious theological issues, certainly responding to views being promoted by Peter Abelard.[37] In some of Bernard's responses, he sought to include his systematic account of Christian doctrine, the *De sacramentis*. Hugh was aware that students raised many questions about doctrine that deserved to be answered. He insisted, however, on the primacy of contemplative reading of the sacred text as a foundation for any theology.[38] Hugh shared with Bernard great respect for Gregory

---

[37] Bernard, Epistle 77, SBOp 7:182–200.

[38] Franklin T. Harkins, "*Lectio exhortatio debet esse*: Reading as a Way of Life at the Twelfth-Century Abbey of St. Victor," in *From Knowledge to Beatitude: St. Victor, Twelfth-Century Scholars, and Beyond*, ed. E. Ann Matter and Lesley Smith (Notre Dame, IN: University of Notre Dame Press, 2013), 103–30.

the Great's exposition of three senses of Scripture, the historical, the allegorical, and above all the moral or tropological. While Hugh was much more interested than Bernard in exploring Hebraic exegesis as a foundation for the historical meaning of Scripture, he also attended to its allegorical and moral implications and composed a series of short treatises on love (*caritas*).[39] Hugh was never exposed, however, to Bernard's homilies on the Song of Songs. For Hugh, the author who was the most important, after Augustine, was Dionysius the Areopagite, on whose *Celestial Hierarchy* he produced a commentary. Drawing on the notion of theophany in this text, Hugh was most interested in how the material world, above all the sacraments, provided a medium for divine revelation. His theological vision was calm and grandly majestic, but not personally engaging in the way offered by the writings of Bernard of Clairvaux.

Richard of Saint-Victor and *On Four Stages of Violent Love* (*De IV gradibus violentae caritatis*)

The figure who perhaps did most to restructure Bernard's thought for non-monastic readers was Richard, a Scot who became a canon regular at Saint-Victor, Paris, perhaps during the 1140s.[40] Sometime before 1153, the abbot of Clairvaux was

---

[39] These treatises are usefully translated in *On Love: A Selection of Works of Hugh, Adam, Achard, Richard, and Godfrey of St. Victor*, ed. Hugh Feiss (Turnhout: Brepols, 2011), 115–32 (*Eulogium sponsi et sponsae*, a commentary on Song of Songs 4:6–8); 151–68 (*De laude caritatis*); 171–81 (*Quid vere diligendum est*); 185–232 (*Soliloquium*).

[40] Dale M. Coulter considers that Richard probably came to Saint-Victor near 1150, possibly as early as 1145 (*Per Visibilia ad invisibilia: Theological Method in Richard of St. Victor (d. 1173)* [Turnhout: Brepols, 2006], 246–47). In his introduction to *Richard of Saint Victor, On the Trinity* (Eugene, OR: Cascade Books, 2011), Ruben Angelici (5), by contrast, repeats the claim of Mario Spinelli, *Riccardo di San Vittore: La Trinità*, Fonti Christiane

sufficiently impressed by Richard to ask him to respond to several important questions: the complexity of the chronology of the kings of Israel and Judah; why anything might be impure for the Hebrews when all creation was naturally good; the meaning of yeast in Scripture; why Augustine attributed unity, equality, and concord to the Father, Son, and Holy Spirit; and why power, wisdom, and goodness might also be assigned to each of the three persons, precisely the claim of Abelard at Sens in 1141.[41] Possibly Bernard was seeking clarification from Richard after failing to win widespread assent for his accusations against Gilbert of Poitiers at Rheims in 1148. Richard distances himself from the theological approach of Peter Lombard, whose *Sentences* (completed by 1157) covered the range of Christian teaching. The first book covered discussion of God as a trinity of three persons and about divine will; the second discussed creation, Adam's Fall, and sin; the third considered redemption; and the fourth examined the sacraments. Rather than engage in a systematic survey of Christian doctrine, Richard preferred to take great stories in the Old Testament (like that of Benjamin) as illustrating the relationship between the active and contemplative life.[42] In this way, his teaching was closer to monastic tradition in being concerned with how to lead a spiritual life rather than with teaching doctrine.

---

per il Terzo Millennio (Rome: Città Nuova Editrice, 1990), 66, that he arrived there between 1120 and 1134.

[41] *Richard of Saint-Victor: De concordia temporum regum conregnantium super Judam et super Israel*, PL 196:241B–48B; *Declarationes nonnullarum difficultatum scripturae ad b. Bernardum Claraevallensem abbatem*, PL 196:255A–61C; *Liber de verbo incarnato*, PL 196:955A–1010C.

[42] Richard's most famous work is *De duodecim patriarchis*, also known as *Benjamin minor*, ed. Jean Châtillon and Monique Duchet-Suchaux, *Les douze patriarches, ou, Beniamin minor*, SCh 419 (Paris: Cerf, 1997), in Richard of Saint-Victor, *Twelve Patriarchs, Mystical Ark, Book Three of the Trinity*, trans. Grover A. Zinn (Toronto: Paulist Press, 1979).

Richard's thought can be compared to that of Bernard through one of his most original works, *The Four Degrees of Violent Love* (*De quatuor gradibus violentae caritatis*), written toward the end of his life, ca. 1170.[43] To speak of *caritas* as violent was unusual in the extreme. Augustine had done so only once, in relation to the violence of death.[44] Richard, by contrast, developed the theme of love as a dynamic force, much greater than ourselves, from his reading of the Song (2:5) about the soul's being wounded by love. In this treatise, he describes *caritas* as fundamentally the same as *amor*, both God's core attribute and a passionate longing that describes our relationship to God. Like Bernard, Richard was drawn to using the Song of Songs as a way of explaining Christian teaching because it draws on the poetry of imagined experience. Yet whereas Bernard, following Origen, interpreted the bride in Song as both the Church and the soul, Richard reads the verse of the Song (2:5) about being wounded by love as a focus for explaining different types of human condition: "Behold, I see some people wounded, others bound, others languid, others growing faint—and all from love."[45] Richard's four stages are existential experiences. He sees the first stage of violent love—of being wounded—as ex-

---

[43] The Latin text was edited and translated into French by Gervais Dumeige, in *Ives, Épître à Séverin sur la charité. Richard de Saint-Victor, Les quatres degrés de la violente charité* (Paris: Vrin, 1955), 127–77. The work is introduced and translated by Andrew Kraebel within *On Love*, ed. Feiss, 263–300. Kraebel (263) follows a date of around 1170, proposed by Pierluigi Cacciapuoti, *Deus Existentia Amoris: Teologia della Carità e Teologia negli Scritti di Ricardo di San Vittore (d. 1173)* (Turnhout: Brepols, 1998), 94–95.

[44] Augustine, *Enarrationes in Psalmos* 47.13, CCSL 38:548: *a contrario enim similitudo data est de morte; quomodo enim mors ad auferendum uiolentissima est, sic caritas uiolentissima est ad saluandum. . . . Quomodo enim mors ad auferendum uiolentissima est, sic caritas uiolentissima est ad saluandum.*

[45] *De quatuor gradibus* 4: *Ecce video alios vulneratos, alios ligatos, alios languentes, alios deficientes; et totum a caritate* (ed. Dumeige, 129; trans. Kraebel, 275).

pressed in the Song, leading to apparent despair. The second stage, of being bound by love, he describes as being unable to forget what one loves. The third stage, of being languid, he sees as resulting from an excess of love, when nothing but love can satisfy the mind and for which there is no remedy other than gazing on divine mercy.[46] While Richard is certainly indebted to Bernard for provoking thought about the degrees of loving, he does not define love initially in terms of the relationship between the soul and God and the stages by which the will is relinquished for the sake of God. Instead, Richard chooses the four stages in terms of psychology and effect on the self. The fourth stage he formulates without reference to God, but rather to a state of mind:

> And so the fourth degree of violent love exists when nothing at all can satisfy the desire of the boiling mind any longer. This degree, unlike the others, knows no limits to its growth, for it has excelled the limits of human possibility and it always finds something else that it can desire ardently. . . . But who can explain the violence of this highest degree? Who is capable of pondering worthily the utter pre-eminence of this degree? What, I ask, penetrates the heart of a man more deeply, crucifies him more harshly, stirs him up more vehemently?[47]

---

[46] *De quatuor gradibus* 12 (ed. Dumeige, 129; trans. Kraebel, 280).

[47] *De quatuor gradibus* 14: *Quartus itaque violente caritatis gradus est quando estuantis animi desiderio jam omnino nichil satisfacere potest. Hic gradus, quia humane possibilitatis metas semel excessit, crescendi, ut ceteri, terminum nescit, quia semper invenit quod adhuc concupiscere possit. . . . Sed hujus superemi gradus violentiam quis digne explicare valeat, quis ejus supereminentiam vel digne pensare sufficiat? Quid, queso, est quod cor hominis profundius penetret, acerbius cruciet, vehementius exagitet?* (ed. Dumeige, 139; trans. Kraebel, 280–81).

The ecstasy of love is thus an experience hinted at through all of these stages rather than reserved for a final stage.

In introducing arguments from the experience, without initially introducing their theological implications, Richard imitates a style of argument from reason alone that had previously been adopted by Saint Anselm in his *Monologion*. Although Anselm had produced remarkable treatises in the late eleventh century, they were never quoted by Peter Lombard. They would not become standard reading in the Parisian schools until the thirteenth century. In drawing on Anselm, Richard may have benefited from scholarly connections in England (where they did circulate). In any case, Richard moves only gradually from psychological stages of love to comparison of human and spiritual versions of the stages of love. Thus he gives particular primacy to conjugal love (*amor conjugalis*), never mentioned by Bernard, as being of the highest value: "For in fact the shared feeling of intimate love tightens the chains of peace between those who are pledged to one another, and it renders that indissoluble and perpetual union pleasing and delightful."[48] Yet in human affairs, Richard observes that the three remaining stages can be potentially destructive, namely, being bound or obsessed by what one loves, with the exclusion of emotions other than love, and never freeing oneself from desire.

Richard moves only gradually to reflect on what these stages mean in terms of love of God. Like Bernard, Richard emphasizes the longing of the heart, thus promoting an affective spirituality that would be developed further by another Victorine canon, Thomas Gallus, in relation to Dionysius, of great influence within a Franciscan milieu in the thirteenth century. Richard would have known the Celestial Hierarchy,

---

[48] *De quatuor gradibus* 19: *Mutuus namque intimi amoris affectus inter federatos pacis vincula adstringit, et indissolubilem illam perpetuandamque societatem gratam et jocundam reddit* (ed. Dumeige, 145; trans. Kraebel, 283).

commented on by Hugh of Saint-Victor, with its driving theme of moving from the visible to the invisible, but he betrays no particular debt to Dionysius except in the more general theme of moving from the visible to the invisible. Richard's habit of refusing to identify any patristic authority in his writing makes it hard to be certain about what exactly he has read. His broad program, however, is to systematize what Bernard had taught in his homilies about the theme of desire for God. He comments that God is first loved, in the words of Scripture, "with the heart, soul, and mind," in a second stage with one's entire heart, in a third with one's entire soul, and in a fourth with all one's strength.[49] He loves devising fourfold categories to describe the process by which the mind focuses on God. The mind enters itself in meditation, then transcends itself through contemplation, and then proceeds into God with jubilation, but in a fourth stage, the mind goes out for its own sake, out of compassion.[50] Whereas Bernard's final stage of loving God is that of loving oneself for God's sake, Richard perceives the process as culminating in compassion for others.

The final part of his treatise deals with the consequences of these steps. A sense of intoxication begins at the very first stages of love. Thus in a first stage the soul is intoxicated with inner sweetness, provoking it to demand loftier things, while the second stage is one of contemplation, lifting the soul to a second heaven. The third degree of love is "when the mind of a man is snatched away into that abyss of divine light so that in this state, the human mind, forgetful of all external things, forgets even itself and passes entirely into God."[51] Richard

---

[49] *De quatuor gradibus* 23 (ed. Dumeige, 149; trans. Kraebel, 284).

[50] *De quatuor gradibus* 29 (ed. Dumeige, 157; trans. Kraebel, 287).

[51] *De quatuor gradibus* 38: *Sic itaque anima divini ardoris rogo intimique amoris incendio absorpta eternorumque desideriorum globis undique circumsepta, primo incalescit, postea incandescit, tandem autem tota liquescit et a priori status penitus deficit* (ed. Dumeige, 167; trans. Kraebel, 291).

evokes the image of molten metal being fully shaped by a metal worker to describe the submission of the soul to God. The final goal, however, is not ecstasy or beatitude but transforming the soul so that it can live fully for others.[52] As he puts it in his final sentence, the mind is in the first stage led back, in the second carried over, in the third transfigured, in the fourth reawakened.[53] When we compare these stages of loving to those of Bernard, we find that Richard is not preoccupied by the moral issue of whether one is loving oneself or loving God, or indeed the experience of sin. Rather, Richard's interest is in different stages of the experience of loving, as a forgetting of oneself, and thus an emergence into ecstasy. Implicit to his argument is his sense that ecstasy is a process that begins in this life, even if it comes to fruition in the next.

Richard of Saint-Victor on the Trinity

Sometime before his death in 1153, Bernard of Clairvaux prompted Richard to write a short treatise about the thorny theological problem of whether individual attributes, in particular power, wisdom, and goodness, could be attributed to the Father, Son, and Holy Spirit.[54] This is precisely the triad of divine attributes that Peter Abelard had defended in his *Theologia*, initially in the *Theologia "Summi boni"* condemned at the Council of Soissons in 1121, and again by Bernard of Clairvaux. Yet whereas Bernard was cautious about the triad, Richard saw no problem with the notion, doubtless because his own mentor, Hugh of Saint-Victor, had introduced precisely this triad within his *De tribus diebus*, a treatise written at about the same time as Peter Abelard first composed his own treatise on the

---

[52] *De quatuor gradibus* 44 (ed. Dumeige, 173; trans. Kraebel, 294).
[53] *De quatuor gradibus* 47 (ed. Dumeige, 177; trans. Kraebel, 296).
[54] Richard, *De tribus appropriatis personis in Trinitate* (PL 196:991B–94C).

Trinity.[55] In his *De sacramentis*, Hugh is more cautious about assigning divine attributes to particular persons of the Trinity, as if responding to the debate provoked by Abelard's *Theologia*.[56] His emphasis was always more on explaining how the mind could be lifted to God than on debating terminology applied to God. Given that Bernard had applied himself to criticizing the trinitarian theology of both Peter Abelard and Gilbert of Poitiers as seeming to undermine God's majesty, it was a bold effort of Richard to tackle the doctrine of the Trinity toward the end of his life, at about the same time as he produced *De gradibus IV violentae caritatis*. The dominant exposition of the Trinity in the schools was then that of Peter Lombard, who had integrated the subject into the first book of the *Sentences* but discussed the subject largely from the perspective of Augustine's analogy of the Trinity to memory, intelligence, and will within the soul.[57] While Lombard opened the *Sentences* by introducing Augustine's distinction between enjoying "the certain supreme thing" (*summa quaedam res*) of God and using what is in the world, he never developed an experiential approach to Christian doctrine.[58] His pedagogical technique was that of Abelard, questioning the meaning of statements made about God by the Fathers, without Abelard's appeal to philosophical authority. Lombard focused on presenting the Trinity as a

---

[55] Hugh presented these themes in his *De tribus diebus*, ed. Dominique Poirel, CCCM 177 (Turnhout: Brepols, 2002), a work that Poirel studies in great detail in his *Livre de la nature et débat trinitaire au XIIe siècle*, Bibliotheca Victorina 14 (Turnhout: Brepols, 2002), proposing that the *De tribus diebus* was written before Abelard's *Theologia Summi boni*, rather than in the mid-1120s, as was previously argued.

[56] Poirel, *Livre de la nature*, 329–33.

[57] Peter Lombard, *Sententiae in IV libris distinctae* 1.d.2–34, ed. I. Brady, *Spicilegium Bonaventurianum* 4, 2 vols. (Grottaferrata: Editiones Collegii S. Bonaventurae, 1971), 1:61–254, especially 1.d.3.2.

[58] *Sententiae* 1.d.2, quoting Augustine, *De doctrina Christiana* 1.5, ed. J. Martin, CCSL 32 (Turnhout: Brepols, 1962), 9.

matter of correct doctrine rather than as what could be known through experience.

Richard's opening assertion in the *De trinitate* is that we learn in a threefold way: "For we perceive some things by experience, we attain others through reasoning, and we hold certitude in other things by believing."[59] The goal to which he aspires is that of mystical experience, imitating Saint Paul in rising to the highest heaven: "Nor does that notice of eternal things suffice for us which is through faith alone, unless we apprehend that which is through intelligence, if we do not yet suffice for that which is through experience."[60] Richard's exposition silently draws on the technique of Saint Anselm in emphasizing how faith leads to understanding, but it also picks up on Abelard's emphasis that unless one exercises understanding, one cannot be led to faith. Richard may well have acquired his familiarity with the writings of Saint Anselm in England. He was not an authority ever alluded to by Peter Lombard in his writings. Yet in speaking about the need for experience alongside intelligence, Richard was combining a core emphasis of Bernard alongside that of Anselm. Whereas Peter Lombard followed Augustine in speaking about God as "a certain supreme thing" (*summa quaedam res*), Richard is much happier with notions of *plenitudo*, above all the plenitude of love. Following an argument raised by Abelard, he argues that God's nature as love (described as both *amor* and *caritas*) requires there to be sociability, manifest in a plurality of persons:[61] "Fullness of goodness could not have been

---

[59] Richard of Saint-Victor, *De trinitate* 1.1, ed. Jean Ribaillier (Paris: Vrin, 1958), 86: *Rerum itaque notitiam, ni fallor, modo triplici apprehendimus: nam alia experiendo probamus, alia ratiocinando colligimus, aliorum certitudinem credendo tenemus.* Trans. Angelici, 73.

[60] Richard, *De trinitate* Prol., ed. Ribaillier, 84: *Nec nobis sufficiat illa eternorum notitia que est per fidem solam, nisi apprehendamus et illam que est per intelligentiam, si necdum ad illam sufficimus que est per experientiam.*

[61] Gregory, Hom in Evang 1.17.1; ed. R. Etaix, CCSL 141 (Turnhout: Brepols, 1999), 177 (PL 76:1139), quoted by Abelard, *Theologia Summi*

present without fullness of charity; and fullness of charity could not have existed without plurality of divine beings."[62] His approach to the Trinity is through appealing to experience: "Similarly there is nothing more joyful than charity. And this is what nature teaches and the manyfold experience reveals to us the same. . . . Spiritual life cannot experience anything more pleasant than the delights of charity."[63] Richard's treatise about the Trinity is about the limitations of language rather than about visions of ecstasy. Yet he seeks to argue from experience to glimpse what is beyond: "We all know what power, wisdom, love, or goodness are, as we verify it every day by experience. Indeed from clear knowledge of these realities, we can go back to the notion of those which transcend the limit of human abilities."[64] Richard was reasserting Abelard's argument about the triad of divine attributes being attributed to the three persons of the Trinity by arguing not through the theory of language (as Abelard had done) but through the testimony of experience, a term dear to Bernard of Clairvaux. In the *De trinitate* Richard was repeating verbatim an argument that he had made in a letter responding directly to a question from Bernard about why he attributed power to the Father, wisdom to the Son, and charity or goodness to the Holy Spirit.[65] Richard's entire *De trinitate* can be seen as developing a response to a question about the

boni 3.89; CCCM 13:196; *Theologia Christiana* 4.117; CCCM 12:323; *Theologia Scholarium* 2.123; CCCM 13:469. Alluded to by Richard, *De Trinitate* 3.2, ed. Ribaillier, 136.

[62] Richard, *De trinitate* 3.2, ed. Ribaillier, 59: *Bonitatis vero plenitudo non potuit esse sine caritatis plenitudine, nec caritatis plenitudo sine divinarum personarum pluralitate.* Trans. Angelici, 117.

[63] Richard, *De trinitate* 3.4, ed. Ribaillier, 139: *Certe, ut dictum est, nil caritate dulcius, nil caritate jocundius. Caritatis deliciis rationalis vita nil dulcius experitur; nulla unquam delectatione delectabilius fruitur.* Trans. Angelici, 119.

[64] Richard, *De trinitate* 6.15, ed. Ribaillier, 247: *Quid sit potentia, quid sit sapientia, quid caritas vel bonitas, omnes in commune novimus, et cotidiano experimento probamus.* Trans. Angelici, 221.

[65] Richard, *De tribus appropriatis personis in Trinitate*, PL 196:991B–1004C, esp. 993D.

Trinity initially put to him by Bernard. In combining appeals to both reason and experience, Richard was showing Bernard that it was possible to reflect on the Trinity using the triad of power, wisdom, and goodness, as both Abelard and Hugh of Saint-Victor had done, but without incurring the accusations of heresy made against Abelard. Bernard's interest in Richard is evident not just from this short treatise about divine attributes but also from other treatises responding to questions from the abbot of Clairvaux, about Scripture and the incarnation of the Word.

In the final book of the *De trinitate* Richard launches a tirade against unnamed contemporaries who questioned the notion that substance begets substance, or wisdom begets wisdom:

> But many arise in our time who do not dare to say this; rather, much more dangerously, they deny and seek in every way to try to refute what is against the authority of the holy Fathers and so many assertions of patristic tradition. They stubbornly deny that which is claimed by all the saints, without being able to exhibit any authoritative proof of their assertions. . . . Your exposition strives to this, that we believe that substance does not beget substance. The faithful exposition, worthy of full acceptance, asserts that what the holy Fathers equally assert, is false, and contends that what none of the saints assert is true. But they say: "If the substance of the Son is begotten, that of the Father is unbegotten, how can there be one and the same substance of both?"[66]

---

[66] Richard, *De trinitate* 6.22, ed. Ribaillier, 259: *Sed multi temporibus nostris surrexere qui non audent hoc dicere, quin potius, quod multo periculosius est, contra sanctorum Patrum auctoritatem et tot attestationes paternarum traditionum audent negare et modis omnibus conantur refellere. Nullo modo concedunt quod substantia gignat substantiam, vel sapientia sapientiam. Pertinaciter negant quod omnes sancti affirmat.* Trans. Angelici, 232.

While Peter Lombard never specifically taught that "substance does not beget substance," Richard was responding to an argument made in the first book of the *Sentences* (on the authority of Augustine) that God cannot beget himself.[67] Peter Lombard had argued that

> In the same way it is not to be asserted that the divine essence generated the Son because, since the Son is the divine essence, the Son would already be the thing from which he is generated; and so the same thing would generate itself. And so also we say that the divine essence did not generate an essence. Since the divine essence is a one and supreme certain thing [reality], if the divine essence generated an essence, then the same thing generated itself, which is not at all possible. But the Father alone begot the Son, and the Holy Spirit proceeds from the Father and the Son.[68]

Joachim's criticism of this passage in Lombard's *Sentences* as implying an unnecessary distinction within God provoked the Fourth Lateran Council to censure his claim in 1215. Nonetheless, Joachim was repeating the same reservation raised both by Bernard and by Richard of Saint-Victor about any attempt to reserve divine substance to God alone as distinct from the divine persons.[69] Like Joachim, Richard was responding to a

---

[67] Peter Lombard, *Sententie* 1.4.1.1, ed. Brady 1:78. That Richard is alluding to Peter Lombard (even if exaggerating his arguments) is observed by Ribaillier in his introduction to the *De trinitate*, 11–12.

[68] *Sent.* I, d. 5. c. 1. no. 6, ed. Brady, 1:82: *Ita etiam non est dicendum quod diuina essentia genuit filium: Quia cum filius sit diuina essentia, iam esset filius res a qua generatur; et ita eadem res se ipsam generaret. Ita etiam dicimus quod essentia diuina non genuit essentiam: Cum enim una et summa quaedam res sit diuina essentia, si diuina essentia essentiam genuit, eadem res se ipsam genuit, quod omnino esse non potest; sed pater solus genuit filium, et a patre et filio procedit spiritus sanctus.*

[69] Joachim of Fiore, *Psalterium decem cordarum,* I, dist. I, ed. K.-V. Selge, Monumenta Germaniae Historica, Quellen zur Geistesgeschichte des

passage in the *Sentences* in which Peter Lombard paraphrased a passage of Augustine in a way that could be construed as implying a distinction between divine essence as *summa quaedam res* and the divine persons.[70] His criticism may have exaggerated the careful analysis of terms introduced by Peter Lombard, but it vented his suspicion of an analysis that explained God as a trinity more through distinguishing the meaning of terms than through reflecting on arguments drawn from experience as much as reason. Richard preferred to explain the Trinity not in terms of "a certain supreme thing" (a potentially unfortunate phrase used once by Augustine) but through consideration "of his omnipotence . . . from the plenitude of his wisdom

---

Mittelalters, Band 20 (Hannover: Hahnsche Buchhandlung, 2009), 20 = ed. Venice 1527; repr. Frankfurt: Minerva, 1965, f. 229[rb]: *Sed nec ut tres olivas que unius sunt nature sed tamen corporum proprietate disiuncte, neque ut tres ramos uni radici infixos; ut substantiam radicem et tres ramos ypostases arbitreris iuxta aliquorum perfidiam, quod est inducere quaternitatem.* Cf. *Decrees of the Ecumenical Councils,* ed. Norman J. Tanner (London: Sheed & Ward, 1990), 231: *Damnamus ergo et reprobamus libellum sive tractatum quem abbas Ioachim edidit contra magistrum Petrum Lombardum de unitate seu essentia trinitatis appellans ipsum haereticum et insanum pro eo quod in suis dixit sententiis quoniam quaedam summa res est pater et filius et spiritus sanctus et illa non est generans neque genita nec procedens unde asserit quod ille non tam trinitatem quam quaternitatem adstruebat in deo videlicet tres personas et illam communem essentiam quasi quartam manifeste protestans quod nulla res est quae sit pater et filius et spiritus sanctus nec est essentia nec substantia nec natura quamvis concedat quod pater et filius et spiritus sanctus sunt una essentia una substantia unaque natura.*

[70] Augustine, *De doctrina Christiana* 1.5, ed. J. Martin, CCSL 32 (Turnhout: Brepols, 1962), 9; ed. W. M. Green, CCSL 80 (Vienna: Tempsky, 1963), 10: *res igitur, quibus fruendum est, pater et filius et spiritus sanctus eademque trinitas, una quaedam summa res communisque omnibus fruentibus ea, si tamen res et non rerum omnium causa, si tamen et causa.* For further discussion of Joachim's critique of Peter Lombard, see Constant J. Mews and Clare Monagle, "Peter Lombard, Joachim of Fiore and the Fourth Lateran Council," *Medioevo. Rivista di storia della filosofia medievale* 35 (2010): 81–122.

and from the plenitude of his goodness."[71] In the Godhead, the divine persons enjoyed each other in permanent ecstasy. Richard's perspective on the Trinity differed profoundly from the detached analysis of Peter Lombard. His argument was that through our experience of plurality we can understand the trinity of divine persons in God. Whether or not we call this theology mystical, it was based on *consideratio* or reflection, a term that Bernard much preferred to *theologia*.

Conclusion

Richard's *De trinitate* formulated a much-expanded response to a question once put to him about the Trinity by Bernard of Clairvaux. Richard wanted to show that it was possible to explain this core doctrine of Christian faith in a way that drew on both experience and rational thought. The treatise explores a different subject from *Four Stages of Violent Love*. Yet both texts of Richard privilege the realm of experience, a notion that Bernard had brought to the fore in the literary genre in which he excelled, that of the sermon. In the case of that treatise, Richard's argument was that *caritas* is not a static concept but a dynamic force of divine origin that is able to transform our lives, sometimes in a way that might seem violent. This same sense of the dynamic quality of love animates Richard's understanding of the triune nature of God. Love, in his view, requires plurality and thus can explain why power, wisdom, and goodness are divine attributes relevant to individual persons, but together illuminating the plenitude that is God.

---

[71] *De Trinitate* 6.25, ed. Ribaillier, 266: *In hujus operis nostri calce illud replicare et memorie commendare volumus . . . quod omnipotentie consideratione facile convinctur, quod non sit, sed nec esse possit Deus nisi unus; ex bonitatis plenitudine, quod sit personaliter trinus; ex plenitudine vero sapientie liquido colligitur quomodo conveniat unitas substantie cum personarum pluralitate.*

Bernard may not have been a systematic theologian, but he did introduce a new way of presenting Christian doctrine, namely, through preaching on the Song of Songs. While steeped in the writing of Augustine, Bernard was inspired by the commentary of Origen on the Song of Songs to find a much more personal way of developing what we might call a mystical theology. Whereas previous monastic explanation of the Song of Songs had focused on understanding the bride as the church, Bernard followed the precedent of Origen in also seeing it as about the soul. Bernard's approach to expounding Christian doctrine was radically different from that of Peter Abelard, who drew on his understanding of what Aristotle had to say about language to reconceptualize the doctrine of the Trinity. Bernard accused Abelard of being excessively intellectual in his theological analysis—unfairly, given Abelard's concern with divine love, manifest in the person of Jesus and through the Holy Spirit. Bernard, by contrast, was a preacher rather than an analyst of words. He focused on the Word of God as the lover of the Soul, presented through the Song of Songs. Bernard may not have been happy with the attempt of Peter Abelard to formulate the doctrine of the Trinity, and he was always cautious about attempts to assign power, wisdom, and goodness to the three persons.

While Richard of Saint-Victor completed his *De trinitate* only around 1170, long after Bernard's death, I would argue that he was still seeking to answer a question put to him about the Trinity by the abbot of Clairvaux. Richard's preferred angle was very different from the analytic technique adopted by Peter Lombard. He sought to draw on Bernard's technique of attending to the voice of experience, as formulated above all in the Song of Songs. In the same way, Richard's treatise *On the Four Stages of Violent Love* took much further a way of thinking that Bernard had initiated in his *De diligendo Deo*. It was a vision inspired by the Song of Songs as a text that uses the language of experience to speak about longing for God. Richard admired the contemplative insights of Bernard but sought to adapt them to the demands of an Augustinian canon, teaching his students in the city of Paris.

Chapter 9

A Mirror for Abbots
The *Pastoral Prayer* of Saint Aelred

Bernardo Bonowitz, OCSO

L ast September, in the course of a trip to Australia, I received an icon card that has been on the desk of my choir
stall ever since and that I look at for a brief moment at the
beginning of each hour of the Divine Office. It is a copy of the
icon of Saint Benedict that Pope Benedict XVI was presented
with during the 2008 World Youth Day in Sydney. What first
struck me about the icon is that Saint Benedict is weeping.
Second, his right hand is extended in a gesture that seems to
express both supplication and self-giving. Finally, the text on
the parchment scroll that he carries in his left hand, rather than
being the citation from the Prologue (and the Sermon on the
Mount), *Whoever hears these words of mine and puts them into
practice is like a man who built his house on rock* (Matt 7:24-25,
cf. RB Prol.33-34), with which I am familiar from other icono-
graphic depictions of Benedict, is a quotation from chapter 27
of the Rule, "He is to imitate the loving example of the Good
Shepherd,"[1] and, finally, along with the scroll he is carrying a
monastic staff (*baculum*).

This conjunction of tears, a humbly outstretched hand, a
text that summarizes the abbatial charge, and a staff seems to
me a marvelous visual translation of the *Pastoral Prayer* of Saint

---

[1] *Et pastoris boni pium imitetur exemplum* (RB 27.8).

Aelred. This could in part be because I have been studying both the icon and the prayer each day during these last few months, but I think that something more than mere subjective meandering is involved in my association.

What I hope to do in this article is to reflect on these elements in Aelred's *Prayer* and then bring them to bear on us, abbots and abbesses, priors and prioresses, of the beginning of the twenty-first century. An insertion from the fourteenth or fifteenth century at the beginning of the text says that besides being composed by the "venerable Aelred, abbot of Rievaulx," this prayer was "frequently recited by him." Frequent recitation has as its aim assimilation and identification—the words of the text become our words, and we become genuinely compenetrated with their sentiments. If it is permitted to have a goal in this kind of article, my own would be that by reading it—and even more, by following Aelred's example and praying the *Pastoral Prayer*[2] frequently—our inward features will come to resemble the features on the icon card: the weeping, loving, trustful face that looks out at us from the icon will be our own.

A Reading of the Prayer

How Can a Sinner be an Abbot?

Aelred begins his prayer with: "To you I cry" (*Ad te clamat*).[3] He is crying out to Jesus, the Good Shepherd, because he knows that he is "good, merciful, and loving,"[4] and he is crying out to him because he knows himself to be none of these things.

---

[2] Where not otherwise indicated, all references are to *Aelred de Rievaulx: La Prière Pastorale*, in *Aelred de Rievaulx: La Vie de Recluse, La Prière Pastorale*, trans. Charles Dumont, SCh 76 (Paris: Éditions de Cerf, 1961).

[3] Aelred de Rievaulx, *La Prière Pastorale*, 184.

[4] Aelred de Rievaulx, *La Prière Pastorale*, 184 (English translations of the Latin text are my own).

If Jesus is the Good Shepherd, Aelred is the "not good shepherd," the "no good shepherd" (*Iste non bonus pastor*).[5] They both have the same job description—shepherd—and they both have the same flock. Many times in the course of the prayer Aelred reminds the Lord that the brothers of the community of Rievaulx are the Lord's flock, the Lord's people. But whereas the Lord is supremely fitted by his holiness for the fulfillment of his pastoral charge, Aelred is woefully lacking in the prerequisites. As a shepherd, he is "wretched, miserable, weak, inexperienced, and useless."[6] And this unsuitability for a task that he has accepted and that he cannot get away from (for all his deficiencies, he recognizes that he is "still and all a pastor of your sheep"[7]), leaves him worried. He is worried for himself, knowing that he will be judged on the basis of a genuine carrying out of his abbatial ministry, and he is anxious for the Lord's sheep,[8] who he knows will go to ruin should he fail in a task that seems utterly to exceed him.

Aelred's sense of inadequacy stems from something much more inclusive and profound than an experience of professional difficulties in his service as abbot. It derives from the tormenting awareness of being unworthy before God, of being irremediably and undeniably a poor, very poor, sinner, someone with many grave sins on his conscience. As a matter of fact, *many* does not go far enough in conveying Aelred's personal conviction of his sinfulness. In his own eyes, Aelred is a man of "countless offences."[9] It is this that has him in tears.

---

[5] Aelred de Rievaulx, *La Prière Pastorale*, 184.

[6] *miser, miserabilis, infirmus, imperitus, inutilis* (Aelred de Rievaulx, *La Prière Pastorale*, 184).

[7] *ovium tamen tuaram qualiscumque pastor* (Aelred de Rievaulx, *La Prière Pastorale*, 184).

[8] *anxius pro se, anxius pro ovibus tuis* (Aelred de Rievaulx, *La Prière Pastorale*, 184).

[9] *innumerabilium criminum* (Aelred de Rievaulx, *La Prière Pastorale*, 184).

He cannot see how his long and heavy history of personal sin can be reconciled with the title of abbot and, even less, with the abbatial office: "If I didn't recognize myself as utterly unworthy of the name of shepherd, I would certainly be a fool."[10] How can a person with all this on his conscience presume to exercise the abbatial charge? For Aelred, holiness—or at least innocence—of life is the indispensable requisite for assuming a pastoral responsibility. And it is just this that he does not have. His self-knowledge, his memory of his past years, carried out in "the bitterness of his soul,"[11] leave this beyond question.

Aelred does not doubt that by God's mercy his sins have been forgiven. He marvels at the fact that the divine mercy has bent down to draw him up from the depths of the abyss in which he wallowed in his youth, that God has not avenged himself on him by definitively condemning him for his misdeeds nor overwhelmed him with dread by threats of future punishment nor even loved him any less as a result of all his multiple infidelities. In fact, the awareness of God's mercy in the face of so much infidelity is an unceasing source of gratitude: "With all my strength and from the depths of my being, I render you thanks and praise."[12]

Yet if God can forget the whole history of Aelred's misdeeds, Aelred himself cannot. As much as he gives thanks to God for his mercy, he cannot leave behind the recollection of his misdoings. It haunts him: "mindful of your goodness— yes—but unable to forget my own ingratitude."[13] This initial inability on the part of Aelred to let the forgiveness of God

---

[10] *Pavesco et contremisco ad nomen pastoris: cui me indignissimum si non sentio, certe desipio* (Aelred de Rievaulx, *La Prière Pastorale,* 184).

[11] Aelred de Rievaulx, *La Prière Pastorale,* 184.

[12] *quantum conari possunt, grates et laudes exsolvunt tibi omnia viscera mea* (Aelred de Rievaulx, *La Prière Pastorale,* 186).

[13] *memor quidem bonitatis tuae, sed non immemor ingratitudinis meae* (Aelred de Rievaulx, *La Prière Pastorale,* 186).

have its full effect and bring him to the experience of pardon
and peace points us to one of the most interesting aspects of
the *Pastoral Prayer*: its dynamism. Exactly because Aelred is
not simply soliloquizing but genuinely praying, and thereby
opening himself to the transforming power and love of the God
with whom he is in dialogue, Aelred's sentiments undergo a
profound change in the course of the *Prayer*. As he continues
to pray, *because* he perseveres in prayer, he is gradually led to
let go of the burden of guilt and to have the spiritual courage
and confidence to desire and then to receive the infusion of
God's own holiness within himself. He who confessed to God
at the outset of his prayer that while he remembered God's
goodness he could not forget his unthankfulness in the face of
this goodness will later ask God, without hesitation or anxiety,
to do precisely this: to be "mindful of your goodness and no
longer mindful of my own ingratitude."[14]

But I have jumped ahead. At this point in the *Prayer*, Aelred
is still weighed down by the memory of the past sins he has
committed. He is even weighed down, in a certain sense, by the
memory of the past sins that he has *not* committed, since he sees
in their avoidance a further debt he has incurred in relation to
God. It is God's providence[15] rather than Aelred's virtue that has
kept him from falling on myriad occasions, whether by God's
removing the occasion of sin, or by delivering Aelred from the
impulse to sin, or by providing him with the virtue to resist
temptation. Not only that: he is also weighed down by the daily
temptations with which he continues to struggle in the present
and which often enough he ends up giving in to, for lack of a
sufficient watchfulness over himself and his inclinations.[16]

[14] *memor bonitatis tuae, immemor ingratitudinis meae* (Aelred of Rievaulx, *Prière Pastorale*, 192).

[15] *te utique gubernante* (Aelred of Rievaulx, *Prière Pastorale*, 186).

[16] *nec pro praesentibus adeo sollicitum ut oporteret* (Aelred of Rievaulx, *Prière Pastorale*, 186).

What makes Aelred's anxiety a genuine agony, however, does not have to do, at the root, with the pangs of his individual conscience. His torment stems from his awareness of the dire consequences his sinfulness has on the flock entrusted to him through his abbatial election. He knows that nothing contributes so much to the ruin of a community as to have a foolish and sinful man set over others as their superior.[17] Yet this is the very situation in which his flock finds itself. Here we see the very core of Aelred's anguish. With this, we pass from the tears of the icon to the scroll. Aelred's tears spring from taking to heart with supreme seriousness the admonition written on the parchment, "And imitate the loving example of the Good Shepherd." That injunction is constantly before the eyes of his soul, precisely because that is the task he has taken on in becoming abbot, to unrestrictedly imitate the Good Shepherd who lays down his life for his sheep, who came so that they might have life and have it in abundance. It is a task that in his own estimation utterly exceeds his capacities.

In his frustration, Aelred enters into a dispute with the Lord. Which of the two of us, Aelred demands to know, brought about this state of affairs in the first place? Aelred recognizes his own contribution to the present predicament, which consists in his acceptance of the abbatial election: "What was I thinking of?"[18] But surely God in his infallible providence could have averted this situation. He too has a share in the responsibility, at least through his permissive will, if not through his absolute will.

To us there can seem something comic, contrived, or exaggerated in Aelred's tearful questioning of God about his motives in allowing him to become superior of his monastery.

[17] *Quod enim maius periculum subditis, quam stultus prelatus et peccator?* (Aelred of Rievaulx, *Prière Pastorale*, 188).

[18] *Miser ego: Quid feci, quid praesumpsi, quid consensi?* (Aelred of Rievaulx, *Prière Pastorale*, 186).

But for Aelred the subject is entirely serious. Convinced that in light of the call to "hold the place of Christ in the monastery" (RB 2.2), which for him means "to carry out the mission of Christ in the monastery," he is wholly inadequate, he feels himself compelled to try to think out why God would have allowed such a scenario to take place. "How is it possible, O Fount of Mercy, that you could have wished to entrust those who are so dear to you to one who has been cast so far from your countenance?"[19]

Two possible reasons come to Aelred's mind. The first, a truly frightening one, is that in permitting Aelred to assume the abbatial office, God's intent has been to abandon him to his own inclinations and give him more scope to yield to his temptations. He recognizes, as every superior must, that if it is dangerous to be the subjects of a sinful superior, it is equally dangerous for the superior himself. He or she does have freer rein than the other members of the community and fewer restrictions, and this freedom and lack of restraint can easily be abused. (This theme of divine punishment expressing itself in a permissive indulgence destined to end in a more severe punishment begins with Saint Paul in Romans 1:28—*And since they did not see fit to acknowledge God, God gave them up to a debased mind and to things that should not be done*—and is frequently found in the writings of Saint Augustine and Saint Bernard.) Aelred does not entirely exclude the possibility that God's permission of his election has in view his final condemnation, though he does significantly relativize the likelihood of this alternative by the use of the titles with which he addresses the Lord in this passage. In the midst of entertaining the theory that by allowing him to become abbot God intends his ultimate ruin, Aelred maintains a dialogue with this same God as "my hope," "my salvation," "my sweet Lord." As a matter of

---

[19] *Cur ergo, fons misericordiae, tales tali, tam caros tibi tam proiecto ab oculis tuis commendare voluisti?* (Aelred de Rievaulx, *La Prière Pastorale*, 188).

fact, these titles, unvaryingly affectionate and intimate, form a thread that runs through the entire *Prayer* and indicate, from the very beginning, something of the *Prayer*'s final outcome. Aelred rapidly passes on to the second possible reason that God might have permitted his election, one that he says does more honor to God and offers more consolation to the superior and that Aelred himself finds more convincing. Aelred theorizes that God is making use of him as an extreme case, as someone chosen for the abbatial office in order to make patent the mercy, wisdom, and power of God in allowing human beings to exercise spiritual authority in his stead.[20] If God has chosen someone so deficient as Aelred and has "set him over your family" (and for Aelred it is impossible to doubt God's love for his family, a love revealed in the cross), it is to show in an incontrovertible way that whenever a community is well governed, it is truly God himself who is doing the governing through his representative.[21] Aelred paradoxically sees himself as rendering a service, precisely through his limitations. If it weren't for superiors like himself, patently "foolish and sinful" (*stultus et peccator*), other superiors more competent and better morally equipped than he might be led to think that they were able to fulfill their sacred office by their own wisdom, justice, and strength. Aelred's ability to see that his own community is prospering spiritually and to recognize that this can in no way be attributed to himself ends up serving as a motivation for all superiors to glorify God and persevere in humility. For this reason, Aelred concludes this part of his prayer with the verse from Psalm 113, *Not to us, O Lord, not to us, but to your name give the glory.*[22]

---

[20] *ut manifesta fieret misericordia tua et notam faceres sapientiam tuam* (Aelred of Rievaulx, *Prière Pastorale*, 188).

[21] *quoniam cum bene regunt populum tuum illi, tu potius regunt quam illi* (Aelred of Rievaulx, *Prière Pastorale*, 186).

[22] *Non nobis, Domine, non nobis, sed nomini tuo da gloriam* (Aelred de Rievaulx, *La Prière Pastorale*, 186).

Acceptance of His Office; Preparatory Prayer for Himself

It is at this juncture that Aelred interiorly consents to the charge that has been laid upon him. From now on, rather than continuing to focus on himself and his unworthiness, he wishes to concentrate on the task that has been given him. This task consists in two interwoven obligations: to care for the flock confided to him and zealously to pray for it.[23] Poor as he is, Aelred is now ready to give himself over to the work for which God has chosen him. His lack of merit becomes secondary in the light of his responsibility to be faithful to his call: "If merit has no right to speak, the abbatial charge cries out."[24]

Before undertaking the care of his brothers and the task of praying for them, however, Aelred believes that it is incumbent on him first to pray for himself. Through "the sacrifice of prayer" (*sacrificium orationis*) offered to the Divine Majesty on his own behalf, he trusts that he will be cleansed in such a way that he can henceforth act both as shepherd and priest for his monks, giving himself to them and making intercession for them. It is evident that he does not expect a miraculously instantaneous answer to this prayer for healing and renovation. Rather, through the repeated offering of this prayer, he hopes to be rendered progressively more capable of fulfilling his pastoral responsibility.

Aelred's initial petition in this prayer is simply to be seen by the Lord: "Behold me, my sweet Lord, behold me."[25] He knows that the instinct of the sinner is to hide himself from the face of the Lord, but he is sure that to do this is to run in the absolutely wrong direction. Flight from the Lord does not

[23] *iubes me sollicitum esse pro illis et attentius orare pro illis* (Aelred of Rievaulx, *Prière Pastorale*, 188, 190).

[24] *Ubi tacet meritum, clamat officium* (Aelred of Rievaulx, *Prière Pastorale*, 190).

[25] *Vide me, dulcis Domine, vide me* (Aelred of Rievaulx, *Prière Pastorale*, 190).

turn one invisible. It leaves the sinner as he is and exposes him to condemnation. To place oneself willingly before the Lord, on the other hand, is to submit oneself to the healing power of God's gaze. God looks at the sinner who presents himself before him with the regard of a devoted doctor, a kindly teacher, an indulgent father. To be seen this way, by "your all-powerful mercy and most merciful omnipotence,"[26] is not only to be forgiven, but to experience an inward cure of the "languors of the soul."[27] Aelred prays that while this healing is in process, he will not obstruct it or render it ineffective by giving in to the passions that still assail him. He asks for the grace to remain stable beneath God's benevolent gaze in the midst of the onslaughts of temptation and to allow God completely to heal his weaknesses, cure his wounds, and, most lovely of all, form anew, make beautiful (*formosa*), everything in him that sin had deformed from its original comeliness.[28]

As he will do again later when he comes to pray explicitly for his community, Aelred here passes from imploring God to fix his gaze upon him to asking him to send his Spirit from on high to dwell within him and to establish in his heart his abiding "dwelling place" (*habitaculum*). I see in the staff that Saint Benedict holds in the icon an image of the indwelling Spirit that Aelred prays for. Benedict holds the staff in the same hand as he holds the scroll. The limitlessness of what is asked for by the injunction of the scroll—"and imitate the example of the Good Shepherd"[29]—is matched by the limitlessness of the gift of the indwelling Spirit. It is the Spirit living in Aelred that will not only pardon and heal him but thoroughly sanctify him, just

---

[26] *omnipotentissima misericordia tua et misericordissima omnipotentia tua* (Aelred of Rievaulx, *Prière Pastorale*, 190).

[27] Aelred of Rievaulx, *Prière Pastorale*, 192.

[28] *donec perfecte sanes infirmitates meas, et cures vulnera mea, et deformia mea formes* (Aelred of Rievaulx, *Prière Pastorale*, 192).

[29] *et pastoris boni imitetur exemplum* (RB 27.8).

as it is the Spirit who will enable him truly to attend to all the necessities of his brothers and as it is the Spirit who, in coming down upon the community, will unify them, enlighten them, and perfect them. Concluding his prayer for himself, Aelred, much more daringly than one might have imagined at the *Prayer's* outset, asks that the Spirit in him make him desirous and capable of orienting every one of his deeds and thoughts according to God: loving God, praising God, praying to God, and living continually in God's presence.[30]

Prayer for Divine Wisdom to Direct His Human Love

Purified by this prayer and the fruits of it, Aelred is ready to ask for the grace to fulfill the first of his abbatial duties: to care for his brethren, to exercise his abbatial authority in ruling them for their salvation. For this he will need the gift of divine wisdom. God knows only too well the ignorance of his "little servant" (*peccatori servulo tuo*).[31] Aelred implores a wisdom from God, the fountain of wisdom (*fons sapientiae*)[32] that will become the living spring from which everything that he needs to do in regard to the community will flow, a wisdom placed so deeply within him that all of his inward and outward activities will emerge already marked and oriented by it. Aelred describes the working of this wisdom with the verb *disponere*. His yearning is that every thought that he entertains, every word that he speaks, every work that he undertakes, every plan that he considers be "ordered" by this divine wisdom to God's good pleasure.[33] Nothing is to be left outside the sphere of influence

---

[30] *Praestet mihi . . . ad te amandum, laudandum, orandum, meditandum, et omnem secundum te actum et cogitatum, devotionem et efficaciam* (Aelred of Rievaulx, *Prière Pastorale*, 192).

[31] Aelred of Rievaulx, *Prière Pastorale*, 194.

[32] Aelred of Rievaulx, *Prière Pastorale*, 194.

[33] *disponat . . . secundum beneplacitum tuum* (Aelred of Rievaulx, *Prière Pastorale*, 194).

of this wisdom. Everything is to be directed by it to God's glory, the brothers' spiritual growth, and Aelred's own salvation. But what is it that this divine wisdom is to work upon, to "dispose of"? What is the substratum underlying Aelred's thoughts, words, deeds, and plans? It is here, I think, that we come to the heart of the *Pastoral Prayer* and discover that central dimension in Aelred that, for all his own negative self-evaluation, has made him a good shepherd from the very start of his abbacy. If, as Saint Paul says in the First Letter to the Corinthians, to be without love is to be nothing and have nothing (see 1 Cor 13:3), then the opposite must also be true: to abound in love is to possess what is most valuable and to be someone whose life is necessarily fruitful for others. This is precisely Aelred's case. In this part of the *Prayer*, Aelred tells the Lord that his whole love, his whole *affectus*, has always belonged to the community. He is so certain of this that he calls God to witness: "Lord, you know my heart" (*Tu scis, Domine, cor meum*).[34] Aelred reveals to God the heart that he already knows so well. Everything that God has given him from the beginning of his ministry, Aelred affirms, he has only wanted to pass on to the brothers. His great desire has always been, and continues to be, to employ and spend (*impendere . . . expendere*) every grace and blessing that he has ever received from the Lord for the benefit of the members of his community.

But this does not succeed in expressing the extent of Aelred's desire. It is not just what he has received from the Lord that he wishes to dedicate to the community; it is the very self that he has received from him that he yearns to be given over and consumed in their service. Aelred uses repetition to make undeniably clear the intensity of his desire—"Let it be so, my Lord, let it be so" (*Sic fiat, Domine mi, sic fiat*)[35]—and he proceeds

[34] Aelred of Rievaulx, *Prière Pastorale*, 194.
[35] Aelred of Rievaulx, *Prière Pastorale*, 194.

to make an inventory of what this "everything" consists of. It begins with a list of his inner and outer doings, goes on to embrace all the possible circumstances and conditions of his existence—"my good fortune and my ill fortune, my death and my life, my health and my sickness"[36]—and culminates in an all-embracing description of everything that makes Aelred, Aelred: "all that I am, all that I live, all that I feel, all that I think."[37] It is all this and not an iota less (*omnino*) that Aelred wants to be used and completely consumed in the service of his brothers. Aelred reveals himself here as a "mystic of the community"—as a monk who lives the "horizontal ecstasy" in perfect union with the "vertical ecstasy" (in the words of my novice master, also named Aelred), as a man completely given to Christ and the monastic church. His model and inspiration for this is the Lord himself, the Lord who likewise was a "mystic of the community," to whom the glory of the Father and the salvation of the brothers formed a single mystery: "Let everything in me be wholly dedicated and consumed in their service, in the service of those for whom you yourself did not refuse to be consumed."[38]

This measureless love of Aelred for his brothers that earlier made him weep because he considered himself so unworthy to serve them in the abbatial office (we now know that the brothers whom Aelred described previously to God as "so dear to you" [*tam caros tibi*] are also "so dear to him" [*tam caros sibi*]) and now makes him pray with an astounding fervor is expressed in the open, outstretched hand of the Saint Benedict icon. Aelred's heart is completely given over to his monks. His

---

[36] *prosperitas mea et adversitas mea, mors mea et vita mea, sanitas mea et infirmitas mea* (Aelred of Rievaulx, *Prière Pastorale*, 194).

[37] *quicquid omnino sum, quod vivo, quod sentio, quod discerno* (Aelred of Rievaulx, *Prière Pastorale*, 194).

[38] *Totum impendatur illis et totum expendatur pro illis, pro quibus tu ipse non dedignabaris expendi* (Aelred de Rievaulx, *La Prière Pastorale*, 194).

only request is to be eaten up by his zeal for God's house. The open hand, as I see it, symbolizes Aelred's total dedication, which in the end has nothing to do with duty and everything to do with spontaneity, with *affectus*. It is this immense love that Aelred asks God to direct and make effective through the infusion of his wisdom. He asks for the wisdom that will make his love discerning, that will form in him the *discreta caritas*.

Aelred needs the Holy Spirit's instruction (*magisterium Spiritus tui*)[39] to know *how* to do what he yearns to do: "Teach me, I pray, through your Holy Spirit, how I am to spend myself on them, how I am to be spent for them."[40] In asking the guidance of the Spirit for the exercise of his pastoral solicitude, Aelred's first concern is to be shown how he can effectively come to the aid of those in the community particularly afflicted by some form of frailty in their monastic living. He is instinctively drawn to the sad, the spiritless, the fallen away, the weak, the unsatisfied. He himself is definitely not satisfied with the idea of simply putting up with these brothers, or even with feeling sorry for them. He wants to really transform their oppressive experience—"to console the sorrowful, strengthen the fainthearted, lift up the fallen, be weak with the weak, and burn with indignation with those who are offended"[41]—and he depends on the Spirit to enlighten him as to how to proceed concretely with each brother. He believes that the key to truly benefiting them consists in the tireless labor of identifying himself with each one, not just with the weak, but with every member of the community.

With this in mind Aelred expands and develops Saint Benedict's idea of the abbot as someone called to "serve a variety of

[39] Aelred of Rievaulx, *Prière Pastorale*, 196.

[40] *Doce me, quaeso, per Spiritum sanctum tuum, quomodo me impendam illis et quomodo me expendam pro illis* (Aelred of Rievaulx, *Prière Pastorale*, 194, 196).

[41] *maestos consolari, pusillanimes robarare, lapsos erigere, infirmari cum infirmis, uri cum scandalizatis* (Aelred of Rievaulx, *Prière Pastorale*, 196).

temperaments" (*multorum servire moribus*, RB 2:31). Rather than simply "serve," Aelred sees himself as called upon to "take on the form" (*memetipsum conformare*) of each of the brothers, adapting himself to the nature, character, disposition, ability, and limitation of each one, including in this process of continual self-adaptation the modifying circumstances of time and place. It is a mammoth task that Aelred proposes for himself, or rather that he believes is integral to his task of imitating the example of the Good Shepherd, incarnating himself anew, as it were, for each of the monks of his community so as to make living and healing contact with each one in his particularity. For Aelred this is the core of pastoral solicitude and the best guarantee of its fruitfulness: to "become everything for everyone in order to gain them all."[42]

Aelred is not unmindful of the importance of the abbot's teaching in the edification of the community. Nevertheless, the instruments he most wishes to employ for the upbuilding of the brothers are "my humility, my charity, my patience, and my mercy."[43] All of these are so many forms of self-emptying, so many forms of laying down his life for his friends. And nothing in Aelred's text indicates that this labor of obedience to the community is anything but a joy to him.

Aelred's Abbatial Prayer for His Brethren

At the end of this consideration on the practical service of his brothers, Aelred asks that his prayer may ever be of benefit to them.[44] With this, he finally comes to offer up his prayer of

---

[42] *Omnibus omnia fieri, ut omnes lucrifaciam* (Aelred of Rievaulx, *Prière Pastorale*, 196).

[43] *humilitas mea, caritas mea, patientia mea, et misericordia mea* (Aelred of Rievaulx, *Prière Pastorale*, 196).

[44] *Prosit illis semper oratio mea* (Aelred de Rievaulx, *La Prière Pastorale*, 196).

benediction and supplication for his community. He knows that he is obliged to pray for them by his office (*officium compellit*), and he feels drawn to pray for them by his affection (*affectus invitat*). What really encourages him to make this prayer, however, is the conviction of God's loving-kindness,[45] that is, God's pleasure in hearing and answering prayer. Aelred prefaces his prayer by declaring to God the spirit in which he wishes to make it. He will pray for them as their superior, as one eager to serve them in love; he will pray for them as their inferior, subject to them in humility; and, best of all, he will pray for them as their equal, as someone whose delight is simply to be among them as one of them.

Aelred's prayer for the brothers is intentionally solemn, possessing something of the deliberate majesty of Jesus' high-priestly prayer or the prayer of consecration at the time of perpetual profession. It begins with a series of invocations: "Hear me, Lord my God, hear me."[46] He asks the Lord to keep the brothers ever in God's sight; he asks God to bless them; he asks God to protect them. And then he asks God to pour forth his Holy Spirit into their hearts. This invocation of the Spirit, rhythmically repeated, constitutes the heart of his prayer for the brethren.

What is the work that Aelred pleads the Spirit to accomplish? He begins with what is of greatest significance: that as a community, the brothers be sustained in the unity and peace of the Spirit himself, and that as individuals, each of them be maintained in chastity of body and humility of mind. This pairing of chastity and humility appears several times in the *Pastoral Prayer* and highlights not only the importance that Aelred attributes to these two virtues in living out the monastic

---

[45] *animat autem consideratio tuae benignitatis* (Aelred of Rievaulx, *Prière Pastorale*, 198).

[46] *Exaudi me itaque; exaudi me, Domine, Deus meus* (Aelred of Rievaulx, *Prière Pastorale*, 196).

204 A Not-So-Unexciting Life

conversatio but their analogous nature as well. For him, humility is a type of inner chastity, and chastity an outward irradiation of humility.

Aelred asks the Spirit to sanctify by his abiding presence the brothers' life of prayer. He desires that through the power of the Spirit's presence, the brothers may come to the intimate savoring of the "marrow and fatness" of the love of God,[47] that their minds may know the sweetness of compunction, and that their hearts may be warmed and enlightened by the light of the Spirit's grace. Aelred prays that through this ongoing cycle of the effects produced by the Spirit's presence—delight, compunction, illumination—his brothers may become more and more grounded in a single unified experience of hope, humility, and love. Here it is worth taking note of Aelred's expression "the sweetness of compunction" (*suavitas compunctionis*).[48] Like Augustine and William of Saint-Thierry, Aelred is never happier, never closer to his Lord, than when he is weeping before him.

The Spirit is then called on to accompany the brothers in the vicissitudes of their daily interior life. Aelred asks the Spirit to permanently "impress himself upon their memory" (*memoriae suae imprimant*)[49] so that whenever they experience doubt, temptation, anguish, or tribulation, they may instinctively sense that it is the same Spirit to whom they should confidently have recourse. Aelred wants the Spirit to reveal himself to them as the "loving Consoler" (*pius consolator*), the One who anticipates their cry to him ("runs to their aid"[50]) in every kind of inward affliction.

---

[47] *adipe et pinguedine dilectionis tuae repleat viscera eorum* (Aelred of Rievaulx, *Prière Pastorale*, 196).

[48] Aelred of Rievaulx, *Prière Pastorale*, 196.

[49] Aelred of Rievaulx, *Prière Pastorale*, 196.

[50] *occurrat et succurat*—a lovely example of Cistercian assonance (Aelred of Rievaulx, *Prière Pastorale*, 196).

Aelred next implores the Spirit to ripen the coenobitic virtues in his brothers, to work within them to make them peaceable, equable, and kind. While he wishes that they habitually demonstrate these qualities in their fraternal relationships with one another and in their relationship with the abbot, he first requests that the brothers may possess them within themselves (*in se ipsis*). I believe that Aelred's mentioning this is not simply his manner of indicating that a monk's inner attitudes will invariably be reflected in his dealing with others. Of course he wants these virtues, fruit of the Spirit's presence and activity in each of the monks, to be continually extended to the other members of the community. But he likewise desires that the brothers themselves be the beneficiaries of the virtues that the Spirit has cultivated within them. May they know the joy of being filled with the peace, patience, and kindness of the Holy Spirit. There is an irreplaceable personal happiness in having these facets of the Spirit's life continually experienced as the tenor and flavor of one's individual existence. Aelred wants to make sure that his brothers are not deprived of this pleasure. It is one more sign of his spontaneous generosity. Aelred goes on to ask, in a passage reminiscent of RB 72 ("On the Good Zeal of Monks"), that the attitudes that he just requested continually express themselves outwardly in a community life characterized by mutual service, obedience, and tolerance.[51]

Aelred puts forth two more requests for the brothers' spiritual life: first, that the Lord who has deigned to bestow the Holy Spirit on the brethren may drive far from their hearts every contrary spirit, every spirit that induces to vice; second, affirming his faith in the Lord's promise to be ever present wherever two or three are gathered in his name, Aelred asks the Lord personally to assume pastoral responsibility for the

---

[51] *invicem obedientes, invicem servientes et supportantes invicem* (Aelred of Rievaulx, *Prière Pastorale*, 200).

community. With his divine intuition into every heart and his boundless power, may the Lord attend to the needs of each brother, and above all, just as Aelred himself has attempted to do, to those most urgently requiring his help: "the sick, the sad, the lukewarm, the wavering."[52] In making this petition, Aelred is obviously not abandoning his post. Rather, he wishes to emphasize once more a theme he has set forth earlier. For all the human effort and dedication of the abbot as Christ's vicar, it is always the Lord who cares for them as the Good Shepherd. This does not make the abbot's task thankless. It makes its exercise more tranquil and its success more certain.

At the end of his prayer for the brothers, in obvious correspondence to the structure of RB 2 on the abbatial charge, Aelred offers a prayer for the brothers' temporal needs. His intention in this brief passage is not to present to the Lord a petition that the brothers may never want for earthly goods. The Lord best knows what he wants to provide for the monks,[53] says Aelred; it would be arrogance on his part to make suggestions to the Lord on this subject. What he wishes is the Lord's assistance in his own administration of whatever temporal goods the Lord sees fit to furnish to the community and in strengthening the brothers in their detachment from the things of this world. He asks the Lord to grant them the liberty that will keep them patient in times of want and temperate in times of abundance.[54]

What is wonderful about this passage is the *non sequitur* with which Aelred ends it. Almost as an afterthought, and just before the closing commendation of the brothers to the

[52] *quod morbidum sanes, quod maestum laetifices, quod tepidum accendas, quod instabile confirmes* (Aelred of Rievaulx, *Prière Pastorale*, 200).

[53] *sicut videris et volueris provide servis tui*s (Aelred of Rievaulx, *Prière Pastorale*, 200).

[54] *Inspira et illis, Deus meus, ut patienter sustineant quando non dederis, moderate utantur quando dederis* (Aelred of Rievaulx, *Prière Pastorale*, 200).

Lord with which the *Pastoral Prayer* concludes, Aelred makes a request with regard to the brothers' relationship to him. This is what he asks: "Let them think of me and feel about me, your servant, and theirs as well for your sake, exactly what will be useful for them. May they love and fear me just to the extent that you know will be beneficial for them."[55] When we remember the outpouring of *affectus* that Aelred has lavished on them (just before initiating the great prayer for them, he says that his *affectus* has been so warmed by them that it has melted and been poured out over them),[56] it is astounding that he asks for nothing whatsoever in return. He refuses to ask for himself the love and reverence he would have every right to expect and hope for, and for which his affectionate personality would naturally yearn. Instead, he deflects this love and reverence from his own person. He instrumentalizes it: "May they love and revere me just in the measure that it will advance their salvation."[57] It is an amazing act of self-abandonment, especially when considered in light of Aelred's emotional intensity. If he really means it (and I am convinced that he does), I believe it might be the most splendid sentiment in the whole text.

The *Pastoral Prayer* comes to a close in a mood of profound serenity. On the one side, Aelred entrusts his brothers completely to the Lord's "holy hands and loving providence."[58] He knows that the brothers are completely safe in these hands and that no one will be able to snatch them away from them. On the other, he accepts that the Lord has entrusted these same brothers

---

[55] *et ut de me servo tuo, et propter te etiam illorum, semper hoc credant et sentient quod utile sit illis; tantum diligent et timeant me, quantum videris expedire illis* (Aelred of Rievaulx, *Prière Pastorale*, 200, 202).

[56] *quomodo liquescat super illos affectus meus* (Aelred of Rievaulx, *Prière Pastorale*, 198).

[57] *tantum diligant et timeant me quantum videris expedire illis* (Aelred of Rievaulx, *Prière Pastorale*, 202).

[58] Aelred of Rievaulx, *Prière Pastorale*, 202.

to his own human hands.[59] This no longer makes Aelred fearful. The brothers' security is absolutely guaranteed, and if God's love and wisdom wishes to confide them to Aelred's care, God's love and wisdom will make of Aelred the instrument of their joyful perseverance in monastic life (*in sancto proposito feliciter perseverant*),[60] a perseverance that will ultimately be transformed into the attainment of eternal life.[61] All of this, Aelred jubilantly recognizes, will come about through the benevolence of the one whom Aelred calls, for the first time, "*our most sweet Lord*" (*dulcissimus Dominus noster*).[62] In reading the *Prayer*, it is impossible not to be struck by the fact that objectively Aelred's task remains the same at the end as it was when he began to pray, and yet he himself has moved from dread to profound peace. Exposing himself to God's gaze, allowing himself to be contemplated by God—the essence of prayer for Aelred—the abbot of Rievaulx has found comfort, strength, and assurance.

An Application of the Prayer

In the past, whenever I have studied a text of the Cistercian Fathers for any length of time, there has always come the moment, unexpectedly but not totally unpredictably, which in Brazil is called an *estalo*, an inner bolt of perception into the central intuition around which a text is composed. This was not my experience with the *Pastoral Prayer*. Instead of obtaining a single unifying insight, what was given to me one day in prayer was an admonition: "This is not a text to be understood, but to be lived." While I hope I have succeeded in presenting Aelred's

---

[59] *Commendo eos sanctis manibus tuis . . . de manu servi tui cui commendasti eos* (Aelred of Rievaulx, *Prière Pastorale*, 202).

[60] Aelred of Rievaulx, *Prière Pastorale*, 202.

[61] *perseverantes autem vitam aeternam obtineant* (Aelred of Rievaulx, *Prière Pastorale*, 202).

[62] Aelred of Rievaulx, *Prière Pastorale*, 202.

prayer in a comprehensible way, I agree with the voice of my invisible and, I believe, beneficent, interlocutor. Aelred's prayer is a mirror in the medieval tradition: it shows us an ideal model and it shows us ourselves in our unvarnished reality. To gaze into the mirror is to be made aware of the distance that separates the two persons reflected in it and to take on the work, through prayer and ongoing conversion, of bringing the two persons into an ever-greater proximity.

Aelred's prayer, with its turbulence, ardent love, and final peace, is the result of his looking into the mirror of the Good Shepherd and immediately perceiving both Christ and himself. This is clear from the very first words of the *Prayer*. In the final part of this article, I would like to invite us to look into the mirror of the *Pastoral Prayer*, with the aim of contemplating both Aelred and ourselves and with the willingness to strive to diminish the distance that separates us from him. As I see it, it will be helpful to look at the mirror from four angles: vocation, preparedness, love, and trust.

Vocation: From the opening lines of the prayer, it is clear that Aelred recognizes that receiving the abbatial charge constitutes a vocation to grow into the likeness of the Good Shepherd, to *be* the Good Shepherd for the brothers or sisters of one's community. This vocation consists of pastoral care (*sollicitudo*) and prayer. Christ has truly commended the brothers to us; we are inescapably responsible for guiding them safely to eternal life. Aelred often uses the word *regere* to describe inclusively the abbot's pastoral activity. But this ruling, as we have seen, implies a continual spiritual discernment of the needs of each of the brothers in his particular monastic journey, and a continual accommodation and re-accommodation of oneself so as to serve each and every brother as he truly requires. It calls for a constant, untiring exercise of humility, charity, patience, and mercy to edify the brothers, both in the sense of revealing Christ to them and in the sense of inspiring and assisting them in their own configuration to Christ. All of our words, actions, personal encounters, and decisions in their regard should emerge from a profound connectedness with the Holy Spirit. Our teaching has to be true, clear, and eloquent.[63] Along with this solicitude, we are called to offer a prayer that truly benefits them, a holocaust of prayer whose value and efficacy are related to our authentic sanctity as Christians and monks.

To put it in another way, Christ did not call us to be shepherds in his image in order to dispense with our services. He has seated us in his place to lovingly exercise his authority. In some real sense, the salvation of our brothers depends on the seriousness and integrity with which we give ourselves over to the responsibility of "imitating the example of the Good Shepherd." Aelred's depiction of the abbatial task goes no further than Saint Benedict's, but it may be that through his intensity and insistence the impact of Aelred's presentation is more forceful.

Preparedness: Given the determinative role Christ has given to the abbot in enabling his brothers to persevere faithfully and joyfully in their vocation and thereby enter into eternal life, we cannot avoid questioning ourselves about our spiritual and moral readiness to carry out our ministry. Dom David Knowles, in his 1971 introduction to the English translation of the *Pastoral Prayer* in the Cistercian Fathers Series, writes of it that, "Any abbot, any religious superior, will find in it his deepest apprehensions."[64] My own apprehension is that for many religious superiors (myself included) these apprehensions will have receded to such a depth as to cease to affect us, at least on a conscious level. We need to be able to regain the ability to *feel* these apprehensions, to know ourselves insufficient to the task that has been given us, and this insufficiency should be

[63] *Da verum sermonem et rectum et bene sonantem in os meum, quo aedificentur* (Aelred of Rievaulx, *Prière Pastorale*, 196).
[64] David Knowles, "Introduction," in *Aelred of Rievaulx: Treatises and Pastoral Prayer*, CF 2 (Kalamazoo, MI: Cistercian Publications, 1971), xii.

a cause of suffering for us, as it was for Aelred. The suffering should proceed from a twofold conviction: "There is nothing more dangerous for a community than to be ruled by a foolish, sinful man," and "That foolish, sinful man is me." Aelred's initial anguish is not unhealthy; it is realistic. When we put together our "job description" and our "spiritual personality profile," the results are not heartening.

What good does it do us to know our unworthiness? In the first place, it puts us in touch with the truth of our poverty. As I like to say to my own community, "The ugliest truth is more beautiful than the most beautiful lie." Secondly, it will have the same effect on us that it had on Aelred; it will make us cry out for help in our affliction.

I will always remember the words of a retired abbot a year or so after I was elected superior: "It took me about six months to realize that I didn't have the intelligence or sanctity necessary to be abbot. That's when I really began praying to the Holy Spirit." Third, it will help us to situate ourselves appropriately among the various weaker brothers whom Aelred includes in the composition of the monastic community. Finally, it can impel us to give ourselves more integrally, a little less unworthily, to what Christ asks of us. Aelred's sense of unworthiness is that of a saint; our own can make us sensitive to those aspects of our monastic and human life that are diminished or disfigured by long-term unfaithfulness, an unfaithfulness that by the intimate link between the abbot and the brothers cannot help but prejudice those we are called "to seek and to save."

Love: As was noted earlier, Aelred's saving grace, which he himself recognized as such, was his overwhelming love for his brothers. It is impossible to be unmoved at the totality of the gift of self that he longed to make to his monks. The irrepressible and self-evident *amor* about which Saint Bernard frequently wrote possessed Aelred completely in his relationship to his community. Aelred's description of all that he experienced himself as inwardly compelled to put at the disposal of each brother as well as that of the whole community is either overheated rhetoric or the fullness of pastoral consecration. In *The Interior Castle*, Teresa of Avila speaks of having a seal impressed on her heart that let her experience "something of that which was Christ's": his absolute zeal for the glory of the Father and his consuming love for other human beings and their salvation. Aelred seems to have been marked with the same seal.[65]

Teresa explains that this seal could only be impressed in her once Christ had (in a citation from the Song of Songs beloved by the Cistercian Fathers) "put love in order within her." If those of us who are abbots and abbesses do not yet possess this kind of dedication to our communities, this is not a state of affairs to be accepted with equanimity. Doubtless, Aelred's extraordinary love for his community was a special gift of the Holy Spirit. But it is a gift that should provoke emulation. Wherever it is fundamentally absent, it is a sure sign of a disorder in our love, of its incomplete ordering, of a dissipation of the vitality of our *affectus* upon an excessive number of objects. Aelred's text pushes us to gather up the fragments of our *eros* so as to employ it productively. We can only know personally what a wholehearted love for the community will be when it has come to be a single-hearted love.

Trust: Aelred pours out his heart before the Lord because he trusts in his love and his healing power. Even in the dark moments of initial confusion and self-accusation, he addresses the Lord as *spes mea, salus mea*. The central section of the *Pastoral Prayer*, the section that makes possible the transition from deep misgivings to his oblation of himself for his brothers, describes him placing himself, in an act of trust, directly in the Lord's line of sight. This he can do fearlessly, because "My hope is

---

[65] Teresa of Avila, *The Interior Castle*, trans. Keiran Kavanaugh and Otilio Rodriguez (New York: Paulist Press, 1979), 95–96.

in your loving-kindness, you who are most merciful. I know that you will look upon me as a good doctor does—in order to heal—or as a gentle teacher—in order to correct—or as a very indulgent father—in order to forgive."[66] Aelred's trust shows itself so audacious that he affirms that God's mercy can go beyond pardoning him to transfiguring his deformities and, even beyond that, to sanctifying him completely in the Holy Spirit.

The demands of our vocation, the awareness of our poverty, the measureless exigencies of a love without measure—these three facets of our office, taken alone, can be experienced as intolerable. What makes the burden light is the gift of trust. This trust permeates the *Pastoral Prayer* in its entirety. In the beginning it comes across as muted and obscured by other concerns. By the end of the *Pastoral Prayer* it is clear and sure. If we are to carry the parchment scroll, to return one last time to the icon of Saint Benedict, we must learn to lean upon the staff, the abiding help of the Holy Spirit.

[66] Aelred of Rievaulx, *Prière Pastorale*, 190.

Chapter 10

Who Wrote the Rule of Walbert?

Terrence Kardong, OSB

Our title may appear nonsensical, like the old radio quiz-show joke, "Who is buried in Grant's Tomb?" However, there is good reason to believe that Walbert, or Waldebert,[1] did *not* write the monastic Rule for nuns that is usually ascribed to him. First let me describe the two things I am talking about: Walbert and "his" Rule.

Walbert was a seventh-century Frankish monk of the Iro-Frankish monastery of Luxeuil, near Besançon in northeast France. He was the third abbot of that abbey, succeeding Eustace in 628 and reigning for forty-two long years. The founder of Luxeuil (about 590) was the famous Irish immigrant monk Columban, who was ultimately driven out of Francia (about 610) by the Merovingian kings and bishops, with whom he regularly tangled. Columban then founded Bobbio Abbey in Lombardy, but Luxeuil itself still flourished and spread its influence throughout Merovingian France.

One of the monasteries Luxeuil helped to shape was Eboriac, just east of Paris, which was founded by Burgundofare, the daughter of a pagan count named Chagneric.[2] Abbot Eustace

---

[1] This name varies from Waldebert to Gaubert, Valbert, and Walbert. The combination *lb* is hard for the Latin tongue to pronounce.

[2] Another name of this famous monastery of nuns, which still exists today, is Faremoutier. *Fare* is short for *Burgundofare*, and *moutier* is an obsolete French word for monastery.

of Luxeuil was also involved in the founding of Eboriac: "On the property of [Burgundofare's] father, between the rivers Morin and Aubertin, he had a monastery built for the virgins of Christ, after having named the brothers who would have the task of building the place. To teach the Rule to the Sisters, he named Chagnoald, the brother of the young woman, and Walbert, who was his successor."[3] To take this passage at face value, Eustace was the founder of Eboriac, but the context shows that Fare herself was the real founder.[4] The author of the *Life of Columban* (*and Eustace*), Jonas of Bobbio, describes at some length how she resisted her father's dynastic determination to marry her off.[5] Eustace came to her rescue (twice), but she herself was the primary impetus. As for "teaching" the Rule, one would assume the reference is to the *Rule of Columban*, since both Chagnoald and Walbert were monks of Luxeuil. As Jonas says, Chagnoald was the brother of Fare. Thus he was a nobleman, and in fact he later became Bishop of Laon.[6]

---

[3] My translation from the *Life of Eustace* 7.2, in the French translation of *Vie de Saint Columban et de ses disciples* (parts 1 and 2), trans. Adalbert de Vogüé with Pierre Sangiani, intro. and notes by Adalbert de Vogüé, Vie monastique 19 (Bégrolles-en-Mauges, France: Abbaye de Bellefontaine, 1988), 190; this book contains both VC I and II, the first modern edition to do so. The original Latin author was Jonas of Bobbio, *Ionae Vitae Sanctorum Columbani, Vedastis, Iohannis*, ed. Bruno Krusch, MGH, SRM (Hannover and Leipzig: Hannoverae Impensis Bibliopolii Hahniani, 1905), 144. Hereafter Jonas's book is called VC.

[4] Jonas no doubt simply follows the patriarchal logic that no woman could found a monastic house. Vogüé seems to take the same route when he claims, on the basis of this text, that Walbert succeeded Chagnoald as the *superior* of Eboriac in 626–627! "Teaching the Rule" and being superior are hardly synonymous. Fare was no child, and she reigned for many years (620–643/55).

[5] VC II 7.1–2. VC I contains the *Life of Columban* itself, while VC II recounts the lives of Columban's successors: Attala (1–6), Eustace (7–11), and Bertulf (23). VC II.12–22 concerns "the miracles of Eboriac."

[6] VC I.30.

Walbert was also a nobleman,[7] who soon succeeded Eustace as abbot of Luxeuil. We will need to take a closer look at Walbert's dates later on.

The Rule of Walbert is actually the modern name for a seventh-century Rule for nuns titled *Regula Cuiusdam ad Virgines*.[8] According to Albrecht Diem, the first historian to connect this document to Walbert was Louis Gougaud in 1908.[9] In Diem's view, this connection is baseless and has led many scholars astray. I have to admit that I belong to that group.[10] In what follows, however, I will join Diem in ruling out Walbert as the author of the *Regula Cuiusdam*. In addition, I agree with him

---

[7] He was the son of Duke Waldelenus of Burgundy. Jonas calls him "count of Guines, Ponthieu and Saint Pol," who had been a military man before joining Luxeuil (J. B. Clerc, *Ermitage et Vie de Saint Valbert, Troisième Abbé de Luxeuil*, 4th ed. (Paris and Lyon, 1861).

[8] For example, Alban Toucas calls it *Regula Waldeberti:* "Regula Waldeberti (regula cuiusdam patris ad virgines)," in *Dizionario degli istituti di perfezione*, 10 vols. (Rome: Edizione Paoline, 1983). No doubt he does so because that is more precise than *Regula Cuiusdam*, which means "Rule of Somebody."

[9] Louis Gougaud, "Inventaire des règles monastiques irlandaises," RBen 25 (1908): 321–31. Albrecht Diem, "Das Ende des Monastischen Experiments," in *Female* Vita Religiosa *between Late Antiquity and the High Middle Ages,* ed. Gert Melville and Anne Mueller (Berlin: LIT, 2011), 81–135, here 83, n. 9. Diem's article provoked this chapter, along with another piece in which I contest Diem's claim that *Regula Cuiusdam* is superior to the Rule of Saint Benedict: "Better than Benedict? Albrecht Diem's Promotion of *Regula Cuiusdam Patris ad Virgines*," ABR 66, no. 4 (2015): 402–18.

[10] This comment refers to my discussion of the issue in *Saint Columban: His Rule, His Life, His Legacy,* CS 270 (Collegeville, MN: Cistercian Publications, 2017), which contains my translations of both the *Rule of Columban* and *The Rule of Walbert*. Actually, I had not seen Gougaud's (or Diem's!) work when I wrote this book. Mostly I was following Sr. Lazare Seilhac and M. Bernard Saïd in their fine study of *Règle de Walbert* in *Règles Monastiques au Féminin* (Bégrolles-en-Mauges, France: Abbaye de Bellefontaine, 1996), 56–95. But on closer examination I find that Seilhac and Saïd themselves have doubts about Walbert's authorship (51–53).

in dropping *patris* from the title.[11] Henceforth I will use the acronym RC for this Rule.

To question the authorship of RC does not question its intrinsic quality: it is in fact an excellent monastic Rule. It was recognized as such very early on by that connoisseur of monastic Rules, Benedict of Aniane (ca. 750–821). In his monumental *Concordia Regularum,* composed about 800 as a sort of commentary on Benedict's Rule, he uses almost every part of RC to parallel the Rule of Saint Benedict. Moreover, Aniane places RC at the very end of the series of Rules in his *Codex Regularum,* of which the Rule of Benedict has the first place. Hence these two Rules are the bookends, apparently comparable in the mind of Aniane.[12]

It has to be reported, however, that the *Regula Cuiusdam* does not seem to have caught on as a famous and influential monastic Rule. We hardly ever hear of it after the time of Aniane.[13] I hope in this article to enhance its modern reputation.

Not Walbert

To return then to our main topic of "Who Wrote the Rule of Walbert?" we have already indicated that it probably was not Walbert of Luxeuil. As I have noted, Diem has shown rather convincingly that Walbert was not the author. Diem's argument is based on literary comparison. He indicates many passages where there is overlap between *Regula Cuiusdam* and the *Vita Columbani,* Part II.[14] This, of course, only pushes the

---

[11] The first editors to add *patris* to the title were Lukas Holste, *Codex regularum* (Rome, 1661); and J.-P. Migne, PL 88:1053–1070 (Paris, 1844–1866). Probably they assume that the author of such a fine work had to be a man. But I am pretty sure that Abbess Fare had her hand in the creation of RC.

[12] *Concordia Regularum,* PL 88:1053–70.

[13] These insights are from Diem, "Das Ende," 84.

[14] VC II has a long section on Eboriac. See n. 5 above.

question back another notch: who wrote the *Vita Columbani II*? Fortunately, we are on more solid ground here. We know that the author was Jonas of Bobbio. Before we explore the background of this interesting and important author, let me say again that I now agree: Walbert probably did not write the *Regula Cuiusdam*.[15]

My argument, unlike Diem's, is mostly based on chronology. If we follow the standard dates for Walbert, he would have written the RC about 626–627,[16] that is, just before he left Eboriac to become Abbot of Luxeuil. We are also told that he reigned as abbot for about forty years: 629–670. That is a very long abbatial reign, but not impossible.[17] What is much more remarkable, at least to me, is that he could have crafted such a sophisticated document as the *Regula Cuiusdam* at such a young age.

What makes RC sophisticated is the great skill of the author at blending his sources into a coherent whole. This is done without quoting them. Rather, the author has fully digested them and so is able to produce a seamless and truly original new version. A comparison with the *Rule of Donatus* is revealing. Donatus may have been a monk of Luxeuil, or at least he was educated in that monastery. Later (ca. 650), as bishop of Besançon, he also wrote a Rule for nuns,[18] but it is very different from the *Regula Cuiusdam*. Donatus also incorporated material from several earlier monastic Rules (Columban, Benedict, Caesarius of Arles), but unlike his practice in RC, he presents these in large chunks of direct quotation.

---

[15] Again, I must confess I got this wrong in my book. See n. 10. I had my suspicions, but I did not follow through.

[16] Seilhac and Saïd, *Regula Cuiusdam*, 51–53.

[17] The date of Walbert's death is generally given as 668–670. This slight vagueness is not unusual for ancient births and deaths.

[18] Adalbert de Vogüé, ed., "La Règle de Donat pour l'abbesse Gauthstrude: Texte critique et synopse des sources," *Benedictina* 25 (1978): 219–313.

My basic question is how Walbert became such an expert on monastic rules at such a young age. If he died at the ripe old age of seventy-five, he would have been only thirty years of age in 627. He may have been a prodigy who had read everything as a monastic novice, but to fuse it into a seamless whole takes maturity that usually comes with experience. Furthermore, there are, as far as I can see, few signs of youthful indiscretion in RC. The author seems as wise as his (or her!) sources.

It also seems to me there are too many loose ends regarding Walbert. For example, if Walbert was abbot of Luxeuil for over thirty years, he must have been a famous man, or at least a well-known one. Why then would he not have been identified as the author of *Regula Cuiusdam*? The use of the term *cuiusdam* itself is curious, since it just means "a certain." Was this title used because everybody knew who the author was, or rather to hide the true identity of the author?[19] We are not sure who devised the title for RC: was it the author or somebody else? If it was the author, it could have been a case of modesty, but if it was somebody else, it is hard to imagine why one would hide such a prestigious name as Walbert.

To tell the truth, there seem to be some details of Walbert's life that do not jibe with his five or so years at Eboriac and his alleged authorship of a monastic Rule for that community. For example, some of the biographies of Walbert claim he was a military man before becoming a monk.[20] It is said that his shield and weapons hung in the Luxeuil church for centuries. What is more, the traditional material claims that he was living as a hermit when he was elected abbot. An interesting aside is that

[19] There is, in fact, another *Regula Cuiusdam* among the ancient Rules, listed by Holste, 220 (n. 11 above) as a sixth-century document (RC is from the seventh century). Moreover, this little Rule (only four pages in Holste) is explicitly labeled *ad monachos*.

[20] Alban Butler, *Butler's Lives of the Saints* (New York: Continuum, 1994), s.v. May 2.

Saint Gall of Switzerland was elected first but turned down the offer. At any rate, all of this leads one to wonder whether there was only one Walbert, or perhaps several.

Another anomaly concerning Walbert and his alleged Rule for nuns is simply this: why is his work not mentioned by Donatus of Besançon in *his* Rule for nuns? As we have seen, Donatus produced a very different sort of mixed Rule from the RC, but he seems to have been a contemporary of Walbert. Could there have been some sort of rivalry between the two men? We know that they were both trained at Luxeuil,[21] but then their paths sharply diverged. At a young age, Donatus was made bishop of Besançon, where he ministered for about forty years.[22] In the midst of his busy life, Donatus composed a female monastic Rule for the monastery of Jussanensis near his see city,[23] but no mention of Walbert!

Although we are arguing here against Walbert's authorship of RC, this does not mean he had no interest in nuns. Probably he was sent to Eboriac around 620 precisely because he did

[21] The sources tell us Donatus was baptized by Columban himself and then "educated" at Luxeuil. That does not have to mean he was a monk, but it could. Donatus was a high Burgundian noble, and such people were often plucked from monasteries to become bishops, as were many monks of Lérins.

[22] According to B. F. Scherer, Donatus was present at the synod of Clichy in 627 ("Donatus of Besançon, St." *New Catholic Encyclopedia* [New York: McGraw-Hill, 1967]). He is also mentioned in a charter of King Clotaire III in 658. Thus his dates approximate those of Walbert. As the two most important church officials of the district, they must have had plenty of contact.

[23] It is no surprise that Donatus was interested in this monastery, for Jussanensis was founded by his mother, Flavia. When her husband died, Flavia entered Jussanensis, but, like many medieval aristocratic foundresses, she preferred to appoint another woman, Gauthstruda, as abbess. If there is any doubt that Flavia was still in charge, the death of Gauthstruda dispels it: Flavia appointed her own daughter, Siruda, as the second abbess.

have such an interest, and that interest seems to have perdured throughout his long abbacy. We know he gave much practical help to women founding monasteries in Francia in those days. Probably the best-known example of this assistance was his aid to Sadalberga, foundress and abbess of Laon.[24] Here are some references to Walbert in the *Vita Sadalbergae*:

> Meanwhile, the fame of Blessed Waldebert, whose reputation for sanctity we noted above, spread to the farthest boundaries of all the Frankish lands. By Christ the Lord without whom no good thing is done, the skill of his preaching enflamed them with the desire to worship God so that monasteries of men and virgins of Christ were established under his rule. . . . [Sadalberga] received him rejoicing as a divine gift conceded by God and eagerly desired to drink words of salvation and fitting medicine for souls from his mellifluous mouth. . . . To ease the work forward, venerable Waldebert offered and committed artisans and laborers to her. . . . Therefore, she took counsel with the wise abbot Waldebert who was so endowed with ingenuity and vigorous wisdom and good nature in all these things. Thereafter, he became her travelling companion and the partner of her labors.[25]

The alert reader will have noted that this chronicler says that Walbert gave Sadalberga "his rule," but that could mean many things. It could be a reference to the very Rule we are talking

---

[24] Actually Sadalberga originated in the general region of Besançon and Luxeuil. Her home was at Langres, on the border of Burgundy and Austrasia. She first founded a monastery there but soon relocated to Laon, north of Paris. Laon was famous as a well-fortified hill city, so it afforded nuns safety.

[25] *Life of Sadalberga* 12 and 14, in *Sainted Women of the Dark Ages*, trans. Jo Ann McNamara and John Halborg (Durham, NC: Duke University Press, 1992), 185, 186.

about here, namely, the *Regula Cuiusdam,* but it need not be. At any rate, I believe the countervailing arguments outweigh it.[26]

Jonas of Bobbio

If Walbert probably did not write *Regula Cuiusdam,* then who did? Diem thinks the answer is Jonas of Bobbio, a name that is not exactly a household word but that deserves to be better known. Jonas wrote an extensive *Life of Columban,*[27] in which he supplies a few autobiographical details. Jonas came from Susa, west of Turin near the French border and about a hundred forty miles northwest of Bobbio. He came to Bobbio as a teenager[28] in about 617, three years after the death of Columban. When he had been a monk for nine years, Abbot Attala ordered him to visit his parents, who had been begging for this for years.[29] Jonas made a quick trip home and returned to Bobbio just in time for Attala's death in 626.

The next abbot was Bertulf, and Jonas seems to have been his secretary, as he had been for Attala. In this role he accompanied Bertulf to Rome[30] in 628 to petition Pope Honorius I (625–638) in regard to the Arian controversy among the north

[26] This *Vita* was probably written by an eyewitness in the late seventh century. Its first modern editor, Bruno Krusch, MGH SRM 5:40–66, considered the account largely spurious, but McNamara, *Sainted Women of the Dark Ages,* 176, defends its authenticity.

[27] The Latin original of *Vita Columbani* is found in PL 87:1014–46. In 1905, Krusch published a critical edition in the MGH. See Vogüé, *Vie de Saint Columban,* 10.

[28] It seems that most of the Columbanian monks came to the monastery as adults and not as child oblates.

[29] VC II.5 (6).

[30] This was a long, arduous journey since Bobbio was hundreds of miles north of Rome and the trip had to be made on horseback. It helped that the Lombard king provided his own wagon and horses for Bertulf. Jonas reports that Abbot Bertulf almost did not make it; he fell ill with fever on the return trip near home. See VC II.23 (8–9).

Italian bishops.[31] The pope was so glad to find an ally in that affair that he granted Bobbio an exemption from episcopal control, apparently the first instance of this controversial arrangement in history.[32] We also know that Jonas spent some time at the nuns' monastery of Eboriac (Faremoutiers) in 633 or 634.[33]

What was he doing at Eboriac? It is a long, long way from Bobbio, across the Alps and hundreds of miles across Francia. We don't know the exact nature of his business (it was not tourism!) at Eboriac, but surely his journey passed through Luxeuil at some point. Bobbio was on the geographical periphery of Columbanian monasteries, but officials like Jonas kept the contacts alive through travel.[34] A few years later, in 638–639, shortly before dying, Abbot Bertulf commissioned Jonas to write the *Life of Columban*. As Jonas tells us in his Prologue,[35] he worked on his book for three years, as well he might have, for it is a considerable work: a hundred fifty pages in Vogüé's French version.

But Jonas also expanded on his original mandate by adding shorter biographies of three abbatial successors of Columban: Attala (eleven pages), Eustace (sixteen pages), and Bertulf (seventeen pages). He also included a long (twenty-five page) section on "the miracles of Eboriac," which suggests he knew those nuns well and probably spent time there on his later travels in northern Francia. In fact, Jonas spent the last years

---

[31] VC II.23 (6).

[32] See *Oxford Dictionary of the Christian Church*, ed. F. L. Cross and Elizabeth A. Livingstone, 3rd ed. (Oxford: Oxford University Press, 1997), s.v. *exemption*.

[33] VC II.12 (5). Jonas was there for the death of the holy nun Gibitrude, a relative of Abbess Fare.

[34] This is not to imply that there was a Columbanian congregation; nor was Bobbio subject to Luxeuil. The fact that Jonas included a section of the VC II (188–204) on Eustace of Luxeuil shows Bobbio wanted to remain close to Luxeuil.

[35] Prol. I. (1–4). Vogüé, *Vie de Saint Columban*, 93–97.

of his life (641–665) around Lille, in Flanders, where he accompanied the missionary monk and bishop Amand.[36] During that time he wrote the *Life of Columban,* plus the lives of two more saints, John of Reomé and Vaast.[37] Moreover, it seems that Jonas was eventually named abbot of Marchiennes, a few miles from Saint-Amand, France. He took the opportunity to transform that house into a double monastery.[38]

At this point I must confess that I have changed my mind about Jonas's travels. When I first read the *Life of Columban,* it seemed as though this Burgundian monk was traveling precisely in order to gather information for his writing projects. As I take a closer look, however, it appears as if Jonas wrote *in spite of* his travels. He had other ecclesiastical duties to attend to, but he must have found time for his writing. No doubt he interviewed people in Francia, but most of his sources must have been monks of Bobbio and Luxeuil.

But our topic here is not Jonas as biographer; it is Jonas as possible author of the monastic Rule for women called *Regula Cuiusdam Patris ad Virgines.* Since we have no conclusive literary evidence as yet,[39] one must work from more general impressions and data. One thing that strikes me about Jonas is his maturity as a writer. Granted that we do not know exactly when the RC was written, I think we can surmise that

---

[36] Saint Amand (585–675) was sent by Pope Honorius I as an at-large bishop missionary to convert the pagans of Flanders. He suffered persecution from both Christian kings and pagan peasants but died the honored bishop of Maastricht.

[37] The lives of Saint John of Reomé and Saint Vaast are found in *Ionae Vitae Sanctorum Columbani, Vedastis, Iohannis,* ed. Krusch, 326, 309.

[38] Vogüé, *Vie de Saint Columban,* 22, notes that this action of Abbot Jonas was characteristic of him, given his "lively interest in women religious." It also strengthens Diem's claim that Jonas wrote the *Regula Cuiusdam.*

[39] At this time (2015) Diem has not completed his comparative study of themes and vocabulary in the RC and the VC, so I cannot judge its probative value. I assume it will be at least plausible.

it was written by an experienced author. Not only did this writer know a good deal of earlier monastic literature, but he or she was capable of reworking it into an original and effective whole. I have already said that I doubt very much if the young Walbert could have managed this.[40] Given the fact that Jonas wrote the VC as a mature man of at least forty, he probably also wrote the RC (if he wrote it) in the same period, namely, when he moved to Saint-Amand.

Another consideration is the target audience. It is easy to assume that RC was written for the nuns of Eboriac, but there is no proof of that. Sometime around 660, Bishop Amand appointed Jonas abbot of the nearby monastery of men called Marchiennes, and he transformed it into a double monastery.[41] In other words, he introduced some nuns to the foundation. Might he not have also written a Rule for them? As their founder, perhaps he felt he owed them a workable monastic Rule, but probably he, and they, found the Rule of Columban inadequate for their purposes.

One question that might surface in regard to Jonas: Was he a good enough writer to bring off the excellent RC? Some of Vogüé's remarks are interesting in this regard, if inconclusive: "Although [Jonas] is relatively cultured, he is not for all that a good writer. From the point of classical art, his prose is full of faults, of which the most blatant is repetition. . . . But still, although he is a mediocre stylist, Jonas has created a remarkable literary work. In the desert of the seventh century, where we can find only stunted trees, he is a giant."[42] In his fine introduction, Vogüé stresses that Jonas is strictly a hagiographer,

[40] This is to take seriously the dates often proposed for RC, that is, ca. 620–628.

[41] Seilhac and Saïd point to RC 5 and RC 22 as clues that it was written for a double monastery. See their "La Règle de Saint Benoît dans la tradition au féminin," RBS 16 (1984): 57–68, here 66.

[42] Vogüé, *Vie de Saint Columban*, 34. My translation of the French.

not a biographer.[43] As such his purpose is edification, not information as to what his subject was *really* like. Jonas has no hesitation in shaping his stories to his purposes, even if that means the avoidance of certain potentially damaging facts.[44]

For example, Jonas says nothing about the date of Easter, although Columban's stubborn insistence on retaining the Irish date in the midst of the conflicting French custom surely lost him the support of the Frankish bishops. Moreover, some scholars think that Jonas largely fabricated the conflict Columban had with King Theoderic II and his grandmother Brunhild. But if these conflicts were nonexistent, then what got Columban expelled from Francia?

I would have to agree that Jonas is a typical early medieval writer, but it still seems to me that he is a better hagiographer than most. To compare him with a far more famous one, I prefer him to Gregory the Great. It seems to me that in *Dialogues II*, Gregory simply buries Saint Benedict under a tsunami of miracles. Even though Jonas includes plenty of miracles, especially at Eboriac, he makes sure they are anchored in a believable context. In regard to Columban, he does not completely hide the fact that the founder could be a difficult man.[45]

---

[43] Vogüé, *Vie de Saint Columban*, 23.

[44] This is the position of Bruno Krusch, the first modern editor of the VC (35). Krusch thought this story looked suspiciously like a similar one in the *Life of St. Didier of Vienne* by Sisebut (*Vita Desiderii*, PL 80:377). Vogüé denies Krusch's theory in *Vie de Saint Columban*, 83–86.

[45] Although Columban fought with the bishops of Gaul over the date of Easter and also rebuked Pope Gregory in a letter on the same point, not all historians take this as cold fact. For example, Joseph F. Kelly, in his article "The Irish Monks and the See of Peter," *Monastic Studies* 14 (1983): 207–24, here 220, says that the Irish did not take the date of Easter nearly as seriously as the "Romans." All they wanted was to be left alone!

Burgundofare

My own suspicion and suggestion is that Abbess Fare herself wrote the *Regula Cuiusdam,* or at least had a lot to do with its composition. There is no direct proof of this, and the evidence for Jonas's authorship is considerable. If Fare wrote this Rule for her monastery, she was the first woman in monastic history to do so.[46] This may have been the reason she preferred to remain anonymous. Recall that the first Rule for nuns was written by a man, namely, Archbishop Caesarius of Arles.[47]

Mention of the *Rule of Caesarius* brings up an obvious question, namely, did the author of RC know this famous[48] Rule and make use of it? According to Diem,[49] whoever wrote RC not only knew the *Rule of Caesarius* very well but apparently conceived RC as a supplement to it. This suggests that the community of the author of RC was already living according to the *Rule of Caesarius*'s pattern.[50] The supplemental nature of RC is seen by the fact that although the spirit of the *Rule of Caesarius* permeates the RC, it is never quoted. Here is Diem's footnote:

[46] In my article "Work in the Convents of the Paraclete: Echoes of RB 48," ABR 63, no. 1 (2012): 49–74, I suggest that Abbess Heloise (fl. 1150) was the author of *Institutiones Nostrae,* an important female supplement to RB. But even the bold Heloise did not sign her work.

[47] To make matters confusing, Caesarius wrote this Rule (about 520) for a monastery of nuns (St. John), of which his sister, Caesaria, was abbess. See the extensive Introduction of Vogüé to his commentary on this Rule in *Caesarius de Arles, Oeuvres Monastiques,* SCh 345 (Paris: Éditions du Cerf, 1988).

[48] For example, Radegunde used *Rule of Caesarius* at her convent founded at Poitiers in about 550. And Donatus of Besançon made heavy use of it in constructing his *Rule for Nuns* in about 650.

[49] "Das Ende des Monastischen Experiments," 108, n. 68. Diem's analysis of the relation between the *Rule of Caesarius* and RC does not lead him in the same direction as I take. He still thinks Jonas, not Fare, wrote RC.

[50] As Diem points out (n. 49 above), these Frankish nuns did not intend to live by the ideal of total enclosure taught by the *Rule of Caesarius.*

"The fact that RC repeats virtually no injunction of the *Rule for Nuns* of Caesarius (if it did, it would come to very different conclusions), while it continually refers to terminology and concepts of this Rule, indicates that this text was thought of as an expansion of Caesarius's Rule. This question will be fully discussed in the planned edition of RC."[51] In my view, whoever accomplished this feat of writing a supplement to the *Rule of Caesarius* that incorporated ideas without directly quoting it was a very sophisticated thinker and writer. No doubt either Jonas or Fare could have done it, or they could have done it together, but my vote is for Fare.

Who would have known *Rule of Caesarius* better than Fare? If she and her nuns actually lived by that southern Rule from the beginning of their foundation, after some years they probably would have found out from hard experience that they needed something more. Moreover, this approach to the monastic tradition was typical of the Columbanian tradition, resulting in the famous "mixed rules" that dominated seventh- to ninth-century Francia.[52] As we have noted, the impetus for this probably came from the inadequacy of the *Rule of Columban*.

Another factor to be taken into consideration here is what is called the redaction history of the document. In this case, there is at least one chapter of RC that suggests that it was written after the target community had a considerable history. RC 21, "On Taking Back a Sister," deals with nuns who have fled the monastic enclosure, and not just once but up to three times.[53]

[51] "Das Ende des Monastischen Experiments," 108, n. 68. My translation of Diem's German.

[52] Seilhac and Saïd, *Règle de Walbert* in *Règles Monastiques*, 61, note that all the ancient Rules, including RB, are essentially "mixed rules," for they take from the tradition what they find useful and adapt it to their special needs.

[53] RB 29 deals with the same problem of repeated flight and comes to the same basic conclusions. But although the author of RC 21 probably knew RB 29, she reworked it in her own language.

In their perceptive notes on RC, Seilhac and Saïd remark that this chapter seems to presume a fair span of communal history.[54] This also implies an author with a long experience of the community. Again, who fits that role better than Fare herself? She not only founded Eboriac, but she also ruled it for a long time, from 620 to at least 643, and possibly 655.[55]

Someone might object that Jonas himself had long experience of Eboriac. To judge from his extensive "Miracles of Eboriac" in the *Life of Columban*,[56] he knew the community better than would a casual or ephemeral visitor. Yet surely he had to rely on information from the sisters, and probably from Fare herself. As superior she would probably have had privileged information on a case such as that of the fugitives. This calls to mind another relevant detail in this matter, namely, that a monk such as Jonas, no matter how well revered by the nuns, hardly had access to the inner life of the convent. Are there elements of RC that would demand direct observation by the author? According to Seilhac and Saïd, there seem to be.

The test case could be the monastic dining room. To put it succinctly, no one but the nuns of Eboriac was allowed to eat in their refectory. This is set out in categorical terms in the chapter on the portress: "They should permit no man or woman to eat or drink within the walls or gates of the monastery. They should attend to the guests who arrive outside in the guesthouse, as their rank demands and the abbess orders. We declare that only those who have made vows of holy religion to

---

[54] Seilhac and Saïd, *Règle de Walbert*, 66.

[55] See Jean Gúerout, "Fare," *Dictionnaire d'Histoire et de Géographie Ecclésiastiques* 16 (Paris: Letouzey et Ané, 1967), 16:506–31.

[56] VC 11.22. Section 19 recounts the sad saga of two nuns who flee Eboriac. They return but are never able to bring themselves to confess their sin; hence they cannot be buried in sacred ground. This story shows Jonas has thought a lot about this problem, but whether his account is completely compatible with RC 21 is not certain, at least to me.

God, and are bound in the unity of obedience under one Rule, should eat and drink within [the monastery]" (RC 3.23–24). What we have here is not at all unusual: the monastic refectory is open only to the members of the community. The corollary is that it is closed to outsiders. Usually such a dining room would be open to visiting nuns, but Eboriac does not seem even to countenance such a possibility. But for our purposes here, the salient thing is that male visitors were certainly not given access to the refectory. That prohibition would surely include Jonas of Bobbio, even though he may have been a long-term guest at Eboriac.

If, then, Jonas could never have been present in the dining room, how could he have been privy to the details of dining for these nuns? "When it comes time to serve the meal, one Sister should arise at each table and proceed calmly to the window of the kitchen. This should be done without any loud stamping of feet or clatter of dishes. They should all serve the senior table first, and only then should they carry the dishes to the table where they sit. The leader of the table should decide how they ought to serve one another, either by turn, or by the youngest in age if there be such." Although our purpose here is not to analyze these texts, we might note here that this method of waiting on table was not something that RC picked up from Benedict.[57] Here the point is simply that these are very specific details that Jonas could not have observed. If he knew about them, it was only through the nuns. But Abbess Fare, of course, would have known all about them.

Another detail of the observance at Eboriac that Jonas could not have seen in person was the arrangement for sleeping. Here I am adding to Seilhac and Saïd's list:

[57] The term "leader of the table" is not something found in Benedict's Rule, but it does turn up in the *Rule of Caesarius* 18.4. So perhaps the table-waiting system given here was typical among Frankish nuns.

We decree that they should sleep two to a bed, except for the sick and the aged. They should do this, however, in such a way as not to speak together, nor look on each other face to face. They should lie down to sleep with their backs to one another. This will prevent the Ancient Enemy, who wants to wound souls with his greedy bite, from hurling any kind of confusing dart. It will also prevent the Devil from arousing deadly desires through pillow talk. It should be arranged that one of them is always a senior Sister whose maturity is well attested. (RC 14.5–8)

The casual reader may be bemused or even amused by this legislation. It is helpful to know that medieval people usually slept together, and rarely in separate beds. Yet Benedict wants each monk to have his own bed (RB 22.1), and Caesarius (RCaes 9.1) and Donatus (Reg 65.1) also provide their nuns with a bed apiece. RC, however, tells the nuns to sleep two in a bed, but it has an important proviso to add: they are to sleep with their backs to each other!

We are perhaps tempted to laugh at this kind of "naïve" micro-management. After all, how could these people maintain this posture all night long? But actually the text just says, "They should lie down to sleep with their backs to each other." And it helpfully adds that this should prevent "pillow talk," which is my fanciful rendering of *colloquendo.* The additional stipulation that one of the two be a senior nun strongly suggests that there is concern for sexual purity in all this. But we do not want to let our imaginations wander too far into lurid speculation. The point here is that Jonas simply could not have known about this arrangement firsthand. It was either the firsthand knowledge of the nun-author, or it was reported to Jonas. Either way, this is simply another detail to bolster my argument.

So then we have reached the conclusion of our study. We have to admit that it has not provided us with any definitive answers. As with many ancient documents, the *Regula Cuiusdam ad Virgines* does not have a label that identifies the author. We might remember that much more famous texts like the *Regula Benedicti* fall into the same category, but of course we have "decided" long ago that it was written by Benedict. It is hard to recall that we are by no means sure who *he* was!

The same holds true for the *Regula Cuiusdam*. Even though Louis Gougaud decided that it was written by Walbert of Luxeuil, and the Belgian monk was followed in this by every author since, except Albrecht Diem, we now know that we do not know. Diem thinks it was written by Jonas of Bobbio; I think it was written by Abbess Fare of Eboriac. Given the nature of literary "proofs," there can be no final answer to such a question. Nevertheless, I hope this trek through the data leaves the reader better informed, and even ready and willing to go back to these texts herself.

Chapter 11

Medieval English Nuns and the Benedictine Rule
The Evidence and Example of Wintney Priory

Elizabeth Freeman

"Medieval society was a 'traditional' society—not in the sense that society was unchanging, because in fact society and culture were highly dynamic. But it was traditional in that tradition legitimized."[1] Surely no truer words have been written. Applicable in all sectors of medieval society, these words carry particular relevance for Benedictine monastic society, as groups of men and women, in hugely varying places and contexts, over vast centuries, chose to live and work and strive together, always drawing guidance from unchanging texts while at the same time applying those texts within their own specific contexts. The Rule of Saint Benedict—an appreciation of which so many of Michael Casey's publications have both derived from and contributed to—is of course a key medieval example here.

[1] Constance Brittain Bouchard, *Rewriting Saints and Ancestors: Memory and Forgetting in France, 500–1200* (Philadelphia: University of Pennsylvania Press, 2014), 1.

233

The Rule of Saint Benedict

Yet for all its centrality as a foundational text for thousands of medieval monasteries of different orders (Benedictine, Cistercian, Gilbertine, and more), surviving medieval copies of Benedict's Rule are comparatively few. For every extant manuscript copy, we must assume the existence of others, supported in our extrapolation by occasional medieval library catalogue references to copies that did exist at the moments of catalogue composition but that have since been lost, and of course supported by all the other medieval documentation (e.g., legislation, customaries, *consuetudines*) that tells us that the Rule of Saint Benedict was the foundation of monastic life, as well as all the many times when the Rule was invoked or quoted in other instances, not to mention surviving visual and architectural evidence of its centrality to medieval monastic life.

If we turn to medieval Britain as an example, it seems extraordinary that David N. Bell's researches into Cistercian libraries have identified only two surviving copies of the Rule from Cistercian abbeys of monks, and yet that is the case.[2] Medieval library catalogues confirm that more copies did once exist,[3] and of course not all monasteries kept catalogues; probably only the larger libraries needed to catalogue their holdings. Another study, this time concerning medieval England and surviving copies of the Rule from male communities of any order, also notes that many copies have disappeared and that those that do survive tend to be small-format booklets for personal

---

[2] *An Index of Authors and Works in Cistercian Libraries in Great Britain*, CS 130 (Kalamazoo, MI: Cistercian Publications, 1992), 44.

[3] But, even accounting for copies that no longer survive, listings of *Regula S. Benedicti* in medieval library catalogues are fewer than we might imagine: see p. 745 of the consolidated "List of Identifications" (latest revision October 15, 2015), at "British Medieval Library Catalogues," http://www.history.ox.ac.uk/british-medieval-library-catalogues#tab-1-2.

use, rather than large service books to be read aloud.[4] As Nigel Ramsay has so eloquently, and somberly, put it, the "market value" of many monastic manuscripts was minimal after the onset of the Reformation in England—this was especially so in the case of a Rule for a way of life that no longer existed—and hence manuscripts containing texts such as the Rule of Saint Benedict were quickly lost over the course of the sixteenth century. The reasons differed—indifference, obsolescence, active mutilation if the manuscript featured any valuable bindings or embellishments—but the result was the same.[5]

Medieval English Nuns and the Rule

Turning to medieval English nunneries—the subject of this essay—there are some notable points concerning Benedict's Rule, specifically the feminized Rules. Here *feminized* means that the text of the Rule has been altered in some ways to explicitly acknowledge a female audience, for example by changing personnel from male to female (e.g., changing references from the abbot to abbess) and/or by changing or omitting parts of the text when these parts are considered unsuitable for, or irrelevant to, communities of nuns (e.g., regarding priests, regarding clothing).[6] Although "feminization" of the written

[4] James G. Clark, "Monastic Education in Late Medieval England," in *The Church and Learning in Later Medieval Society: Essays in Honour of R. B. Dobson*, ed. Caroline M. Barron and Jenny Stratford (Donington: Shaun Tyas, 2002), 27–28.

[5] Nigel Ramsay, "'The Manuscripts Flew about like Butterflies': The Break-Up of English Libraries in the Sixteenth Century," in *Lost Libraries: The Destruction of Great Book Collections Since Antiquity*, ed. James Raven (New York: Palgrave Macmillan, 2004), 125–44.

[6] The best introduction to the small number of manuscripts and early printed texts (medieval and sixteenth-century) of feminine versions of the Benedictine Rule (Latin, English, German, French) is the resource by Frank Henderson and contributors, "Feminine Versions of the Rule of St. Benedict," http://www.osb.org/aba/rb/feminine.

Rule of Saint Benedict need not necessarily involve translation out of Latin and into the vernacular, it is important to note that in the High Middle Ages it almost always did.[7] Today, seven feminized versions of the Rule survive from medieval England, six in English and one, unusually, in Latin.[8] This may seem a small number, but it is in fact notably high when compared with other countries and, certainly, it is high when compared with the relative dearth of other texts that survive from England's medieval nunneries. Moreover, of these seven surviving copies, three relate to the Cistercian nunnery of Wintney. A thirteenth-century manuscript from Wintney (London, British Library, Cotton MS Claudius D iii) contains two feminized Rules—one in Latin and one in English—while in 1516 another English translation of the Rule was made for Wintney. The thirteenth-century versions are the earliest known feminized Rules from medieval England; in fact, they predate any other surviving English feminized Rule by two centuries.[9] The 1516 version is the latest known feminized Rule from medieval England. As one scholar has perceptively noted: "the medieval

---

[7] As studied by John E. Crean, Jr., with regard to German-language Rules; e.g., "A Comparative Study of Three Manuscripts of The Rule of St. Benedict for Women," *Vox Benedictina* 10 (1993): 157–78.

[8] http://www.osb.org/aba/rb/feminine, and J. Frank Henderson, "Feminizing the Rule of Benedict in Medieval England," *Magistra* 1 (1995): 9–38. The seven listed by Henderson are Wintney Latin, Wintney Middle English, Northern Prose, Northern Metrical, Lyminster Rule, Caxton printed Rule of 1491 (more strictly a "gender-neutral" Rule, with its use of what would today be called gender-inclusive language, e.g., "he or she"), and Foxe's printed Rule of 1516.

[9] This is not to say that the Rule was the first ever produced for nuns in England; there has been significant debate on the existence of a (now-lost) tenth-century or eleventh-century Old English version for nuns; see Rohini Jayatilaka, "The Old English Benedictine Rule: Writing for Women and Men," *Anglo-Saxon England* 32 (2003): 147–87, esp. 149; and Mechthild Gretsch, "Aethelwold's Translation of the *Regula Sancti Benedicti* and its Latin Exemplar," *Anglo-Saxon England* 3 (1974): 138–39.

English tradition of translating the Benedictine Rule for nuns begins and ends in the same priory," namely Wintney.[10] But the significance of all this is yet to be probed. What exactly might the example of Wintney priory teach us about the meaning of Benedict's Rule in the Middle Ages?

Wintney Priory

Wintney was a female religious community in the county of Hampshire and the diocese of Winchester.[11] It was founded before 1159, a period of huge expansion in female monastic communities in England.[12] At the time of Wintney's foundation, Hampshire already had three other nunneries: Nunnaminster, also known as St. Mary's, in Winchester; Wherwell; and Romsey. These were all founded in the tenth century with strong links to Anglo-Saxon, indeed Wessex, royalty, and all would eventually be known as belonging to the Benedictine Order. Unlike northern England, southern England had a number of pre-Conquest nunneries; these communities survived and thrived right through to the Dissolution in the sixteenth century. Wintney, then, was an exception. It was surrounded by much older and wealthier nunneries that dated back almost to the days of King Alfred, but it must nevertheless have

[10] Jeanne Krochalis, "The Benedictine Rule for Nuns: Library of Congress, MS 4," *Manuscripta* 30 (1986): 32.

[11] The best information about Wintney appears in Diana K. Coldicott, *Hampshire Nunneries* (Chichester: Phillimore, 1989). As a convenient summary, the hundred-year-old entry in the Victoria County History retains some value, although it has naturally been superseded on some points of detail: "House of Cistercian Nuns: Priory of Wintney," in *A History of the County of Hampshire: Volume 2*, ed. Herbert Arthur Doubleday and William Page (London: A. Constable, 1903), 149–51, at http://www.british-history.ac.uk/vch/hants/vol2/pp149-151.

[12] Christopher N. L. Brooke and Denis M. Smith, "Addenda and Corrigenda to David Knowles and R. Neville Hadcock, *Medieval Religious Houses, England and Wales*," *Monastic Research Bulletin* 6 (2000): 33.

responded to certain needs and provided certain functions in order to have warranted foundation in the post-Conquest period and then continued until the Dissolution.

The size of Wintney's community is known for certain periods only: over twenty-seven nuns in 1315, fifteen in 1414, and ten in 1536, with unknown numbers of lay sisters and, often, lay brothers.[13] These small figures are consistent with those for other post-Conquest foundations in England and a stark contrast to the larger numbers in Winchester diocese's other nunneries. But, despite its modest size and wealth, Wintney did survive for almost four hundred years, just as, strikingly, almost all of England's other small and poor post-Conquest communities of nuns survived. Wintney remained a functioning community until it was closed in July 1536. It was one of the earliest English nunneries to be dissolved, and its ten nuns were perhaps transferred to other local nunneries for a few extra years of communal life before all English nunneries were closed by 1540. In the 1960s there were still farm buildings remaining from Wintney's monastic complex, but more recent motorway construction has destroyed much evidence.[14] According to a recent survey, there are no extant remains of the nunnery, although some rubble foundations were noted in 1956.[15]

Whenever medieval documents stated to which monastic order the community belonged, which was not a consistent priority, the Wintney community was sometimes referred to as

---

[13] On population numbers, see references later in this essay, and Coldicott, *Hampshire Nunneries*, 43.

[14] Coldicott, *Hampshire Nunneries*, 148–50.

[15] See "Hartley Wintney with Hartley Row," at http://documents.hants.gov.uk/landscape/historic-settlement/HartleyWintneyHistoric Rural Settlementpublication.pdf, 135. This report seems to have been completed in 1998. See also the archaeological survey at http://www.pastscape.org.uk/.

Benedictine and sometimes as Cistercian. In this the community was not unusual. One of the features of female monastic life in medieval England was the fact that affiliations with particular monastic orders were not fixed; this was particularly the case for nunneries that claimed membership in the Cistercian Order.[16] At different times in a community's centuries-long existence, there might be a concerted campaign publicly to assert a membership in the Cistercian Order. At other times, we see such membership recorded uncontroversially as an unchallenged fact, only to find that in later years the same house might just as uncontroversially be referred to as belonging to the Benedictine Order. Some nunneries in Lincoln and York dioceses took active steps as early as the late twelfth century to be recognized as Cistercian. In the case of Wintney, the connection with the Cistercians first comes to our attention in the thirteenth century, and not as a point in dispute but, instead, as one that seemed to have been accepted in practice at the local level.

Connections with Waverley Abbey

The first undisputed connection between Wintney and the Cistercian Order comes from the pen of "frere Symon," a brother from nearby Waverley Cistercian abbey. In the early thirteenth century Simon copied out a martyrology, added instructions on how to use it, and donated this text to the Wintney community. In the same manuscript he included a poem in octosyllabic couplets that he had written. Writing in French (strictly Anglo-Norman, the so-called French of England), he pointed out that he was ill and "unable to be cured in this life,"

---

[16] For this and what follows, see my "'Houses of a Peculiar Order': Cistercian Nunneries in Medieval England, with Special Attention to the Fifteenth and Sixteenth Centuries," *Cîteaux: Commentarii Cistercienses* 55 (2004): 245–87.

and that "because of this" he was entreating the prioress and convent of Wintney to secure his soul, receive him into chapter, and add his name and obit to their memorial book (to "this book").[17] The opening lines of the poem are a request to Jesus Christ, in the name of the brother Simon, to "guard the convent of Wintney and the convent of Waverley."

Waverley, founded in 1128, is best known today for its status as the first Cistercian monastery in England. In the Middle Ages it wore its status as England's founding Cistercian house somewhat shakily. In terms of influence it was soon overtaken by northern houses such as Rievaulx and Fountains, not to mention the legitimate argument from another northern house, Furness, that it in fact was England's first Cistercian community. Furness's foundation date was before 1128, at a time when it had been part of the Savigniac Order.

Of course, there is more to a productive monastic community than high-profile influence, and here we might look afresh at Waverley. Located in the same diocese as Wintney and in the neighboring county of Surrey, Waverley was geographically the closest Cistercian community of monks to Wintney. Possibly the monks at Waverley had some involvement in Wintney's foundation in the mid-twelfth century, although the evidence is from over a century later and not definitive.[18] But, at the very least, by the thirteenth century there was the belief that Waverley's monks had been involved in the process of Wintney's foundation, and this itself is significant. For it was in the

[17] The poem is at London, British Library, Cotton MS, Claudius D. iii, fol. 3ᵛ; it is printed in Paul Meyer, "Bribes de littérature anglo-normande," *Jahrbuch für romanische und englische Literatur* 7 (1866): 45–47. See "Pur ço requer devotement / La prioresse e le cuvent/ Ke á ma alme securrez / Que est de peché mut chargetz. / E en chapitre me recevez / E de ester frère me grantez. / E ke mun nun e mun obit / En ceste livre seit escrit."

[18] *Calendar of Charter Rolls*, 1–14 Edward III, AD 1327–1341 (London: HMSO, 1912), 4:392.

thirteenth century that a clear connection between Waverley and Wintney certainly arose, for which the unlikely claim concerning Waverley's involvement in Wintney's foundation is but one of multiple examples.

It is probably no coincidence that the vexed issue of Cistercian primacy in England (Waverley or Furness?) was settled in 1232;[19] the thirteenth century certainly shows Waverley taking on a more confident role. Waverley began looking outward toward female monastic communities in the thirteenth century. In the years leading up to 1244, Waverley's abbot certainly played a role in the incorporation of the newly founded Cistercian nunnery of Marham in distant Norfolk. Brother Simon (who was clearly an active poet) was probably still alive at this time, as he seems to have added poems to various entries in the Waverley Annals between 1201 and 1240.[20] The poem that Simon wrote for Wintney suggests mutual support and an ongoing connection. Simon concluded his poem by telling the prioress and convent that he had "great trust" in them, as he urged them not to forget him,[21] something that suggests both that there had been preexisting contact between Simon and the Wintney community and that Simon wanted his connection to continue. Simon's wish to enter into confraternity with the nuns foreshadowed a community of memory that linked past, present, and future.

British Library, Cotton MS, Claudius D. iii

The French poem and prayer from brother Simon of Waverley appear in British Library, Cotton MS, Claudius D iii. This

---

[19] "Annales Monasterii de Waverleia," in *Annales Monastici*, ed. Henry Richards Luard (London: HMSO, 1865), 2:311.

[20] Richard Sharpe, *A Handlist of the Latin Writers of Great Britain and Ireland before 1540* (Turnhout: Brepols, 2001), 619.

[21] "Ne me metez en ubliance / Kar en vus ai grant affiance."

important manuscript, made for and owned by the Wintney community, contains three main items, all written in the first half of the thirteenth century—a martyrology; two feminized versions of Benedict's Rule (Latin and English), copied out as one integrated item with a given Latin chapter succeeded by its English equivalent; and a calendar. Before the commencement of the martyrology, the opening folios of the manuscript contain some short texts: Simon's poem *cum* prayer to Wintney, an inventory of items in the Wintney refectory, and instructions in French—by Simon again—on how to use the martyrology. These texts confirm both that the entire manuscript was housed at Wintney and that it was a manuscript designed for community use.[22] Numerous elements of the manuscript lead to the clear conclusion that the entire manuscript was used and consulted at Wintney over at least two centuries after its creation in the thirteenth century—the kitchen inventory is dated to 1420 and includes the name of Wintney's obedientiary in charge of the refectory, Alice Preston, who had just died, while the calendar names numerous prioresses who can be identified as those of Wintney, including later entries explicitly dated to the early- and mid-fifteenth century. The combination of the three main texts—martyrology, Rule (Latin and English), calendar—as well as the fact that the manuscript is a physically large item rather than of small pocket size for personal reading, indicate that this book was very much to be used in a communal setting. This leads us to the chapter house and recent research by Anne Lawrence-Mathers.

---

[22] The British Library manuscript catalogue entry dates the manuscript to "the 1st half of the 13th century to the middle of the 15th century" and lists the folios for the entries as fols. 6^r–51^v for the martyrology, 52^r–140^r for the bilingual Rule of Saint Benedict, and 140^v–162^v for the imperfect obituary calendar. The short texts at the start appear at fols. 3^v–5^v.

The Martyrology

In providing the only detailed study of the Wintney martyrology, Anne Lawrence-Mathers has emphasized the communal nature of this text, as well as Simon of Waverley's effort to ensure that the Wintney community could make best use of the material included within the text.[23] The martyrology was in fact Bede's martyrology. Simon wrote some instructions in French for this Latin text—what Lawrence-Mathers calls a brief "user's manual"—and here he specifically stated that the martyrology was to be read in chapter (*Sachez uus ke lire deuez in capitule*). He also explained how to calculate the lunation and age of the moon for each day over the nineteen-year Metonic cycle, how to use this to compute the date of Easter, and, in relation to that, how to calculate other feast days that depend on the date of Easter. Lawrence-Mathers suggests that this was Simon's attempt to help the nuns, that is, to help them calculate Easter and hence to know the dates of other feasts that depended on the date of Easter. As she writes, Simon of Waverley had a role in "inducting the nuns (or some of them) into the 'mysteries' of their institutional life."[24] She suggests that Simon helped the nuns to get a good copy of the martyrology and helped them work out how to use it. Here then we can see an aspect of practical care, practical *cura monialium*.

In addition to evidence that Simon of Waverley helped the nuns to use the martyrology, we need to consider what this usage involved. First and foremost, a martyrology was a text for ongoing use, one that reflected past communities and traditions and also perpetuated them. It was a text in which the annual timetable was a constant over the centuries. We can

[23] "Books, Religion and Literacy in Medieval English Nunneries," http://www.palaeographia.org/apices/papers/mathers.htm. Lawrence-Mathers has studied the martyrology in particular, and I direct the reader to her fine discussion of the details of dating calculations.
[24] Lawrence-Mathers, "Books, Religion and Literacy," 5 of 7.

244 A Not-So-Unexciting Life

expect that the Wintney nuns continued to use this martyrology for the rest of the Middle Ages, aided by the explanatory text that the Cistercian Simon had provided them. Their use of the martyrology would have taken place in the daily chapter meetings as they noted the saints to be celebrated each day. This location in the chapter house takes us to the next element of the Claudius manuscript, the two versions of Benedict's Rule.

The Feminized Rules

To turn now to the manuscript's two Latin and English thirteenth-century versions of the Rule of Saint Benedict that are addressed directly to nuns, as is indicated by the introductory rubric:[25] *In nomine sancte trinitatis incipit regule prologus sanctimonialium eximii patris & beatissimi benedicti abbatis* (In the name of the Holy Trinity, here begins the prologue of the Rule for nuns of the excellent father and most blessed abbot Benedict).[26] The opening words of the Rule indicate from the outset that the Latin has been feminized, with the command to listen being given to the daughter (*Asculta o filia*) rather than to the son. What follows is a twofold presentation of the Rule, in which each chapter is presented first in Latin, with changes of male personnel and male grammatical forms to female.[27]

[25] The consensus is that they were written in the early thirteenth century; Neil R. Ker, *Catalogue of Manuscripts Containing Anglo-Saxon* (Oxford: Clarendon, 1957), xix, n. 2; "The Production and Use of English Manuscripts 1060 to 1220," at https://www.le.ac.uk/english/em1060to1220/mss/EM.BL.Clau.D.iii.htm.

[26] The standard edition of the thirteenth-century Wintney Rule (including both the Latin and English texts) is Arnold Schröer, ed., *Die Winteney-Version der Regula S. Benedicti*, rev. Mechthild Gretsch (1888; Tübingen: Max Niemeyer, 1978). The Latin text (with corrections of Schröer's text, and with a good survey of the text's key qualities) is also available at http://www.osb.org/aba/rb/feminine/winteney/index.html.

[27] E.g., chap. 2 changes *discipulus* to *discipula*.

Chapter headings are also changed from male to female[28] and are then followed by a Middle English translation with, again, male personnel from the Latin Rule being usually changed to female, before the following chapter is then included in Latin followed by English, and so on.[29] The only exception to this alternating chapter sequence is chapter 7, which is broken down into sections and in which the first step of humility in Latin is succeeded by the first step in English, to be followed by the second step in Latin and then English, and so on.

The unusual fact that the Claudius manuscript contains not just one but two feminized versions of Benedict's Rule has already prompted scholarly analysis,[30] but more remains to be done, not least in terms of examining what purpose the joint presentation of the two copies of the Rule was meant to serve. The English translation of the Rule has attracted some interest from linguists, who note that the form of English used was already quite archaic for the early thirteenth century;[31] in fact, it has even been referred to as an Old English version as opposed to the more common reference to it as a Middle English version of the Rule.[32] Whether or not the thirteenth-century community

---

[28] E.g., see the titles of chapters: *Qualis debet esse abbatissa* (chap. 2); *Quomodo dormiant sanctimoniales* (chap. 22); *Si debeant iterum recipe sorores exeuntes de monasterio* (chap. 29); *Si debeant monache proprium aliquam habere* (chap. 33); *De infirmis sororibus* (chap. 36); *De disciplina suscipiendarum sororum* (chap. 58); *De sanctimonialibus peregrinis* (chap. 61); *De sororibus in via directis* (chap. 67).

[29] Biblical quotations that refer specifically to men are not changed, but other quotations are indeed feminized; see Henderson, "Feminizing the Rule."

[30] E.g., by Frank Henderson; see "Feminizing the Rule."

[31] Jayatilaka, "The Old English Benedictine Rule," 158.

[32] Jayatilaka, "The Old English Benedictine Rule," 148, refers to it as one of the nine versions of the Old English translation of the RB. For Maria Artamonova, the version is a "revision" of the Old English Rule, perhaps revised on more than one occasion: "Construing Old English in the Thirteenth Century: The Syntax of the Winteney Adaptation of the Benedictine Rule," *Leeds Studies in English*, n.s. 40 (2009): 27–46.

at Wintney considered this English translation to be archaic and/or found it to be an impediment because of its earlier linguistic structures is a different matter. Perhaps the linguistic ability of nuns was greater than we have imagined, and perhaps the thirteenth-century nuns could still read a text that modern scholars, with the benefit of hindsight, refer to as archaic. From the arrangement of the two texts, one chapter of Latin followed by the same chapter in English, it is not possible to read both the Latin and English of the same sentence or verse at the same time. To compare the same sentence or verse one must turn back and forth between folios. So this manuscript could not have been intended to provide a facing-page translation for nuns who were poorly literate in one or the other of the two languages. The physical arrangement of the chapters on the folios suggests instead a situation in which there was at least some competent knowledge of each language. Whether one or the other of the texts was the favored version is impossible to know.

The very decision to modify the Rule of Saint Benedict—be it to change male personnel to female in the Latin version, or to translate the text from Latin to English—deserves our consideration. It is by no means self-evident that a foundational text should be modified, even when it could be linguistically. What does it mean to change a Rule? And, returning to the opening words of this essay, what does it mean to change a Rule in a society in which tradition legitimized?

I think it is no accident that the alternating sequence of Latin and English feminized chapters starts with the Latin. In other words, it starts with the version that is closest to the sixth-century Latin original. To create a feminized version of the Rule but to retain the Latin language was highly unusual. In fact, of the seven feminized Rules surviving from medieval England, the Wintney Rule is the only one in Latin. While feminized versions of Benedict's Rule from England, and from other places such as Germany, typically involved translation into the vernacular, the Wintney example shows that here nuns were expected to be able to understand Latin.[33] Although we cannot know to what extent the Wintney community members favored the Latin or English version in this manuscript, or indeed if their preferences changed from the thirteenth century to the Dissolution, this manuscript certainly indicates a dedication to knowledge of the Rule, with various linguistic abilities of the community being anticipated, and a dedication to ensuring that as many people could read it as possible.

The Latin version uses feminine forms consistently throughout—*abbas* is changed to *abbatissa*, *frater* to *soror*, *monachus* to *sanctimonialis* or *monacha*, *discipulus* to *discipula*, *magister* to *magistra*, and *cantor* to *cantrix*. This might seem to be the easy part—a simple and direct transferral from a male monastic community member to the female equivalent. But there are some unexpected changes. At chapter 11, the Latin Rule changes the person who reads from the Gospels after Vigils on Sundays. While the original Rule has the abbot do this reading, Wintney's Latin version does not have the abbess but, instead, a priest assigned to the task. The abbess, however, does lead the hymns *Te Deum* and *Te decet*. Strangely, the English version has the priest leading the *Te decet*. Hence there is inconsistency between the two versions—as the reader turns the folio from one side to the next, two different situations are presented. A small change of wording—abbot to priest—provides us with a large insight into life in a female community and the nuns' interactions with the outside world, since the reference to a priest immediately alerts us to fact that the Wintney nuns must have had regular contact with such individuals.

Other matters of translation required even bigger decisions and can again inform us about internal details within the

---

[33] In fact, the Claudius manuscript overall indicates that some knowledge of Latin and/or English and/or French was assumed.

community in question. All feminized versions of Benedict's Rule have to work out how to deal with the issue of priests, juggling adherence to the text with practical applicability. We might say that here tradition as changelessness and tradition as practical applicability rub up against each other. In Wintney's Latin Rule there are changes in chapter 55 (on clothing) and in chapters 60 and 62 (both on priests). Making changes to these three chapters was entirely common in medieval feminized versions of the Rule, but the types of changes could vary. In Wintney's case, chapter 60 has been rewritten to refer not to priests who enter the community, as the original Rule has it, but instead to women who come from other orders, especially canonesses. This is ambiguous; perhaps the translator (whoever that may have been) believed that such canonesses might have been common, but there is no evidence that Wintney or indeed the local area had canonesses.

The issue of canonesses arises again in chapter 62. This chapter (on members of the monastery being ordained as priests) naturally presented difficulties for all feminized versions of the Rule. Different medieval versions took different paths, sometimes omitting both this chapter and chapter 60 entirely.[34] As Henderson has noted, in the Wintney manuscript, both the Latin and English versions take the "radical step of completely rewriting chapter 62 to fit the circumstances of communities of women."[35] But there is more to it than this. As recent scholarship has pointed out, the rewriting in chapter 62 is in fact drawn heavily from the ninth-century Carolingian guide for canonesses known as the *Institutio sanctimonialium Aquisgranensis*.[36] Possibly what happened here was that the translator, while knowing that chapter 62 needed revision, was not prepared to venture too far into the field of originality but, instead, wanted to retain

---

[34] Henderson, "Feminizing the Rule."

[35] Henderson, "Feminizing the Rule," 31–32.

[36] Jayatilaka, "The Old English Benedictine Rule," 164–66.

adherence to some kind of authoritative guide for cenobitic life, even if that meant using a text for canonesses when canonesses were not present in Wintney. Significantly, the English version of chapter 62 in the Claudius manuscript is almost the same as the manuscript's Latin version, which leads to the suspicion that there was a deliberate attempt at creating equivalence between the two versions. In both the Latin and English versions, chapter 62 deletes the Rule's original discussion on the place of the priest within the order of other monks and instead focuses on the decision-making of the abbess in choosing the priest and the qualities such a priest should possess. Quite bluntly, the priest must do as the abbess tells him. Little by little, we are gaining a picture of priests at Wintney, their presence and their roles, not to mention a sense that the traditional authority of cenobitic guides was valued and that reliance on an earlier written guide was preferable to original composition.

Overall the English version does not deviate much from the original Rule, certainly not as much as later fifteenth-century feminized versions do. In all the sections referring to psalms, the English Rule adds the Latin incipit to the number of the psalm, to make it clear exactly which psalm should be sung, but, other than this and the changes to chapter 62, modifications are few. Given then its lack of deviation from the original Rule and the fact that the changes that do appear are replicated in the Claudius manuscript's feminized Latin version of the Rule, it may well be that the English version was included as a teaching tool to familiarize novices with the Latin text and not intended to be read as a modification of the Rule but, rather, as a pointer for the reader to go back to the original.

The Calendar

The English text of the last chapter of Benedict's Rule ends on the *recto* of folio 140. On the *verso* of the same folio is the start of the obituary calendar. So the scribe of the calendar must already have had the text of the Rule in hand when he (probably not she) began the calendar. From the outset, then, the calendar belonged to the Rule, as it physically existed alongside the feminized Latin and English versions of it, thus contributing to a manuscript compilation that combined knowledge of the Rule with knowledge of people to be commemorated.

The calendar appears at fols. 140ᵛ–162ᵛ of the manuscript and covers the period from January until mid-December, when the manuscript as we have it today ends abruptly. The calendar was a living document, added to over the years, as more and more deceased individuals were incorporated into the living community of memory.[37] Benefactors of the house, deceased nuns and prioresses and sisters, three separate individuals each of whom was named as the "founder" of the house, local abbots and bishops—the calendar presents a clear picture of the community of memory within Wintney. Although it rarely refers to years, the calendar does specify that the church of Wintney was dedicated in 1234, and another dated entry refers to 1446. Periodic additions from the thirteenth to fifteenth centuries are also evident in the use of different scribal hands. Each month was allocated two folios, and plenty of space was left next to each date for such later additions to be made.

One group of people commemorated were the female community members. For example, in January the obit of the professed nun Gunnora was noted (*O. Gunnora monacha et professa*), as were the obits of the professed nuns Maria and Matilda. A later hand added an additional entry for January, Emma of pious memory, *quae fuit quondam priorissa*. Turning to other evidence, we can cross-reference this entry and identify the individual as Emma of Winterburn, who was elected in

---

[37] The obituary calendar is printed, with inaccuracies, by Thomas Hearne, *Johannis de Trokelowe Annales Edwardii II* (Oxford: E Theatro Sheldaniano, 1729), 384–93.

1349.[38] On 7 Kalends February the professed nun Amicia was listed; on 4 Nones March it was Cristina the professed nun. Overall, the calendar includes approximately ninety named *monacae* (nuns), eleven named prioresses, many of whom can be independently dated to the thirteenth century, with the earliest, Roisa, being in office in 1219,[39] and one sub-prioress named Eleanor Werbington. There is also inclusion of a *cantrix* named Margaret Brakenham. Clearly, then, at one point the community of Wintney was sufficiently large to be able to allocate time and effort to the dedicated liturgical role of *cantrix*, something that not all nunneries could manage.[40] From other documentation, we know that Eleanor Werbington was still alive in 1414 and that Margaret Brakenham was also a member of the community in that year,[41] so this indicates that the calendar was certainly still in use and being updated after 1414. The calendar also refers to Alice Preston, described as a professed nun and *refectoratrix*. As we know from the kitchen inventory at the start of the Claudius manuscript, Alice was in charge of the kitchen in 1420, again indicating that the calendar was very much in use in the early fifteenth century. For many of the nuns listed I have been unable to find any corroborating information, such as when they lived, but the information in the calendar certainly tells us that the Wintney community had not forgotten about such individuals as Cristina de Ekcetre

---

[38] David M. Smith and Vera C. M. London, eds., *The Heads of Religious Houses: England and Wales II 1216–1377* (Cambridge: Cambridge University Press, 2001), 622.

[39] David Knowles, et al., eds., *The Heads of Religious Houses: England and Wales I 940–1216*, 2nd ed. (Cambridge: Cambridge University Press, 2001), 298.

[40] On the difficulties of filling the cantrix role, given other heavy demands in English nunneries, see Anne Bagnall Yardley, *Performing Piety: Musical Culture in English Nunneries* (New York: Palgrave, 2006).

[41] See discussion below of Joanna Benbury's election.

(Exeter), Drusiana, Billehalda, Isabella, Isilia, Rosamunda, Eva, and many others.

In addition to providing us with an internal picture of the Wintney community members unavailable to us from administrative documents, the calendar also expands our knowledge of the types of personnel present at, and indeed considered integral to, the Wintney community. I refer here to lay sisters, women whose shadowy presence in medieval English nunneries has confounded modern scholars. But it is clear from the calendar that the Wintney community did include lay sisters and that these individuals were considered deserving of commemoration alongside nuns and others. Interestingly, and confusingly, sometimes the Latin term used is *monacha et conversa* (nun and conversa), rather than simply *conversa*, and it is not clear what this dual designation meant. The calendar also provides no help in terms of what tasks these individuals might have performed, but it clearly embeds Cristina, Edelina, and Eluiua (each described as *monacha et conversa*) as equal members in the community, worthy of commemoration.

As well as nuns and lay sisters, the calendar also refers to six men as *frater noster* (our brother). These were probably lay brothers, men who certainly did live in England's Cistercian nunneries but about whom details are elusive at best. The limited information, such as it is, refers to lay brothers in the more common areas for Cistercian nunneries (York and Lincoln dioceses) and indicates that lay brothers were certainly present in the twelfth and thirteenth centuries.[42] But evidence of lay brothers after the thirteenth century is lacking. The absence of dates in the Wintney calendar means that I cannot add anything to the dating of lay brothers. If evidence from northern English nunneries is anything to go by, then these brothers too would

---

[42] The discussion by Sharon K. Elkins is a useful starting point: *Holy Women of Twelfth-Century England* (Chapel Hill and London: University of North Carolina Press, 1988), 86–88.

have lived no later than the thirteenth century. Whenever they lived, the lay brothers remained continual members of the Wintney community for centuries, via the annual commemorations listed in the calendar.

The calendar also shows that various people were received into fraternity with the community, with the ceremonies specified as taking place in the chapter house. William de Rale, bishop of Winchester, is listed as such, and the date (1446) is helpfully included. Others who were remembered were the community's confessors. Who these men were would be wonderful to know, particularly insofar as it could inform us about where Wintney's pastoral care came from, but their names are rather general, and I have had no luck in tracking them down. Were these confessors members of the mendicant orders as, for example, we know was sometimes the case with Cistercian nunneries in Yorkshire?[43] Somewhat strangely, the calendar contains only one reference to a monk from Waverley, *Adam Abbas de Waverle quondam*, who according to other evidence died in 1229,[44] although it does record obituaries for John the Bishop of Winchester and various abbots of Reading. Finally, on 12 Kalends February the calendar also mentions *Simon sacerdos*—this Simon the priest may or may not have been the same "brother" Simon from Waverley who wrote the poem at the start of the manuscript asking to be remembered at Wintney (*Ne me metez en ubliance*). In any case, nowhere else in the manuscript is Simon's name mentioned, a fact that suggests that his request in his prayer may or may not have been answered, at least in written form.

To conclude thus far: the evidence of Cotton Claudius D. iii indicates that a community of memory was developed and maintained at Wintney. The Rule of Saint Benedict was part of this, but in fact the meaning is confirmed and enhanced by

[43] See my "'Houses of a Peculiar Order.'"
[44] Smith and London, eds., *Heads of Religious Houses*, II:320.

the other items in the manuscript also. As the calendar shows, many and varied people played a role in Wintney's history, some of them listed as "benefactors." In fact, on 12 Kalends November the calendar recorded the commemoration of "all brothers and sisters and benefactors of our order," indicating a culture of inclusion on the widest possible scale.

Wintney and the Bishops of Winchester

Despite the fact that the Wintney calendar explicitly commemorates only one member of Waverley (Abbot Adam), this is not to say that connections with the Cistercian Order were weak, as indeed the annual commemoration on 12 Kalends November reminds us. Indeed, by the end of the thirteenth century the connection between Wintney and the Cistercian Order was sufficiently pronounced to be recognized by others. I refer here to evidence in the Winchester episcopal registers. Indeed, in 1295 the bishop of Winchester identified Wintney as a Cistercian community in his episcopal register, citing a letter from the king to the same effect.[45] This is the earliest register from Winchester to survive, and one wonders what earlier bishops might have thought. The same register refers to Wintney as Cistercian again in 1301, in which instance the bishop ordered the nuns to obey the new prioress whose election he had just confirmed.[46] An episcopal register entry from 1329 identifies the house as Cistercian, at the election of the new prioress Alicia Westcote.[47] A later bishop did the same in 1349,[48] and so on into the fifteenth century.

---

[45] *Registrum Johannis de Pontissara Episcopi Wyntoniensis A.D. MXXLXXXII–MCCCIV*, 2 vols., ed. Cecil Deedes (Oxford: Oxford University Press, 1924–1925), 2:509.

[46] *Registrum Johannis de Pontissara*, 1:98.

[47] Hampshire Record Office (hereafter HRO) 21M65/A1/5 = Register of John Stratford (1323–1333), fol. 115.

[48] *The Register of William Edington Bishop of Winchester 1346–1366*, Part 1, ed. S. F. Hockey (Winchester: Hampshire Record Office, 1986), 97.

Here it is important to note a characteristic feature of Cistercian nunneries in England. Bishops retained a certain degree of interest in them, despite the (modern-day) assumption that all medieval Cistercian communities were exempt from episcopal control. English bishops certainly did accept nunneries as belonging to the Cistercian Order and at the same time had significant influence in their running. For example, an early episcopal register entry from 1301 includes a firm letter from the bishop of Winchester announcing, with no hesitation at all, his upcoming visitation of the house.[49] From the other perspective, the Cistercian nuns' communities themselves (of which there were approximately thirty-five in England) seemed to interpret their relationships with bishops rather pragmatically, sometimes accepting episcopal oversight (no doubt when it was helpful). At the same time, they were also sufficiently aware of the theoretical Cistercian exemption from episcopal control as codified most influentially by Pope Lucius III in 1184. They invoked this exemption numerous times when it was to their advantage.[50] In the case of Wintney, unlike some other English Cistercian nunneries (in northern England), I am not aware of any instances in which the nuns argued publicly for independence from episcopal control. The evidence, such as I have examined, indicates a satisfactory, indeed cooperative, relationship between Wintney and the local bishops.

In fact, Winchester's episcopal registers provide quite a lot of evidence of the connections between the Wintney community and bishops. As was the case with Simon's textual support, and as is also evidenced by the memorials to bishops and others in the calendar, a spirit of cooperation can be detected between Wintney and clerics. Throughout the fifteenth century the bishops of Winchester continued to take responsibility for, and care of, the Wintney community. Reports of the elections

[49] *Registrum Johannis de Pontissara*, 1:112.
[50] As discussed in my "'Houses of a Peculiar Order.'"

of new prioresses feature regularly in the episcopal registers, as for instance at the election of Joanna Benbury as prioress in 1414. This was an instance in which episcopal involvement in the community's affairs was no doubt welcome, since a possible reason a new prioress was needed was that the existing prioress (now of infirm body) had apparently been causing major disruptions for decades, including financial and physical damage to the monastery.[51] In reporting the election of the new prioress Joanna, the lengthy entry in the episcopal register provides the modern scholar with invaluable information about the Wintney community, as it lists the names of fourteen nuns who were present at the election.[52] For example, we learn that the outgoing prioress was Alice Fyshide, and that other nuns were called Leticia, Elinora, Anna, Alicia, Christina, and Agnes, and that there were multiple nuns named Margaret and Joanna. No doubt these same nuns, and their prioress, would have returned to the copies of the Rule of Saint Benedict, and the calendar, in the Claudius manuscript. The episcopal register entry describes the election ceremony in some detail, recording that the nuns all sang *Veni creator spiritus* and *Te Deum laudamus*. The register also quotes the words that Joanna spoke at her election, "Ego Joanna Benbury," of the *convent sancte Marie Magdalene de Wynteney ordinis Cistercien Wynton dioc electa*. From these words, we can see that Joanna saw herself as a member of, and committed herself to serving, a community that was specifically Cistercian.

Later episcopal registers show continued episcopal attention to Wintney's affairs.[53] There is the confirmation of the election

---

[51] *Calendar of Entries in the Papal Registers Relating to Great Britain and Ireland: Papal Letters*, AD 1404–1415, ed. Jessie A. Tremlow (London: HMSO, 1904), 6:55 (*sub anno* 1405), 485 (*sub anno* 1415).

[52] HRO, 21M65/A1/12, Register of Henry Beaufort 1405–1447, fol. 50[r+] to fol. 51[r+.]

[53] E.g., HRO, Register of William Waynflete (1447–1486), part 1, fols. 102[v]–103[v], from 1460.

of prioress Alicia Somerset in 1452.[54] In 1497, the confirmation of prioress Anne Thomas is included. Interestingly, the vow professed by Anne was to the "regular order of Saint Bernard,"[55] reflecting a late-medieval English trend of referring to the Cistercians in this way. Only six nuns were named as being present at Anne's confirmation, a soberingly small number on the one hand but also evidence that medieval nunneries were able to sustain their community life with relatively few members.

Bishop Fox and the Rule

Anne Thomas remained prioress until 1534.[56] Her community of nuns may have been small, but she took active steps to provide for it. At some stage between 1501 and 1516/1517—probably toward the end of this period—she asked Bishop Richard Fox (Foxe) of Winchester for a translation of Benedict's Rule. She was not alone in her request; the abbesses of the three other nunneries in Hampshire did the same. Our knowledge of this comes not from the pens of the four women in question but, rather, from Bishop Fox himself. In January 1517 he published (in print form) an English translation of the Rule.[57]

---

[54] Register of William Waynflete (1447–1486), part 1, fol. 58ᵛ.

[55] HRO, 21M65/A16 (Bishop Langton 1493–1501), fol. 51ᵛ.

[56] David M. Smith, ed., *The Heads of Religious Houses: England and Wales III: 1377–1540* (Cambridge: Cambridge University Press, 2008), 708.

[57] The most recent edition (along with a thorough study) is in Barry Collett, ed., *Female Monastic Life in Early Tudor England: With an Edition of Richard Fox's Translation of the Benedictine Rule for Women, 1517* (Aldershot: Ashgate, 2002). The Fox version is also available at http://www.osb .org/aba/rb/feminine/foxe/wwwfoxe.htm. Collett has completed other studies on the translation; e.g., "Here Begynneth the Rule of seynt Benet: Richard Fox's Translation of the Benedictine Rule for Women, 1517," TJ 36 (1989): 10–25, and "Holy Expectations: The Female Monastic Vocation in the Diocese of Winchester on the Eve of the Reformation," in *The Culture of Medieval English Monasticism*, ed. James G. Clark (Woodbridge: Boydell, 2007), 147–65.

As he wrote in the preface to the translation, he had made the translation, *into oure moders tonge, commune, playne, rounde Englisshe*, in response to the "instant" (i.e., urgent) request of the superiors of the four nunneries in his diocese, and he also wrote that he had already sent manuscript versions of the translation to the four communities before organizing the printing.

Assuming that the four heads of Hampshire's female monasteries did ask Fox for a translation, and there is no reason that we should not, this raises all sorts of possibilities concerning the reading of the Rule of Saint Benedict at Wintney, as well as the relationship between the house and its bishop. We know that the community was experiencing poverty at this time.[58] Perhaps the request was an appeal to Fox to show charity in providing them with a text they could not afford for themselves. The Wintney community would still have possessed the manuscript now known as Claudius D. iii.[59] Could the nuns no longer read the English, which even at its point of composition in the thirteenth century had been old-fashioned?[60] Could they no longer read the Latin? Rather than assuming an incapacity on the part of nuns, I prefer to think that they were simply taking the initiative, that is, their community was now adding some members to its small body of nuns, and it was time to get an updated easy-to-read copy of this key text. In requesting another copy of Benedict's Rule, and requesting it in English, prioress Anne Thomas recognized something of which Michael Casey has reminded modern readers on multiple occasions, that is, that traditions at their best are living,

---

[58] Gerald Bray, ed., *Records of Convocation*, vol. 7, Canterbury 1509–1603 (Woodbridge and Rochester, NY: Boydell, 2006), 56–60.

[59] Strictly speaking, we cannot prove this, but there is no reason to believe that the manuscript would be anywhere else.

[60] Krochalis suggests that this was the reason a new English one was needed; "The Benedictine Rule for Nuns," 32.

active, and forward-looking.[61] Rather than being a sign of incapacity to read the Latin and English versions of the Claudius manuscript, I think it is worth considering that the Wintney prioress's request for another translation of the Rule was a sign of ongoing engagement with the Rule and an acknowledgment that traditional texts could not live unless they were updated.

While in the thirteenth century Wintney had gained textual material from Simon, the brother of Waverley, increasing interactions with bishops had occurred over the fourteenth and fifteenth centuries, leading to a situation in which it made sense to seek textual support from Bishop Fox and not from Cistercian personnel, particularly given the additional fact that Fox was extraordinarily devoted to both education and monastic life. In 1517—the very year of publication of Fox's Rule—the abbot of Waverley was involved (as a witness and decision-maker) when two English Cistercian abbots worked out which monasteries were to be "divided to them" for purposes of monastic oversight. Some female houses were included in the list that was subsequently produced, but Wintney

---

[61] See, for example, some of Casey's earliest contributions to TJ: e.g., "The Hermeneutics of Tradition," TJ 5 (1973): 39–50, the aim of which was to "propose a system of hermeneutics in which fidelity to the past is not opposed to fidelity to the present but dependent on it" (39), and which was prompted very much by the challenge posed by the Benedictine Rule, a challenge that Casey put starkly as the difference between an overly traditionalistic "keeping" of the Rule and a more reflective and forward-looking "understanding" of the Rule. Likewise, see Casey's more recent contribution, "Autonomy: An Address to the 2012 Congress of Benedictine Abbots," TJ 84 (Easter 2014): 5–19, especially, "As Benedictines we are heirs of a significant spiritual tradition; there is a tendency to define ourselves so strongly by our links to the past that we do not always attend to the importance of belonging also to the present and of being, as it were, a bridge between past and present, drawing our energy from both a return to the sources and an attention to the signs of the times" (12).

was not.[62] Perhaps Bishop Fox was doing a sufficiently good job of providing pastoral care that the Cistercian abbots did not need to assert a formal link with Wintney, and the prioress did not need to turn to the Cistercian abbots, but to her bishop, to provide support.

Richard Fox was no everyday bishop.[63] Between 1487 and 1516 he was also the keeper of the privy seal, juggling this same position with his role as bishop of Exeter, Bath and Wells, and Durham successively, and then finally Winchester from 1501 until his death in 1528. While bishop of Winchester he also took a strong interest in Oxford University, revising the statutes of Balliol College and, famously, founding Corpus Christi College with its focus on the *studia humanitatis*. As a humanist scholar he was in contact with Erasmus and Thomas More. Upon relinquishing the privy seal in mid-1516, he retired from politics and settled in Winchester; his translation of Benedict's Rule was published shortly thereafter, in January 1517. Although we cannot be sure when he made the translation and offered the (now-lost) manuscript copies to the four communities of nuns, it would make sense that it was between his retirement and the 1517 publication date, perhaps near the top of his "to do" list now that he could devote himself solely to his episcopal duties for the first time.

Fox's rather liberal English translation of the Rule, which was Fox's own translation and not based on any earlier versions (not even the Claudius manuscript housed then at Wintney), has drawn some very useful analysis by modern scholars, focusing most of all on what Fox's conception of the female

---

[62] Charles H. Talbot, *Letters from the English Abbots to the Chapter at Cîteaux 1442–1521* (London: Royal Historical Society, 1967), 236–38.

[63] For a good biography, see Cliff S. L. Davies, "Fox, Richard (1447/8–1528)," *Oxford Dictionary of National Biography*, online edition Sept. 2010, http://www.oxforddnb.com/view/article/10051. There is also Clayton J. Drees, *Bishop Richard Fox of Winchester: Architect of the Tudor Age* (Jefferson, NC: McFarland and Co., 2014).

monastic life might have been and the influence of his humanistic attachment to education, based on the ways in which he modified aspects of the original Latin Rule in the process of translating it.[64] Fox clearly believed in setting up a firm foundation from the outset, as he was particularly concerned that novices should know and understand the Rule before they professed to it. In the preface to the translation he pointed out that reading without understanding was of no value whatsoever. Scholars have focused on Fox's interests, suggesting that his stress on the abbess's being learned and capable of teaching others reflects Fox's own humanism.[65] Fox went out of his way to emphasize that nuns could and should read. Fox did not believe in censorship. Even when he believed that a certain section of the Rule did not apply to nuns, he still translated that whole section before then proceeding to state that the section was irrelevant.[66] Alternatively, perhaps he did not believe that Benedict's Rule should be cut into pieces. Rather, he believed it should be presented in its integrity. Indeed, he regularly added, *sayth seint Benet*, to stress the voice of Benedict himself.

[64] For Collett, Fox's four key concerns were poor leadership, ignorance, uncertainty, and misunderstanding of the task at hand; see Barry Collett, "The Civil Servant and Monastic Reform: Richard Fox's Translation of the Benedictine Rule for Women, 1517," in *Monastic Studies: The Continuity of Tradition*, ed. Judith Loades (Bangor: Headstart History, 1990), 211–28, esp. 216.

[65] See Collett's studies, and also Nancy Bradley Warren, *Spiritual Economies: Female Monasticism in Later Medieval England* (Philadelphia: University of Pennsylvania Press, 2001), 42. In chap. 64, Fox expands on the Rule's qualities of an abbot and writes of the abbess, *she must be well lerned in the lawes of god & hir religion & that she vnderstonde & be that person that can shewe & teche the lawes rules and constitucions of the religion with suche histores of holy scripture & seyntes lyues as be moste expedient.*

[66] As discussed in Elizabeth A. Lehfeldt, "Gender, the State, and Episcopal Authority: Hernando de Talavera and Richard Fox on Female Monastic Reform," *Journal of Medieval and Early Modern Studies* 42 (2012): 621–22.

It has been pointed out that Fox's translation is wordy, and that perhaps this was Fox's attempt to clarify and humanize the Rule, which he thought was too direct.[67] From the outset in the Prologue to the Rule, Fox elaborated on words, providing synonyms and explication. There was certainly an element of Fox the teacher here. Whether he was asserting his authority as a male ecclesiastic over the nuns in his care and mediating their access to the Rule, as has been suggested,[68] is perhaps in the eye of the beholder.

In the translation he referred to the feminine *minchin* (nun) and *suster* and *abbasse* in place of the masculine Latin terms of the original Rule, and at some places he made changes to the Rule. In the important section of chapter 2 in which the Latin original speaks of the abbot occupying the place of Christ, Fox's translation states that the abbess "occupies the place of almighty god in the monastery." An interesting change![69]

Fox's attention to enclosure has been noted by modern scholars. According to Henderson, "Bishop Foxe intruded into Benedict's text to a greater extent than did the other revisors."[70] For Henderson, Fox's insistence on female enclosure betrays an attempt to control the women, and not just to meet their spiritual needs. Other scholars have argued likewise,[71] although not all. Surely this is open to interpretation, and Collett's more generous interpretations of Fox's motives are just as likely.

What do we know about the reception of Fox's translation? As he wrote in his preface to the translation, Fox had first of

[67] John E. Crean, Jr., "British Bishops, Austrian Abbots and Benedictine Nuns: RB 1500," *Magistra* 19 (2013): 21–22.

[68] Lehfeldt, "Gender, the State, and Episcopal Authority," 618.

[69] Collett suggests that Fox wanted to distance the abbess from the priesthood, that is, from the sacrificial role of Christ with which the priesthood is connected; see "Here Begynneth," 14. Even so, the end result of equating the abbess with God is somewhat unexpected.

[70] Henderson, "Feminizing the Rule of Benedict," 36.

[71] Warren, *Spiritual Economies*, 34–35.

all given "books" of the translation to the "said monasteries," and then later, in order that there should be no shortage, he arranged for the text to be printed. From the context, then, by "books" Fox surely means manuscripts. These manuscript copies do not survive. But it is important to note that they did once survive, that is, that Wintney once owned a manuscript copy of Fox's translation, even though there is no evidence that a printed copy ended up there.

Only two copies of Fox's translated Rule survive today.[72] These are both printed copies. One copy survives in mint condition. It could hardly therefore have been used. Either it never made its way to a monastic library, or if it did it was never handled (which is hard to imagine). The other copy contains the handwritten *ex libris* of an early sixteenth-century prioress. This woman was not, interestingly, a member of any of the four nunneries whose leaders had requested the translation. The *ex libris* and a signature added elsewhere in the printed book refer to prioress Margaret Stanburne of St. Michael's Stamford, a Cistercian nunnery in the county of Northampton and diocese of Lincoln. Stanburne was prioress from 1523 to 1529.[73] Somehow, Fox's English translation of the Rule became known outside his own diocese and made its way to Stamford, and Stanburne's annotations show that it was put to some use in the decade before the Dissolution. Perhaps the now-lost manuscript version given to Wintney also had annotations to show its use?

Wintney and the Dissolution

In 1536 Wintney was visited by royal commissioners, in the rapid buildup to the Dissolution. The commissioners were fully

---

[72] See discussion at Collett, *Female Monastic Life*, 70–75. As I have not examined these books personally, my discussion relies on Collett's comments.

[73] Smith, *Heads of Religious Houses: III*, 694.

convinced that Wintney was a Cistercian house: *A heed howse of nunnes of thordre of Cisteaux*. They reported that there were ten nuns at Wintney, that the ten were by report all of "good conversation," and that all ten wished to continue in monastic life.[74] Wintney was dissolved in July 1536, very soon after monastic closures began. Because no names were listed in the 1536 commissioners' reports, we know nothing about the later lives of nine of the ten nuns and whether or not they did manage to transfer to another nunnery before all England's religious houses were ultimately closed by 1540. We do know about the last prioress, however. Half a century after the Dissolution, in 1584, Elizabeth Martin, "sometime Prioress of Wyntney," specified in her will what her grave should look like.[75] She wanted a stone placed on the grave and this stone should feature an image of a woman (herself?) in a long garment with wide sleeves and the hands joined together, as well as the following text: *In te domine speraui non confundar in aeternum. In iusticia tua libera me et salua me.* That is, she wished her grave to record words from the psalms, in this case, Psalm 70/71: "In you, O Lord, I take refuge: let me never be put to shame. In your righteousness deliver me and rescue me" (vv. 1-2). She would have sung these words many times in her life as a nun fifty years earlier, and evidently they remained important fifty years later.

Traditions: Medieval and Modern

As the opening words of this essay noted, tradition was ubiquitous in the Middle Ages. And medieval tradition was a

[74] Francis A. Gasquet, "Overlooked Testimonies to the Character of the English Monasteries on the Eve of the Suppression," *Dublin Review* 14 (1894): 268.

[75] This is printed in Charles H. Mayo, "Last Prioress of Wyntney, Hants.," *Somerset and Dorset Notes and Queries* 3 (1892–1893): 55–56.

changeable, tangible, and prized possession. But the tangible, valuable, and active force of tradition is not a matter confined to the medieval past. How notable that some of Michael Casey's earliest contributions to *Tjurunga: An Australasian Benedictine Review* discussed precisely this issue of tradition in monastic communities. In calling for "a more creative understanding of tradition,"[76] Casey advocated specifically for the ways in which the undeniable presence of tradition, a community's "fundamental integrating principle,"[77] with all its pluses and minuses, might be embraced as an active force rather than as a solely backward-looking one. Even more specifically, he pointed out how Benedict's Rule can play a key role in this despite (or, more likely, because of) the fact that in the modern monastic context it has now been supplemented by so many texts that its "legal" force is ever diminished.[78] In the first volume of *Tjurunga*, Casey asked a provocative question in a context in which other texts had taken on legislative force in the modern monastic environment: "Why read the Rule of St. Benedict?"[79] In posing such a daring question, Casey opened the reader up to being challenged and changed, aided, of course, by the admirably clear and straight-to-the-point prose in which he has always excelled.

In many respects Wintney was an unexceptional nunnery among medieval England's approximately 150 female religious

---

[76] "Community and Tradition," TJ 4 (1973): 56.

[77] Casey, "The Hermeneutics of Tradition," 46.

[78] Michael Casey, "Variation on a Theme—Approach to the Rule," TJ 1 (1972): 5–11. See also his "Principles of Interpretation and Application of RB," TJ 14 (1977): 33–38. Casey's "The Hard Sayings of R.B.," TJ 3 (1972): 134–43, also had its basis in the question of how a text originally written as a Roman legislative document (and one with little focus on the "development of the individual," to boot) could be most profitably read in the modern world when the text no longer retains its original legislative primacy.

[79] Casey, "Variation on a Theme," 6.

communities. Certainly, it rarely rates a mention when modern students of monasticism examine medieval England. In its Hampshire context, it has been overshadowed by attention to Nunnaminster, Wherwell, and Romsey, the three quite different (that is, richer, and pre-Conquest) nunneries, of which, interestingly, each had significant library collections and histories of manuscript possession.[80] At the Dissolution Wintney was the poorest of all Hampshire's fifteen houses of monks, nuns, and canons.[81] But is it the aim of a monastic community to be somehow exceptional or financially wealthy? In the case of Wintney, an unexceptional and poor nunnery maintained a centuries-long engagement with the richness of the Rule of Saint Benedict and the liturgical memorialization of its own community members. At Wintney, traditions were inherited, made, and remade in the Middle Ages, and their presence continues to this day, accessible to us via the links that are the Cotton Claudius D. iii manuscript and Bishop Fox's Rule.

[80] E.g., on Nunnaminster's library, see David N. Bell, "What Nuns Read: The State of the Question," in *The Culture of Medieval English Monasticism*, ed. James G. Clark (Woodbridge: Boydell, 2007), 117.

[81] Joseph Kennedy, "Laymen and Monasteries in Hampshire, 1530–1558," *Proceedings of the Hampshire Field Club* 27 (1970): 65.

Chapter 12

Some Benedictine Legacies

Austin Cooper, OMI

The Vatican II Decree on Ecumenism happily noted that among churches and communions that retained some Catholic institutions and traditions, "the Anglican Communion occupies a special place."[1] In more recent times this continuity has been given a more specific focus. It is best seen, perhaps, as coalescing around the Benedictine tradition, a view given wide prominence when Pope Benedict XVI was welcomed to Westminster Abbey in 2010. On that occasion, the then-archbishop of Canterbury, Dr. Rowan Williams, noted, "For many centuries the daily office of the Church has been celebrated here, first by the Benedictine monks, then by the new foundation of the sixteenth century, always with the same rhythms of psalmody and petition and the same purpose of glorifying God in all things."[2] It was a clear recognition of continuity despite the ravages of Reformation debates and divisions. In his homily, the archbishop recalled Pope Saint Gregory the Great, who in the year AD 597 sent missionary monks to England under the leadership of Saint Augustine:

---

[1] Decree on Ecumenism, *Unitatus Redintegratio*, no. 13.

[2] *Order of Service*, p. 9; http://www.westminster-abbey.org/__data/assets/pdf_file/0007/42748/web-WA-Papal-service.pdf, accessed Nov. 18, 2015.

St Gregory was the first to spell out for the faithful something of the magnitude of the gift given to Christ's Church through the life of St Benedict . . . in [his] Dialogues, we can trace the impact of St Benedict—an extraordinary man who, through a relatively brief Rule of life, opened up for the whole civilisation of Europe since the sixth century the possibility of living in joy and mutual service, in simplicity and self-denial, in a balanced pattern of labour and prayer in which every moment spoke of human dignity fully realised in surrender to a loving God. The Benedictine life proved a sure foundation not only for generations of monks and nuns, but for an entire culture in which productive work and contemplative silence and receptivity—human dignity and human freedom—were both honoured.[3]

Simplicity . . . balance . . . dignity in worship and in living. Perhaps that captures something of the essential qualities of this continuing Benedictine tradition. But far more eloquently than mere words, the "action" of this liturgy spoke powerfully of Benedictine continuity: the splendid monastic setting of the abbey, the measured dignity of the service, centuries-old prayers including psalms and the Magnificat, the moving strains of the chants. All witnessed an enduring beauty.[4] The pope, who seemed enthralled at this liturgy, admirably summed up the experience. He expressed his gratitude at being welcomed at Westminster Abbey where "architecture and history speak so eloquently of our common heritage of

---

[3] 2015; http://rowanwilliams.archbishopofcanterbury.org/articles.php/945/the-visit-of-archbishop-rowan-williams-and-pope-benedict-xvi-to-westminster-abbey-for-evening-prayer, accessed Tuesday, Nov. 17, 2015.

[4] The entire service is available on YouTube: https://www.youtube.com/watch?v=SYmwvLOoQRU, accessed Wednesday, Nov. 18, 2015.

faith. . . . Here we . . . are forcibly reminded that what we share, in Christ, is greater than what continues to divide us."[5] It is all too easy to see the most obvious monastic legacy in the choral office celebrated in so many Anglican cathedral and collegiate churches around the world. But it also survives in the many smaller and quite humble communities. A similar legacy of a monastic tradition is seen too in the approach to the Eucharist. A notable example can be found in the case of the priest-poet George Herbert (1593–1633). This seventeenth-century vicar of Bemerton wrote his poetry as a form of private prayer. More than seventy poems were assembled to form *The Temple*. In this work a whole spirituality is based on reflections on the church building, its furnishings, and liturgical functions. That could well pass muster as a monastic approach. For Herbert, liturgical practice and a deep personal prayer combine: a very Benedictine attitude indeed. And at the conclusion of his long poetic work Herbert placed his remarkable poem "Love III," which his latest biographer and commentator has judged his "masterpiece."[6] All the many and varied aspects of church life are brought together in the Eucharist. The poem is utterly simple, yet profoundly prayerful. The uncluttered dialogue between Love and the imperfect self maintains a marked restraint, almost understatement. Love, which here is obviously the redemptive mission of Christ, can effect a change. Here at last, the hesitant sinful self finds acceptance through the mercy of God. This measured and humane dialogue effects a change. Simone Weil judged it "the most beautiful poem in the world" and thought it made one aware of a "presence, more personal,

[5] https://w2.vatican.va/content/benedict-xvi/en/speeches/2010/september/documents/hf_ben-xvi_spe_20100917_celebrazione-ecumenica.html, accessed Wednesday, Nov. 18, 2015.

[6] John Drury, *Music at Midnight: The Life and Poetry of George Herbert* (London: Penguin Books, 2013), 136.

more certain, more real than that of any human being."[7] Her view speaks eloquently of the Holy Spirit's effecting the action of the Eucharist and, through that action, effecting conversion in the sinner. Uncertainty gives way to a simple statement of belonging; a sense of sin is met with mercy; the discourse terminates with a deep sense of peace. And this simplicity maintains a great dignity throughout:

> Love bade me welcome. Yet my soul drew back
> Guilty of dust and sin.
> But quick-eyed Love, observing me grow slack
> From my first entrance in,
> Drew nearer to me, sweetly questioning,
> If I lacked any thing.
> A guest, I answered, worthy to be here:
> Love said, You shall be he.
> I the unkind, ungrateful? Ah my dear,
> I cannot look on thee.
> Love took my hand, and smiling did reply,
> Who made the eyes but I?
> Truth Lord, but I have marred them: let my shame
> Go where it doth deserve.
> And know you not, says Love, who bore the blame?
> My dear, then I will serve.
> You must sit down, says Love, and taste my meat:
> So I did sit and eat.[8]

Despite the fact that Herbert, as an Anglican vicar of the seventeenth century, would not have celebrated the Eucharist daily, infrequent celebration is not incompatible with a very lofty notion of the Eucharist and its place in the Christian scheme of things. One senses that maintaining a sense of

[7] Cited in Drury, *Music at Midnight*, 359, 320.

[8] *George Herbert and the Seventeenth-Century Religious Poets*, ed. Mario A. Di Cesare (New York: W. W. Norton and Company, Inc., 1978).

simplicity, balance, and dignity in worship is a matter requiring some effort, some training. Liturgical rites could so easily degenerate into mere routine. In his treatise on pastoral care Herbert says the priest must set an example of "reverence" in leading worship. But more is needed, and Herbert provided it: "Besides his example, he . . . often instructed his people how to carry themselves in divine service, exact[ing] of them all possible reverence."[9] How much this continues the ethos of the older medieval monastic practice is difficult to say. However, the architectural legacy of those days (which Anglicans inherited), the beauty of surviving service manuscripts so lovingly and elaborately illuminated, and the chants that we still cherish all suggest that medieval monastic worship must have afforded many folks a glimpse of the beauty of holiness. Maybe the English (and specifically Anglican) penchant for excellence in liturgical rites is as much a monastic legacy as a national trait.

Closely allied to this is what Rowan Williams referred to as "contemplative silence and receptivity." Indeed that would provide the atmosphere in which the liturgical prayer could develop and flourish to the full. In the seventeenth century the Church of England produced another pastor whose approach to prayer would seem to ideally capture the spirit of chapter 48 of the Holy *Rule:* namely, the *Preces Privatae* of Lancelot Andrewes.

Andrewes (1555–1626) was a remarkably learned man. A student, then Fellow and eventually Master of Pembroke Hall, Cambridge, he became skilled in fifteen languages. James I, who succeeded to the throne in 1603, held him in high regard and successively appointed him bishop of Chichester (1605), Ely (1609), and finally Winchester (1619). He played a leading

---

[9] George Herbert, "The Country Parson," chap. 6 in George Herbert, *The Country Parson*, ed. John N. Wall, The Temple Classics of Western Spirituality (New York: Paulist Press, 1984), 60–61.

part in the formation of the King James Bible.[10] And his works include numerous sermons that have left their imprint on the poetry of T. S. Eliot. He had a broad catholic outlook that was sharply at odds with the vocal and powerful Puritan presence in Parliament.

Andrewes' *Preces Privatae* was written purely for private use. Based on a wide range of biblical and patristic sources, it has exercised an attraction for successive generations of English-speaking Christians. The prayers have been re-edited in English on several occasions through the last three hundred years. One of the most influential, and perhaps best-known and loved, editions is that produced by John Henry Newman in 1840 and published as one of the *Tracts for the Times (No. 88)*. As such it was intended primarily as a book of devotions for clergy and so forms an essential element in the Tractarian program for clerical renewal. For Newman this work marked a "rediscovery of *lectio divina* as practiced by the ancient Christians," and he used it throughout his lifetime.[11]

Lancelot Andrewes was well practiced in the ages-long approach to prayer based on slow, reflective divine or sacred reading. As such he has an obvious affinity to, if not a literal dependence on, the approach of Saint Benedict's chapter 48 of the Rule. In this form of prayer, to use the homely image of C. S. Lewis, one takes "a little bit at a time, more like sucking a lozenge rather than eating a piece of bread."[12] Such prayer therefore eschews the modern tendency to read quickly. It seeks rather to allow a text to seep into one's awareness, much as we should linger over a beautiful landscape rather than simply

[10] Helen Moore and Julian Reid, eds., *Manifold Greatness: The Making of the King James Bible* (Oxford: Bodleian Library, 2011), 93–94.

[11] Louis Boyer, "Introduction," in John Henry Newman, *Prayers, Verses and Devotions* (San Francisco: Ignatius Press, 1989), xvi.

[12] "C. S. Lewis to Mrs Margaret Gray, 9 May 1961," in W. H. Lewis, ed., *Letters of C. S. Lewis* (London: Geoffrey Bles Ltd., 1966), 299.

click a camera to record and store it. Newman's translation (used here) is faithful to Andrewes, though it does not include all sections of the work, and it makes some slight changes in the order of the texts. But Newman faithfully followed Andrewes in adopting the practice first used by Saint Anselm (d. 1109), Benedictine, archbishop of Canterbury, and theologian.[13] Anselm, in his reflective works, introduced the practice of writing short, well-spaced lines, which prompt the eye and mind to pause and reflect rather than rush through a text. Newman felt that previous editions had turned it from a "book of prayers into a collection of texts."[14]

The work opens with a section headed "Preparation." There is a series of texts gathered under three headings: 1. Times of Prayer, 2. Places of Prayer, and finally 3. Circumstances of Prayer. This last is the shortest of the three and gives some sense of how, slowly pondered, the texts would introduce one to a reflective attitude:

3. Circumstances of Prayer

1. Kneeling,   *humiliation.*
>   He kneeled down and prayed. *Luke* xxii. 41.
>   He went a little further, and fell on His face,
>   and prayed. *Matt.* xxvi. 39.

---

[13] Newman also chose not to clutter his version with overly numerous references to sources. These can be found in the edition by Frank E. Brightman, ed., *The Private Devotions of Lancelot Andrewes* (Gloucester, MA: Peter Smith, 1983). In 1989 the Ignatius Press republished Newman's *Meditations and Devotions* and included the *Preces Privatae* of Andrewes in light of Newman's love of this text.

[14] Newman to Miss Holmes 10 June 1840, in *The Letters and Diaries of John Henry Newman* (Oxford: Clarendon Press, 1995), 7:341. A 1957 SCM Press edition used Newman's translation but managed to turn it back into a "collection of texts." See *The Private Prayers of Lancelot Andrewes*, trans. J. H. Newman and J. M. Neale, ed. Hugh Martin (London: SCM Press, 1957).

> My soul is brought low, even unto the dust,
> my belly cleaveth unto the ground.
> 2. Sinking the head,   *shame.*
>   Drooping the face. [*Ezr.* ix. 6.]
> 3. Smiting the breast, [*Luke* xviii. 13.]   *indignation.*
> 4. Shuddering, [*Acts* xvi. 29.]   *fear.*
> 5. Groaning, [*Isai.* lix. 11.]   *sorrow.*
>   Clasping of hands.
> 6. Raising of eyes and hands, [*Ps.* xxv. 15. cxliii. 6.]
>   *vehement desire.*
> 7. Blows, [*Ps.* lxxiii. 14.]   *revenge.*

2 Cor. vii. 11

Typical of this Reformation age is the stress on one's sinfulness and frailty. Humiliation, shame, fear, and vehement desire are prominent. Of course the Western liturgy has always commenced in a similar spirit with the penitential rite. Prayer time is not simply creating a cozy and comfortable space for oneself. Yet overall one has a sense that, through the mercy of God, a reflective reader has the possibility of adopting a calm, meditative approach to prayer, setting one's face against the rush and noise of modern life in which the "still small voice" might well be muffled and eventually silenced. So Andrewes is a realist. We often come to prayer with a variety of emotional states, yet each can be an opening to the grace of prayer. We create for ourselves a space of silence and peace in which to be attuned to the Spirit whose temples we are.

Lancelot Andrewes' beautifully structured set of prayers also introduces us to another aspect of prayer: the need for a daily discipline. He is a splendid example of a well-ordered, "regular" life. This also stems from the old Benedictine idea of sanctifying time and place in the daily sevenfold office. For Andrewes this had now been simplified into something that could well be common to both clergy and laity: the twofold Office of Matins and Evensong of *The Book of Common Prayer.*

So Andrewes faithfully reflects the stress on order, regularity, and moderation that are hallmarks of that approach to the daily Office. Indeed these prayers and meditations form a bridge between the set forms of the church and the deeply personal aspects of prayer.

Andrewes has an "Order for Matin Prayer" that consists of a Litany, Confession, and Commendation. Here is the "Confession" from this "Order of Matin Prayer":

> Essence beyond essence, Nature increate,
> Framer of the world,
> I set Thee, LORD, before my face,
> and I lift up my soul unto Thee.
> I worship Thee on my knees,
> and humble myself under Thy mighty hand.
> I stretch forth my hands unto Thee,
> my soul gaspeth unto Thee as a thirsty land.
> I smite on my breast
> and say with the Publican,
> GOD be merciful to me a sinner,
> the chief of sinners;
> to the sinner above the Publican,
> be merciful as to the Publican.
> Father of mercies,
> I beseech Thy fatherly affection,
> despise me not
> an unclean worm, a dead dog, a putrid corpse,
> despise not Thou the work of Thine own hands,
> despise not Thine own image
> though branded by sin.
> LORD, if Thou wilt, Thou canst make me clean,
> LORD, only say the word, and I shall be cleansed
> And Thou, my SAVIOUR CHRIST,
> CHRIST my SAVIOUR,
> SAVIOUR of sinners, of whom I am chief,
> despise me not, despise me not, O LORD,

despise not the cost of Thy blood,
who am called by Thy Name;
but look on me with those eyes
with which Thou didst look upon
Magdalen at the feast,
Peter in the hall,
the thief on the wood;—
that with the thief I may call on Thee humbly,
Remember me, LORD, in Thy kingdom;
that with Peter I may bitterly weep and say,
O that mine eyes were a fountain of tears
that I might weep day and night;
that with Magdalen I may hear Thee say,
Thy sins be forgiven thee,
and with her to love much,
for many sins yea manifold
have been forgiven me.
And Thou, All-holy, Good, and Life-giving Spirit,
despise me not, Thy breath,
despise not Thine own holy things;
but turn Thee again, O LORD, at the last,
and be gracious unto Thy servant.[15]

Likewise the "Order of Evening Prayer" has three parts:
Meditation, Confession, and Commendation. But following
these are seven sets of meditative prayers for each of the days
of the week. Like Saint Bonaventure in *Itinerarium mentis in
Deum* (but lacking Bonaventure's serious theologizing between
his prayers), the structure follows the themes of the creation
story in Genesis. Each of these in turn is well ordered into
sections: Introduction, 1. Confession, 2. Prayer for Grace, 3.
Profession, 4. Intercession, and finally, 5. Praise. The days of
creation are not treated in any literal sense. Indeed each offers

---

[15] Newman and Neale, eds., *Private Prayers*, 7–8.

a key or symbol that is used to unlock a wide variety of themes for prayer. There are graces and blessings for which we must be thankful, misuse of them that prompts one to plead for mercy, and a remarkable series of intercessions that display something of the wide interests and sympathies of Andrewes. So this creative week commences with "Light" on the first day:

Introduction.
Through the tender mercies of our GOD
the day-spring from on high hath visited us.
Glory be to Thee, O LORD glory to Thee.
Creator of the light,
and Enlightener of the world,—
of the visible light,
the Sun's ray, a flame of fire,
day and night,
evening and morning,—
of the light invisible,
the revelation of GOD,
writings of the Law,
oracles of Prophets,
music of Psalms,
instruction of Proverbs,
experience of Histories,—
light which never sets.
GOD is the LORD who hath showed us light;
bind the sacrifice with cords,
yea even unto the horns of the altar.

O by Thy resurrection raise us up
unto newness of life,
supplying to us frames of repentance.
The GOD of peace,
who did bring again from the dead
the great Shepherd of the sheep,
through the blood of the everlasting covenant,

> our LORD JESUS CHRIST, perfect us in every good work,
> to do His will,
> working in us what is acceptable before Him,
> through JESUS CHRIST,
> to whom be glory for ever.

> Thou who didst send down on Thy disciples
> on this day
> Thy Thrice-Holy SPIRIT,
> withdraw not Thou the gift, O LORD, from us,
> but renew it in us, day by day,
> who ask Thee for it.[16]

At the conclusion of the prayers for the days of the week there is a valuable collection of "Additional Exercises" comprising Deprecation, Forms of Intercession, Christian Meditations (on Christmas Duty, On the Day of Judgement, and On Human Frailness), and finally A Preparation for Holy Communion.

The old monastic practice of *lectio divina* is finding a renewed popularity among many Christians. And Andrewes can still make a contribution to this renewal. He can wean us from an unhealthy individualism typified by comments such as "I pray when I feel like it." This is all very well in its own way. It indicates a religious faith and a sense of dependence on God, and it shows a response to some promptings of the Spirit. Yet even deeply personal prayer ought never be totally individualistic and cannot simply be dictated by personal and passing fads and whims. Andrewes takes us out of such a mind-set and places us within the wider context of the entire cosmos. At times he may jolt the modern reader. His sections on penitence and deprecation ensure that one is made aware of the sinfulness that surrounds us and that has penetrated our own hearts. The world of Andrewes was one in which sin and re-

---

[16] Newman and Neale, eds., *Private Prayers,* 17–19.

demption were pressing concerns, made all the more so by the comparative brevity and harshness of life. We who doubtless prefer a more cozy and reassuring religion can still do well to ponder the prevalence of human evil and the availability of divine mercy. But there are also challenging and encouraging prayers on the works of mercy and intercessions reminding us of our social, ecclesial, and cosmic context. And there are also passages of sheer delight. The weekly round terminates, most appropriately, with an outburst of joyful praise totally in tune with the last of the Psalms (150).

(5) *Praise.*
Now unto Him that is able to do
exceeding abundantly
above all that we ask or think,
according to the power that worketh in us.
to Him be glory
in the Church in CHRIST
unto all generations
world without end. Amen.
Blessed, and praised, and celebrated,
and magnified, and exalted, and glorified,
and hallowed,
be Thy Name, O LORD,
its record, and its memory,
and every memorial of it;
for the all-honourable senate of the Patriarchs,
the ever-venerable band of the Prophets,
the all-glorious college of the Apostles,
the Evangelists,
the all-illustrious army of the Martyrs,
the Confessors,
the assembly of Doctors,
the Ascetics,
the beauty of Virgins,
for Infants the delight of the world,—

for their faith, their hope,
their labours, their truth,
their blood, their zeal,
their diligence, their tears,
their purity, their beauty.
Glory to Thee, O LORD, glory to Thee,
glory to Thee who didst glorify them,
among whom we too glorify Thee.
Great and marvellous are Thy works,
LORD, the GOD ALMIGHTY;
just and true are Thy ways,
O King of Saints.
Who shall not fear Thee, O LORD,
and glorify Thy Name?
for Thou only art holy.
for all the nations shall come and worship before Thee,
for Thy judgments are made manifest.
Praise our GOD, all ye His servants,
and ye that fear Him,
both small and great.
Alleluia,
for the LORD GOD Omnipotent reigneth;
let us be glad and rejoice, and give honour to Him.
Behold the tabernacle of GOD is with men,
and He will dwell with them;
and they shall be His people,
and GOD Himself shall be with them,
and shall wipe away all tears from their eyes.
And there shall be no more death;
neither crying, neither pain any more,
for the former things are passed away.[17]

How then might the contemporary person at prayer make use of this particular monastic legacy? The prayers certainly

[17] Newman and Neale, eds., *Private Prayers*, 74–76.

should not merely be read through from start to finish. They require an unhurried approach. For us moderns who seem to have so little time, it might be very useful if just a single section is taken up on any one day. What Andrewes would surely advise is that we seek some regularity. He would be a wonderful guide over a period of some three or four weekly cycles. And he is the sort of writer to whom one would frequently return for spiritual nourishment.

Placed in a wider context, these prayers can take their place among the classics of the tradition. T. S. Eliot remarked that "The prayers . . . should take . . . a place beside the Exercises of St. Ignatius and the works of St. Francois de Sales."[18] They can indeed be the means of schooling one in the Lord's service. And the Orthodox writer Nicholas Lossky noted that this form of prayer is of the highest order: "This theology is mystical in the sense that it is not an abstract reflection, but a way of living the mystery in the deepening of faith through prayer and the renunciation of one's own will. . . . This is only possible in fidelity to the data of revelation, that is to say in the biblical and patristic tradition, that is, in the catholicity of the Church."[19] Teresa of Avila would agree with this, particularly in the relevant chapters of *The Way of Perfection*. This devotion to "prayers" can lead one to the heights of contemplation.[20]

If Andrewes provides a prayer context for worship and life, then John Cosin shows the importance of a clearly structured form of prayer. Andrewes was fortunate in serving under the

[18] T. S. Eliot, *For Lancelot Andrewes: Essays on Style and Order* (London: Faber & Gwyer, 1928), available at http://mariannedorman.homestead.com/eliot.html, accessed Wednesday, Nov. 18, 2015.

[19] Nicholas Lossky, *Lancelot Andrewes Le Predicateur (1555–1626)* (Paris: Éditions du Cerf, 1987), 327, cited in Stephen Sykes and John Booty, eds., *The Study of Anglicanism* (London: SPCK, 1988), 317.

[20] See Teresa of Avila, "Way of Perfection," in *The Collected Works of St. Teresa of Avila,* trans. Kieran Kavanaugh and Otilio Rodriguez (Washington, DC: ICS Publications, 1980), 2: chap. XXX, 123–26.

first of the Stuart sovereigns. By the time of John Cosin (1594–1672), church and nation saw the more tempestuous reign of Charles I: the civil war, the execution of the king, and the establishment of the Protectorate under Oliver Cromwell. Cosin was irrevocably ensnared in the fractious politics of the day.

His talents had been recognized early, and he became master of Peterhouse (Cambridge) and later dean of Peterborough. But powerful forces militated against him. In 1644 the Long Parliament deprived him of his benefices. The harsh political realities that unfolded meant years of exile in Paris for the likes of John Cosin. After the Stuart Restoration (1660), he was soon given appropriate recognition once again and was made bishop of Durham. Like Andrewes, he engaged in controversies with continental Catholics, though his own theological and liturgical preferences were of a decidedly catholic nature. And like Andrewes, he eschewed the prevailing Calvinism of his university and political life. He would be among those who would have subscribed to the comment by Richard Hooker that in some matters "Rome keepeth that which is ancienter and better."[21] In the approach of this particular Anglican movement we can also discern the presence of an incipient ecumenical approach.

Cosin's spiritual writings are undoubtedly less significant than those of Lancelot Andrewes, yet he is not without his importance. His translation of the *Veni Creator* is still widely used and deeply appreciated. However, his contribution to English-speaking spirituality also has to take account of his insistence on the importance of the set liturgy of the Church.

In terms of a personal spirituality, the corollary of this was that one's private devotion should be fed on prayers reflecting the liturgy of the church. Such books of prayers had a long history. They were known throughout the Middle Ages as *primers*.

---

[21] Richard Hooker, *The Laws of Ecclesiastical Polity* (Oxford: Oxford University Press, 2013), book V, chap. xxviii, section 1.

These enabled lay folk, particularly, to have prayers that were related to, and in some sense reflected, the Divine Office, the official prayer of the church. Cosin's work, therefore, reflects an Anglican continuation of a much older Catholic practice. Thus this tradition stresses the central role of the official liturgy of the church (in this case the *Book of Common Prayer*) and the need to see it as a model for all prayer; it also stresses the need for regularity and form in prayer. In his emphasis on the primacy of worship Cosin followed the example of the archbishop of Canterbury, William Laud (1573–1645), who suffered the same fate as his sovereign, Charles I. His work also contains the stress on the suffering and death of Christ, so typical of his time, and a rich sacramentalism. These are undoubted strengths, and we would do well to ponder their significance for us today. However, a more negative side of the work of Cosin is that it tends to equate prayer with the saying of prayers. The reader does not sense any longing for, or any opening to, deep personal prayer or contemplation, such as that in Lancelot Andrewes and George Herbert.

Cosin's best-known work, *A Collection of Private Devotions*, was first published in 1627.[22] It is a much more formidable tome than the work by Andrewes discussed above. Its original title page indicates something of its ambitious scope: *A Collection of Private Devotions in the Practise of the Ancient Church, Called the Houres of Prayer, As they were after this manner published by Authoritie of Q. Eliz., 1560. Taken Out of the Holy Scriptures, the Ancient Fathers, and the divine Service of our own Church.*[23] The brief but learned preface clarifies the threefold aim of the work: "to continue & preserve the authority of the ancient *Lawes*, and old godly *Canons* of the Church"; to refute those "who give

---

[22] There is a more recent edition: *John Cosin, A Collection of Private Devotions*, ed. P. G. Stanwood (Oxford: Clarendon Press, 1967).

[23] From a photograph of the title page of the first edition. Cosin, *A Collection*, Plate III opposite, 1.

it out, & accuse us here in ENGLAND to have set up a *New Church*, and a *New faith*"; and finally to foster the devotional life of the faithful, especially those unable to attend a Church service.[24] In these few packed pages, reference is made to several early church councils and fathers of the church.

In addition to the strong appeal to religious continuity, one also detects the impact of increasing interest in patristic studies. The volume comes with a complete calendar, as in the Breviary and the *Book of Common Prayer*. Festivals newly included in the latter are printed in red by Cosin, and one finds a few ancient and Anglo-Saxon names appearing: Hilary, the bishop of Poitiers in France, on January 13 (indicating the growing importance of patristic studies); Blaise, an Armenian bishop and martyr, on February 3 (perhaps indicating a memory of and hankering after an old medieval devotion); and Chad, bishop of Lichfield, on March 2 (among the Anglo-Saxon saints included). This is followed by *The Summe of the Catholike Faith*, which includes the Apostles Creed, the Lord's Prayer, and the Ten Commandments. Then follows a detailed list of the duties these latter impose.[25]

The most interesting part of the work is that devoted to prayers for the different times of the day. These follow the old order of the monastic breviary: "The First Houre, or The Morning Prayers," etc., then an order of prayer for the third, sixth, and ninth hours, "Prayers at the Vespers, or the Time of Evensong," and finally "The Compline, or Final Prayers to be said before Bed-time." In each case the similarity to the hours of the Office as celebrated in the monastic tradition is evident. The interesting addition to each is the series of short quotations before each hour. It is not clear whether these are intended for something like *lectio divina* as a preparation for the praying of the hour that follows or as an *apologia* for what Cosin's contemporaries would doubtless have considered unusual, leaving him open to the charge of mere Romanism.

The Third Hour offers a typical format. It opens with twelve relatively short texts, three biblical and the remainder patristic. Each has some reference or allusion to prayer at the third hour. Thus, from Saint Basil, "At the THIRD HOUR of the day, let us give our selves to holy Supplications and Prayers, having in continuall remembrance, the most glorious Gift of the Holy Ghost, which was then bestowed upon the Apostles of Christ, as they were devoutly met together at their Prayers and holy Exercises. And let us beseech Almighty God, that we may also bee made fit to receive the like blessed Sanctification of the Spirit, to bee our Director and Instructor in all things that we doe."[26]

This prelude is then followed by "Prayers for the Third Houre": The Lord's Prayer, the Hymn *Veni Creator*, then three psalms: Psalm 15 (14), Psalm 25 (24), and Psalm 145 (144), each being followed by the "Glory bee to the Father." Then there is a short benediction: "Blessed be the Lord God of Israel from everlasting & world without end."[27]

The accent throughout is on the coming of the Holy Spirit, and the Office terminates with a short reading from Ephesians 6:11, 14-18 (adapted).[28] The Hour terminates with two prayers, the second of which relates expressly to sacramental grace:

> Almightie God, the fountaine of all goodness, and the wellspring of divine Graces, who hast vouchsafed to regenerate me, being borne in sinne, by water and the Holy Ghost in the blessed laver of Baptisme, thereby receiving me into the number of thine elect Children, and making mee an Heire of everlasting life, in the

[26] Cosin, *Collection*, 109–10.
[27] Cosin, *Collection*, 110–15.
[28] Cosin, *Collection*, 116.

Communion of thy glorious Saints: strengthen me, *I
beseech thee*, O Lord, with that blessed Spirit of things,
the Ghostly Comforter: and daily increase in mee thy
manifold Gifts of Grace, the Spirit of Wisdom and
Understanding, the Spirit of Councell and Ghostly
Strength, the Spirit of Knowledge and true Godlinesse
and fulfil me, O Lord, with the spirit of thy Holy Feare,
even through him who hath sent down the Spirit upon
his Church, Jesus Christ our Lord. Amen.[29]

Cosin's manual of prayers concludes with a lengthy selection of prayers for various persons and occasions. Needless
to say, prayers for the king and queen figure prominently. But
there is also a section entitled "A Devout manner of Preparing
our selves, to receive Absolution."[30] One could well argue that
this is not merely a very Catholic book of private devotions but
also one largely inspired by the central role of an ordered Office
that is at the heart of the monastic tradition. In medieval times
every parish priest had a commitment to the Divine Office that
was hardly likely to have been a very visible aspect of medieval
English life. It was otherwise with the monastic Office. The
very number of the great monastic churches in England meant
that for many people the celebration of the Divine Office as a
liturgical rite was a very visible feature of life indeed. Maybe
the sense of the loss of something good and beautiful lingered
long. Cosin instinctively felt it was opportune to recast the
tradition for the devout of his day.

It is doubtless a sense of loss that inspired much of Cosin's
interest in the great monastic cathedral he inherited at Durham
and in its liturgical practices.[31] The place obviously had a great

[29] Cosin, *Collection*, 117.
[30] Cosin, *Collection*, 238–40.
[31] See Canon Fowler, ed., *Rites of Durham, Being a Description or Brief
Declaration of All the Ancient Monuments, Rites, and Customs Belonging
or Being within the Monastical Church of Durham before the Suppression.*

deal of fascination for the bishop, and his work contributed much to the introduction of a more catholic tone to the 1662 *Book of Common Prayer*. Monastic life does indeed speak to us of a sense of the importance of place. Benedict was insistent on stability for his followers. One can be schooled in God's service at *this* time, in *this* place, and with *these* people. Such an affection for place has a long history in Christendom. We find that Saint Antony of Egypt, coming to the remote desert, "fell in love with the place."[32] Some notable English spiritual writers of the post-Reformation period take up this strand of Christian thought. The best known and loved is undoubtedly Thomas Traherne (1647–1674). In his *Centuries* he gives rhapsodic expression to his love for the cosmos: "To conceive aright and to enjoy the world, is to conceive the Holy Ghost. And to see His love: which is the mind of the Father."[33] And again:

> You never enjoy the world aright, till the Sea itself floweth in your veins, till you are clothed with the heavens, and crowned with the stars: and perceive yourself to be the sole heir of the whole world, and more than so, because men are in it who are every one sole heirs as well as you. Till you can sing and rejoice and delight in God, as misers do in gold, and Kings in sceptres, you never enjoy the world. . . . You never enjoy the World aright, till you see all things in it so perfectly yours, that you cannot desire them any other way: and till you are convinced that all things serve

---

Written 1593, Surtees Society 107 (Durham: Andrewes and Co., 1903), ix, xiii, xix, 163, 233.

[32] Robert C. Gregg, ed., Athanasius, "The Life of Moses," in *Athanasius, The Life of Moses and The Letter to Marcellinus* (London: SPCK, 1980), 68.

[33] Thomas Traherne, *Centuries* (London: Mowbray, 1975), no. 10:6.

you best in their proper places. For can you desire to
enjoy anything a better way than in God's Image?[34]

However, such references are perhaps more a development
and reflection on a reasonably common thread of Christianity,
that "the heavens proclaim the glory of God" (Ps 8). Thus
William Law (1686–1761): "all that is sweet, delightful, and
amiable in this world, in the serenity of the air, the fineness
of seasons, the joy of light, the melody of sounds, the beauty
of colours, the fragrancy of smells, the splendour of precious
stones, is nothing else but Heaven breaking through the veil
of this world, manifesting itself in such a degree and darting
forth in such variety."[35]

For the purposes of this essay, William Law is even more
important than the foregoing for articulating an explicit debt
of gratitude for the monastic tradition. Coming as he did in an
atmosphere less fraught than that dominated by Puritans, he
breathed some of the more tolerant air of the "Age of Reason,"
though not without some very strongly held views. Educated
at Emmanuel College, Cambridge, he became a fellow of the
college, but on the accession of George I (1714), he declined to
take the Oath of Allegiance, being convinced that the Stuarts
were the legitimate sovereigns. He joined the Nonjurors and
spent the greater part of his life as chaplain and spiritual guide
to two wealthy ladies at Kings Cliffe, Northants. He organized
schools and charitable works and spent his life in great simplicity. His major work was titled *A Serious Call to a Devout and Holy
Life*, first published in 1729. Quoting Eusebius, the early church
historian, he admitted the value of monastic life, saying that
those who live that life should not be criticized unreasonably:

[34] Traherne, *Centuries*, nos. 29, 38:14, 18.
[35] Stephen Hobhouse, ed., *Selected Mystical Writings of William Law*
(London: C. W. Daniel Co., Ltd., 1938), 44.

> If, therefore, persons of either sex . . . and desirous of
> perfection, should unite themselves into little societies,
> professing voluntary poverty, virginity, retirement,
> and devotion, living upon bare necessaries, that some
> might be relieved by their charities, and all be blessed
> with their prayers, and benefited by their example;
> or if, for want of this, they should practise the same
> manner of life, in as high a degree as they could by
> themselves; such persons would be so far from being
> chargeable with any superstition, or blind devotion,
> that they might be justly said to restore that piety,
> which was the boast and glory of the Church, when
> its greatest saints were alive.[36]

William Law, like the generality of Nonjurors, tended to see things relating to the Catholic past in a much more benign light than did the generality of Anglicans in these centuries. But his admiration for things monastic did not go so far as to seek to reestablish religious communities, as was to happen under the influence of the nineteenth-century Oxford Movement. Yet terms like *monk, monastery, cloister*, and *rule* frequently enter his discourse. He saw the value of the regular life as a practical lesson for all devout Christians. He begins his lengthy tome with the simple assertion, "Devotion is neither private nor public prayer; but prayers, whether private or public, are particular parts or instances of devotion."[37] Here is no mere legalistic approach to a series of religious practices but what Rowan Williams referred to as "a balanced pattern of labour and prayer in which every moment spoke of human dignity

[36] William Law, *A Serious Call to a Devout and Holy Life—The Spirit of Love*, ed. Paul G. Stanford, Classics of Western Spirituality (London: SPCK, 1978), 131.
[37] Law, *A Serious Call*, 47.

fully realised in surrender to a loving God."[38] At times, doubt-less, William Law can be overly severe, but he does speak with moving conviction of the primacy of love for others, addressed to his likely readers, the rich and powerful: "If there be noth-ing so glorious as doing good, if there is nothing that makes us so like to God, then nothing can be so glorious in the use of our money, as to use it all in works of love and goodness, making ourselves friends, and fathers, and benefactors, to all our fellow-creatures, imitating the Divine love, and turning all our power into acts of generosity, care, and kindness to such as are in need of it."[39]

Such an attitude requires one to be regularly open to the Spirit of Love. Law does not recommend any particular form of office, such as Cosin had so carefully organized, but he does recommend prayer at nine in the morning, noon, and three in the afternoon as well as morning and evening prayers and those "at bed-time."[40] Yet here again, this is no mere legalism, nor the performance of specific tasks. Law clearly recognizes that one's duties in life may demand work at these hours, and not times of prayer. One must do whatever one can do in the circumstances: "this method of devotion is not pressed upon any sort of people, as absolutely necessary, but recommended to all people, as the best, the happiest, and most perfect way of life."[41] This recommendation is, in effect, the old canonical hours of the monastic office but in an approach adaptable to people of all walks of life. One senses that Kings Cliffe had its own school of the Lord's service.

[38] 2015. http://rowanwilliams.archbishopofcanterbury.org/articles.php/945/the-visit-of-archbishop-rowan-williams-and-pope-benedict-xvi-to-westminster-abbey-for-evening-prayer, accessed Tuesday, Nov. 17, 2015.
[39] Law, *A Serious Call*, 97.
[40] Law, *A Serious Call*, 225–79, 280–315, 316–27, 328–39, 339–40.
[41] Law, *A Serious Call*, 280.

In his address of welcome to Benedict XVI, Rowan Williams referred to the Benedictine legacy as "a sure foundation . . . for an entire culture in which productive work and contemplative silence and receptivity . . . were both honoured."[42] It might well be argued that the humane and balanced approach of William Law exhibits those characteristics in a marked degree. So much rests on a realistic and healthy realization of one's role in the scheme of things. Such a basic Christian realism is traditionally termed "humility": "Humility does not consist in having a worse opinion of ourselves than we deserve, or in abasing ourselves lower than we really are; but as all virtue is founded in truth."[43] Indeed Law suggests humility as a suitable theme for the third hour each day because "an humble state of soul is the very state of religion, because humility is the life and soul of piety, the foundation and support of every virtue and good work, the best guard and security of all holy affections; I shall recommend humility to you, as highly proper to be made the constant subject of your devotions."[44] And this attitude comes to its full flowering in a real connection between prayer and dealings with other human beings. Our relationship to God in a life of regular prayer is productive of a truly humane and loving attitude toward others. Law casts this understanding in terms that would do justice to the best of monastic humanists. The Christian love he envisages is a truly humane and courteous virtue indeed:

> If therefore you should always change and alter your
> intercessions, according as the needs and necessities

---

[42] 2015, http://rowanwilliams.archbishopofcanterbury.org/articles.php/945/the-visit-of-archbishop-rowan-williams-and-pope-benedict-xvi-to-westminster-abbey-for-evening-prayer, accessed Tuesday, Nov. 17, 2015.
[43] Law, *A Serious Call*, 229.
[44] Law, *A Serious Call*, 228.

of your neighbours or acquaintance seem to require; beseeching God to deliver them from such or such particular evils, or to grant them this or that particular gift, or blessing; such intercessions, besides the great charity of them, would have a mighty effect upon your own heart, as disposing you to every other good office, and to the exercise of every other virtue towards such persons, as have so often a place in your prayers.This would make it pleasant to you to be courteous, civil, and condescending to all about you; and make you unable to say or do a rude or hard thing to those, for whom you had used yourself to be so kind and compassionate in your prayers.

For there is nothing that makes us love a man so much as praying for him; and when you can once do this sincerely for any man, you have fitted your soul for the performance of everything that is kind and civil towards him. This will fill your heart with a generosity and tenderness, that will give you a better and sweeter behaviour than anything that is called fine breeding and good manners.[45]

Law sees this process as being grounded and fostered in an atmosphere of temperate and disciplined language: "Let truth and plainness therefore be the only ornament of your language."[46] Indeed the gift of the Holy Spirit in the believer must be given "peace in solitude."[47] As Law insists, this silence and solitude are necessary aspects of growth in the Spirit: "The spiritual life is nothing else but the working of the spirit of God within us, and therefore our own silence must be a great part of our preparation for it, and much speaking or delight in it will be often [a great] hindrance of that good which we

[45] Law, *A Serious Call*, 302.
[46] Law, *A Serious Call*, 258.
[47] Law, *A Serious Call*, 91.

can only have from hearing what the spirit and voice of God speaks within us."[48] William Law's very civilized Christian approach was worked out in the narrow confines of a remote manor house and its surrounding society. In chapter 7 of *A Serious Call*, Law discusses the imprudent use of an estate that corrupts the Christian heart, whereas in the next chapter he shows how a "wise and pious use of an estate naturally carries us to great perfection in all the virtues of the Christian life."[49] Given that in the eighteenth century one's "estate" still generally meant a rural-based society, we can find echoes of life on a great monastic estate. It was in such a rural setting and society that Law spent the greater part of his life, a practical example of stability, surely. Can Law's life and example be a continuing inspiration to those who would seek to translate monastery into marketplace and still find there the *pax* that should mark the life of those who seek to follow Saint Benedict in the world? One can only point to the example of numerous authors such as Esther de Waal and Kathleen Norris. The simple monastic life of regularity, balance, and a sense of service can give the individual Christian a practical framework of growth in what often seems like the jungle of modern life.

William Law had died before the birth of both William Wordsworth (1770–1850), who was to be enthralled by the enchanting ruins of Tintern Abbey, and Walter Scott (1771–1832), whose medieval-style home, Abbotsford, was named after the ford over the Tweed River used by the abbot of the nearby Melrose Abbey. Such allusions are among the first dawning of the Romantic Movement, which was later to make such associations commonplace. But the Movement was to have its

---

[48] "Sayings of William Law," http://sozein.org.uk/Pdf/Lawfold.pdf, accessed Dec. 6, 2015.

[49] William Law, *A Serious Call*, 111–20.

full impact when people realized the destructions wrought by the French Revolution. This fact is succinctly summed up by historian Christopher Dawson:

> [The French] Revolution, which was the child of the Enlightenment [or "The Age of Reason"], also proved to be its destroyer. The philosophic rationalism of the eighteenth century was the product of a highly civilized and privileged society which was swept away by the catastrophe of the *ancien régime*. In the salons of Madame de Pompadour, Madame du Deffand, or Madame Geoffrin, it was easy to believe that Christianity was an exploded superstition which no reasonable man could take seriously. But the same men and women felt very differently when the brilliant society that had worshipped at the shrine of Voltaire was decimated by the guillotine and scattered to the four winds. Many of them, like Chateaubriand, recovered their faith in Christianity by the stress of personal suffering and bereavement, but even those who did not recover their faith in God, lost that faith in man and in the law of progress that had been characteristic of the previous age. Rationalism flourishes best in a prosperous age and a sheltered society; it finds few adherents among the unfortunate and the defeated.[50]

The nineteenth-century Romantic Movement provided the immediate context for the resurgence of the catholic tradition in the Church of England and in so many ways was intertwined with the catholic renewal after the Revolution. John Henry Newman was clear in his *Apologia* about the debt owed to such authors: "First I mentioned the literary influence of Walter Scott, who turned men's minds in the direction of the middle

[50] Christopher Dawson, *The Gods of Revolution* (London: Sidgwick & Jackson, 1972), 118.

ages."[51] But the evident impact of that movement in stressing elements of catholic continuity in the Church of England should not diminish one's respect and admiration for those who valiantly, and at times courageously, kept alive memories of earlier times. The question remains: Can these few authors we have discussed have any role in shaping the twenty-first century? Given that this is a time that is not noted for its religious sense and is one in which (at least in the Christian West) no charismatic figure seems to be a Bernard-like leader, carrying large numbers to novitiate doors, the average Christian can still be instructed, encouraged, and brought close to God and others by a prayerful use of these old writers so obviously influenced by the monastic tradition. If some of them have enriched a Newman in the nineteenth century and a Simone Weil in the twentieth, they may serve a purpose still. While the dust storm of secularism may cloud much that is good in the tradition, their message may quietly survive and nurture many until called forth by another spring. May their words live on.

[51] John Henry Newman, *Apologia Pro Vita Sua: Being a History of his Religious Opinions*, ed. Martin J. Svaglic (Oxford: Clarendon Press, 1967), 94.

Chapter 13

Cloister and Community

Katharine Massam

Concepts of place have a resonant history within monasticism. Touchstones of monastic life often have a spatial dimension: stability and pilgrimage, boundaries and hospitality, even the balance of solitude and corporate life. Paying attention to the way monasticism is lived, in and across spaces, enlivens our understanding of the values that inform it. As Philip Sheldrake has suggested for monasteries in general, the cloister in particular is what Foucault might have called a *heterotopia*: one real location that represents several different sites at once.[1] Balanced by controlled entry between isolation and accessibility, a *heterotopia* throws other locations into relief and challenges definitions of normal. Foucault had in mind museums, libraries, and Japanese gardens representing a cosmos within themselves, but for the medieval world the cloister also stood at the heart of the monastic commitment and, on at least one reading, *was* that heart.

This essay outlines the development of the medieval cloister as an architectural form, for nuns as well as monks. Acknowledging the "spatial turn" in the humanities more broadly, I explore the "cloister" as part of the paradox in Christianity where any particular location is potentially both a place of encounter with God and a liminal boundary between "here"

---

[1] Michel Foucault, "Of Other Spaces" (1967), cited in Philip Sheldrake, "The Practice of Place: Monasteries and Utopia," ABR 53 (2002): 10, n. 18.

and the "beyond" of discipleship.[2] In tracing concerns to set aside the space and also to protect and control it, I argue that the cloister was not only a real and specific location but also a space that carried allusions beyond itself. The cloister reflected choices within the monastery and also became a resource for those choices and a value in monastic life.

The monastic cloister echoed with meaning in the Middle Ages. It continues to resound with significance today, not only in religious communities that maintain a physical cloister, but also beyond them. As political responses to the refugee crisis of the twenty-first century falter and churches in Australia revive the ancient pledge of "sanctuary" in the face of threat,[3] the cloister remains potent as both a haven and a source of faithful discipleship.

Place, Space, and Values

As the British theologian Timothy Gorringe observes, "to be human is to be placed."[4] Bodies take up space, being a person involves "being there,"[5] and building shelter is an intensely

[2] Key resources include Philip Sheldrake, *Spaces for the Sacred: Place, Memory and Identity* (Baltimore, MD: Johns Hopkins University Press, 2001); Belden C. Lane, *Landscapes of the Sacred: Geography and Narrative in American Spirituality* (New York: Paulist Press, 1998); Yi-Fu Tuan, *Space and Place: The Perspective of Experience* (Minneapolis, MN: University of Minnesota Press, 1977).

[3] Justin Glynn, "Offers of Sanctuary Brighten Australia's Refugee Dark Age," *Eureka Street* 26 (2), http://www.eurekastreet.com.au/article.aspx?aeid=45954#.V0Y2W2Y3JFU, accessed May 25, 2016; Peter Catt, "Why I Offered Sanctuary to Asylum Seekers," *The Melbourne Anglican*, March 23, 2016, http://tma.melbourneanglican.org.au/opinion/sanctuary-peter-catt-230316, accessed May 25, 2016.

[4] Timothy J. Gorringe, *A Theology of the Built Environment: Justice, Empowerment, Redemption* (Cambridge: Cambridge University Press, 2002), 1.

[5] Phillip Sheldrake, *Spaces for the Sacred*, 7, draws on Martin Heidegger to elaborate this point. See Heidegger, "An Ontological Consideration of Place," *The Question of Being* (New York: Twayne Publishers, 1958), 26.

human activity. For the Roman architect and engineer Vitruvius (d. 15 CE), writing in the first century BCE, humanity became itself by building, and the geometry of the human body became the geometry of classical architecture, rediscovered by Leonardo da Vinci (1452–1519) in the Italian Renaissance and remembered now by proponents of human-scale "vernacular" town planning in Scandinavia and elsewhere.[6] When we build shelters, we build symbols.

"Bodies themselves generate spaces," argued Henri Lefebvre in 1991.[7] His pathbreaking work *The Production of Space* warned against overuse of the term *space* by linguistic philosophers who gave too little attention to the human decisions that create both intellectual and physical realities. His firm reminder of the need to bridge mental and material space, not least by attention to everyday life, pointed to market halls, porticos, sports grounds, cemeteries, houses, and basilicas as well as cloisters as places "produced by and for" the "ritualised and codified gestures" of human bodies.[8]

The monastic cloister shared a monastic language with the monks; it produced and was produced by a set of ritualized gestures (of walking, reading, praying, working).[9] Lefebvre

---

[6] Marcus Vitruvius Pollio. *The Ten Books of Architecture 2.II.i*, trans. Morris Morgan (Cambridge, MA: Harvard University Press, 1914), 38; on da Vinci, see M. J. Ostwald and John R. Moore, *Disjecta Membra: Architecture and the Loss of the Body, or, The Architect, the Serial Killer, his Victim and her Medical Examiner* (Sydney: Archadia Press, 1998); on contemporary theology and architecture, see Seppo Kjellberg, *Urban Ecotheology* (Utrecht: International Books, 2000), 26; all of these cite Gorringe, *Built Environment*, 1–11, who promotes "vernacular" architecture as the ethical way forward.

[7] Henri Lefebvre, *The Production of Space*, trans. Donald Nicholson-Smith (Oxford: Blackwell, 1991), 216.

[8] Lefebvre, *The Production of Space*, 3–7, accuses Foucault, Chomsky, J. M. Rey, Kristeva, Derrida, and Barthes of disregarding the gap between mental and physical or social space.

[9] Lefebvre, *Production of Space*, 216–17.

sees it as "a grand creation" in which signs and symbols give physical expression to a worldview, "mooring a mental space . . . to the earth"[10] and sustaining practices of that flow from that mental space:

> Here, then is a space in which a life balanced between the contemplation of the self in its finiteness and that of a transcendent infinity may experience a happiness composed of quietude and a fully accepted lack of fulfilment. As a space for contemplatives, a place of promenade and assembly, the cloister connects a finite and determinate locality—socially particularized but not unduly restricted as to use, albeit definitely controlled by an order or rule—to a theology of the infinite. Columns, capitals, sculptures—these are semantic differentials which mark off the route followed (and laid down) by the steps of the monks during their time of (contemplative) recreation.[11]

It is a simple enough point, that the environment shapes and reflects meaning, but the code is not an end in itself; rather, "it reproduces itself within those who *use* the space in question, within their lived experience."[12]

Mircea Eliade's concept of a sacred location as an *axis mundi*, a metaphorical center of the world separated from secular surrounds but linking earth to heaven, opened up discussion of place as a dynamic and a variable in spiritual encounter. With Edith and Victor Turner, who drew on the *axis mundi* to explore what they called the *communitas* of individuals formed by their experience of a site or a pilgrimage to it, Eliade implied that such sites were both universal and carried a single

[10] Lefebvre, *Production of Space*, 217.
[11] Lefebvre, *Production of Space*, 217.
[12] Lefebvre, *Production of Space*, 137.

meaning.[13] As social geographers and cultural historians as well as theologians have engaged with the experience of space and place, the many interpretations of a location and the idea of single readings have been overtaken by attention to the multiple meanings potentially embedded in a single site and to the political contest that validates some readings over others.[14] Place is multidimensional, and Christian theology can explore it fruitfully.

Traditionally Christian thinkers have paid more attention to time in relation to God than to place, but both are similarly complex. The distinction between the regular tick of *chronos* and the elastic experience of *kairos* as moments of revelation unfold is relatively well known. There is a parallel distinction to be made in relation to concepts of place captured in the Greek terms *topos* and *khora*. On the one hand there is the map, the topography of location, and on the other there is the site of encounter, the "interval" between the locations or the notes on a musical score.[15] For Christians attention to the particularity of the experience of a single place of revelation is in paradoxical tension with the reality of God, who cannot be confined to local sites. There is both place, the experience of being on "holy ground," and placelessness, of moving toward what is to come. There is both the incarnation and the empty tomb of Jesus Christ, who has gone ahead to Galilee. Christianity holds that the particular is the doorway to the universal, the beyond.

---

[13] Mircea Eliade, *The Sacred and the Profane* (New York: Harcourt Brace, 1959); Victor Turner and Edith Turner, *Image and Pilgrimage in Christian Culture: Anthropological Perspectives* (Oxford: Blackwell, 1978). See also the discussion in Sheldrake, *Spaces*, 5.

[14] Sheldrake, *Spaces*, 6 n. 13.

[15] See also Katharine Massam, "Creating Space Between: Women and Mission in Oceania," in *Explorations in Practical Theology: Bridging the Divide Between Faith, Theology and Life: The Church in Oceania*, ed. Antony Maher (Adelaide: Australian Theological Forum, 2015), 123–33, http://repository.divinity.edu.au/1943/.

The unique "this-ness" of God's creation calls Christian disciples to live into the reality where all things are reconciled in Christ. The boundary between "here" and "elsewhere" is the creative place of Christian faith and action.[16]

Being secure enough to engage with others and to reflect on the world fruitfully is to be "at home." In trailblazing work from 1958 Gaston Bachelard argued that we can take the pulse of the world more accurately if we understand the images of house and home that shape our experience of shelter.[17] Coining the term *anthropocosmic*, he sought to pay attention to what he called the "poetics of space." Out of a background in the philosophy of science, he was interested not so much in the description of houses or other inhabited spaces, but in what it meant to people to inhabit a place. In particular, the symbolic universe of human dwellings as a first "resting place" not only fosters definitive relationships with wider community and reality itself at its farthest horizon but also provides a key for reading them. As the political historian Hugh Stretton would remark of Australian suburban houses in the 1970s, they deserved focused attention because "above all, people are produced there and endowed there with the values and capacities which will determine most of the quality of their social life and government away from home."[18]

Contrasting his work as a phenomenologist with other rather more scientific approaches, Bachelard insisted that we could read inhabited spaces for the "germ of well-being" they enclose. He defined that well-being as essentially the capacity to dream, to be protected enough to slip into reverie. This shelter and safety that is the essence of a "home" for human

---

[16] Sheldrake, *Spaces*, 22–32.

[17] Gaston Bachelard, *The Poetics of Space* (1958; Boston: Beacon Press, 1994).

[18] Hugh Stretton, *Capitalism, Socialism and the Environment* (Cambridge and Melbourne: Cambridge University Press, 1976), 183.

beings also affirms the need to be sheltered, and constitutes a fundamental experience of the "non-I" that protects the "I." Bachelard's terminology invites comparison with Martin Buber's emphasis on the I-Thou relationship of humanity with God. The implicit parallel between a literal home, as the place that protects our capacity to dream and to integrate experience, and God, as the home who protects our capacity to hope and locates our deepest and most daring dreaming, is rich.

Home, sanctuary, and any kind of shelter in which to dream are increasingly contested and luxurious realities. Refugee camps and detention centers are chilling examples of non-places, or "de-territorialized" sites. Like other much more benign instances (airports, freeways, supermarkets, and digital screens), they affirm function above all. The French anthropologist Marc Augé has pointed to the increasingly pervasive experience of non-places in contemporary cities, experienced as "both everywhere and nowhere."[19]

In contrast, places are specific. They both result from and sustain community, they are interwoven with personal and collective identity and history, they draw forth commitment and aspiration.[20] Like the spiritual geography that is *Dakota* for the American writer Kathleen Norris, places enable us to "wrestle my story out of the circumstances of landscape and inheritance."[21] Like the cloister embedded with meaning to connect with the community's history and hope, places create relationships and focus energy.

---

[19] Marc Augé, *Non-places: Introduction to an Anthropology of Supermodernity* (London: Verso, 1997), 66, cited in Sheldrake, *Spaces*, 8.

[20] Sheldrake, *Spaces*, 9 n. 22 and 12–13 n. 23.

[21] Kathleen Norris, *Dakota* (Boston, MA: Houghton Mifflin, 1993). See also Sheldrake, *Spaces*, 15.

Cloister in the Rule of Saint Benedict

The cloister has a long monastic history as formative space set apart. The sixth-century Rule of Saint Benedict used the word *claustra* twice, both times in the classical sense of a boundary that secured a focus against distraction rather than referring to a particular feature of monastic architecture.[22] Benedict's concern to set aside space for the school of the Lord's service, and consequently to restrict access from the outside and control egress from the inside, became a priority that shaped "the most enduring feature of the monastic builders" of the Middle Ages.[23] The internal cloister, in the form of a square courtyard surrounded by covered walkways, was set apart as "a haven of peace at the heart of the monastery."[24] It was clearly part of the monastic ideal by the early ninth century[25] and became a powerful and enduring symbol of religious life in the West.[26]

We know very little about buildings in which Benedict's community lived, but the assumptions in his Rule are credited with shaping the central square cloister with a surrounding U of arcades that became characteristic of Western monasticism. In his instruction in the Rule on "Tools of Good Works," the enclosure itself (*claustra monasterii*) created an arena for seeking God. Benedict summed up his approach to monastic holiness in chapter four by observing that "The workshop [*oficina*] where we are to toil faithfully in all these tasks is the enclosure of the monastery [*claustra monasterii*] and stability in the community" (RB 4.78). The enclosure was spatial, but also closely linked to

---

[22] See RB 4:78; 67.7.

[23] Roger Stalley, *Early Medieval Architecture* (Oxford and New York: Oxford University Press, 1999), 182.

[24] Stalley, *Early Medieval Architecture,* 182.

[25] Stalley, *Early Medieval Architecture,* 185. See also Walter Horn, "On the Origins of the Medieval Cloister," *Gesta* 12 (1973): 42, 48.

[26] Horn, "On the Origins of the Medieval Cloister"; Paul Meyvaert, "The Medieval Monastic Claustrum," *Gesta* 12 (1973): 53–59.

a quality of life that was focused and productive within the boundaries. Benedict's second explicit use of *claustra*, in chapter 67.7, underlined the good effect of the boundary against disruption by provisions to punish "anyone who presumes to leave the enclosure of the monastery [*claustra monasterii*] . . . without the abbot's permission" (RB 67.7). This sense of danger outside the bounds had informed Benedict's instructions to the monastery gatekeeper in the preceding chapter, where a "wise" (*sapiens*) old monk was delegated to welcome the visitors and effectively given the role of managing potential disruption sensibly (see RB 66.1-5).

Between the guarding of the boundary and the punishment for crossing it, Benedict offered his vision in chapter 66 of a self-sufficient community that would supply all that the monks needed to seek God. Here the same concept of space set aside was implied as core to monastic practice itself without *claustra* being specified. If possible everything necessary should be within the enclosure (*intra monasterium execeantur*), so there was no need to leave the space set aside: "The monastery should, if possible, be so constructed that within it all necessities such as water, mill and garden are contained, and the various crafts are practiced. Then there will be no need for the monks to roam outside, because this is not at all good for their souls" (RB 66.6-7). Benedict also used the spatial image of enclosure against disturbances in his discussion of silence in 6.8. His focus was on establishing a permanent but internal boundary, closed to distracting chatter. Ribald and frivolous talk was to be shut out with a perpetual ban (*aeterna clausura*), so that the monk's mouth would be kept shut "like the door of an inner cloister,"[27] and the focus made possible by silence could be maintained. The allegorical development of the cloister in the Middle Ages

---

[27] Timothy Fry, *RB 1980: The Rule of St Benedict in Latin and English with Notes* 6.8 (Collegeville, MN: Liturgical Press, 1981), 191.

reflected a similar interchangeability between individuals and the monastic spaces that shaped their lives.[28]

As Paul Meyvaert observes, it is likely that Benedict's use of *claustra* influenced the word's connotations, so that a monk became a *claustris*, and *cloister* became synonymous first of all with the whole monastery and later with the central area of covered arcades.[29] Read allegorically, as in the influential account by Hugh of Fouilloy in the twelfth century, the cloister reminded alert monastics of the dimensions of contemplative life.[30] The four sides spoke of love of God, love of neighbor, contempt for self, and contempt for the world, and were each supported by pillars that evoked component attributes—such as preferring subjection and avoiding praise or fame.[31]

Archaeologists and historians interested in material culture have traced the shift from a general monastic enclosure to the development of the cloister as "a monastery within a monastery."[32] From Pachomius (292–348), who built a wall around his monastery in fourth-century Egypt,[33] through monastic buildings laid out with a cloister in fifth-century Syria[34] and the round enclosures of fifth-century Ireland,[35] monasteries have defined their ground. On the continent, early founders converted domestic

[28] Ulrike Wiethaus, "Spatial Metaphors, Textual Production, and Spirituality in the Work of Gertrude of Helfta (1256–1301/2)," in *A Place to Believe In: Locating Medieval Landscapes* (University Park, PA: Pennsylvania University Press, 2006), esp. 140–41.

[29] Meyvaert, "Medieval Monastic Claustrum," 53–54; Horn, "On the Origins of the Medieval Cloister," 34.

[30] On *De Claustro Animae* by de Fouilloy and other interpretations, see Christiania Whitehead, "Making a Cloister of the Soul in Medieval Religious Treatises," *Medium Aevum* 67 (1998): 1–29.

[31] Whitehead, "Making a Cloister of the Soul," 3.

[32] Horn, "Origins of the Medieval Cloister," 34.

[33] Horn, "Origins of the Medieval Cloister," 15–16 n. 6.

[34] Horn, "Origins of the Medieval Cloister," 21.

[35] Horn, "Origins of the Medieval Cloister," 25, 42.

villas with characteristic courtyards into monastic space,[36] but
Walter Horn sees the Benedictine mission under Charlemagne
as more important than these precedents. He argues that the
cloister is a product of the Benedictine commitment to cenobitic
life in the context of the medieval manor system:

> [Development of the cloister] was dependent, for one,
> on the rejection of the semi-eremitic forms of living
> of the Irish monks in favour of the highly controlled
> and ordered forms of communal living prescribed by
> St Benedict. It was an answer also on the other hand,
> to the need for internal architectural separation of the
> monks from the monastic serfs and workmen, who had
> entered into an economic symbiosis with the monks
> when the monastery, in the new agricultural society
> that arose north of the Alps, acquired the structure of
> the large manorial estate.[37]

The self-sufficiency of the monastic house, so prized by Benedict, required the monastery to administer its own estates and
employ its own workforce. The paradigmatic plan of St. Gall
showed the lines of tradesmen and workshops, animals, and
visitors all within the monastic gates; the separate cloister was
"the architectural solution allowing the monks to perform their
sacred task in quarters isolated from those of serfs and laymen."[38] The cloister was then particularly important as a place
of seclusion for houses that had a large resident workforce
(including lay brothers for the Cistercians), as a place of community and turning inward together for the Carthusians who
gathered there from separate cells,[39] and "houses of mercy" run

---

[36] Horn, "Origins of the Medieval Cloister," 48.

[37] Horn, "Origins of the Medieval Cloister," 48.

[38] Horn, "Origins of the Medieval Cloister," 42.

[39] Roberta Gilchrist, *Contemplation and Action: The Other Monasticism*
(London: Leicester University Press, 1995), 198, 205.

by Hospitaller groups.[40] Even the military orders retained them when they took over older houses or grouped buildings around a central space or garden,[41] while the preachers, teachers, and active groups without vows took the goal of an "interior cloister" of the heart as the model of Gospel spirituality; the form itself remained powerful as universities grew.[42] Within these variations, the paradigmatic physical cloister was a hundred feet square, to allow comfortable work but discourage gossip,[43] and became the unit of measurement especially for Cistercian sites to create a monastic "kit-home" of extraordinary aesthetic balance and serenity.[44]

The variations from the pattern have also interested historians. Cloisters in women's communities have been less closely studied until recently, but seem to be characterized by a lack of uniformity.[45] Roberta Gilchrist argued on the basis of initial British archaeology in 1994 that the communities of women were making choices in design of their houses that were different from those of men and could not be explained by their

[40] Gilchrist, *Contemplation and Action*, 19–22, 60.

[41] Gilchrist, *Contemplation and Action*, 71, 75 on preceptories, fig. 38 on earlier inherited buildings, fig. 30 on later enclosed yards.

[42] Whitehead, "Making a Cloister of the Soul," 16.

[43] Walter Horn and Ernest Born, *The Plan of St. Gall: A Study of the Architecture & Economy of, & Life in a Paradigmatic Carolingian Monastery*, California Studies in the History of Art 19 (Berkeley, Los Angeles, London: University of California Press, 1979), 246; at St Gall Monastery Plan. Codex Sangallenis 1092, http://www.stgallplan.org/horn_born/index.htm, accessed July 19, 2010.

[44] I am grateful to Colmán Ó Clabaigh, OSB, for this point in conversation, July 16, 2010.

[45] James D'Emilio, "The Royal Convent of Las Huelgas: Dynastic Politics, Religious Reform and Artistic Change in Medieval Castile," in *Studies in Cistercian Art and Architecture vol. 6: Cistercian Nuns and their World*, ed. Meredith Parsons Lillich (Kalamazoo, MI: Cistercian Publications, 2005), 6:191–282, here 217.

smaller size and relative poverty.[46] She points especially to the higher proportion of north-facing cloisters, which may have reflected a gendered connection between women and the darker colder north reflected in the positioning of saints' images, and in some cases women's seating and burial.[47] The depiction of Mary on the right hand of the Cross in the rood screens of the churches also puts her on the north, or to the "right hand" in the church itself imaged as Christ's body.[48]

Reading the Cloister as Christ

The metaphorical significance of the cloister itself was important to medieval writers, and in one unusual but telling example it was imagined as Christ's body. Gertrude of Helfta (1256–1302), who wrote of her spiritual experience from the 1280s, was a member of an observant and talented Benedictine community probably influenced in its practice by Cîteaux.[49] The secluded places of the monastery appear in Gertrude's writing as locations of spiritual experience,[50] but she skipped over better-known allegories of the cloister as the soul in contemplation[51] to read the body of Christ as the cloister in which the faithful community would live. She reported that while she was singing

---

[46] Roberta Gilchrist, *Gender and Material Culture: The Archaeology of Religious Women* (London: Routledge, 1994).

[47] Gilchrist, *Gender and Material Culture,* 133–49.

[48] Gilchrist, *Gender and Material Culture,* 135, 139–43. See also Corine Schleif, "Men on the Right—Women on the Left: (A)Symmetrical Spaces and Gendered Places," in *Women's Space: Patronage, Place, and Gender in the Medieval Church,* ed. Virginia Raguin and Sarah Stanbury (New York: State University of New York Press, 2005), 207–49.

[49] Sr. Maximilian Marnau, Introduction to *Gertrude of Helfta: the Herald of Divine Love* (New York: Paulist Press, 1993), 10.

[50] For example, *Herald* 2.3, her vision near the fish pond; 1.1, her withdrawal as a child to the "perfumed garden" and "bridal chamber"; 1.7, her turn to the "inmost chamber."

[51] See Whitehead, "Making a Cloister of the Soul."

Vespers with the community, Christ said to her, "Behold my heart; now it will be your temple. And now look among the other parts of my body and choose for yourself other places [*oficinas*] in which you can lead a monastic life, because from now on my body will be your cloister."[52] Gertrude did not know how to choose other places, protesting that she would not find rest or refreshment ("both of which are necessary in a cloister"[53]) if she left Christ's heart. Assured she could stay but should still choose other "places to have in your cloister," Gertrude chose "The Lord's feet for a hall or ambulatory; his hands for a workshop; his mouth for parlour and chapter house; his eyes for a library where she might read; and his ears for confessional."[54] The word *oficinas* for "places" in Gertrude's vision echoed the Rule of Saint Benedict and the description of enclosed corporate life. Significantly, the locations she finds in the body of Christ relate to maintaining the community (assuming that the activity of hands and eyes is for the common life). Her vision is corporate not only in image but also in what it draws her toward.[55] Rather than self-absorbed mysticism she is directed to the love of God for the service of neighbor "in Christ" that the four sides of the cloister traditionally enshrined. Gertrude tells her readers that the cloister of Christ is itself the life of service.

While a papal decree of 1298 saw "dangerous and abominable" consequences for society if nuns breached their enclosure,[56] and the cloistered life as a prison for unwanted women

[52] Gertrude of Helfta, *Herald* 3.28.
[53] Gertrude of Helfta, *Herald* 3.28.
[54] Gertrude of Helfta, *Herald* 3.28.
[55] See also E. M. W. Pedersen, "The Monastery as a Household within the Universal Household," in *Household, Women, and Christianities in Late Antiquity and the Middle Ages*, ed. Anneke B. Mulder-Bakker and Jocelyn Wogan-Browne (Turnhout: Brepols, 2005), 167–90.
[56] Elizabeth Makowski, *Canon Law and Cloistered Women: Periculoso and Its Commentators* (Washington, DC: Catholic University of America, 1997). The decree is Appendix 1, 131–36.

was a reality and a literary trope,[57] Gertrude's writing, also from the end of the thirteenth century, suggests a richer reality. She points to the dynamic that Sheldrake with Foucault holds is *heterotopia*, the microcosm that holographically holds and becomes the macrocosm. Within the ordered life of what appears to have been an extraordinary community, Gertrude moved to incorporate herself into the cloister that was Christ.

Hospitality and the Heart of Christ

Gertrude's prayerful discovery of the many locations of the cloister suggests that to withdraw to the heart of Christ is to discover a new kind of openness. As "border protection" gathers political momentum around the globe, there are vital issues here. The cloister is not for any sectarian guarding of the heart of Christ; it is to enable those who gather metaphorically or physically within its precincts to embody that heart. Australian churches taking decisions to provide sanctuary to refugees who face deportation have not only called on ancient privileges of "cloistered" space but also pointed to the scriptural tradition of "cities of refuge" within, not apart from, the civic space.[58] The resident alien in Israel was not to be sequestered, but sheltered and treated with equal justice by the law. It would be a familiar spiritual trap to confine the vision of cloister (or monasticism or faith itself) to an institutional limit when its full purpose is to unsettle norms and disrupt assumptions.[59] The whole story of the cloister includes a wider vision of reconciliation for the world.

[57] Jo Ann McNamara, *Sisters in Arms: Catholic Nuns Through Two Millennia* (Cambridge, MA: Harvard University Press, 1996), 317, 321.

[58] Sean Winter, "Sanctuary for Asylum Seekers is an Offer with an Ancient Pedigree," *The Conversation*, Feb. 5, 2016, https://theconversation.com/sanctuary-for-asylum-seekers-is-an-offer-with-ancient-pedigree-54234, accessed May 25, 2016.

[59] Sheldrake, "The Practice of Place," 12.

For Benedict, the cloister is closely related to the capacity to offer hospitality. There are checks and balances in his Rule to ensure that the focus of the permanent community is not disrupted or undermined by guests and new arrivals.[60] Both chapter 53 of the Rule, on the reception of guests, and chapter 58, on the reception of new members, assume that the surrounding structures of monastic life remain in place. From that stability, hospitality flows. The community that is secure and at home is able to reach out. Confident of their own place in the heart of Christ, they see that same Christ embodied in the guest and the newcomer. The cloister is at the heart of community as Christ is, for the community.

---

[60] John H. Smith, "*All guests who present themselves are to be welcomed as Christ* (RB 53.1): An Investigation of RB 53.1-15 and Some Thoughts on its Implications for Today," TJ 88 (2015): 23–35.

Chapter 14

Aequo animo:
With a Quiet Mind

Margaret Malone, SGS

At the end of chapter 31 of the Rule of Saint Benedict, which concerns the cellarer, Benedict uses a phrase that I consider very significant. He notes that if the community is rather large, help is to be given to the cellarer so that he may calmly perform the duties of his office (RB 31.17). The phrase translated in RB 1980 as "calmly" is *aequo animo*.[1] Terrence Kardong translates this phrase as "peacefully," and George Holzherr and Justin McCann translate it as "with a quiet mind," while Luke Dysinger has "a peaceful soul."[2] Aquinata Böckmann in her commentary on this phrase notes that Hildemar maintains that it means "quietly, with good will, patiently, with even temper and balance."[3] John Cassian speaks of patience that must be observed not by words but

---

[1] Unless otherwise indicated, all references to the Rule of St. Benedict will be taken from *RB 80: The Rule of St. Benedict*, ed. Timothy Fry (Collegeville, MN: Liturgical Press, 1981).

[2] Terrence Kardong, *Benedict's Rule: A Translation and Commentary* (Collegeville, MN: Liturgical Press, 2000), 259; George Holzherr, *The Rule of Benedict: A Guide to Christian Living* (Dublin: Four Courts Press, 1994), 175; Justin McCann, *The Rule of Saint Benedict* (London: Sheed and Ward, 1976), 39; Luke Dysinger, *The Rule of Saint Benedict: Latin and English* (California: Source Books, 1997), 85.

[3] Aquinata Böckmann, *Around the Monastic Table: Growing in Mutual Love and Service* (Collegeville, MN: Liturgical Press, 2009), 38.

by "the inner tranquility of the heart."[4] This idea of having a "quiet mind" underpins many aspects of the Rule; I would like to explore some of these connections, particularly in dialogue with Quaker spirituality.

The first thing to note is that in the context of the end of chapter 31, "Qualifications of the Monastery Cellarer," Benedict gives a reason behind the need for help to be given, so that the development of a quiet mind is possible. All must be done in due order: "Necessary items are to be requested and given at the proper times so that no one may be disquieted or distressed in the house of God" (RB 31.18-19). The emphasis on *disquieted* (*perturbetur*) is significant because one of the qualities of the cellarer at the beginning of the chapter is that he not be excitable (*turbulentus*) (v. 1). Benedict considers it important to stress that there be a quality of peace on the part of the cellarer; then it will follow that there will be peace in the community. One affects the other; this fact will be of note throughout this paper. It is obvious that this peacefulness of mind is very important to Benedict both for individuals and for the community: for all who dwell in the house of God.

We are reminded here of a text from John's gospel. In chapter 14 there is a similar context to that described above. In the same way that Benedict does not want anyone troubled in the house of God, John's mention of not having troubled hearts is followed by a message of Jesus about dwelling places in the Father's house. The chapter begins, *Do not let your hearts be troubled. Believe in God, believe also in me. In my Father's house there are many dwelling places* (John 14:1-2). This idea is repeated in another place in this gospel: *Peace I leave with you; my peace I give to you. I do not give as the world gives. Do not let your hearts be troubled and do not let them be afraid. You heard me say to you*

---

[4] *Conferences* 16.XXII.3; Boniface Ramsay, *John Cassian: The Conferences* (New York: Paulist Press, 1997), 571.

"I am going away and I am coming to you" (John 15:27-28). So the promise of the Father's house, which is our ultimate destination, should quiet our restless hearts in the here and now, in the house of God. We need to find ways of living peacefully, that is, with a quiet mind and a peaceful heart, conscious of our goal—the dwelling places in the Father's house.

There are also many connections to this idea of a quiet mind in the psalms, and a verse in Psalm 116 in particular stands out. In the NRSV translation it reads, *Return, O my soul to your rest, for the Lord has dealt bountifully with you* (Ps 116:7). The ICEL translation has, *Rest once more my heart, for you know the Lord's love.* The Lord's goodness in the present, and knowledge of God's love, are certainly steps toward a peaceful heart and a quiet mind.

It is worth making a connection with the Quaker tradition at this point. A clear description of this quietness of mind is given by Daniel Seeger: "This inner silence consists of a gentle releasing, a letting go of mental movies, of preoccupation with events of yesterday, of plans for the next steps to take on an important project at work, of all inward thoughts and desires, cravings and dislikes, erratic thoughts and inner conversations. By releasing such transient concerns we begin to make a space within ourselves where universal and eternal things can be heard. Inner silence has the quality of alert listening."[5]

Dependence on God

Benedict often notes that we are to be secure in our dependence on God. Certainty of God's never-failing help is a sure way of maintaining peace in our minds and hearts. Christ is the one on whom we can dash our evil thoughts (RB Prol.28). It is by God's grace that we are what we are, and those who

[5] Daniel Seeger, *The Mystical Path: Pilgrimage to the One Who Is Always Here* (Millboro, VA: Quaker Universalist Fellowship, 2002), 19.

boast should make their boast in the Lord (RB Prol.31-32). At all times we ask the Lord to supply, by the help of his grace, what is not possible to us by nature (RB Prol.41). We are never to lose hope in God's mercy (RB 4.74); in difficult times we are to rely on the Lord (RB 7.37), and in all this we overcome the difficulties of life "*because of him who so greatly loved us*" (RB 7.39). We even need God's help to do our duties of service, so the monks ask for help at the beginning of their time of kitchen service, and at the end of it they thank God who has helped and comforted them (RB 35.16-17).

At the time of profession the monk knew he needed God's help and prayed, "*Receive me, Lord, as you have promised and I shall live; do not disappoint me in my hope*" (RB 58.21). Then, throughout the journey, the monks were to keep Benedict's little rule with Christ's help (RB 73.8). Finally when they set out to reach "the loftier summits of teaching and virtue," this journey was always under God's protection (RB 73.9). How else but with God's help are we to follow the advice of the fourth step of humility, "that in this obedience under difficult, unfavorable or even unjust conditions, his heart quietly [patiently] embraces suffering and endures it without weakening or seeking escape" (RB 7.35)? Kardong notes that a more literal translation might read, "One embraces patience quietly in the heart." He also notes that the root of the text is from the fourth sign of humility in the *Institutes* of John Cassian: "If he maintains in everything obedience and gentleness and constant patience."[6] All the invitations in these texts call us to the development of a quiet mind.

This profound belief in the help of God at all stages of life is no doubt a way to ensure that our minds are not disquieted or distressed even in difficulties or hardships. With this attitude there is peace of mind and restfulness of heart. It is the kind

[6] Inst 4.39, cited from Kardong, *Benedict's Rule*, 147.

of peace that is expressed in the Psalms: *But I have calmed and quieted my soul like a weaned child with its mother* (Ps 131:2). In relation to this stance, George Fox, the seventeenth-century founder of the Quaker tradition, wrote the following: "Friend, Be still and cool in your own mind and spirit from your own thoughts, and then you will feel the principle of God to turn your mind to the Lord God, from whom life comes; whereby you may receive his strength and power to allay all blusterings, storms, and tempests. That it is which works up into patience, into innocence, into soberness, into stillness, into quietness, up to God with his power."[7]

One way to maintain our awareness that God is always with us is by living with an attitude of mindfulness. In the first step of humility we are exhorted to keep the fear of God always before our eyes, never to forget it, and constantly to remember all God's commandments (RB 7.10-30). Thus we will live always in God's presence. This is the attitude of those who are impelled by love (RB 5.10). It is also the reason for Benedict's frequent reference to the word *vacare* in chapter 48 of the Rule, "The Daily Manual Labor." The word is used eight times in this chapter in relation to prayerful reading. One has to be free for and empty of what would disturb such prayerful reading. Kardong has an interesting comment on this: "While one can admit that *lectio* demands concentration and effort, it is not just another labor, but rather something akin to contemplation. Thus it is in the class of leisure: something that has meaning but no purpose."[8] So we are reminded of the connection between this lack of disturbance and the awareness of God, gathering ourselves to be in the presence of God, growing in mindfulness of God. As Seeger reminds us, "One who practices inner silence

---

[7] George Fox, "A Message of Comfort to the Troubled Soul," from *The Letters of George Fox*, 1658, http://www.hallvworthington.com/George_Fox_Selections/foxtroubled.html; accessed Sept. 29, 2015.

[8] Kardong, *Benedict's Rule*, 386.

has the quality of being thoroughly present here and now."[9] All this we need as preparation for prayerful reading, and a corresponding outcome is a deepening of such mindfulness and a path to a peaceful mind, or, as Mary Margaret Funk describes it, "The unspeakable joy of simply resting in God."[10] In the William Penn Lecture of 1942, Kenneth Boulding expresses this idea well: "There is a quiet, open place in the depths of the mind, to which we can go many times in the day and lift up our soul in praise, thankfulness and conscious unity. With practise this God-ward turn of the mind becomes an almost constant direction, underlying all our other activities. As a compass swings towards the north immediately after each disturbance, so we swing towards the Pole that draws the life of our being the moment a temporary distraction is removed."[11]

Qualities of Community Members

As was already noted above, one of the qualities the cellarer in the Rule is to possess is a quiet mind. He is to be *non turbulentus*. This is expressed as "not excitable" in the *RB 1980* translation and even more strongly worded in Kardong's translation as "not violent."[12] The cellerer is also to be temperate and well disciplined, *sobrius* (RB 31.1). But he is not the only one who must be like this. The abbot is also to be temperate (RB 64.9), not excitable or anxious (RB 64.9), and as Kardong's translation reads, "He should not be restless and troubled, not extreme and headstrong, not jealous or oversuspicious for then he will have no peace" (RB 64.16). As such the abbot is "not to

[9] Seeger, "The Mystical Path," 20.

[10] Mary Margaret Funk, *Thoughts Matter: The Practice of the Spiritual Life* (New York: Continuum, 1999), 17.

[11] Kenneth Boulding, "The Practice of the Love of God," *William Penn Lecture, 1942,* http://www.quaker.org/pamphlets/wpl1942a.html, accessed Feb. 5, 2017.

[12] Kardong, *Benedict's Rule,* 259.

disturb the flock entrusted to him nor make any unjust arrangements as though he had the power to do whatever he wished" (RB 63.2).

It is obvious that Benedict connects the quiet mind, or lack of it, in the abbot with the prevailing atmosphere in the community. Thus the abbot's "goal must be profit for the monks, not pre-eminence for himself" (RB 64.8). He is also to show mercy, as it is more important than judgment (RB 64.10). Extremes are to be avoided: the vessel is not to be broken by excessive effort: the bruised reed is not to be crushed (RB 64.10-14). Even when he must deal with faults, "prudence and love" are to be the characteristics that he displays, and these will ensure peace in the individual and in the community (RB 64.14). The abbot himself, having acted in this way, will also rest secure and peacefully in the knowledge that he has done his best (RB 64.21; 2.8-9). Whatever is done in the community is to be done so that the community is not upset and the humanity of all is maintained.[13]

Benedict seems to see the position of the prior as a threat to community peace, so he states, "For the preservation of peace and love we have, therefore, judged it best for the abbot to make all decisions in the conduct of the monastery" (RB 65.11). He also notes that if the running of the monastery is maintained via deans, and with the abbot's direction, "no one individual will yield to pride" (RB 65.12-13). Indeed, so important is the community's peace that if the prior is not "a peaceful and obedient member of the community" himself, he is to be expelled (RB 65.21).

It seems significant for the peace of the community that when guests are welcomed the community is to pray and be "united in peace" and that "prayer must always precede the kiss of peace because of the delusions of the devil" (RB 53.4-5).

---

[13] So, for example, the fast can be mitigated if the summer heat is too oppressive (RB 41.1).

Visiting monks are to be content with the life as they find it and "not make excessive demands that upset the life of the monastery" (RB 61.2).

Order in the Community

Benedict believes strongly in due order in the community, perhaps precisely because he sees order as a way of maintaining peace. Just as a quiet mind in an individual member can work toward peace in the community, so too ordered arrangements can help toward the peace of individuals and hence of the community. In this present age, we may have reservations about the apparent hierarchical structure expressed in chapter 63 of Benedict's Rule, which concerns community rank. However, Benedict is making an important point here. Rank does not depend on wealth or influence or age but on date of entry into the community. This is the first criterion. The other criteria for ranking are virtue and the decision of the abbot. It is in this context that he places the prescription already mentioned, that is, "the abbot is not to disturb [conturbet] the flock entrusted to him nor make any unjust arrangements as though he had power to do whatever he wished" (RB 63.2).

For Benedict, the concern that due process be maintained is clear in chapter 65, on the prior. There is a process to be followed in relation to this appointment. Although Benedict has reservations about the position of the prior, he does suggest a process for the appointment that contains great wisdom: "But if local conditions call for it, or the community makes a reasonable and humble request, and the abbot judges it best, then let him, with the advice of God-fearing brothers, choose the man he wants and himself make him his prior" (RB 65.14-15). The prior then is to carry out his duties respectfully and not in any way that is disruptive of the community's peace.

There are similarities in this process to that which occurs when the brothers are called to counsel about important decisions to be made; this is obviously a process that helps maintain peace. In chapter 3, "On Summoning the Brothers to Counsel," a careful and ordered process is laid out. The abbot calls the community together, explains the business, hears the advice of the brothers, and then only after pondering this advice will he do "what he judges the wiser course" (RB 3.2). Throughout this chapter there is a sense that there is great care being taken to use due process, including prescriptions about how the community members are to express their opinions and, in the end, how they are to accept the decision that the abbot eventually makes. Additionally, there is a description of the integrity with which the abbot ponders the advice and arrives at a decision with "foresight and fairness" (RB 3.4-6). If community members know that real listening and careful consideration have taken place, the peace of individuals and the community as a whole will not be disturbed.

Benedict describes another wise process when a brother is asked to do something that seems impossible. First he is to accept what is asked. But if this proves to be too much for his strength, he must choose the right moment to express his concern. As in chapter 3, there are ways that this is to be achieved. It will always be done "without pride, obstinacy, or refusal" (RB 68.1-3). If the abbot still requires that the task be undertaken, the brother is to accept it and with trust in God fulfill what is asked of him (v. 5). History has many examples when what is asked of someone seems outside the capabilities of the person. However, if obedience asks this and due process is followed, such a one often discovers that it is possible to be stretched and to carry out things that one thought were not possible.

There is also an ordered process in handling things when monks fail in living out the prescriptions of the Rule (RB 23-28). There are two warnings, then a public rebuke, and, if this does not bring about the required conversion, exclusion from the community ensues in order to give the erring monk time to reflect (RB 23.2-4). He is supported by visits from mature and wise brothers lest his equanimity be disturbed by "excessive sorrow" (RB 27.2-3). The procedure includes a series of efforts to lead him to repent of his failings: encouragement, Scripture, and the prayers of the brothers. If these processes do not work, then the final judgment is made, where "amputation" is considered the only course of action (RB 28).

Details of the return to the community after a monk has completed his time of exclusion also follow due process. In chapter 44, "Satisfaction by the Excommunicated," after fulfilling the various demands of the time during which he has been excluded, the monk can be readmitted to the community, but only gradually, and he can only be readmitted to the rank that the abbot assigns him. He cannot lead a psalm or reading without further instructions from the abbot. He must prostrate himself in his place as the hours of the Work of God are completed. And then finally, at a word from the abbot, this punishment may cease, so he will be at rest (*ut quiescat*) (RB 44.5-8). All of this course of action would indicate a true understanding of the fact that reconciliation is a process that can only come about in stages, and that if this procedure is adhered to, there will be a peaceful resolution.

Peace Disturbed

Benedict was a realist and knew that the peace of both individuals and the community could be disturbed at times, no matter what processes were set in place to avoid it. The Rule enumerates many possible faults, and Benedict seems to identify them as things that will disturb the community or the individual member. For example, the faults listed in chapter 46, "while working in the kitchen, in the storeroom, in serving, in the bakery, in the garden, in any craft or anywhere else—either by breaking or losing something or failing in any other way in any other place" (RB 46.1-2), are corrected so that the peace of the community does not continue to be disturbed. Individual failings are thus seen to impinge on community peace, as are the failings listed in the beginning of chapter 23: stubbornness, disobedience, pride, grumbling, defiance of the Rule, and the orders of the seniors. These too require correction.

At this point, I would like to place an emphasis on three things that stem from a lack of peace of mind in the individual and that have ramifications for community peace: the vice of private ownership, murmuring, and lack of reconciliation.

1. Private Ownership

Private ownership, which is about not relying on the leader of the monastery for one's needs, is strongly condemned in the Rule. In chapter 33, private ownership is called a "most evil practice," and there is a strong emphasis that this vice is to be cut out from the roots (v. 1), showing how seriously Benedict considers it. For those who at their profession gave up "the free disposal even of their bodies and wills" (RB 58.25; 33.4), it would seem to be a great anomaly to want to possess things.

Meg Funk traces how thoughts about possessions can grow and grow and finally possess a person so that all one's efforts go into amassing even small things, so that finally "No number of things can satisfy our desire." She goes on to remind us that "a monastic's thoughts about things—whether they are material things, or 'things I must do'—need to be focussed on the single idea that God alone satisfies. As long as one's thoughts are filled with 'things' the mind is fragmented and its energy out of control."[14]

This reminds us of Mark's gospel account of the man who was apparently seeking a genuine answer to his question about

---

[14] Funk, *Thoughts Matter*, 62–63.

what he must do to inherit eternal life. He had kept all the commandments, and then Jesus, looking on him with love, said to him that there was one thing he was lacking. He must sell what he owns and give to the poor, and then he will have treasure in heaven. Then he might follow Jesus. Mark's passage ends dramatically: *When he heard this, he was shocked and went away grieving, for he had many possessions* (Mark 10:17-22). This is indeed what undue desire to own things can do. It disturbs our peace and affects or prevents the living out of our discipleship. Saint Augustine also knew this danger of private ownership. In a well-known passage from his *Confessions* he notes, "Lo, you were within, but I outside, seeking there for you, and upon the shapely things you have made I rushed headlong, I, misshapen. You were with me, but I was not with you. They held me back far from you, those things which would have no being were they not in you."[15]

Benedict emphasizes the other way in which things can completely disrupt peace of mind in chapter 34, "Distribution of Goods According to Need." The understanding that distribution is to be made according to need is a difficult challenge, perhaps often the most difficult challenge to individual and community peace. The first impulse can be to call on the right to equality, with the interpretation that what one person has is also another's right. This can happen whether it concerns the possessions of others or perceived privileges given to others. Benedict takes a different view. There is to be "consideration for weaknesses," and in these cases more may be needed. This extra need should bring about humility in the recipient, and in those who need less, gratitude for the gift of not needing more. If these attitudes are present, "all the members will be at peace" (RB 34.3-5). In any case Benedict knows that the needs

---

[15] Augustine, *The Confessions* 10.38, trans. Maria Boulding (New York: New City Press, 1997), 262.

of individuals differ with each community member and should be recognized and accepted by all.

2. Murmuring

It is in this context of particular needs that Benedict again condemns murmuring or grumbling, and this condemnation is often in regard to possessions. He insists that, "First and foremost, there must be no word or sign of the evil of grumbling, no manifestation of it for any reason at all" (RB 34.7). In one of his addresses, Rowan Williams speaks of a conversation in which the issue of the atmosphere in a community was discussed. He notes that the following question can be asked: "Is the climate in a community one of a currency of grievances or one of goodness and kindness?"[16] I think this is what Benedict is speaking about when he condemns murmuring, because he knows how destructive and corrosive murmuring can be. In relation to the different needs expressed within a community this insight is particularly relevant. It can be easy to forget the gifts one already has and develop the desire for more, and this desire leads to murmuring, just as the Israelites murmured in the desert when they forgot the blessings of God (Exod 16:2-12).

Earlier in the Rule, Benedict also spoke of murmuring in relation to prompt obedience. Here he refers to grumbling not only aloud but also in the heart. One who murmurs in the heart certainly does not have a quiet mind (RB 5.7). A quiet mind will result if each person is content with what can be obtained locally. This point is made in reference to provision of wine but can equally apply to all circumstances (RB 40.8-9). The same thing is implied in the eighth step of humility, where a mark of humility is living by "the common rule of the monastery"

16 Rowan Williams, "God's Workshop," http://rowanwilliams .archbishopofcanterbury.org/articles.php/654/shaping-holy-lives-a -conference-on-benedictine-spirituality, accessed Sept. 29, 2015.

(RB 7.55). This requires contentment with what is available where one lives and not longing for what is better or more convenient elsewhere.

3. Lack of Reconciliation

In chapter 4 of the Rule, Benedict gives us a list of the tools for good works, or *Seventy-Four Tools for Good Living,* as in the title of Michael Casey's recent book.[17] In the address of Rowan Williams already mentioned, there is a reference to what tools mean in our ordinary life. A workman uses tools in such a way that the tools become part of him, so to speak—an extension of his hand: "the hand fitted to the wood forgetful of the join."[18] In this way, so too does the bow of a violin or cello become very much part of the musician. Williams notes that the tools are "worn smooth with long use and skillfully patched up over time."[19] The point is that Benedict's tools are to become so much a part of us that we will use them even without effort. This is particularly important in the case of differences that can occur in relationships in the community. Experience shows that if a first reaction is to try to remedy the situation immediately after a misunderstanding, or even a hurt, long-term antagonisms are cut off from the root. Otherwise anger grows, hurt deepens, and relationships are damaged.

We are warned about what can happen when the tools are not used in this internalized way. Many of the tools, expressed either negatively or positively, refer to ways of living peacefully. Conversely, without the use of these tools there is disruption of the peace in the community. So it is clear that many of the negative prescriptions refer to things that will destroy

---

[17] Michael Casey, *Seventy-Four Tools for Good Living: Reflections on the Fourth Chapter of Benedict's Rule* (Collegeville, MN: Liturgical Press, 2014).

[18] Williams, "God's Workshop."

[19] Williams, "God's Workshop."

peace of mind in the individual and often in the community. Anger, for example, nourished and expressed in aggression, is particularly destructive in this regard. Casey notes that Benedict's tool, "You are not to act in anger" (RB 4.22), might be better expressed today as, "Not to go all the way with anger."[20] Feeling the anger is not the problem; however, when it becomes an action of aggression or violence it is indeed a problem: "Anger is a passion that disturbs our equanimity and makes us feel bad: aggression is an action by which we hope to make someone else feel bad. Anger arises independently of the will; aggression comes about only with the will's consent given at the moment or prepared in advance by a habit or history of violent responses."[21]

Similar violent responses can result from other tools connected with anger in this chapter of the Rule, for example, nursing a grudge, deceit, grumbling, speaking ill of others, hatred, envy, jealousy, gossip (RB 4.22-28). All of these, if harbored and acted upon, do indeed prevent us from having a quiet mind as well as often causing divisions in a community so that people end up living with unresolved differences. What can happen then, unless reconciliation is brought about, is what Casey describes as a continuance of "long-lasting animosities," if not "underground guerrilla warfare."[22]

In one of the tools for good living, Benedict also instructs us not to give a false peace (RB 4.25). The peace toward which we must strive is not one that simply covers up underlying resentments. Williams describes what is needed for the real peace that we are to seek and pursue as "a habit of stable determination to put into the life of the body, something other than grudges."[23]

---

[20] Casey, *Seventy-Four Tools for Good Living*, 76.
[21] Casey, *Seventy-Four Tools for Good Living*, 77, 78.
[22] Casey, *Seventy-Four Tools for Good Living*, 85, 79.
[23] Williams, "God's Workshop."

This leads us to the final three tools near the end of Benedict's chapter 4 that I think need to be taken together in order to change this situation: "Pray for your enemies out of love for Christ. If you have a dispute with someone, make peace with him before the sun goes down. And finally, never lose hope in God's mercy" (RB 4.72-74). Ideally we would hope to be able to make peace before the setting of the sun, but if that is not possible there is always the recommendation to "pray for your enemies out of love for Christ." Prayer and the help of Christ can sometimes be the only thing that makes reconciliation possible in difficult situations. And finally we are "never to lose hope in God's mercy" (RB 4.74), for others and for ourselves. À propos of all this, Casey lends us wise advice:

> Peace will not happen of its own accord. It has to be created. All peacemaking begins in the head. We have to start thinking differently. First of all, I have to renounce all those violent imaginative scenarios in which I visit misfortune on those who offended me. Then I have to step back and recognize some degree of complicity in any misunderstanding that has developed. Then I need to acknowledge that any continuance of war (whether it be cold war or a more open exchange of hostilities) will be a war of attrition, which will erode the integrity of all parties, cause serious scandal, and bring impairment to the quality of life within the community. It is a no-win situation. At this point, I must begin to think about what I can do to resolve the matter peaceably and move toward reconciliation.[24]

At the very end of chapter 4, Benedict reminds us that the workshop where we learn to use these tools, and in fact do use them, is "the enclosure of the monastery and stability in the

[24] Casey, *Seventy-Four Tools for Good Living*, 242.

community," and here we toil faithfully at the task (RB 4.78). Williams confirms this when he states, "Stability requires this daily discipline of mending."[25] It is yet another reminder that what disturbs the peace of individuals in the community can also affect the peace of the community as a whole.

At the beginning of this essay I referred to the text of John's gospel, which reminds us not to let our hearts be troubled, and suggested that this relates to the question of a quiet mind. I am reminded here of a homily given by Pope Francis, at Mass on February 10, 2015. He noted that "people will not find the face of God by relaxing at home on the couch, surfing online or reading encyclopedias. Only people with a restless heart that thirsts for God will find him as they strike out on the road, taking risks and overcoming fatigue, danger, and doubt."[26] This comment would immediately call to mind the well-known passage of Augustine at the beginning of the *Confessions*: "You stir us so that praising you may bring us joy, because you have made us and drawn us to yourself, and our heart is unquiet until it rests in you" (*inquietum est cor nostrum donec requiescat in te*).[27] We may ask if there is a contradiction in the two ideas: the restless heart that thirsts for God and moves us to strike out on the road, that is, the unquiet heart that can only rest in God—and on the other hand, the need for a quiet mind. I do not believe there is a contradiction here. In fact it will only be with a quiet mind, with equanimity, which brings peace, that we are enabled to know where our true home lies in our seeking of God—the Father's house of John's gospel. It also makes it possible for us to have the strength to strike out on the road of discipleship. With a quiet mind and a peaceful heart we

[25] Williams, "God's Workshop."

[26] Pope Francis, "Homily at Santa Marta, 10 February 2015," http://en.radiovaticana.va/news/2015/02/10/pope_at_santa_marta_the_courage_of_a_restless_heart/1122532, accessed Sept. 29, 2015.

[27] Augustine, *Confessions* 1.1.4; Boulding trans., 39.

are able to live without undue disquiet in Benedict's house of God, while nonetheless responding to the call to discipleship, whatever that may entail.

We also know that the acquisition and maintenance of this quietness of mind can happen only with God's help in much the same way that Mark's gospel narrates the story of Jesus calming the storm. The New English Bible translation of this incident reads as follows: *Now he was in the stern of the boat asleep on a cushion; they roused him and said, "Master, we are sinking! Do you not care?" He awoke, rebuked the wind, and said to the sea, "Hush! Be still!" The wind dropped and there was a dead calm* (Mark 4:38-39). At the word of the Lord, the sea is still, the fear of individuals is assuaged, and then calm and quiet rests on all. Indeed, "no one is disquieted or distressed."

A Quaker poem by Geoffrey Weeden, entitled *Draw Breath,* expresses much of this biblical tradition and also expresses what it means to have a quiet mind and to grow into its full experience. It seems to sum up much of what I have been trying to express here:

> Breathe in the quiet purpose of this place;
> Through outward stillness, seek a calm within.
> Here we can find forgiveness and forgive;
> Here find the healing miracle begin.
>
> Breathe out the busy world, the teeming mind,
> The follies, fears and failures of the week;
> Breathe out contention, pettiness and pride,
> And wait in trust for "that of God" to speak.
>
> Breathe in communion, friend with quiet friend,
> Each drawing closer in this timeless hour;
> As all our different needs and gifts are drawn
> To the one source of comfort, love and power.

Breathe out at last, to God, the heart's full thanks
That we have seen this vision, known this grace;
Renewed through love, let us that love extend
Through all our daily life beyond this place.[28]

---

[28] http://www.quakerquaker.org/profiles/blogs/draw-breath-a
-poem-by-geoffrey, accessed Feb. 5, 2017.

Chapter 15

Monasticism in an Age of Transition
A European Perspective

Bernhard A. Eckerstorfer, OSB

Michael Casey is no stranger to European monasticism of today. His publications are read in refectories, his books are used in formation, his talks are handed on by individuals who find his thoughts provoking and enriching. In 2016, a prior and novice master of an Austrian monastery even went so far as to spend three months under Father Michael's guidance on the other side of the globe. Australia as a hub of monastic renewal? At least for an Austrian this seems awkward. When traveling outside of Europe, we Austrians are frequently identified as coming from the very nation where the kangaroos are at home; likewise Australians are sometimes confronted overseas with the idea of being Austrians with a strange English accent. While often confused with one another, the two countries on the opposite side of the globe do not in fact have much in common. In Europe there is hardly any awareness of Benedictine or even Trappist life in Australia, and Tarrawarra sounds like an exotic dance or a brand of an African tea rather than the name of an abbey. But when the name Michael Casey is mentioned in monastic circles, it is immediately associated with serious scholarship and a keen awareness of our time.

In a catalogue of the EOS-Verlag (St. Ottilien) listing seven of Fr. Michael's books in German, the Australian Trappist is aptly depicted as "transmitting the spiritual traditions of monasteries." Note the plural of *geistliche Traditionen* in this citation. Michael Casey is profoundly rooted in monastic traditions and able to reformulate them for our time. He does this with an erudition typical of Bernard of Clairvaux and with the comprehensible language that makes Anselm Grün so accessible. Whereas there are writers who are more widely received (like Anselm Grün, Notker Wolf, or David Steindl-Rast, to name just a few from my own surroundings), Michael Casey may be the most fruitful contemporary writer on monastic studies in the narrow sense.

This essay in honor of Michael Casey aims to consider thoughts about the transitory nature of contemporary monasticism. We can hardly capture the enormity of the changes our monasteries are undergoing currently, nor fully describe what it means for the monks and nuns of today to adapt to ever newly emerging situations. To reflect upon the present state and possible future of monasticism, we need various perspectives and a dialogue that spans the world. I do not claim to give *the* European perspective, but can only offer *a* European insight. It is not only limited geographically but also finds its limits in the writer of these lines, that is, a monk who entered monastic life in the year 2000 at the age of twenty-nine and who tries to make sense of what he himself experiences and observes in his own environment.

1. Trapped in the Past

In what condition do we find our monasteries, and what can we expect from the future? Nothing is as it used to be! The present situation is not how things were at a time when numbers flourished and monastic life and its enterprises expanded. In recent years I undertook an experiment in a variety of settings, for example, in a parish council and in a community of religious. I split the gatherings into two parts. The first group was to identify signs of deep crisis, and the second to name signs that showed how lively the parish or religious order was. The groups that were dedicated to a disastrous reading of the crisis within the church had usually twice as many entries as those groups describing signs of a healthy development. Does this not show that we are conditioned to see more the negative side than the positive in our time of transition?

What makes this experiment so interesting is especially this: The first group took into account primarily quantitative arguments, such as lower church attendance and fewer vocations. The second group, on the contrary, pointed out mostly qualitative traits, for example, the high relevance of the church in periods of personal crisis, and the spiritual competence of religious. This difference leads to the key question: Does the past have to be normative for the future?

In Austria we judge the present situation of the church and its religious orders largely with reference to the past. We regularly learn of statistics that show how rapidly our situation is changing. However, the statistics are not usually received as a mere statement about the transitional nature of our time. Rather, being often employed in an anti-religious perspective, they are used to point out that the church and its institutions are falling apart, without signs of hope. Time and again, a picture is being drawn that shapes us and that, in turn, we ourselves carry on, whereby we concentrate on the loss of numbers—fewer priests and religious, reduced church attendance, and thus fading faith in our congregations. No wonder we get depressed.

I do not deny that the figures used are right, nor do I ignore the deep change and crisis of church and religious orders in the world I come from. The drastic change can be gauged when we look at a recent development for consecrated women in Austria. In 1970 there were 13,800 as compared to 3,600 in 2015. This decline is strongest in religious houses that run hospitals and schools, whereas the few new vocations we have can mainly be found in contemplative communities. We should not be fixated on this apparent collapse, but rather challenge the underlying hermeneutics by which we judge our situation. I am convinced that we paralyze ourselves if we focus too much on falling numbers and put too much effort into explaining why things have changed.

Precisely because we are in the midst of an enormous upheaval that is drastically changing the ecclesial and monastic landscapes, we should resist the temptation to concentrate on what no longer works in the way it used to. In an insecure time such as ours, it is all too tempting to find an orientation in unquestionable statistics and an attitude that principally laments that our world is not as it once was. The concentration on numbers, to be sure, fits our time, with its domination by the natural sciences, which suggest that what count are things that we can measure. The predominance of the economy is also adopted in the prevailing outlook, that is, the perspective of church and monasteries to a great extent follows the dynamic of profit and loss.

When we ask members of a parish council, or monks and nuns of a given community, what a bright future might look like, we most likely get a picture of the past. The assumption is that "If we once more had as many vocations, ordinations, and church attendees as we used to have, then the parish or the religious institute could again . . . ." This logic of "again" shows how much we are oriented toward the past and indicates that we measure success mostly with regard to figures from of old. Therefore the word *still* is often used: "How many monks *still* live in this abbey?"

The hermeneutics of diminishment entail the implicit assumption that the future would be mastered if it could be just like the past. Of course, nobody would say this so bluntly, but it seems to be the underlying belief. And this is only natural. A community where most members are above the retirement age of the secular world is naturally inclined to take the past as the norm for the future. In other words, to a large extent we wish that a world with which we are already familiar would reemerge. In this way, the logic of *still* and *again* prevents us from discovering new ways that would lead us forward.

2. The Vice of Comparison

It is true that church and religious orders are losing ground, losing ground and moving to the fringes of society in my part of the world. But I want to draw attention to the danger of staring too much at painful losses. I pointed out that we should be cautious not to confine our attention to numbers and not too easily to compare our time with a past situation. A merely quantitative investigation of how the church and our communities develop does not capture vigorous forms of religious practice that emerge ever new. Such a narrow perspective sees success and flourishing communities only in comparison with the past. Thus we are prone to be blind to new developments in religious life.

The Catholic milieu of the 1950s in Austria, for instance, cannot be compared with an increasingly pluralist world of the twenty-first century. When one-third of my community entered the monastery (and that was in the 1950s!), 90 percent of Austrians officially belonged to the Roman Catholic Church. To grow up as an Austrian meant, to a great extent, to be automatically socialized into the Catholic worldview. At least on an exterior level, it was part of the culture to attend church; indeed most personal and cultural events also had an ecclesial dimension. This brought forth a beautiful Catholic culture that also, of course, had its downside. Nowadays 60 percent of the population are members of the Catholic Church. Church attendance is only half what it used to be thirty years ago. Religious practice has become an option. To be Catholic demands a deliberate decision and all too often a firm stand against the *Zeitgeist*.

Nobody would claim that the church and society are the same today as in the past, but we are still comparing figures between times that have utterly changed. This practice leads to a static view that demonstrates comparison as a vice. For the monastic tradition, comparison prevents life and brings forth the vice of murmuring. As the Desert Fathers teach, "Do not compare yourself with others, and you will find peace."[1] This advice is usually taken on the individual level, according to its literal meaning: Do not compare yourself with this confrere, that sister or preacher, for that only enhances jealousy and envy. The exhortation not to compare oneself with others can lead to humility as well as a new appreciation of one's own gifts and strengths, whereas mere comparison leads to an unhealthy concentration on traits and successes we find in others. The command not to compare oneself with others can also, I would claim, be taken as advice not to compare our time and situation with past times and situations: If you limit yourself to the past, you might constrain your view so that you are not open to new developments and only look out for something to reemerge from the past. However, if we look at the current

---

[1] Paphnoutios 3 in the alphabetic collection no. 788 from Bonifaz Miller, ed., *Weisung der Väter* (Trier: Paulinus-Verlag, 1986). My German translation reads, "Vergleiche dich nicht mit anderen, und du wirst Ruhe finden." A new German translation reads, "Miss dich nicht, und du wirst Ruhe haben." See *Apophthegmata Patrum*, ed. Erich Schweitzer (Beuron: Beuroner Kunstverlag, 2012). Benedicta Ward, however, translates the saying in English as "Do not judge yourself and you will be at peace," whereas in *Apophthegmata* no. 165 (Bessarion 10) she has, "Keep silence and do not compare yourself with others." See *The Sayings of the Desert Fathers*, CS 59 (Kalamazoo, MI: Cistercian Publications, 1975). The Italian edition always has "non misurare se stessi" and explains the wide range of meaning with regard to *Apophthegmata* 610 (Poimen 36), that is, that comparison should not lead to putting oneself down or feeling better than others, but leaving everything to God's judgment. See *Vita e Detti dei Padri del Deserto*, ed. Luciana Mortari (Roma: Città Nuova, 1971), 381, n. 37.

form of monasticism we detect a "de-form" that cries out for a "re-form." Often something has to vanish in order that something else can appear.

We have to break free from the past as a determinative norm; that would enable us more easily to let go of what has already run its course. To give something up does not mean capitulation. Letting go is difficult for a culture where long traditions reign, and change is often seen as something we would be better off without. But we need to establish new things. The new things need not be something extra! We must be careful of placing extra straws on the camel's back. I think we have to study best practice, where monasteries have succeeded in giving something up in order to make room for something new. For example, Altenburg Abbey for many years ran family weeks. In fact, although my baptismal name is Andreas, one of the reasons that I put the name *Bernhard* at the top of suggestions for a new name at my profession was that we went as a family a few times to Altenburg, where I liked to chase "Pater Bernhard," so this name became familiar for me. There must have been many experiences like this associated with the family week at Altenburg, and it must have been hard for the monks to give it up. However, fewer and fewer families came, so the abbey decided not to offer the family week anymore. Then a new project emerged, the "garden of religions," dedicated to the world's five major religions, because the few remaining monks of this abbey had time enough to think about a new focus.[2] Another example is the Abbey of Göttweig. Their boys' choir was not doing too well, so they abandoned a century-long tradition. The empty rooms were instead dedicated to a youth center that is principally run by lay people,[3] whereas previously the boys' choir demanded much manpower on the part of the monks.

[2] See www.stift-altenburg.at/begehbarebibel.htm.
[3] See www.jugendimstift.

Monasticism has arrived in the twenty-first century and can help shape the contemporary culture, if achievements that were once meaningful are not held sacrosanct forever but can make way for future developments. A leading question in this regard is: what will be important in fifteen or twenty years' time? To deliberately adopt a future perspective enables a clearer vision of what is ripe for the time. A young mind-set (whatever age one is) does not see it as loss when things change, particularly if former numbers are not considered so important. Rather, a young mind-set wants change and sees in it a promise for the future. Therefore it is important to let younger people be associated with monasteries in one way or another, for they do not have fixed ideas of what monasticism should look like today. They do not find the high point of the twentieth century—the period after World War II—as the only role model for the future. Theirs is a totally different world; they long to be different in another way. New times need new standards! A young mind-set thus frees us from false expectations, which often stem from the vice of comparison.

3. The Message of an Ancient Abbey for Our Time

Before we look at the development of my abbey and point out what we might learn from it, I have to admit that we are inevitably (at least to some extent) trapped in the past and cannot escape from it too easily. I have already mentioned the demographical situation that we cannot alter ourselves. Likewise, we have to acknowledge that we are standing on the shoulders of our mothers and fathers, those who have gone before us. Writing these lines, I realize that I am sitting in the wing of the novitiate and of junior monks, a building that dates back to the sixteenth century. Most of my confreres live in the main Baroque building. The walls of our church are from the Romantic epoch, even though the interior decoration has undergone many changes. How much the past is present, and shapes our life, became clear to me when a twenty-four-year-old novice looked at the directory of our community from 1965 and exclaimed, "Most of today's community were already here then!" He was right. The majority of the confreres had entered before the Second Vatican Council—which to a young man is prehistory. When we looked at the books telling the history of our abbey for the classes in the novitiate, this very novice was astonished that there were hardly any publications from recent years. This is in sharp contrast to the life he had led before coming to the monastery, when pretty much all the publications he was familiar with were dated after the year 2000, especially because of the influence of technology.

We currently have about fifty monks who run a school and take care of twenty-seven parishes, and the numbers will decrease even further into the future. The average age of my community is sixty, with one-third between seventy-five and eighty-five. During the reign of Empress Maria Theresia we reached the climax of one hundred fifteen monks in the late nineteenth century, and in the 1950s there were around a hundred monks in my abbey. The high number of confreres during the last two hundred fifty years shaped today's perception of the Benedictine community at Kremsmünster. According to these statistics we run the danger of dying out.

However, if we look at not only the last two hundred fifty years but the last four hundred years, we get quite a different picture. Three hundred fifty years ago we had the same number of monks as today, and before that we were even fewer. There were fewer monks before the Baroque period than today. After the Reformation only a few kept up monastic life, yet they handed it on to future generations. In this larger perspective, it becomes clear that our present situation is not such a disaster. If we go even further back, we can see that between the eighth and fifteenth centuries, there were probably never more than twenty monks.

In Kremsmünster, when young confreres suggest changing a tradition or wish to invent something new, the argument of the older generation goes like this: "Why should we change what has worked since 777!" I find it interesting that we identify ourselves with the abbey's 1,200-year history, saying, "We have done it like that for 1,200 years; why should we change our habits because a few young people think so?" Of course the traditions we hold sacred are much younger, perhaps from the time after World War II, or, at the earliest, from the eighteenth or nineteenth centuries. Sometimes our communities give the impression that the Benedictine vows are not stability, *conversatio morum*, and obedience but rather the commonly held assertions "It has always been like that! We have never done it that way! Where would this lead to, if we altered this?"

4. Interpreting the Crisis Spiritually

This overview of the history of just one ancient European abbey shows us that developments of a given time have to be understood in relative terms. However, the historic change remains a reality that rightly lets us speak of a profound crisis of monasticism. I once wrote the term *Ordenskrise* into my breviary, meaning "crisis of religious life." I encounter this entry during Vigils on Tuesdays, next to the passage from Psalm 74:9: *Now we see no signs, we have no prophets, no one who knows how long.* The desert experience we are currently undergoing can be connected to the lack of orientation in other times.

The Bible and our monastic traditions teach us that we do not have to hold back our feelings of disappointment and failure. We can and should find the right expression of lamentation in the presence of God. Far from the depressing murmuring that Saint Benedict seeks to banish, acknowledging our difficult situation with a view of the eternal God is both promising and hopeful. Thus we can escape the temptation of expecting a bright future only from our own efforts. Authentic monastic renewal does not start with programs but with a new awareness of God's loving care. Paradoxically, this happens in the desert. The Lord says, *So I will allure her. I will lead her into the desert and speak to her heart* (Hos 2:16). The place of love is the desert, where God wants to renew his covenant. The prophet continues: *She shall respond there as in the days of her youth, when she came up from the land of Egypt* (Hos 2:17). Israel forgot God precisely in the land where milk and honey flow, at the worldly feasts and in the sedate life of the bourgeoisie (see Hos 2:15). In the desert, God and his people are together again. They return to their first love, which will lead them into the future. Thus renewal is a matter of an interior conversion. It is God's initiative, not ours.

If we only murmur, we leave reality where it is and remain focused on the surface of things. No single monk should prevent the whole community from moving forward. We point out what is not going well, complain about it—without seeing deeper and realizing that there might be a call for conversion. Indeed, the crises can lead us to a deep conversion. What we might experience is the call for an exodus. We might have to leave the self-secured lands that we could not give up on our own.

Again the Old Testament has something to say to us, telling us to stand up and move forward. Genesis 12 starts with this line from God to Abram: *Go forth from your country* (v. 1). This was not easy for him and Sarah, with the prospect of dwelling in tents and accepting a lower standard of living. Yet it is also our call: *Go forth from your country . . . to the land which I will show you* (v. 1). And then comes the promise that we should perhaps understand in a different way: *And I will make you a great nation* (v. 2). Interesting also is the reference to Abram's age: *Now Abram was seventy-five years old when he departed from Haran* (v. 4). To start anew as an elderly person demands much faith. Abram and Sarah trusted God, and they found what God had promised to be true: *To your descendants I will give this land* (v. 7).

342 A Not-So-Unexciting Life

Holy Scripture supplies us with abundant riches to move forward and interpret our crisis theologically, while every line can be interpreted existentially. Isaiah 43 starts with this pledge, which is the basis of monastic consciousness: *But now, thus says the LORD, who created you, O Jacob, and formed you, O Israel: Fear not for I have redeemed you; I have called you by name: you are mine* (v. 1). Then God expands what he is willing to do for his chosen ones: *because I love you* (v. 4). God loves our communities and wants us to be free from self-determined dependence, and he wants to lead us into a new world that monks and nuns are called to testify to with all of their being: *Remember not the events of the past, the things of long ago consider not. See, I am doing something new! Now it springs forth, do you not perceive it?* (vv. 18-19).

5. Reading the Signs of the Times

It is precisely a biblical concept to read the signs of the times, as the Second Vatican Council urged us to do.[4] Now it is awkward to make this proposition to the monastic world in a volume that is dedicated to Fr. Michael Casey. He is a master when it comes to identifying current issues and relating them to the riches of the biblical and monastic traditions. However, it is precisely the aim of this volume to examine whether and how Benedictine spirituality can shape the twenty-first century. For this it is vital to ask what the signs of the times might be for monasticism and to exchange ideas about this issue.

Do we have time and space enough to contemplate the signs of the times? Looking at the German-speaking world, I am compelled to admit that we plan so much in our monasteries, putting an enormous effort into restoration work and exhibitions, as well as into educational and pastoral projects, that

[4] For the argument employed here see in particular *Gaudium et Spes*, numbers 4, 11, and 44.

there is hardly any room for sedate reflection. Is this not already a sign of our times? Perhaps our reaction to falling numbers and the partial breakdown of the living tradition leads to a desperate busyness. We try at all costs to be doing something, to build for the future, and to escape the apparent decline. As a consequence, we can visit one newly restored Baroque abbey after another with astonishing cultural activities. A closer look behind the polished facades, however, reveals spiritual fruitlessness and worn-out communities. It might be easier to negotiate with construction companies than to take pains to build up a monastic community for the twenty-first century.

Such an exterior activism is not convincing for our contemporaries. On the contrary, they expect to find in monasteries an alternative concept of being in the world today. Monastic life has in itself an enormous pastoral potential.[5] The new fascination with monasticism that we find in Europe testifies to this. There are ample interviews with monks or nuns, every year new documentaries about monastic life, and many books issued about the wisdom of monasticism for our time. Whereas adherence to the Roman Catholic Church as an institution seems old-fashioned, and there is hardly anyone under the age of fifty involved in parish life, visiting a monastery either as a tourist or as a guest appears attractive to (post)modern sensitivities.

The gift, but also the burden, of a centuries-old monastery is its tradition. In Austria, for instance, we are still shaped by the Enlightenment's emphasis on the usefulness of consecrated life. The Habsburg emperor Joseph II suppressed many contemplative monasteries in the 1780s and commanded the

---

[5] I have spelled this out in detail in "The Monastery as a Pastoral Site: The Meaning of Benedictine Living Witness," ABR 65 (2014): 94–109. Terrence Kardong translated this text from the original version: "Das Kloster als pastoraler Ort. Die Bedeutung des benediktinischen Lebenszeugnisses," *Geist und Leben* 82 (2009): 321–35.

remaining religious houses to take up ever more active work. While geared toward this understanding of monasticism, we are challenged by contemporary developments to offer an utterly different concept. A monastery does not make sense only if it carries out educational, pastoral, and charitable work in an obvious way. Monastic life should not make sense in terms of what monks or nuns achieve in worldly terms, but it should make sense in and of itself. Hence monasteries exert their influence on concentrating on their own resources. This new understanding can be detected in a remarkable shift from the old to the new constitutions of the Austrian Benedictine Congregation.[6]

The constitutions of 1986 have a chapter heading "Die Aufgaben des Klosters," a section that deals specifically with the principal occupation of a Benedictine monastery in Austria. In constitution no. 227 it says that our vocation has at its core an apostolic character. The main service to the world is pastoral work (no. 228). According to this rather functional view, community life serves as a source of strength for the monk's successful work in parish, school, or research (no. 229). The constitutions issued twenty years later have quite a different definition under the same heading. Here we read that the Benedictine monks see their monastery as a spiritual center (no. 239). No. 240 urges each monastery of the Austrian congregation to evaluate old and new tasks in order that they be appropriate to the needs of the church in our time. The following section, no. 241, is also newly written; it suggests priorities according to which the monastery's workforce should be organized.

Whereas the constitutions of 1986 talked about and limited themselves to exterior fields of work, the constitutions of 2006 quite prophetically state that the prime focus should be on the

---

[6] "Die Satzungen der Österreichischen Benediktinerkongregation," 1986 and 2006.

monastery as a spiritual center. Hence the first and foremost task of a Benedictine community is to offer a lively and livable place for the individual monk. His vocation should flourish in his community in a certain setting. Second, the monks should be there for people who visit their monastery, with liturgy, pastoral counseling, and retreats. Third, the employees should be offered the same resources that are vital for the monks themselves. Only as a final point do the constitutions also mention tasks outside of the monastery, such as work in a parish, insofar as these jobs can be carried out without compromising the primary purpose of the monastery.

Obviously this emphasis on monastic life itself might appear superfluous to monks and nuns outside of the Austrian-Bavarian region, let alone a Trappist monastery on the other side of the globe. However, it might be instructive to witness this shift and see it tightly connected with trends that we find in contemporary culture. Reading the signs of the times demands the interpretation of changing situations in the light of the Gospel.

6. Weak Communities for a Transitional Age

In Europe, monasteries have for centuries been part of the ecclesial and thus societal establishment. Monasticism was not so much a counterculture or a driving force for distancing oneself from the *Zeitgeist* in both church and society. Rather, monasteries were founded by the aristocracy to help build up a Christian civilization. During the Counter-Reformation it was necessary to appoint abbots from the outside. Time and again, monasteries were used to establish law and order in civil society and in matters of faith. Hence their schools were supported by state authorities. As in the other large abbeys of Austria, we have an Emperor's Hall, and the governor of Upper Austria has portraits of the abbots of Kremsmünster Abbey in his office, because some of them were his predecessors!

As was mentioned above, the tight connection between church, state, and consecrated life was in many ways very fruitful for all sides. But being supported and employed by the establishment of a given time can cause a dependence that deprives one of a critical role. If the population of the area surrounding an abbey experiences religious life not only as sustaining the faith but also as a worldly power (occasionally oppressive), we can well understand that monasticism can be conceived of in ways that turn out to be a real problem today. Even now, younger monks who devote themselves to an erudite monastic life are still regarded and addressed as *Stiftsherren*, a word related to *Herr*, meaning Lord. However, monastic landlords with a traditionalist spin do not fit the postmodern landscape.

The Second Vatican Council states: "The church is not unaware of how much it has profited from the history and development of humankind."[7] Historians and sociologists sympathetic to the Christian faith keep reminding us that the seedbed of European secularization is to some degree the wealth and power of the church through the centuries. Can we thus dare to say that perhaps our current crisis is a gentle way of God's loving care to deprive us—through the developments in the modern world—of might and power that has also compromised monastic life and its prophetic witness? This claim seems all too risky, but I have a source that is above suspicion: Pope Benedict XVI, who had experienced and cherished Bavarian Christendom as a theologian and the archbishop of Munich, stated clearly in his last speech in Germany as the reigning pope what would sound outrageous if a liberal theologian had said it: "One could almost say that history comes to the aid of the Church through the various periods of secularization,

---

[7] *Gaudium et Spes* 44, cited in Austin Flannery, ed., *Vatican Council II: Constitutions, Decrees, Declarations* (New York: Costello, 1996).

which have contributed significantly to her purification and inner reform."[8]

In a post-Constantinian era, a church that has become weak and powerless probably has a stronger message for a world in danger, a more compelling message for its people with their broken lives. In both society and church we are prone to holding fast to something that has already slipped away from our grasp. Could not monasticism with its inherent logic testify to the freedom that comes from giving way rather than claiming everything as one's own, that being willing to lose oneself can lead to a fulfillment this world cannot give, that poverty enables us to have a freedom that worldly riches and control are not able to provide?

7. Reimagining Our Future

Looked at in this larger perspective, we might devote ourselves more freely to probable signs of the times. Yes, there is a severe vocation crisis in European monasteries and beyond. Things will not continue as they used to be. But is it not also true that at the same time the interest in monasticism has not vanished? Perhaps it has even increased? There are fewer vocations to monastic life in the narrow and immediate sense—vocations that will be necessary if monasticism is to continue. On the other hand, there are serious people willing to let Benedictine life shape their lives in whatever they do and wherever they live. Should we as monks and nuns not cherish and foster these new vocations? I have heard from several older persons that they plan to move to within the vicinity of a monastery when they retire, because they want to be close to a lively spiritual center. We need to inquire about the

[8] Speech in the Concert Hall of Freiburg on September 25, 2011. The full text, which was heavily criticized by the ecclesial and theological establishment of Germany, can be found at www.vatican.va.

possibility of associated members, of individual men, women, and families who might, in part, carry on the monastic charism.[9]

Young persons who feel tightly connected with a monastery can exert a good influence. Young monks or nuns need peers in their own generation who sustain their vocation, even if those who support them did not enter monastic life. Likewise, when vocations have become fewer, contacts across monasteries are increasingly important. In Germany, Switzerland, and Austria the formation programs for novices and juniors include weeks for members of various communities, for either one congregation or across Benedictine congregations, both male and female. Still, formation happens principally in one's own community. Here it will be a question of the future, particularly if we can find the right balance of acknowledging the individual and immersing him or her thoroughly into the monastic realm.[10]

Finally, I want to raise, as a sign of the times, the topic of a healthy balance in monastic life. In the monasteries of the "Old World" that I am familiar with, we have a pressing issue of overwork.[11] Our contemporaries expect a lifestyle from monasteries that inspires their quest for peace and quiet. Monks talk and write about the balance between work and prayer, but they find it hard to live out what they teach. The rush of our time does not stop at the walls of a monastery. What then

---

[9] Fr. Hugh Feiss, for one, has made proposals in this regard. See his "Review Article: In the Cloister and in the World: Charles De Miramon, Les 'Donnés' au Moyen Age. Une forme de vie religieuse laïque, v. 1180–v. 1500," ABR 59 (2008): 20–34; Feiss, "Reconfiguring Monastic Life," ABR 61 (2010): 63–80; also, from an associate member, Michael Downey, "A Half Commitment? Toward a Reconfiguration of the Cistercian Charism," CSQ 40 (2005): 191–203.

[10] I tried to develop this for a General Chapter of the American Cassinese Congregation, printed as "The Future of Monastic Formation: Reflections from an Austrian Monk," ABR 64 (2013): 282–305.

[11] For an engaging essay from North America, see Terrence G. Kardong, "Work Is Prayer: Not!" ABR 62 (2011): 430–42.

are the best ways both to work hard and also to find the right amount of spiritual leisure? For in such leisure we find the necessary atmosphere for reflection and *lectio divina*, without which communal prayer goes dry. Michael Casey has extensively written about the basis of sound monastic life. He is a source of inspiration both by his way of life and by his writing, which we hope will continue for many years to come.

Chapter 16

Musings of a (Post)Modern Monastic Historian

Columba Stewart, OSB

M y aim is to suggest that the study of monasticism can serve as a mirror of both the movement it examines and the one examining it. I will do so by sketching the evolution of monastic historiography, speaking about my own development as a student of monasticism, and then describing the present moment with its advantages for the study of monasticism and for the renewal of the monastic charism itself. It is a pleasure to write in honor of Michael Casey, who though not a historian has brought to all of his work a deeply historical consciousness and sensitivity.

Monastic Historiography

Until the modern era there was no such thing as academic study of monasticism considered as a historical or religious phenomenon. There were always monastic hagiographies and chronicles, but these were internally generated accounts of significant events and figures in the life of particular communities or congregations, intended primarily to edify adherents. Occasionally there were also intra-monastic dialogues, whether in self-justification, such as those undertaken by Benedictines and Cistercians in the early period of that reform, or more directly polemical, such as the seventeenth-century dispute between the founder of the Trappist Cistercians, Armand Jean de Rancé (1626–1700), and the learned Maurist Jean Mabillon

(1632–1707) about the balance between manual and intellectual labors in monastic life.[1] The birth of external critique came with the Renaissance, whether from the inside-outsider Erasmus's satire *Stultitiae Laus* (1509, published 1511) or Martin Luther's critique of monasticism as a non-evangelical distortion of Christian discipleship when based on the assumption that vows were meritorious works earning salvation, which he pursued in *De votis monasticis* (1521).[2] Thanks to David Hume (1711–1776) and Edward Gibbon (1737–1794), in the Anglophone-Protestant world, monasticism, by then long gone in the British Isles, became synonymous with degeneracy and ignorant fanaticism. Hume dismissed monasticism for its lack of social utility.[3] Gibbon wrote, "these unhappy exiles from social life were impelled by the dark and implacable genius of superstition. . . . The operation of these religious motives was variously determined by the temper and situation of mankind. . . . They acted most forcibly on the infirm minds of children and females."[4] Antiquarians such as William Dugdale (1605–1686), whose *Monasticon Anglicanum* (1655 and 1661) was

---

[1] Started by De Rancé's *De la sainteté et des devoirs de la view monastique* (Paris: François Muguet, 1683), to which Mabillon responded in his justly famous *Traité des études monastiques* (Paris: Ch. Robustel, 1691). Their dispute continued in other publications.

[2] See *The Book of Concord*, Article 26:1–12, and the *Smalcald Articles* III.15.

[3] "Celibacy, fasting, penance, mortification, self-denial, humility, silence, solitude, and the whole train of monkish virtues; for what reason are they everywhere rejected by men of sense, but because they serve to no manner of purpose, neither to advance a man's fortune in the world; neither qualify him for the entertainment of company, nor increase his power of self-enjoyment? We observe, on the contrary, that they cross all desirable ends; stupefy the understanding and harden the heart, obscure the fancy and sour the temper. We justly, therefore, transfer them to the opposite column, and place them in the catalogue of vices." From David Hume, *Enquiry Concerning the Principles of Morals* (1751), chap. 9.

[4] *Rise and Fall of the Roman Empire* (1781), vol. 3, chap. 37.

based on the research of Roger Dodsworth (1585–1654), gathered evidence for monasteries and monuments, but with little interest in their religious life or spiritual practice.

On the continent, wherever monasticism survived the Reformation it tended to focus on internal reforms, playing little role in ecclesiastical affairs or theological matters. In the intellectual sphere there was the outstanding exception of the Maurists, who expressed the deep humanism of Benedictine life using the tools and critical spirit of the early modern era as they searched for, edited, and published the essential texts and documents of the Christian and monastic tradition.[5] They established the precedent for later, non-monastic projects of vast scope that brought together and published the sources needed for the scientific study of Latin ecclesiastical and monastic history (and, in some cases, the Greek sources as well). The launch of the *Acta Ordinis Sancti Benedicti* by Luc d'Achery (1609–1685), finished by Jean Mabillon, harnessed monastic interest in ancient texts to modern scholarly technologies. Mabillon also laid the foundations of scientific Latin paleography and diplomatics,[6] extended by Bernard de Montfaucon (1655–1741) to Greek texts.[7] The Maurists undertook ambitious "voyages littéraires" to find manuscripts scattered in monasteries and churches across Europe. Their editions of patristic and medieval texts made possible the wholesale plagiarism of the abbé Jacques-Paul Migne (1800–1875) in his astonishing *Patrologiae cursus completus* (1844–1858).[8]

---

[5] See the still-compelling overview of their work in David Knowles, *Great Historical Enterprises: Problems in Monastic History* (London and New York: Nelson, 1964), 32–62.

[6] *De re diplomatica* (Paris: L. Billaine, 1681).

[7] Bernard de Montfaucon, Joannes Komnenos, and Jean Bouhier, *Palæographia græca* (Paris: apud Ludovicum Guerin [etc.], 1708).

[8] R. Howard Bloch, *God's Plagiarist: Being an Account of the Fabulous Industry and Irregular Commerce of the Abbé Migne* (Chicago: University of Chicago Press, 1994).

The Maurists had been preceded, and perhaps inspired, by the Jesuit Heribert Rosweyde (1569–1629), whose compendium of Latin translations of early monastic texts, *De vita et verbis seniorum* (1615), sits on my desk as I write this essay. It was Rosweyde who began the *Acta Sanctorum*, a great compendium of lives of the saints arranged by feast days, published in sixty-eight volumes over almost three hundred years (1643–1940), and continued by his successor Jean Bolland (1596–1665), founder of the "Bollandists."[9] In the Roman Catholic world, the study of monasticism and hagiography was of great interest to members of the newer orders, who were often active in the formal academic world in a manner untypical of the Benedictines and Cistercians.[10]

With abundant, if not complete, sources now available, the scientific study of monasticism could begin. As a result, the nineteenth century proved to be a watershed for the study of monasticism as for so many other things, with serious efforts to examine the literature and a growing willingness to contextualize it, even if religious affiliations and controversies still shaped interpretations. In this modern study of monasticism and its literature one can observe a demarcation of interests between those scholars who focused on monastic *spirituality* and the explication of monastic texts that acquired canonical status (usually monks or religious) and those who employed a historical or phenomenological approach, often sustained by a wider scope of interests. The latter were typified by the great German historians of the Classical and Early Christian periods, beginning with Theodor Mommsen (1817–1903) and

---

[9] See Knowles, *Great Historical Enterprises*, 2–32.

[10] In the Prussian Protestant world one can find a project of even greater magnitude, the *Monumenta Germaniae Historica* (1826–), whose title must be understood in the broadest sense, encompassing historical texts from 500–1500 across much of Europe, a reminder of the Germanic cast of the Frankish and later Carolingian Empire. See Knowles, *Great Historical Enterprises*, 64–97.

the towering Adolf von Harnack (1851–1930), both in Berlin. The latter, particularly, absorbed the historical-critical method of contemporary German biblical scholarship and applied it to the full range of early Christian literature. His penetrating analysis of the development of monasticism,[11] which concludes in a manner revealing of his Lutheran formation, is still essential reading for those interested in monastic historiography.

Harnack's insistence on free inquiry inspired his contemporaries and later followers, many of whom were more sympathetic than he to monasticism, despite their Protestant affiliation. This was true of the historians influenced by the so-called History of Religions School (*Religionsgeschichtliche Schule*), with their sensitivity to spiritual motivations allied to a comparative method that recognized and explored the influence of Hellenistic philosophy, Gnosticism, and other movements on the development of Christian asceticism and monasticism. Richard Reitzenstein (1861–1931) wrote analyses of the *Life of Antony*[12] as well as of the *Historia Monachorum in Aegypto* and of Palladius's *Lausiac History*, placing them in their classical literary and philosophical contexts.[13] Wilhelm Bousset (1865–1920) published the first major study of the *Apophthegmata Patrum* (1923).[14] Both attempted to describe a pre-Christian

---

[11] Adolf von Harnack, *Monasticism: Its Ideals and History, and the Confessions of St. Augustine: Two Lectures by Adolf Harnack*, trans. E. E. Kellett and F. H. Marseille (London: Williams & Norgate, 1901).

[12] *Des Athanasius Werk über das Leben des Antonius: ein philologischer Beitrag zur Geschichte des Mönchtums*, Sitzungsberichte der Heidelberger Akademie der Wissenschaften, Philosophisch-Historische Klasse, Jahrg. 1914, 8. Abhandlung (Heidelberg: C. Winter, 1914).

[13] *Historia Monachorum und Historia Lausiaca: Eine Studie zur Geschichte des Mönchtums und der frühchristlichen Begriffe Gnostiker und Pneumatiker*, Forschungen zur Religion und Literatur des Alten und Neuen Testaments, 24 (n. f. 7) (Göttingen: Vandenhoeck & Ruprecht, 1916).

[14] *Apophthegmata: Studien zur Geschichte des ältesten Mönchtums* (Tübingen: J. C. B. Mohr [P. Siebeck], 1923).

"Gnostic" movement that found varied expression in early Christianity such as in the Johannine movement and in monasticism. Their effort—continued by numerous others up to the present—is now considered mistaken in its assumption that "Gnosticism" as such can be used as a meaningful category for comparative study and the tracing of intellectual influence.[15] The importance of their work, however, apart from the enduring value of their philological and textual analysis, was its demonstration that the *Sitz im Leben* of Christian monasticism was not one of isolation but of intellectual and cultural engagement, as was obviously true of early Christianity as a whole. By the same token, *Der Ursprung des Mönchtums* ("The Birth of Monasticism," 1936), the study of monastic beginnings by *religionsgeschichtliche* scholar Karl Heussi, acknowledged the Christian inspiration of monasticism while recognizing the elements borrowed from Hellenistic philosophy and culture. As a result of the work of these scholars, what had been received within the ecclesiastical tradition as a canon of authoritative monastic texts was now viewed as part of an array of unbundled sources available for historical assessment undertaken in dialogue with philosophical and other non-Christian writings.

Such academic rigor—shaped as it inevitably was by the explicit affiliations of these scholars—in turn affected writers within the Roman Catholic intellectual world as well. The tools of historical criticism had become normative, even if the agenda were different. This was notably the case among French Catholic scholars, who comfortably acknowledged the influence of philosophy on Christianity in general and monasticism in particular and were as comfortable as their German counterparts in moving between non-Christian Greek philosophical

---

[15] See most recently the balanced critique in Hugo Lundhaug and Lance Jenott, *The Monastic Origins of the Nag Hammadi Codices* (Tübingen: Mohr Siebeck, 2015).

and Christian theological literature. It was they who laid the groundwork for much monastic scholarship in the twentieth century. The important point to note is that once again the Benedictines did not take the lead. It was work such as that of the great Alsatian Jesuit Irénée Hausherr (1891–1978), at the Pontifical Oriental Institute, that was vitally important for the study of monastic spirituality. In addition to recovering a full view of the writings and profound influence of Evagrius Ponticus, an achievement that required mastery of several ancient languages, Hausherr contributed many articles to the Oriental Institute's journal, *Orientalia Christiana Periodica*, and its monograph series, Orientalia Christiana (along with its successor Orientalia Christiana Analecta). It was again the Jesuits—this time in Toulouse—who launched the monumental *Dictionnaire de spiritualité ascétique et mystique. Doctrine et histoire* in 1928. This initiative required sixty-three years and nine thousand articles to survey the field (with volumes appearing from 1932 till 1995).

Hausherr's Dominican contemporary, André-Jean Festugière (1898–1982), worked with both philosophical and Christian ascetic texts and wrote an enduringly valuable work on the religious world of Antioch at the time of John Chrysostom and Libanius.[16] As a young friar he was exposed to the archeological awareness cultivated at the École Biblique in Jerusalem, whose venerable founder, Marie-Joseph Lagrange (1855–1938), wrote the foreword to his first book. Festugière had the unusual ability to work both philosophically/theologically and historically, as is evidenced by his publications on the Hermetic corpus, translations of monastic texts (*Moines d'Orient*), and editions of the ecclesiastical historians Sozomen and Evagrius Scholasticus.

---

[16] André Marie Jean Festugière, *Antioche païenne et chrétienne; Libanius, Chrysostome et les moines de Syrie,* Bibliothèque des écoles françaises d'Athènes et de Rome, fasc. 194 (Paris: E. de Boccard, 1959).

For the most part, monastic scholars tended to work either entirely within the tradition or from the inside out, starting with the core texts and then seeking links to cognate texts or practices in philosophy. Their interest went more explicitly to deepening familiarity with and appreciation of the received literature, and to more fully understanding its implications for actual monastic life. This time French and Belgian Benedictines led the way, with the *Revue Bénédictine* (1894–), published by the Abbey of Maredsous in Belgium, as the flagship journal for research on the Rule, related texts, and later history. The standard view of Benedictine history from this tradition was expressed in the *Histoire de l'Ordre de Saint-Benoît* of Philibert Schmitz (1888–1963), published by Maredsous in the mid-twentieth century.[17] The Cistercians established their own review, the *Collectanea Cisterciensia*, founded by the general chapter in 1933. For many years monastic history was a largely French enterprise. From that tradition came the prolific Adalbert de Vogüé (1924–2011) of La Pierre-qui-Vire in France and Jean Leclercq (1911–1993) of Clervaux in Luxembourg, both of whom worked with the traditional canon of monastic literature—the former concerned with Late Antique and Early Medieval texts, the latter with a range of medieval topics.

The small English Benedictine Congregation produced two notable scholars important for Anglophone monasticism throughout the world. Cuthbert Butler (1858–1934), abbot of Downside for many years, published three significant works: the *Lausiac History of Palladius* (1898), *Benedictine Monachism* (1919), and *Western Mysticism: The Teaching of SS Augustine, Gregory, and Bernard on Contemplation and the Contemplative*

---

[17] Published in seven volumes between 1942 and 1956, with the final volume devoted to the history of Benedictine women. He also published a handy edition of MS Sangallensis 914, the best manuscript of the Rule: *Regula Monachorum: Textus critico-practicus sec. cod. Sangall. 914, Edito altera emendata* (Maredsous: Abbaye, 1955).

Life (1922), as well as a remarkably useful pocket-sized edition of the Rule[18] with important sources not simply cited but fully quoted in the footnotes. David Knowles (1896–1974) was a historian of medieval English monasticism who ended up spending most of his monastic life in Cambridge, ironically because of disagreement with his Congregation's orientation toward teaching and running schools. Although famous for his works on medieval English religious life,[19] he wrote more popularly with a wider historical scope. The small paperback *Christian Monasticism* (1969) featured the first photograph of the Saint John's Abbey Church that I ever saw. His remarks about American Benedictine life were not very complimentary, but I remembered that photograph.

Here I Join the Narrative

My immersion in monastic history began in 1980, when I spent a summer at Saint John's Abbey. I was there to grind through German grammar to satisfy a requirement for my doctoral program at Yale. Providentially it was the sesquimillenial celebration of the birth of Benedict (and of Scholastica, who was regularly invoked, especially when sisters were present). Saint John's hosted a symposium featuring Cardinal Basil Hume, the abbot primate (then Victor Dammertz), prominent scholars, and hundreds of monks and nuns. It was the zenith of post–Vatican II optimism about the renewal of religious life, the liturgy, ecumenism, and engagement with the modern world.

---

[18] *Sancti Benedicti Regula Monachorum*, Friburgi Brisgoviae (St. Louis, MO: B. Herder, 1912); subsequent editions (1927, 1935) appeared under the title *Sancti Benedicti Regula Monasteriorum*.

[19] *The Monastic Order in England: A History of its Development from the Times of St. Dunstan to the Fourth Lateran Council, 943–1216* (Cambridge: Cambridge University Press, 1940; 2nd ed., 1963); and David Knowles, *The Religious Orders in England*, 3 vols. (Cambridge: Cambridge University Press, 1948).

It was still possible to think and dream big. Relegated for the summer to a sleepy corner of the monastery, I spent much of my time with the summer-school students, at that time consisting mostly of teaching sisters from various congregations working on an MA in theology, as well as several seminarians and priests pursuing degrees in liturgy or Scripture. I didn't know much about Benedictine monasticism at that point. I had a cursory familiarity with the Rule and had plowed through Jean Leclercq's classic *The Love of Learning and Desire for God* at the suggestion of an Irish priest at Yale (who, in the way of the far-flung but small Benedictine network, had baptized a good friend from Glenstal Abbey, a fact discovered only twenty-five years later). I had a wonderful time. I loved the architecture (that photograph!), the liturgical style, and the natural setting of the abbey. But most of all I loved the monks: in a community filled with such intelligent and generous men I could imagine a monastic future for myself.

Before that summer, my experiential familiarity with religious life had been with the Anglican brothers of the Society of Saint John the Evangelist at their houses in Cambridge, Massachusetts, and in Cowley, a suburb of Oxford. I had written my Harvard AB thesis on their founder, a representative of the nineteenth-century Catholic renewal of the Church of England. Although they tended to avoid calling themselves monks, they really were. With them I first prayed the Office, ate in monastic silence, and experienced a reverent and contemplative celebration of the Eucharist.

As much as I liked them (and still do), I wasn't an Anglican and had no interest in becoming one. My research about nineteenth-century English church history, however, was leading me to the early Christian centuries so important for John Henry Newman and the other Tractarians. Their view of Catholicism owed little to that medieval era that had been so influential for the monastic revival in Europe and for the various Gothic revival movements in art and architecture in Great Britain. The turn to the early period had also introduced me to the study of liturgy, which required expanding my view of the Christian world to encompass the Christian East, first in its Byzantine form and then, some years later, the Syriac. As it happened, the first serious study of liturgy I read was the classic *The Shape of the Liturgy* by the Anglican Benedictine monk Gregory Dix. His historical theories are now largely discounted, but his moving final chapter on the spirit of the liturgy can still move one to tears. Dix was feeding me a monastic view of liturgical continuity and practice, though I did not realize it at the time.

My entry into monastic life at Saint John's in 1981 coincided with the dawn of a new era of interest in pre-Benedictine monastic history and its shaping of the Benedictine Rule and tradition. The Cistercian Studies series had begun to publish translations of early monastic texts, notably for me those about the Egyptian desert monks, the works of Evagrius, and the Pachomian literature translated by Armand Veilleux. The Liturgical Press at Saint John's had just released *RB 1980*,[20] which brought the critical edition and analysis of the Latin textual tradition published by Adalbert de Vogüé and Jean de Neufville[21] to a much wider audience, accompanied by a fresh English translation, abundant notes, excellent introductory essays and appendices, and useful indices. Butler's emphasis on the sources of the Rule was evident in the textual apparatus, augmented by further detection of parallel and source texts. The dust of earlier twentieth-century controversies over the relationship between the Rule of the Master and Rule of Benedict and the lesser concern about which form of the Latin text to prefer—whether the common *Ausculta* or the more original but less widely disseminated *Obsculta* tradition—had settled.

---

[20] Timothy Fry, ed., *RB 1980: The Rule of St. Benedict in Latin and English with Notes* (Collegeville, MN: Liturgical Press, 1981).

[21] *La Règle de Saint Benoît*, SCh 181–83 (Paris: Les Éditions du Cerf, 1971). The remaining volumes were Vogüé's commentary on the Rule.

Benedict's dependence on the anonymous text known as the *Regula Magistri* was now obvious, having been thoroughly demonstrated by Vogüé after the original suggestion of Augustin Genestout in 1940.[22] The turn to the purer, though less familiar, text of the Rule signified how firmly the textual criticism with which biblical studies had long been conversant had become standard practice also within the monastic field. The fact that the difference between the two textual traditions of the Rule concerned its first and most important word gave the turn to *Obsculta* added weight.

I lapped it up. My own historical and literary training at Harvard had strongly emphasized textual criticism and close reading in the French tradition of the *explication du texte*, making me naturally oriented to these problems and interested in their details. Tracing the sources of the Rule seemed to be the obvious way to approach it. (Only later did I become interested in its reception as well.) I spent part of the novitiate reading Evagrius for the first time in Antoine and Claire Guillaumont's Sources Chrétiennes edition, using John Eudes Bamberger's translation as backup when neither the Greek nor the French was comprehensible. This began a long intellectual exploration of Evagrius's thought and pedagogical techniques. With my fellow novices I read the *Life of Antony*, taught to us by a young monk then in graduate school. He had been taught to view it alongside its Late Antique parallels, particularly Philostratus's life of the Pythagorean hero Apollonius of Tyana. Our teacher referred

---

[22] Augustin Genestout, "La Règle du Maître et la Règle de S. Benoît," *Revue d'Ascétique et de Mystique* 21 (1940): 51–112; Vogüé's *La communauté et l'abbé dans la règle de saint Benoît*, Textes et études théologiques (Paris: Desclée de Brouwer, 1961), was his initial proof, followed later by his notes and commentary in the Sources Chrétiennes edition of the Rule. For an overview, see now Bernd Jaspert, *Die Regula Benedicti-Regula Magistri-Kontroverse*, 2nd exp. ed., Regulae Benedicti studia 3 (Hildesheim: Gerstenberg, 1977).

to the *Life of Antony* as "the document," which suggested his detached methodology. He may have mentioned Peter Brown's groundbreaking work on the holy man, but I wasn't yet paying attention to such things. I was more inclined toward reverence for the text, puzzled as I was about how to extract meaning from the seemingly crude demonology of the *Life*. I read other monastic literature on my own, especially after the novice master told me toward the end of the novitiate that I'd be teaching some classes in early monastic history to the following year's novices.

Every teacher knows that we really learn something only by teaching it, both because of necessary preparation and of the act of teaching itself. This was memorably expressed by Gregory the Great in one of his homilies on Ezekiel: "I know that frequently *many things in the sacred text that I was unable to understand alone I did understand when standing before my brethren.* . . . I freely admit, *I am often listening along with you to what I am saying.*"[23]

It was then that I first tackled Cassian, who had been curiously neglected in our program thanks to an earlier era's misuse of his *exempla* of obedience (the notorious watering of a dead stick). An overly literal reading of Cassian had led to the view expressed by my novice master that Cassian was a theoretician and an advocate of the anchoritic life, and thus of dubious benefit for an aspiring cenobite. When I actually read Cassian, however, it was a revelation. He combined psychological acuity (which he shared with Evagrius, from whom he would have learned at least some of it) with a mystical sensitivity in his teaching on prayer and biblical meditation. I was so inspired that he became the subject of my first published article, which was about his teaching on unceasing prayer as described in *Conferences* 9 and 10.[24] During those years both

---

[23] *Homilies on Ezekiel*, II.2.1 (PG 76:948D–49A; SCh 360:92). Translation my own.

[24] "John Cassian on Unceasing Prayer," *Monastic Studies* 15 (1984): 159–77.

Adalbert de Vogüé and Jean Leclercq spent time at Saint John's, and I was fortunate to get to know both of them and to remain in contact with them until the end of their lives. With a plethora of sources becoming available year by year both in decent editions and in translation, the conditions for critical study of the tradition had never been better. Our School of Theology had recently introduced a program in monastic studies, and I was asked to divert my interest in early liturgy toward early monasticism. After solemn vows I spent four years in Oxford, where scholarship on ancient texts in the theology and Oriental faculties was still being done on traditional lines. At that point I had little exposure to literary theory. Auerbach's *Mimesis* and a little bit of Walter Benjamin had made it into my undergraduate study of comparative literature, but that was about it. Nor had I heard much about more recent theoretical approaches while combing through Syriac and Greek texts in the pre-internet era that required actually reading (or, more truthfully, skimming) hundreds, if not thousands, of columns of the Patrologia Graeca looking for the terminology important for my thesis on the Messalian controversy.[25] This was still the era of the massive volumes of the Bodleian Library's catalogue with their pasted-in slips for each entry and a whole team of librarians who shifted and repasted the labels as necessary. Books published before 1920 were typically listed in elegant copperplate handwriting on one set of catalogues; the later series of volumes had printed slips. Hefting one of those massive tomes up onto the reading ledge was like handling a great medieval Bible. The very act of research had a liturgical solemnity.[26]

[25] *Working the Earth of the Heart: The Messalian Controversy in History, Texts, and Language to A.D. 431*, Oxford Theological Monographs (Oxford: Clarendon Press, 1991).

[26] Sometime in the early 2000s I saw those massive volumes lined up along a basement corridor in the New Bodleian on the other side of Broad Street. I wonder if they are still there.

Being out of the American academic scene and focused on my own research and its relevance for teaching monastic studies in Collegeville, it was only after I returned home in 1989 that I first heard about Michel Foucault and discovered the rising surge of interest in asceticism, understood as a category inclusive of non-Christian philosophical movements as well as monasticism and its Christian antecedents. This interest encompassed traditional monasticism but took a broader view, with a particular interest in female asceticism, bodily disciplines, and unusual expressions of the ascetic impulse such as stylitism. The surge rose from several sources. Among them were Peter Brown's 1971 article "The Rise and Function of the Holy Man in Late Antiquity"[27] and his 1988 book, *The Body and Society*, which I had read and reviewed at the time it was published.[28] The aim of the former was to place ascetic figures and practices within specific social contexts. The latter revealed the multiple forms and interpretations of early Christian sexual asceticism, adding to the social sensitivity of the earlier article an engagement with the changing philosophical and theological rationales of each ascetic instantiation or theorist. This move away from an abstracted, timeless, and monolithic understanding of the motivations for Christian asceticism to see instead its many expressions, each embedded in particular places and relationships, may seem obvious now, but was revolutionary at that time.

In the mid-1990s I began to attend the annual meetings of the North American Patristics Society, and through my en-

---

[27] *The Journal of Roman Studies* 61 (1971): 80–101; *The Journal of Roman Studies* 61 (1971): 80–101; cf. his later reconsideration in "The Rise and Function of the Holy Man in Late Antiquity, 1971–1997," *Journal of Early Christian Studies* 6 (1998): 353–76.

[28] *The Body and Society Men, Women, and Sexual Renunciation in Early Christianity: Lectures on the History of Religions*, n.s. 13 (New York: Columbia University Press, 1988). A revised edition with a new introduction appeared in 2008.

counters there and at other conferences I learned more about this new and, frankly, at times threatening approach to a tradition in which I had a deep personal investment. For a while in the 1990s it seemed that every paper, article, and book on asceticism or monasticism had to include the word *body* somewhere in its title to merit serious consideration. This trend was exemplified in the fascinating compendium entitled *Asceticism*, published on the basis of papers presented at a conference held at Union Theological Seminary in August 1993.[29] I didn't know about the conference until it was over, but I wrote two review articles about the volume and other contemporary publications that hinted at my unease.[30] There was on the part of some scholars an iconoclastic zeal in taking on the church fathers, and at times an almost juvenile delight in emphasizing the peculiar sexual fixations of early theologians or ascetics.

I felt keenly a growing divide between those working along traditional theological and church historical lines on the one side and those who approached "our" texts and people with a purely academic perspective on the other. At times the atmosphere at professional gatherings grew tense. Those most strongly identified with one camp barely spoke to their counterparts in the opposite one. Unkind things were assumed and said. I felt then, as I have so often in life, that my place was somewhere in between rather than on either side. Figuring out how to live that liminal state was not simple. My affinities with the traditionally minded scholars were obvious enough, even if we might have disagreed on particular points of doctrine or

[29] Vincent L. Wimbush and Richard Valantasis, eds., *Asceticism* (New York: Oxford University Press, 1995).

[30] Columba Stewart, "Asceticism and Spirituality in Late Antiquity: New Vision, Impasse, or Hiatus?" *Christian Spirituality Bulletin*, Summer 1996, 11–15, and "Three Recent Studies on Ancient Monasticism," *American Benedictine Review* 50 (1999): 3–11, originally published in the *Christian Spirituality Bulletin* in Spring 1997.

practice. But I was coming to know my other colleagues as generous and kind people, and my largely secular education had hardly sheltered me from those who did not share my beliefs. Some of them, in fact, were practicing Christians but were not professionally in that space. They taught at secular institutions in which the approach to the topic was that of "Religious Studies" rather than "Theology" or "Church History." Others had reasons for no longer identifying as Christian, having left fundamentalist churches that they felt were not intellectually credible or having experienced rejection because of their sexual orientation, divorce, or other personal situation. Most of them seemed to take their human and social commitments seriously, and their intellectual interest in the Christian tradition surely signified something. I could see aspects of myself, and of my own struggles, in all of them.

By the mid-1990s, I was deep into my book on John Cassian, which required me to engage more thoroughly with Hellenistic philosophy. It was then that I first read Pierre Hadot's limpid "Exercices spirituels" (1981)[31] and its companion article, "Exercices spirituels antique et 'philosophie chrétienne.'"[32] Hadot's combination of careful reading and breadth of view was like Festugière's, but with a simplicity that I still find compelling. As I learned more about him—his early career as a priest, abandoned after the ferocious condemnation of Modernism in the encyclical *Humani generis* in 1950; his conversations with, and gentle chiding of, Michel Foucault—he entered my personal pantheon of intellectual heroes.[33] I owe to Hadot my understanding and then em-

---

[31] Subsequently available in a fine English translation: Pierre Hadot, "Spiritual Exercises," in *Philosophy as a Way of Life: Spiritual Exercises from Socrates to Foucault*, ed. Arnold Ira Davidson, trans. Michael Chase (Oxford and New York: Blackwell, 1995), 81–125.

[32] Translated in the same volume, 126–44.

[33] I touch on his dialogue with Foucault in "Three Recent Studies."

brace of the decisive influence of Hellenistic philosophy, both theoretical and practical, on the development of monastic spirituality. This was true not only of the refined theology of Evagrius Ponticus, but much more broadly in terms of the pedagogical techniques, literary forms, terminology, and practices of attention and remembering, adapted to monastic use. Understanding monasticism as the Christian analogue to "philosophy as a way of life," however indissolubly bound with doctrine and imbued with biblical themes as it may have been, was an important step for me. It located monasticism in a Late Antique marketplace of ideas, exchanging and competing with alternative spiritual paths.

My work has also coincided with shifts in prevailing ways of conceiving the broader canvas. The traditional periodization of Late Roman—Early Christian—Medieval/Byzantine/Early Islamic—Renaissance/Reformation—Modern now has the feel of dusty cases in a dated natural history museum, imposing a brute taxonomy that leaves little room for nuance. The shift to "Late Antiquity" as a way of eliding artificial chronological and religious distinctions had a corollary in the expansion of "Patristics" to "Early Christian Studies," complementing doctrinal analysis of canonical writings with social and cultural investigations. Heretofore neglected texts and figures were brought out of the shadows to which triumphant orthodoxy had consigned them.[34] Placing the development of Christian asceticism and its monastic form within a wider frame has been very helpful indeed.

---

[34] Late Antiquity has become such a dominant way of conceiving a broad sweep of centuries and geographies, overwashing as it does the frontiers between East and West, paganism and Christianity, and then Christianity and Islam, that some are starting to push back. See Anthony Kaldellis, "Late Antiquity Dissolves," *Marginalia: A Los Angeles Review of Books Channel*, September 18, 2015, http://go.shr.lc/2b2eAGw.

A sabbatical in 2009–2010 after some years spent chasing manuscripts in various parts of the world[35] brought me back into sustained dialogue with recent scholarship. I reengaged with the Syriac tradition that had been part of my doctoral research, and also read more deeply in canonical and legal sources to trace the growing regulation of monasticism. As a corollary I returned to heresiology, which had also been an aspect of my work at Oxford, to understand the development of what would become the dominant form of Christian doctrine (viz., "orthodoxy") and the role of monasticism in that process. Monasticism was often involved in the growing tendency to categorize and label theological views and practices deemed to be deviant. Sometimes, especially before the fourth century, ascetic and monastic people or communities themselves were the target, but increasingly they became the agents of doctrinal enforcement. The late fourth-century firestorm of the first Origenist controversy, which remains murky despite much good scholarship,[36] was a watershed in this regard, with the philosophically inclined monks in the line of Origen, Didymus, Evagrius, and the "Tall Brothers" becoming suspect. The influence of their intellectual masters remained indelible despite the loss of many writings in their original Greek and the concealment of other texts by reattribution to unimpeachable figures.[37] As monasticism became a recognized and duly regulated component of the Byzantine theocratic state, charged with maintaining the Orthodox faith, the zeal for doctrinal purity

[35] On behalf of the Hill Museum & Manuscript Library (www.hmml.org), a sponsored program of Saint John's University.

[36] See most recently Krastu Banev, *Theophilus of Alexandria and the First Origenist Controversy: Rhetoric and Power* (Oxford: Oxford University Press, 2015).

[37] For Evagrius, see Columba Stewart, "Evagrius Beyond Byzantium: The Latin and Syriac Receptions," in *Evagrius and His Legacy*, ed. Robin Darling Young and Joel Kalvesmaki (South Bend, IN: Notre Dame University Press, 2016), 206–35.

increased. The simultaneous monasticizing of the episcopate reinforced the new focus. After the fifth-century divisions of the Church, the non-Chalcedonian monasteries did the same within their particular set of theological convictions. I would like to do some further probing of how this evolution affected monastic spirituality and practice. The history of monastic prayer and mystical theology is an area noticeably neglected in the flurry of recent publications on asceticism and monasticism. The distancing from Origen had an impact on monastic spirituality in the East, and one could trace similar effects in the West as well. For example, one can see the Greek translator of John Cassian's writings not only severely trimming the texts chosen for translation but also purging them of any trace of Evagrian contemplative theology or mysticism.[38] In the Syriac tradition, the timing of large-scale translations of Greek Christian literature meant that Evagrius was amply translated, but Origen was reviled as a heretic, with only a few paragraphs scraping into Syriac.[39]

Most of my work has been in the period before the Rule of Saint Benedict, moving between East and West as both people and texts did in Late Antiquity. As a result of being asked to write several surveys of Western monastic literature and spirituality I have become more interested in the period *after* the writing of the Rule of Saint Benedict, with particular

---

[38] Suggested in my review of Panagiotes Tzamalikos's two books on the Greek tradition of Cassian, "Another Cassian?," *Journal of Ecclesiastical History* 66 (2015): 372–76. Further details are forthcoming in a conference paper, "The Reception of the Writings of John Cassian in the Christian East," to be published by the SS Cyril and Methodius Theological Institute for Post-Graduate Studies in Moscow, and my essay in the planned Brill *Companion to John Cassian.*

[39] See my "Psalms and Prayer in Syriac Monasticism: Clues from Psalter Prefaces and their Greek Sources," forthcoming in *Prayer and Worship in Eastern Christianities, 5th to 11th Centuries*, ed. Derek Krueger and Brouria Bitton-Ashkelony (London: Routledge, 2017).

appreciation for Gregory the Great and the Carolingian reboot of Benedictine monasticism.[40] The early medieval commentaries are a tremendous resource for the monastic historian, now finally getting the attention they deserve.[41] Here, too, one discovers that the monastic terrain is more varied, and the dominance of the Rule later, and less pervasive, than traditionally assumed.[42] Because modern Benedictines owe their existence as much to the "Second Benedict"—Benedict of Aniane—and the promotion of the Rule by Charlemagne and his successor Louis the Pious, this period is of tremendous interest and importance. Thanks to Kassius Hallinger's launch of the *Corpus consuetudinum monasticarum* and the access it provides to the earliest sources, the work of Josef Semmler on Carolingian monastic reform, and the tracing of the textual history of the Rule by Klaus and Michaela Zelzer, a much fuller picture is now available, even if not yet widely disseminated in the English-speaking monastic world.[43]

I have been thinking a lot about these historiographic and personal issues, and their intersection, as I undertake a new and foolishly ambitious project, writing the history of the first millennium of Christian monasticism, East and West.

---

[40] E.g., "Benedictine Monasticism and Mysticism," in *The Wiley-Blackwell Companion to Christian Mysticism*, ed. Julia A. Lamm (Chichester, UK, and Malden, MA: Wiley-Blackwell, 2013), 216–36; and "Prayer Among the Benedictines," in *A History of Prayer: The First to the Fifteenth Century*, ed. Roy Hammerling (Leiden and Boston: Brill, 2008), 201–21.

[41] See, for example, the online *Hildemar Project*, with a fresh translation of the longest and most detailed early medieval commentary: http://hildemar.org/.

[42] See my overview in "Re-Thinking the History of Monasticism East and West: A Modest Tour d'Horizon," in *Prayer and Thought in Monastic Tradition: Essays in Honour of Benedicta Ward SLG*, ed. Santha Bhattacharji, Rowan Williams, and Dominic Mattos (London: Bloomsbury, 2014), 3–16, at 10–15.

[43] Albrecht Diem's many recent publications in English are making this area of research more widely known.

For monastic historians, or at least for this one, the deconstruction of the received narratives and the broadening of study beyond the traditional canon of monastic literature has been very fruitful. As I share it with a broader audience, it seems clear to me that the suitable time frame for my survey is roughly 250–1250 CE, with a generous lean across the earlier boundary to explore the philosophical, Jewish, and Christian ascetical antecedents without which monasticism could not have existed. Equally, I will at least hint at what was to come after my cutoff point. By then the respective situations of Eastern and Western monasticism had become quite different, both from their origins and from each other.

Geographical scope was another issue. To think of monasticism purely in terms of the "Roman Empire," whether viewed from Rome itself or from the New Rome of Byzantium, was much too narrow a focus. The Roman Empire and its later Byzantine successor were just one—or better, two—among several empires and kingdoms where Christian monasteries were located. So we must add the Sassanian, Axumite, Himyarite, Rashidun, Umayyad, Tang Chinese, Abbasid, Bagratid (both Armenian and Georgian), Seljuk . . . Christian monasticism was everywhere, tied into the social and political realms in complex ways. We also need to reckon with the reality that monastic people and texts had an unusual mobility, crossing boundaries both physical and linguistic, and, once Christianity had begun its long fissuring in the fifth century, often confessional as well. For example, current scholarly debates about "center" and "periphery" with respect to writing about the Byzantine Empire[44] need concern us only in a limited way, since monasticism never had a center, and thus did not have a periphery. Wherever a monastery was, or even just a hermit,

---

[44] See the helpful overview of this and other neuralgic issues in Averil Cameron, *Byzantine Matters* (Princeton: Princeton University Press, 2014).

there was monasticism, and we have to meet each monastic place, each monastic person, on its own terms.

Why Now? A New Monastic Moment

My project seems to have a timeliness in terms of my own development and the current state of the discipline. But that would not be enough for me to set aside other attractive projects—a history of monastic prayer, for example—to concentrate on this one. I am convinced that this is a particular monastic moment, the beginning of an important if uncertain phase in monastic history. Since the late twentieth century, scholars of the humanities and other fields have been writing, in an often celebratory tone, about the postmodernist era, in which traditional taxonomies of knowledge or authoritative definitions have given way to a world in which there can be no imposed order. The intellectual liberation promised by postmodernism, while genuine in many respects, has proved illusory in others. Traditional religious beliefs and practices have perdured, though within a more diverse landscape. Having lost much of the social reinforcement they previously enjoyed, they have nonetheless demonstrated their coherence and value. In some ways, Christianity and its monastic expressions have returned to their *status quo ante*, in which they competed against other belief systems and ways of life.

In many countries in the developed world, there are new freedoms of personal and social identity, freedom to experiment, to blur boundaries, to create a deeply personal mix of styles and views. Underlying this individual exploration and experimentation is a hunger for authenticity, an authenticity felt as both a personal and a social imperative. The emergence of the transgender movement in the wake of campaigns for gay and lesbian rights is one example of this phenomenon in the contentious realm of sexuality. The rise of the "nones" in religious affiliation and the growth of those who claim to be "spiritual but not religious" bring it closer to those of us who find our home in increasingly fragile historic religious traditions. Monasticism, as an ancient and successful form of covenanted community with well-tested spiritual and ritual practices, has much to offer in this fluid environment. It can also provide a counterbalance to the individualism characteristic of contemporary Western culture.

Even as long-established monasteries and monastic congregations diminish, we see a host of new communities, ranging from hyper-traditional to a "new monasticism" that includes families and exists outside of confessional and canonical structures. The precarious situation of the consumerist global economy and of the natural environment makes one wonder who will keep things going if current social and economic structures—or the technologies that support them—begin to fail. If this suggestion seems jarringly pessimistic or even apocalyptic, remember that we monks and nuns have been there before. Should our natural role as guardians of memory and sustainers of community once more become essential for the survival of Christian—or any—culture, we should be ready. A fresh look at our origins and development could be a small contribution to such readiness.

Chapter 17

Father Michael Casey, OCSO
A Teacher of Monks for Our Time

An Interview

Francisco Rafael de Pascual, OCSO

W hen I first met Michael Casey in our Generalate in Rome, I was surprised by both the sincerity and the discernment in a man so discreet and straightforward. In truth I had only read a few articles by him, but my attention was taken by both his fine intuition and his broadmindedness in addressing various spiritual themes as well as topics in monastic history.

Since then I have been following the various teachings he has given to monks and nuns in different courses, seminars, and conferences. In Viaceli in 1990 we were given a course by Michael on "Cistercian Heritage," which I was unable to attend. Nevertheless, I read about the content of the course, noting that his bibliography contained an important pedagogical reference to a couple of books by Parker J. Palmer.[1] The style of Michael Casey's teaching produced a great impression among those present, and as far as I could tell these impressions fell into three main categories:

---

[1] Parker J. Palmer, *To Know as We Are Known: Education as a Spiritual Journey* (San Francisco: HarperCollins, 1993), and *The Active Life: Wisdom for Work, Creativity and Caring* (San Francisco: HarperCollins, 1991).

1. A marking of realistic and precise boundaries around the subjects that were studied
2. A friendly approach to the particular context of those in the audience
3. A relentless following of the method that had been previously laid down for the course of study

Years later, in 1999, I translated into Spanish a text by Michael from the first newsletter for the "Institute of Cistercian Heritage," entitled "Learning in the Monastery." The truth is that it was an authentic manual of his methodology for study and teaching. It is one of the best works I know of in this respect; it had a great impact on me at the time, and indeed I often return to it even now and have almost memorized some of its paragraphs. This text has given me the key to a deeper understanding of the more dense and technical aspects of Michael's writings. The "heuristic learning" he proposes is not only valid for an individual but can also sustain the program of ongoing formation for an entire community.

When I got the invitation to contribute to this celebratory volume, my first thought was to compile a collection of some of his work, but the truth is that little of his vast literary output has been translated into Spanish. This led me to think of a more personal approach to the task that would be very helpful to me and to others. So I suggested the idea of a personal interview with Michael himself. I would send him some questions on his ideas, and he would respond to these in his own words. Michael's friendly response to my request encouraged me, and I felt very fortunate, first because I believe his work and words are of great monastic value. They are both exemplary and pedagogical. Second, I thought that this task would give me a sort of ownership of an intellectual biography of Michael.

This task would not have been difficult, but it would have been costly in time and effort for me to produce a summary of the main themes contained in all the writings of Michael Casey, so I chose another path, and I believe that the results have been better. A summary of the interview here seems to me to be of more use to the reader than a work of mine (which in fact would only rehash what was previously said by Michael anyway, but with less clarity and brilliance). So I leave it to the reader to take the plunge into the deeper waters of Michael's writings, wherein lie pleasures and much profound satisfaction.

Finally, and without any presumption, I believe that this method of approaching someone's body of work may lead us to try something similar with other writers and pillars of our monastic tradition, whose ideas we have only known from extracts of their writings without actually reaching the existential reality of their lives, or the roots of their literary and human formation. We miss, therefore, the more personal and intimate demonstration of their thoughts and ideas.

An Interview with Michael Casey, OCSO

Question One.

When did you start writing? Do you have any recollections as to how you felt about it then?

I think the components of my writing capacity are the following. First of all I have a great love for learning and for new knowledge. Secondly, I am gifted with a very good memory, and so whatever goes in seems to stay there for a long time, and to be available for recall whenever I wish. Thirdly, the way my mind works is that it seems to have the ability to put together disparate elements of information so that often there are original connections in my thought that lead to surprising conclusions. Once I have arrived at such a point, then it becomes imperative for me to be able to express what is inside my head in the clearest possible way. This means in a way that corresponds to what I am feeling and thinking, a very personal way, an original way. This is the basic equipment that I use as a writer.

When I say I have a great love for learning, I do not mean that I have an ambition to become a walking encyclopaedia. What I have always desired is existential or experiential knowledge. What I am looking for is a truth that helps me to find meaning in my own life and my own experience. I suppose you could call it wisdom rather than science, although this seems to me rather a flash way of describing my own aspirations. In a sense my lifelong pursuit of learning appears to me a little like doing a jigsaw puzzle. Unlike most people I do not start at the edges, but first build up little islands of conjuncture at different points within the whole. As I go through life these islands grow and come closer together and eventually begin to join up. Because there are no edges, the frontiers of my thoughts are always expanding. I do not quite know where everything will end up. It seems that one thing leads to another, and the whole body of my own thought and philosophy are continually expanding. Somehow it makes sense. Somehow each part of what I know adheres to, complements, supports, and sustains the other parts.

With regard to the actual business of producing text, I have to say also that technology has played its role. Because I changed schools between years three and four I was caught at a very formative stage between two different approaches to handwriting. As a result I have always been a bad hand-writer, and what I have produced has never been a source of very great satisfaction to me. All this changed when I had access to a typewriter. The clarity on the page was, I felt, expressive of the clarity of the thought that I was trying to put on paper. Since 1986 I have been using a computer, and, of course, this has led to a greater facility in writing and revising. I can change words around, modify the vocabulary and syntax, to make sure that what I am writing expresses what I really want to say.

As far as I know, I didn't do very much writing as a boy apart from what we had to do as school work, and I have to say that English expression was always one of the subjects at which I was good.

I have never been a particularly ardent keeper of journals. From time to time I do use a journal kind of entry as a means of clarifying my own thought about what is happening inside me. But I have never kept a regular journal. I often think, let it be said as an aside, that too much journal writing destroys personal style, because it is so subjective and introspective that it ceases to be an objective communication with the outside world. This is especially so when the journal becomes a sort of record of a stream of consciousness.

When I entered the monastery I did no more writing than anybody else, but I suppose the birth of my interest in writing for publication came during the three years that were given to the study of philosophy. I really enjoyed the comprehensiveness, the clarity, and the logic of Scholastic philosophy. I enjoyed it so much that I began to try to seek further possibilities by outside reading, and so I read Bernard Lonergan's book *Insight*, an achievement that took me two years. I also read quite a bit of Karl Rahner. The world of thought that was opened to me by these two great thinkers was wonderful, but they played havoc with my English prose. Whatever I wrote at that time became inexorably complicated. And it also became difficult for me to compose straightforward sentences, because there were so many clarifications and definitions to be built into even the simplest statement. So I decided I had to do something to lighten up my writing style and to get it back to the level of facility that I had always enjoyed. So I began to do book reviews for the local Catholic newspaper. Over the next few years I must have done seventy or eighty of these. What this did was that it gave me the opportunity simply to write what I was thinking and feeling without a great deal of agonizing over accurate definitions and without the need for long complicated sentences.

Publication is an addictive drug, it seems to me. It's a delight to see on paper what has originated within oneself. And even these simple little reviews gave me the taste for doing something a bit more complicated.

In the late 1960s Basil Pennington started up Cistercian Publications and was looking for translators. My abbot seemed to consider that I was the only possible candidate locally, and so he sent my name to Basil Pennington. My first experience in translation was the *Apologia of Bernard of Clairvaux*. I really enjoyed this and enjoyed the research that was necessary to be able to accompany my translation with suitable notes. This was the first of my works to be published as part of a book.

From 1969 onward I was also involved in teaching, and this gave me scope not only for the research into whatever I was teaching but also into its delivery and into the preparation of some sort of handouts to give to the students, and so I became, more or less, a man of words. In 1971 I was the founding editor of our Australian Benedictine periodical, *Tjurunga: An Australasian Benedictine Review*.

From 1971 to 1973 I studied Scripture at Louvain. This was an eye-opening experience for me. I was exposed not only to the work that was necessary for my thesis in Scripture but also to many other topics that were, strictly speaking, outside the immediate range of my specialization. It was a time in which my intellectual outlook was irreversibly enhanced. It was there that I started writing a few short articles on monastic topics. These were published initially in our Australian periodical, *Tjurunga*. From the early 70s onward there was interest in publishing my articles in an ever-growing range of other periodicals. It was not, however, until the late 1980s that my first books were published, although I had finished my doctoral thesis on desire for God in Bernard of Clairvaux in 1979.

I think that is about all that can be said about the start of my writing career insofar as it is a career. At least, it is all that comes to mind at this moment.

Question Two.

When you started the monastic life, had it occurred to you that you would eventually become a writer-monk?

The short answer to this question is no. From a very early age I had a strong sense of vocation, but it was a vocation that for many years had no definition. When by chance I came into contact with the monastery at Tarrawarra, I suddenly realized that this is what I had been looking for all along. I didn't really know a great deal about monastic life, but I was attracted by the sacredness of the place, and my intuition was that it was here that God wanted me to be. Shortly before I entered, my sister-in-law offered to give me some of Merton's books to read so that I would be more fully informed about what I was entering. My reply to her was "I shall find out soon enough." In other words I knew virtually nothing about monastic life when I entered. I entered because I was convinced that it was to this life that God was calling me. I had no sense that there was any necessity for me to define the parameters of my own future career.

In fact I do not define myself even now as a writer-monk. I regard myself simply as a monk, perhaps a monk who happens to write at this stage in his life. Of course, it has not always been so. I give priority in my day to monastic observance: I am present at all the Offices and all the other community events, and I never write after Compline. Like every monk in a small community I hold down a variety of jobs that expand and contract according to the demands of the season and of a particular day. One of the great blessings that I have enjoyed for the last thirty years or so is to have an office separate from my monastic cell. My work of writing happens only in the office. For the most part, I go to my office during the morning work period and in the afternoon as the opportunity allows, but by no means am I a full-time writer. And, in fact, members of my own community don't refer to me as a writer or give me any special concessions in that regard. I think sometimes that they regard my writing as a kind of private vice, as though I were a secret drinker. They all know about it, but they are too polite to mention it, much less to engage with it. When a new book appears and is put into the library nobody mentions it. I don't know if anybody reads what I write, whether book or article, but I have to accept that this is part of the way that a community operates.

What I write is mostly done in response to requests from others. Sometimes people ask me to conduct a program on a particular topic, and the way I prepare myself is to write an article on it. I don't read the article to them. I talk around it, and present the material in a more pedagogical and user-friendly way, but the article forms an important part of my own preparation, and eventually I will have it published somewhere. Sometimes this is quite exciting. I am asked to prepare a program on a particular topic about which I know very little and which I have not considered previously. This means that I have to do a large amount of work reading, thinking, experimenting with a way of approaching the topic, and so it is not only something fresh that I eventually deliver but is also a voyage of exploration for myself. It is another island that has started to form in the jigsaw puzzle.

I should also say that my writing career, such as it is, has been complemented by my contact with people. Sometimes this has been with monastic communities around the world, sometimes with people as individuals. These contacts have provided me with new agenda. They have opened my eyes to questions and issues and aspects of questions and issues that perhaps previously I have not considered. And it gives me a chance to try out my thoughts on other people to see their reactions and their responses, and to receive feedback from them. Writing is by nature a very solitary activity. Without this interchange with qualified people it can become a little detached from reality. I have been lucky in that my work in many monasteries all over the world has provided me with incentives and opportunities to explore further the questions that are closest to my own interests.

Later in life I have found that I have a little bit more freedom to pursue avenues of inquiry that correspond to my own present interests and are personally gratifying. These I am eventually able to market in some way or another either in talks that I give, or in a homily or perhaps in publications of one sort or another. After fifty years or more of working in the field of monastic spirituality and monastic authors, I feel that I am somewhat entitled to vent my opinions as well as give the results of my research.

So I don't really like the idea of being called a "writer-monk" especially if there is a hyphen between the two words. I think I would prefer the phrase "a monk who writes." Even better is the phrase "a man of words," because I love words and I love writing (at least, when all goes well), but I do not define myself thus.

Twice my book on Saint Bernard, *Athirst for God*, has been translated into French in Canada, but neither has ever seen the light of day as far as I know. Fr. Graham Touchie of Calvaire (Rogersville) was asked to review one of the versions. Before doing so he read the English original and put together a list of the characteristics of my literary voice—which a true translation ought to maintain. He sent it to me, and when I read it to two of my older brothers, who happened to visit together, they fell about laughing, because they thought it was accurate. Here is the text he sent me, for what it is worth:

Seven Traits of Michael Casey's Literary Voice

1. A Conflictual World. The world is in his face, as it were; he is not excluded from its conflicts and confusion, but encounters those aspects of the world just as he tries to delve more deeply into it. The risk of

error looms large around him. We can hear, then, quiet melancholy if we listen. However, at the very same level of the writing there is a quiet hope. It is a complicated world, but also one in which he is moving toward clarity and resolution. He has a critical eye and a critical edge which serve him well.

The six traits following can be traced back to this one. The world is a wonderful place and a threatening place.

2. A contained sense of humor
3. Knowledge as adventure
4. A passionate unsentimentality
5. A penchant for literary order and structure . . . and distrust of it
6. A contained drive toward the concrete and the matter-of-fact
7. An abiding concern for fairness in tension and trait

Question Three.

Was there any decisive influence, an event or a person, that pushed you to study in depth and write about the Cistercian heritage? What was monastic formation like when you entered the monastery?

I entered the monastery in 1960 on 2 February. I think it was in 1963, as a junior professed, that I first began to take a more intense personal interest in Bernard of Clairvaux. He was my point of entry into the Cistercian patrimony. My novice master's main heroes were Saint Francis de Sales, Saint Therese of Lisieux, and, of course, Abbot Marmion. Saint Bernard was not exactly a favorite with the seniors of the community, because the abbot of the mother house, Dom Camillus Claffey, was an enthusiast and had even written a slight devotional book on Saint Bernard. This had the effect of driving all his monks in the opposite direction. None of them wanted anything to do with Saint Bernard.

What happened, as I remember it, was that I was greatly attracted by the reading for vigils on the Saturday memorial of the Blessed Virgin. This was, as you might remember, the famous reading from Saint Bernard's treatise *Missus est*, with the line "Look to the star." I decided at that point that I wished to read more. I took out from the library the book by Père Bernard Martelet of Sept-Fons, *Saint Bernard et Notre Dame*. This contained all the Bernardine texts about Our Lady with the Latin on one page and a French translation on the other. This was my initiation into reading Bernard in Latin.

From there I continued to read the works of Saint Bernard and gradually to extend the focus of my reading to include other writings of the Cistercian Fathers. This was not my main interest at the time. At this stage of my life the study of Scripture was what attracted me the most. I had wanted to learn Greek, but the abbot, who was also the junior master, was very opposed to this. Perhaps my attraction was fueled by his opposition. I kept pushing the point, and eventually he gave in and permitted me to start studying Greek on my own. After about a year I had gained sufficient facility with Greek to be able to begin reading the New Testament. I then took up Hebrew and the following year German. This meant that, with the Latin and French I had from my school days, I had a good foundation for a future study of Scripture. I am very glad that I had the energy in those days when my brain was still fully operational to acquire these languages. They are more useful to me than anything else that I have done over the years. It is a great blessing to be able to read the New Testament in Greek and the Cistercian Fathers in Latin.

My experience in reading the Cistercian Fathers is that one thing always leads to another. You read one work and feel compelled then to look into another, and, attracted by it, you begin to read a little more. And so gradually one begins to move freely throughout the whole wide pasture of the Cistercian patrimony. It is not as though I was ambitious to acquire a mastery of this area. I don't think I will ever acquire such a level of expertise. Every time I begin to read or to reread a text of that period I discover something new, I discover how little I know about it, and how much more there is to discover. It is all rather exciting. I have never found the study of the Cistercian Fathers in any way boring except, maybe, for William of Saint-Thierry. Parallel with this I was also reading the church fathers. It is very hard to draw a line of demarcation between the area of the Cistercian patrimony and that of the writings of the church fathers, particularly those of the Western church.

When I entered the monastery in 1960 the formation followed a basic apprenticeship model. This is what we do, do it and everything will be okay. Don't ask too many questions because, as my novice master used often to say, "A fool can ask questions that a wise man cannot answer." There were studies especially after simple profession. These were a nod in the direction of canon law, since in those days most choir monks were intended for the priesthood, and to be ordained you had to put in several years of appropriate study. This was minimalist and very amateurish up to the time that I began. In 1963, however, men started returning from postgraduate studies in Rome, and they had something more to offer: a more rigorous method, better content, and a whole lot more enthusiasm. Until then studies had seemed to be secondary to the main work of the monastery; manual work enjoyed a much higher prestige. The two later years of my three years of philosophy really sparked my interest and gave me a foundation for much of the way in which I have thought in the intervening fifty years. Moral theology was solid and Roman and of a fair amount of utility, though it was not exactly thrilling. Dogmatic theology was very much oriented to Scripture and to patristics, though the one teaching it was hopeless, inclined to chase after every red herring that bedeviled his path. For example, when he was teaching the novices monastic history it was discovered that after a year's classes he had not yet reached Christian monasticism. He taught about Qumran and the Pythagoreans and raved on about East Asian monastic traditions, because these were the things in which he himself was interested. I don't think he ever thought about what might be useful to those starting off, what might be helpful in their own monastic lives, what might be instructive in initiating them into the monastic tradition. Since we had nobody who was qualified in Scripture at that time, the Scripture classes, such as they were, were conducted by external teachers, a Sacred Heart father and a Dominican. The library as I recall it was poor enough, though this was a fairly common occurrence in monasteries at the time, especially in new foundations. We were very economically challenged for the first ten or fifteen years of our existence, and buying a book, a single book, was not a thing lightly to be considered. We relied mainly on gifts and the supply that we had been given at the time of our foundation, though, because we were the second foundation made from Mount St. Joseph, Roscrea, in Ireland, the number of spare books that could be given to us was not great. And the distance they had to be transported was an issue also.

When Dom Gabriel Sortais, at the behest of the Roman authorities, began to insist on greater intellectual rigor in the formation of young monks, especially those destined for the priesthood, things began to change. I was a beneficiary of this initiative. Dom Kevin, our first abbot, was, like many of the Irish, greatly a lover of education, and so he began to send most of the young Australians overseas for study. When my turn came I was informed by the two students already in Rome not to go there, mainly because they said living at the Generalate was like living in a madhouse. It was impossible to give oneself fully to study because whatever was done had to be fitted into an unrealistic monastic daily timetable. At a time when some of the universities started having evening and night sessions, this caused a great hullabaloo at the Generalate; it was considered inappropriate that monks should be out at nighttime—who knows what they would get up to? And, I believe, there was much quarreling about whether the doors should be locked and who should have a key given to them. All this worked to my benefit. It was decided that I would not go to Rome but would go somewhere else. And so I ended up at Louvain. I found the approach there, especially in Scripture study, to be much more in line with what I myself desired. It was very rigorous, there was much insistence on a good knowledge of Greek and Hebrew, and it was very much text-based. It was not a kind of generalizing, devotional, or theologizing exegesis of the text but something far more scientific and far more satisfying as far as I was concerned.

The kind of methodology I learned at Louvain served me very well when I came to reading, understanding, interpreting, teaching, and expanding the ancient monastic texts. This meant an insistence on close reading of the text, reading them in the original language, reading widely their immediate and remote contexts. So I see in my years at Louvain a very strong, formative influence on the way I approach things, even though the way I present them is probably more due to my own personality and perhaps to some of our national characteristics.

In 1976, I became conscious that I was becoming a little bit jaded in the monastery, and so what I decided to do was to look for something that would rekindle my own zeal and freshen my life. So I got permission to begin a doctorate, and I decided to do that doctorate on Saint Bernard. I didn't really get any time for this; I was still holding down a number of jobs in the monastery. I was teaching Scripture and was wardrobe keeper and tailor, I was librarian, I was cooking a couple of days a week, and there were many other odds and ends that made demands on my time. But whenever I did have time I worked very consistently reading everything on, or of, Saint Bernard and eventually managed to complete the thesis within the three-year time limit. This was a great grace in my life. To spend time with Saint Bernard, to spend a lot of time with Saint Bernard, is a very formative experience. I never became jaded with Bernard; he always seems to have something fresh to say to me.

I find it very hard to imagine what monastic life would have been for me without my great exposure to the wisdom of Saint Bernard. He has been my master *par excellence.* I did have a very good and very formative relationship with my junior master, and this not only served me well in the five years that we were together but has given me a foundation for the rest of my life. But it is hard for me to think of any living person who has had the sort of influence on me that Bernard has had. Jean Leclercq was very encouraging and supportive, and always ready to respond to queries and to share his vast world of knowledge, but my contact with him (between 1973 and 1990) was inevitably dependent on our being in the same part of the world at the same time and so was necessarily sporadic.

Question Four.

How have you been educating yourself as a monk and a writer?

One of the things that I like about canon law is what it says about formation. It says that those in formation are responsible for their own formation; they are co-responsible. It's no use complaining that the community doesn't provide a good education or a good formation. It is important that each person, as an adult, take active responsibility for educating themselves to the fullest level of their capacity. And this means more than a butterfly approach. It involves disciplined learning, laying foundations, persevering in times of difficulty, and using one's imagination to make the topic under study a very personal item. I remember reading in a nineteenth-century commentary on the Gospel of John by an exegete named Schmiedl, if I remember correctly, who said that one of the prime characteristics for a potential commentator on the Gospel of John was a long life. I think the same is true of anybody venturing into the field of monastic studies. Spending years at the coalface almost inevitably gives a good knowledge and a broad knowledge of one's topic.

I think also that there is a need for a basic confidence in one's own ability to learn, one's own ability to grapple with the topic and to arrive at reasonable conclusions. I must admit that I don't have a lot of sympathy for those whose intellectual life consists mainly in dashing off to seminars or lectures, as it were, drinking in the wisdom from others, and never making the effort to generate their own. I think it was Bernard Lonergan who said that we can never be sure that we really understand something unless we can express it in our own words—and the more original the expression, the more likely that real understanding has occurred. Yes, outside lecturers can be helpful at appropriate moments in one's intellectual journey, but there is always the need to be prepared to spend time alone working quietly and consistently at whatever one is striving to learn. As in prayer, so in study: regularity and perseverance are the key components of progress.

In my own case I am grateful that I got a good fundamental education in Scholastic philosophy and theology. It is not a very cuddly kind of approach to spiritual studies, but it has a certain austere integrity about it that serves very well as a framework for future thought. It provides a skeleton, as it were, that supports the whole structure. The skeleton is not necessarily a very attractive object, but it is necessary, and without it the flesh just collapses into a heap of jelly. My time at Louvain, as I have said, was a great period of formation for me both in exposure to a wider world of content and also in terms of methodology. Finally, in the area of academic training, the three years I spent writing my doctoral thesis were very important for me. It meant spending time consistently working on a single stream of thought, venturing abroad only to the extent that whatever I was exploring had some connection with the basic flow of the work that I had undertaken. I have already mentioned that I am very grateful that I had the opportunity and the energy at a fairly young age to pick up a few important languages: Latin, French, Greek, Hebrew, some German, in particular, although I am no master in any of them. Because I am introverted by nature, my knowledge of the language translates into conversational fluidity only with great difficulty. Living in Australia without much opportunity to be in a foreign-language ambience certainly doesn't help either. But a good reading knowledge is probably the most important thing for a monastic student. I did do some Dutch and Ugaritic in Louvain, but my attempt to learn these did not have the same level of penetration as the others. I am able to stumble through a text in Italian or Spanish without a great deal of difficulty, so long as it is not too complicated, on the basis of my knowledge of Latin and French and because by nature I am intuitive and so I am not averse to a little bit of guesswork.

For the present how am I working on my continuing education? Well, I have a mind like a magpie's nest, which is to say that I very easily accumulate information even without thinking about it very much or trying to do so. Things just seem to stay embedded in my memory and to be ready to come forth without very much prompting. Usually what I have stored in my memory is not totally random, but most often it relates to something that is important to me or that figures strongly in whatever I'm doing at the moment. Fifty years in a monastery means that I have been exposed willy-nilly to a large amount of reading, in the liturgy and the refectory and elsewhere. I usually try to pay attention to what is being read. For my own reading, apart from *lectio divina*, I'm always reading something else, preferably something that has very little to do directly with whatever I am involved in at the time. I read novels for relaxation, classical works of literature, some history, and a little popular science. As librarian I get to browse through every book that I access. I have a friend who gives me copies of *The Times Literary Supplement, The New York Review of Books, The Literary Review,* and the journal financed by the CIA, *Foreign Affairs.* I enjoy reading these even though I may not ever get to read the books which they are reviewing, but I do get a general notion of cultural movements in our own times. On medical advice I try to take a walk of about an hour every day to see if I can extend my miserable life a little bit further, and during this time I habitually listen to podcasts downloaded from the national radio network, usually on cultural or scientific topics. Very often as soon as I get back I jot down a few notes of something that has struck me while I was listening, something that will inevitably crop up in a footnote or a talk that I give. In other words I'm always trawling for things that add a little bit of light, and perhaps a little bit of humor, to the topics that I am researching and presenting.

And of course, as everybody knows, teaching is a great way of learning. I find that it is only when I have to teach others that I discover how little I myself know about a particular topic, and so I have to get to work to learn more. It is one of the ironies of teaching, it seems to me, that the teacher spends much more time learning than the students do; this is more than immediate preparation for the presentation of a class. It is more like the preparation of one's own mind, asking more questions, finding some answers. The same is true, and even more true, of writing. When I write something I may be simply repeating what I have already presented in classes or in lectures or in workshops, but I usually discover that what is presented orally is much looser than can be permitted in writing. There are gaps that need to be bridged. There are references that need to be clarified. And there is the endless effort required to document the assertions that I make.

So I educate myself as a monk by giving myself as fully as possible to living the monastic life, to reading monastic sources, to exploring the different questions that arise in the living of daily life, and to finding some answers to the questions that others raise or seek my guidance about. I don't think this work of ongoing formation ever ceases until death. At the time I was writing the constitutions, there was one abbot who was very critical of the idea of ongoing formation. He said it was a contradiction in terms. There was a period of formation, after which the monk was formed. End of the story. He did not like the idea that one was continually undergoing change, undergoing formation, undergoing reformation. But I think experience tells us that if we are alive and are still possessed of our faculties, then it is necessary for us to be constantly reformed, constantly reeducated, constantly changed to accommodate new situations: the situation outside oneself, and also the changing interior situation that is the mark of spiritual progress.

As I have said previously, I don't consider myself as defined by the term *writer*. I don't try to educate myself as a writer although I'm constantly interested in questions of style and grammar, and I love collecting new words, which I then try to use. This is more a matter of amusing myself and following my own interests than in seriously trying to make myself a better writer. "What I have written, I have written," as someone once said. There is something very exposing about the written word. Whatever one writes one exposes oneself at the same time, no matter how one tries to hide (because the hiding itself then becomes revealing). If I were to give advice to someone who wanted to write it would be a matter of some very simple precepts. Here are my ten commandments:

1. Be alive.
2. Be yourself.
3. Be prepared for a certain amount of solitude and detachment.
4. Be interested in everything.
5. Don't write what you don't know.
6. Know what you want to say—have a passion, a message to deliver.
7. Acquire a taste for elegant simplicity.
8. Don't waffle.
9. Avoid self-indulgence.
10. And don't forget humor!

Question Five.

In light of your experience, which three monastic writers would you recommend to young monks today?

I suppose that you mean contemporary writers, and I can really only speak of those whose work is available in English. I would have to say that I can really only speak to myself; choice of reading is a very personal thing; what speaks to one may be absolutely silent to another. Of course, Thomas Merton must be at the head of most lists. There is much that he has written that is still of great relevance today, fifty years afterward. I would, however, suggest that a certain amount of maturity is necessary to be able to read Merton in context. Many of the issues that he was dealing with in his lifetime are less urgent now. But he is a wonderful writer and he has much to say even now.

Anything that André Louf wrote I have found engaging, insightful, and challenging. He had a great deal of experience of monastic life, and of dealing with monks and nuns. He writes well and with a world of theology behind every page.

In terms of reading about the Rule of Saint Benedict, the writings of Terrence Kardong are excellent. He has a wide background in Benedictine studies, he is the author of a major commentary on the Rule, and he grapples with the way in which the Rule and its conventional interpretation interface with contemporary issues. I enjoy the fact that he writes with a certain amount of vigor and is not afraid to share his opinions, but these are always educated opinions based on years of solid work in scholarship.

Another author whose work on the Rule I like is Aquinata Böckmann. A former professor at the University of Sant'Anselmo in Rome, she has great experience working with groups at every level to help them to understand what the Rule is saying. She is very strong on a methodological approach to the Rule. I think this is important today because there are so many people propagating what they term "Benedictine" spirituality who have not done their homework. They have read a little bit of this and that, and from this they go on to enunciate a "Benedictine" spirituality that is in fact very much of their own making. There is not sufficient evidence to show that they have listened carefully to the Rule or read widely among its key commentators. It seems that Benedictine spirituality has become marketable, and so there are many people offering expositions of it who are not really qualified to speak. Both Kardong and Böckmann are qualified.

In the broader world of monastic spirituality I like the works of Meg Funk, particularly because she applies the teachings of the ancient monastic authors to modern situations and writes in a way that is very accessible to the normal contemporary reader.

A relatively recent book by Brendan Freeman, *Come and See*, is worthwhile, even though I wrote the foreword to it. It is a collection of his chapter discourses over many years as abbot and reveals a good theological foundation, a wide knowledge of monasticism, and a deep experience of monastic life as it is lived in his own community.

You asked for three authors and I have given you six; perhaps this indicates that my arithmetic is not as well developed as some other areas of my intellectual activity. I should say also that most of my own monastic reading is done in primary sources, and although I do read through most of the monastic periodicals that we receive, I cannot really say that I am strongly influenced by them. In fact I find that when I am writing it is very necessary to keep my own particular perspective relatively untainted by what others think about the subject I am discussing. Not because they are wrong or worthless, but simply because it is important for me to develop my own train of thought without getting sidetracked into alternative ways of approaching the same topic.

If you are thinking about which of the monastic writers of the past have influenced me, then the answer is relatively easy. The big three: Bernard, Aelred, and Guerric. Recently I have been reading some of the writings of Abbot Armand-Jean de Rancé and, granted the historical context in which he operated, I think that these are certainly worthy of more attention than they currently receive.

Question Six.

Which texts from monastic writers have left the deepest mark in your life and thought? And which others from non-monastic writers?

Not such an easy question, is it? After all I have been reading pretty consistently for over fifty years in the monastery. Thinking back, Bernard Lonergan's book, *Insight*, would certainly be a key text in the development of my thought. I suppose you could also include Hans Georg Gadamer's work, *Truth and Method*. These have not been permanent companions in my life, but I have come across them at important transitional periods, and they have directed my attention in a particular way that has ongoing influence.

Regarding monastic texts, Bernard's *Sermons on the Song of Songs* have been a key influence in my life. Some years ago the BBC ran a program, a radio program entitled *Desert Island Discs*, in which they asked celebrities which records they would take with them if they were confined on a desert island for a year. So if I were to be locked in jail or dropped onto a desert island with only limited resources, one of the texts that I would want to take as well as the Bible would be Bernard's *Sermons on the Song of Songs*. There is an enormous depth of wisdom here, great humanity, and a very large and profound theology—all expressed in elegant Latin. Nearly everything that Bernard wrote is well worth reading and has played a strong role in my own intellectual, spiritual, and monastic development. These past years I have also learned to appreciate the chapter discourses of Aelred of Rievaulx. Guerric of Igny's work is likewise a beautifully crafted series of sermons that one can read and reread. Beatrice of Nazareth is one of my favorites. Her *Seven Modes of Love* is a wonderful text in which, in simple language, she has embedded so much spiritual insight and wisdom. I am also indebted to the writings of Saint Augustine, particularly his commentary on Saint John's gospel and his treatises on the Psalms, but to many of his other works as well. And Gregory the Great. And, of course, the Rule of Saint Benedict; it is so familiar from frequent community readings that unless one pays close attention to it, a lot of its wisdom can go unnoticed. I have been lucky enough to have been obliged to give courses on the Rule and so have worked closely with the text and been greatly enriched by it.

As I said earlier I read fairly widely from ephemeral sources, and this keeps me somewhat in contact with contemporary culture. This reading is important to me, and it certainly leaves traces, but I doubt very much whether it is strongly formative of my own personal philosophy of life.

Question Seven.

In your role as a teacher, what have been the biggest obstacles you have found to transmit your teachings?

In general, groups have been very receptive to what I have to say. Here I am speaking mainly about people from other monasteries and from the Benedictines, which usually means an international audience since there are not many monasteries in Australia. They have habitually been very hospitable to whatever I have to say, and by interacting with them I have learned a lot.

Teaching in one's own monastery is a challenge. There is a Gaelic proverb that says "Foreign cows have long horns," and this, I suppose, is the same as the English proverb "Familiarity breeds contempt." It is very difficult to teach one's own confreres, people who see you every day in good times and in bad and whose opinion of you is determined by so many factors that are extraneous to the classroom. This is especially true when the same person is acting as formator, with its rather specific interpersonal dynamisms, and as teacher, or the same person is teaching several different subjects. In this case people get tired of you, or at least they get tired of me. So there is always this pressure on you to keep delivering something fresh week after week, year after year, not losing the goodwill of the students, keeping them entertained, and at the same time imparting the useful information and formation that they need. So overexposure is a great obstacle.

For the last few years we have been outsourcing some of the classes that have to be done. This is because of small numbers both in teachers and in students. So we have divided the monastic education program into two streams: a theological stream and a monastic stream. The students do an undergraduate degree in theology by distance education. Formerly we taught this theology ourselves, but now there are too few students to justify such an effort, and in addition there is the advantage that these are courses that are recognized at a theological institution, which means they eventually get a degree, which provides a foundation for postgraduate work later on.

We continue to teach the monastic stream ourselves, this is to say monastic spirituality, monastic history, and the various monastic authors. I have noticed, especially among those who are a little bit competitive or ambitious, that they give much more attention to their external studies than to the intramural courses that they do. For these they sometimes devote a minimum of effort, whereas they work extravagantly hard to achieve good marks in the external courses. I don't know exactly what we can do to remedy this situation, because we have always made a point of not encouraging any sort of competitiveness in studies but encouraged each to do as well as he can in order to enrich his own monastic life. So it is a great discouragement for the teacher when he finds that the students, although very intelligent and enthusiastic about other studies, are not really devoting sufficient personal study to the subjects that they are teaching. My rule always has been that for each hour of class time there should be three hours of private study. And we allow this for the students. But very often if they are doing two parallel streams the external studies get far more attention than those done with community teachers.

For some of the students the whole study program is simply something that they have to do, another burden that is imposed upon them. They come to class simply because they are obliged to come, and while there they do no more than the minimum. Their participation is lukewarm, to say the least, and sometimes they can be positively destructive. The potential teacher needs to understand all these situations and to learn some tactics to deal with them. When a teacher is not a formator, often a student who is going through hard times will express a lot of his negativity in the classroom, because he does not want to get into trouble from his formator by making a scene in front of him.

There is always the question of excessive passivity. A teacher who tries to have an interactive and participative class is reliant on the goodwill of the students. Generally novices are very cooperative. Juniors are for a while, but then things start happening in their own lives, and some of their own uncreative energies begin to make themselves known. More often than not these appear in the classroom. They refuse to get personally involved. Sometimes there is a fair amount of passive aggression, arms folded, looking out the window, not taking any notes, not having one's book open at the right page, ending class with a histrionic yawn. Sometimes this is just an expression of the way they feel about life in general. At other times it is an expression of political protest about something or other in the structure of the monastery that is not to their liking. I think it would be unwise also to omit to say that there are some people who are just plain lazy, who do not want to make any effort, whose main energies are directed at finding excuses for not doing what they are supposed to do, not only in the classroom but everywhere.

Another difficulty is the variety of educational levels that one meets in a typical group of monastic students. Some will have been very highly educated indeed, others not at all. And sometimes those who have been formed in scientific disciplines have little appreciation of the skills and techniques that are needed for a more historical approach to research. Trying to cater for everyone in a single class is quite a challenge, especially if novices and juniors are mixed together. A particular difficulty that is encountered nowadays is that many do not have a good knowledge of foreign languages and, particularly, a knowledge of Latin. Some wish to learn Latin, some begin to teach themselves Latin or ask others to help them to learn Latin, but even if they persevere in their efforts, they rarely reach the point where they can easily read texts. And this condemns them to relying always on secondhand sources.

Thinking back over more than forty years of teaching in a monastery, I cannot name a single student who habitually presented as enthusiastic about what he was learning, or who expressed any sort of gratitude for the efforts exerted on his behalf by the teachers, at least over a long period of time. One gets the impression that they are doing the teacher a favor by attending their courses. Some of those who have left, including some who gave a certain amount of trouble while they were going through the system, have afterward expressed great gratitude for what they learned when they were with us. They boast about the quality of their monastic education, though while they were with us they were pretty hostile. In several monastic writers including Saint Bernard I have come across the characterization of a certain type of monk as one who wishes to teach before he himself has been a learner. I have come across a few of those in my time. In the four decades I have taught, I have tried very many different ways of communicating my material, attempting to make the classes interesting and useful to those who were attending; a great deal of effort has gone into this. Sometimes it seems that people do not want to put themselves into a position of being grateful to anyone for anything. Maybe it will all be expressed at my funeral!

Already, and perhaps an even greater problem in the future, is the relationship of the student with books. Traditional reading is a cool medium; most younger people today prefer something hotter and would rather do research on the internet than in a library. Even the existence of traditional books may be under threat. Just as when computers began to be used for word processing, they often tried to mimic typewriters (though by that time electronic typewriters were moving the gap closer), so today e-books mimic paper books. So reading them is not much different from reading books. In the future e-books may well be connected to the internet so that reading will offer a variety of hypertexts as well. Nicholas Carr in his book *The Shallows* points to the danger in this. He regards it as systematic distractedness. Instead of reading a text straight through we are sidetracked into pursuing all sorts of explanations and expansions so that the line of argument is lost. In a book on Saint Bernard, his name will prompt a series of images, including those of Saint Bernard dogs; mention Burgundy and you will get a tourist video showing the main sites and, perhaps, a selection of Burgundian folk tunes and a listing of the local culinary specialities. This is, obviously, a hindrance to serious, logical study—but in the sphere of *lectio divina*, utterly disastrous.

As I review these remarks, I am conscious that a lot of what I have said sounds pretty negative, but you did ask me about obstacles. I enjoy teaching most of the time, but, like most of the activities of monastic life, teaching is a matter of continuing to stumble forward, doing one's best, without expecting huge tidal waves of adulation.

We have to remember that monastic education is only part of the formation that newcomers receive. They are formed principally by their participation in the fraternal life of the community and in the use of the monastic means: the observances that characterize our way of life. It is also important that they receive help from their relationship with the formator: accompaniment, counsel, mentoring, modeling, and coaching. Somehow or other the monastic education has to sit alongside these two more significant sources of formation; it has to ground them and help to make them more meaningful. And it also has to give the newcomer the possibility of pursuing monastic spirituality as a personal project for the rest of his life.

So I understand that there has to be a basic framework to give some structure to our instruction, but what we are really trying to do is to make young monks and nuns lovers of learning, lovers of reading, people who understand the richness of the monastic tradition and desire to participate in what it has to offer, and to hand it on to the next generation. So there always has to be an element of heuristic learning whereby people are encouraged not simply to receive what they are given but to undertake the adventure of new learning, of moving out in the direction to which they feel attracted and which in some way sustains their own interior fire.

Conclusion

The universality and depth of Michael's educational work, over the period of twenty-five years that I have known him, is unsurpassed in the history of modern monastic literature. Personally, three aspects of Michael's work impress me deeply: first, his ability to modernize the monastic tradition with expert and experienced hands, opening the doors not only to ancient texts but to situations and concepts of the tradition that few others have been able to apply to the lives of all people today, not just monks and nuns; second, his own evident satisfaction in dealing with subjects that give him a profound admiration for their objective value as well as their intrinsic value for people today who are exposed to very different cultural influences from those of earlier centuries, especially those of the Middle Ages; and third, the desire for clarity and organization of the thought manifested in the texts he writes and the classes he organizes. These provide modern interpretations of monasticism in a way that remains available to all, not just the privileged few or those already initiated into the intricacies of the monastic tradition.

Father Michael Casey knows how to infuse his writings with the wisdom and perseverance of a learned man, with the love and dedication of the master for his disciples, and with a keen ear for modern needs in a culture of changing values and spiritual uncertainties.

End Note

Michael Casey
A Poet of the Logos

Bishop Graeme Rutherford

The opening paragraph of Michael Casey's editorial *"Ex Cathedra,"* in *Tjurunga: An Australasian Benedictine Review*, May 2006, reads as follows: "Rereading the Epistle of James recently I was struck by the phrase usually translated 'doers of the word.' In Greek it is *poetai logou*, which might be rendered a little more imaginatively as 'poets of the logos.' This translation suggests that James is admonishing us to become not merely deferential doers of the word but its creative and exuberant proclaimers, welcoming it with meekness and transmitting it to others with intelligence and verve."[1] I can think of no more apt description to sum up Michael's own contribution to monasticism and to the broader ecumenical community than to employ the way in which he has suggested that phrase in James might be translated.

Michael's lectures, homilies, and books are all characterized by an elegant, intelligent, and imaginative use of language. In his contemplative monastic vocation, Michael has served others as a "poet of the logos." He once suggested that there are three different approaches to doing theology. *Orthodoxy* is concerned with right teaching (or literally, with right worship). On its own, it can easily lead to barren intellectualism.

---

[1] *"Ex Cathedra,"* TJ 70 (2006): 3.

Orthopraxy is concerned with correct behavior. But again, this can lead to sterile moral activism. Truth involves deeds as well as creeds. Michael has suggested the need for a third level of truth. For this he coined the word *orthomorphy*. What he had in mind is theology that is characterized by beauty as well as cognitive truth and embodied action. I recall Michael once saying, "Theology is not necessarily dull, feeling-less, and irrelevant to godly living. If it has become so, then let us strive to make of it not only something true and practical, but also 'something beautiful for God.'"

Discovering the superlative value of the Kingdom is the discovery of something of such surpassing worth that the joy of it is irresistible. As our Lord put it, *Where our treasure is, there your heart will be also* (Matt 6:21). Benedict expected his monks to be obsessed with Christ. He says, "Prefer nothing whatever to Christ" (RB 72.11). It is out of the appreciation of the love and beauty of Jesus that Christian joy and peace flow. The heart of Benedictine spirituality is a value judgment concerning Jesus. The hymns of the book of Revelation resound with the words "You are worthy." This is the language of valuation.

As a young scholarly monk, Michael enthusiastically embraced the call of the Second Vatican Council for Religious Communities to return to their original charism. The Benedictine practice of *lectio divina* has always required that monks immerse themselves in the Scriptures. In this respect, Benedictine spirituality has generated commitments and enthusiasms across historic confessional lines. The Evangelical theologian Kevin Vanhoozer reflects this Benedictine spirituality when he writes, "Any theology that is not a response to revelation is, strictly speaking, *irresponsible*, in the sense that it is not a response to God's own self-presentation."[2] Michael's many

---

[2] Kevin J. Vanhoozer, *Remythologizing Theology: Divine Action, Passion, and Authorship* (Cambridge, UK: Cambridge University Press, 2010), 469.

books reflect an appreciation of the continuing relevance of the ancient, precritical approach to the Bible. He also clearly writes with an awareness of the insights of recent biblical scholarship, even if at times he is not backward in advising the young novice simply to turn the page of a biblical commentary if he discerns that it is only intended to show how erudite the author is!

No doubt Michael's concern for *orthomorphy* has been shaped by the poetic and mystical biblical writers themselves. John of Patmos struggled to capture in words something of what he saw when he was given a peep through an open door into heaven. His symbolic language is marked by restraint, particularly when it comes to depicting God. Repeatedly he finds himself resorting to the use of qualifying words and phrases. In writing about his opening vision of the risen Lord, he says, "his face was *like* the sun" (Rev 1:16). He employs suggestion rather than description to convey the dazzling, staggering majesty, and "unfathomableness" of God. The one seated on the throne "*looks like* jasper and carnelian, and around the throne is a rainbow that *looks like* an emerald" (Rev 4:3). This is language showing the weight it bears, the weight of a Word from outside ordinary categories. John's vision is full of exclamations. He is utterly overwhelmed by the experience of God. As one commentator on Revelation puts it, "it is a great mistake to read this fiery, passionate and poetic spirit as though he were composing a pedantic piece of scientific prose. He is painting vivid pictures and it does not matter in the slightest that the details do not harmonize readily."[3] Revelation is a book that offends human rationality. But what is upsetting to the theologian concerned simply about *orthodoxy* is thrilling to the contemplative who is also concerned about *orthomorphy*.

What is true of the biblical seers can also be said of the psalmists. The psalms are the heartbeat of the monastic Offices.

[3] Leon Morris, *Revelation* (London: Tyndale Press, 1969), 123.

Michael has often said that in order to appreciate these ancient poets we must "befriend" them. Such befriending involves recognizing, in the first place, that the psalms belong to the overall category of poetry, and they contain the nonrational components that are typical of poetry, such as strong imagery, exaggeration, exuberance, repetition, and frequent divergence from the canons of rational thought. Artistic involvement and intuition are associated with the nondominant right side of the brain, whereas the left hemisphere specializes in analytic, sequential, and logical thought. Poetry helps us to relate to God as whole persons, with the right hemisphere as well as the left hemisphere of the brain.

Michael further suggests that "befriending" these ancient poets can be aided by an appreciation of more recent Old Testament scholarship that classifies the psalms into recognizable categories such as songs of praise, laments, thanksgivings, or wisdom psalms. In this way, he maintains, the psalter becomes a less impenetrable mass of confused and confusing elements. To have this kind of understanding in advance helps the reader to latch onto the wavelength of a particular psalm so that it becomes a stepping-stone to prayer rather than a stumbling block. The psalms touch the whole spectrum of human emotions. There is no human experience that cannot be turned back to God in prayer. Even the words of imprecation or cursing, such as those at the end of Psalm 137 that describe what the Babylonians did to the Hebrew children can be used in this way: *O daughter of Babylon, you devastator! Happy shall they be who pay you back what you have done to us! Happy shall they be who take your little ones and dash them against the rock!* (Ps 137:8-9). These words need not be read as a call to violent action—to put someone to death. When they are "befriended" the words can be used for turning the very real human hurt of the Hebrew mothers whose children had been bashed to death back to God in prayer. The psalms, as the heartbeat of the monastic horarium, provide the means whereby diverse human experience can be offered to God.[4]

Appreciation of the beauty and existential dimension of the Scriptures is aided by reading aloud. Michael somewhere points out that Peter the Venerable had not read his Bible for some days because he had laryngitis! Ruminating on the Scriptures was primarily an oral function. In a similar way, Saint Augustine highlighted the values of chanting the psalms when he said, "whoever sings, prays twice." In order for the words to affect the soul, they need music. Music integrates the soul, uniting reason, beauty, and passion.

In his doctoral studies, Michael immersed himself in the mystical writing of Bernard of Clairvaux. As a result, he has frequently drawn attention to the way in which Bernard's homilies are characterized by beauty. An example of this can be seen in the *Ode to Eternal Day* within one of Bernard's sermons on the Song of Songs, in which he depicts heaven in terms of the sights and seasons familiar to him in the valleys around his monastery in Clairvaux, France. In one of his many sermons on the Song of Songs, Bernard waxes elegant: "O true noontide, fullness of warmth and light, trysting place of the sun; noontide that blots out shadows, that dries up marshes, that banishes evil odors! O perpetual solstice, day that will never decline to evening! O noontide light, with your springtime freshness, your summer-like gracefulness, your autumnal fruitfulness and . . . your winter of quiescence and leisure."[5]

---

[4] See Michael Casey, *The Undivided Heart: The Western Monastic Approach to Contemplation* (Petersham, MA: St Bede's Publications, 1994), 79–94.

[5] Bernard, SC 33:6; SBOp 1:237; *On the Song of Songs II*, trans. Kilian Walsh, CF 7 (Kalamazoo, MI: Cistercian Publications, 1976), 149. For Michael's translation of this passage, see *Athirst for God: Spiritual Desire in Bernard of Clairvaux's Sermons on the Song of Songs*, CS 77 (Kalamazoo, MI: Cistercian Publications, 1987), 222.

Commenting on this passage, Michael, with his own inimitable wit, draws attention to the fact that the valleys around Citeaux were full of stagnant swamps that would give off a foul odor. Only the warmth of the sun could disperse the stench. Likewise, only the warmth of divine love could disperse the stench of human sin. Moreover, Michael added, heaven, like Melbourne, contains all four seasons in one, each a facet of overall beauty!

Michael often makes truth attractive by punctuating his lectures and writing with a wry sense of humor. It may be just a brief aside, as for instance when he quotes a few words in Latin in the midst of a lecture and then warns his listeners, "I charge more for Latin!" or makes reference in a lecture on the Benedictine vow of stability to the fact that his view of heaven is the view of the monastery in the *rearview* mirror of the car! He also has an eye for an amusing illustration in the writings of the Fathers. He tells us that Saint Bernard often likened prayer to a belch, *ructus*: "A person ate his bread, devoured God's word and allowed it to percolate through his whole being, assimilating it through the process of rumination. When he had made God's word fully his own a response builds up within him and finally bursts forth; this is prayer. *Eructavit cor meum verbum bonum*; my heart belched out a good word."[6]

In the spirit of the Second Vatican Council, Michael has taken the charism of the founder of his Order to heart. Bernard, he tells us, wrote that a likely candidate for contemplation must be one who "has not only lived for Christ, but has done so for a long time." May Fr. Michael continue to persevere as a *poet of the logos* for many more years for the sake of the "spiritual ecumenism" that his lectures and publications have encouraged.

---

[6] Michael Casey, "The Pilgrim's Lament," TJ 13 (1977): 352.

Contributors

David Barry, OSB, has been a monk of Trinity Abbey, New Norcia, in Western Australia since 1955. He studied at Sant'Anselmo in Rome, gaining the licence in theology. He has worked as a monastic formator and retreat director for many years. He earned his BA (Hons) in classics at the University of Western Australia in 1975, and later a Dip. Ed. from Murdoch University. He spent 1997 teaching English in China and 2002 doing archival research in Europe, scanning or photocopying letters and other documents written by or about New Norcia's founders, Dom Serra and Dom Salvado. His publications include the translations of Smaragdus of Saint-Mihiel's *Commentary on the Rule of Saint Benedict*, CS 212 (Kalamazoo, MI: Cistercian Publications, 2007), and Smaragdus's *The Crown of Monks*, CS 245 (Kalamazoo, MI: Cistercian Publications, 2013).

Bernardo Bonowitz, OCSO, became a Roman Catholic in 1968. He entered the Society of Jesus in 1973 and transferred to the Cistercians at Saint Joseph's Abbey, Massachusetts, in 1982. He served as novice director until his election as superior of the monastery of Novo Mundo in Brazil in 1996. He has written several books in Portuguese, and his book *Saint Bernard's Three-Course Banquet* was published by Cistercian Publications (MW 39) in 2013.

Mary Collins, OSB, has been a member of the Benedictine community of Mount St. Scholastica, Atchison, Kansas, since 1957.

She earned her PhD in sacramental and liturgical studies at The Catholic University of America in Washington, DC, where she later became a full professor and has served as professor emerita in the School of Theology and Religious Studies since 1999. She has also taught on the faculties of Benedictine College, Atchison, and the University of Kansas at Lawrence. From 1999 to 2005, she served as prioress of Mount St. Scholastica in Atchison. Mary has been a pioneer in the liturgical renewal in the United States since Vatican II. She has written or edited some fourteen books and written numerous articles and essays in collected works and in journals both scholarly and pastoral. She also served on the advisory commission of the International Commission on English in the Liturgy and directed its Psalter project. She is one of North America's premier liturgical theologians.

Austin Cooper, OMI, has been a priest with the Oblates of Mary Immaculate since 1956. He holds a master of arts from The Catholic University of America and a doctorate of philosophy from Monash University. He was the first master of Catholic Theological College in Victoria, Australia, and also president of the Melbourne College of Divinity (now the University of Divinity). He has taught Reformation History and Christian Spirituality at Monash University, and English Spirituality at Trinity College in the University of Melbourne and at the Centre for Christian Spirituality, Randwick, New South Wales. He is presently the senior fellow of Catholic Theological College and member of the Departments of Church History and of Pastoral and General Studies. His main academic interests are the Oxford Movement and the English tradition of spirituality. He has published works on Julian of Norwich and *The Cloud of Unknowing* and many articles on modern history and the history of English spirituality. His most recent publication is a book entitled *John Henry Newman: A Developing Spirituality* (St Pauls Publications, 2012). In 2004 he was made a member of the Order of Australia (AM) for services to theological education.

Elias Dietz, OCSO, has been a monk of the Abbey of Gethsemani since 1988. He has published studies on early Cistercian authors in various journals, including *Cistercian Studies Quarterly*, of which he was editor from 2003 to 2007. Since 2008 he has served as abbot of his community.

Bernhard A. Eckerstorfer, OSB, is a monk of Kremsmünster Abbey in Austria. He studied theology and geography in Salzburg, Vienna, and the United States. He earned an MTS at Mount Angel Seminary College, Oregon, with a thesis on Benedictine missionaries on Vancouver Island and a *Magister theologiae* degree at Salzburg University. For his doctoral dissertation on American theology (Salzburg, 1999) he studied at the Universities of Duke and Yale. He is the author of *Kirche in der postmodernen Welt. Der Beitrag George Lindbecks zu einer neuen Verhältnisbestimmung* (Innsbruck/Vienna: Tyrolia-Verlag, 2001), S. 403, and *Unterwegs im Geist des Konzils*, Mit einem Vorwort von Bischof Maximilian Aichern (Pettenbach: Micha-Verlag, 2014), S. 132. Dom Bernhard serves his monastery as director of vocations, novice master, and formation director. His lectures and articles focus on how the Church and monastic life can both fulfill their mission in the postmodern world.

Elizabeth Freeman is senior lecturer in Medieval European History at the University of Tasmania. Her research focus is the medieval Cistercian monastic order, especially the Cistercians in England. Her earlier work examined Cistercian historical writing, while her more recent work examines Cistercian nuns in their own right as well as the interactions—both institutional and personal—between the male and female expressions of the medieval Cistercian Order. She is the author of *Narratives of a New Order: Cistercian Historical Writing in England 1150–1220*, and she has published articles in *Cistercian Studies Quarterly* and *Cîteaux: Commentarii Cistercienses*. She has published recent chapters in *The Cambridge Companion to the Cistercian Order*, ed. Mette Birkedal Bruun (Cambridge: Cambridge University Press, 2013), and in *The Cistercian Arts: From the 12th to the 21st Century*, ed. Terryl N. Kinder and Roberto Cassanelli (Montreal: McGill-Queen's University Press, 2015).

Terrence Kardong, OSB, has been a monk of Assumption Abbey in Richardton, North Dakota, since 1956. Since 1982, he has served as editor of the *American Benedictine Review*. His many books include *Pillars of Community: Four Rules of Pre-Benedictine Monastic Life* (Collegeville, MN: Liturgical Press, 2010) and *Day by Day with Saint Benedict* (Collegeville, MN: Liturgical Press, 2005). He has also produced highly regarded translations and commentaries of the Rule of Saint Benedict and Saint Gregory the Great's *Life of Saint Benedict*.

Helen Lombard, SGS, entered the Good Samaritan Sisters in 1961. In 1978 she was appointed to facilitate community renewal, and during this time, together with Cistercian monks from Tarrawarra Abbey, she developed and administered study programs on the Rule of Saint Benedict and its sources, now published by Michael Casey and David Tomlins as *Introducing Benedict's Rule: A Program of Formation* (St. Ottilien: EOS Verlag, 2006). She was superior of her congregation from 1981 until 1993. During this time, she served as president of the Major Superiors of Australia and was involved in the establishment of the *Communio Internationalis Benedictinarum* (CIB). Helen was provost at Notre Dame University in Western Australia from 1994 to 1998 and taught and developed programs for the study on the Rule and its sources for both the sisters of her congregation and the monks of New Norcia. She was sought after as a speaker both in Australia and overseas. Tragically, Helen died in a car accident in 2000.

Margaret Malone, SGS, is a member of the Sisters of the Good Samaritan of the Order of Saint Benedict. She has been a lecturer at Australian Catholic University, where she taught sacraments, liturgy, and social justice. In 1980–1981 she studied at Catholic University of America, completing an MA with a specialization in spirituality. She completed her doctoral studies at Australian National University in 2000 with a thesis titled "Things Both Old and New—A Study of Authority in the Rule of Benedict." Her main work now is in teaching the Rule of Saint Benedict throughout her Order and at the Benedictine Community of New Norcia. She also gives retreats and workshops both internationally and nationally.

Katharine Massam is coordinator of Studies in Church History and associate professor at the University of Divinity, Melbourne. Her research explores intersections between Christian tradition and wider culture in postcolonial settler societies, including Australia. She writes on the history of Christian spirituality (especially Benedictine traditions), cross-cultural encounter in the Australian mission context, and the dynamics of work and leisure. She is especially interested in methodologies that open up neglected sources and experience. Her publications include *Sacred Threads: Catholic Spirituality in Australia* (UNSW Press, 1996), a range of refereed articles, and a forthcoming monograph: *Between: Benedictine Missionary Women in Australia*. Katharine is an oblate of the Benedictine Community of New Norcia. She brings twenty years of experience in offering workshops and retreats on Benedictine themes to community groups.

Constant J. Mews is professor within the School of Philosophical, Historical and International Studies, Monash University, where he is also director of the Centre for Religious Studies. He has published widely on medieval thought, ethics, and religious culture, with particular reference to the writings of Abelard, Heloise, Hildegard of Bingen, and their contemporaries, including *Abelard and Heloise* (New York: Oxford University

Press, 2005) and *The Lost Love Letters of Heloise and Abelard: Perceptions of Dialogue in Twelfth-Century France*, 2nd ed. (London: Palgrave Macmillan, 2008). His research interests range from the early Middle Ages to late medieval religious and intellectual culture, as well as the interface between various religious and ethical traditions.

Francisco Rafael de Pascual, OCSO, is a monk of the Abbey of Viaceli, Cantabria, Spain. He is lecturer and professor on the Monastic Formation Program in Spain. His writings about Cistercian life, history, and spirituality are well known in Spain, and he has been the editor of *Cistercium: Revista Monástica Cisterciense* since 1992. His research interest focuses on the life and works of Thomas Merton, a number of whose works he has translated. He also coordinates a number of "Thomas Merton Encounters" in Spain.

Carmel Posa, SGS, has been a sister of the Good Samaritan of the Order of Saint Benedict since 1989. She completed a master of arts in theology in 1996, from Saint John's University, Collegeville, Minnesota, majoring in monastic studies, and was awarded a doctorate from the Melbourne College of Divinity in 2009. She has been a senior lecturer in theology at Notre Dame University of Australia, and is a founding dean of the New Norcia Institute for Benedictine Studies and coeditor of *Tjurunga: An Australasian Benedictine Review*.

Graeme Rutherford was the assistant bishop of the Anglican Diocese of Newcastle in NSW, Australia. While in that role, he was the Anglican cochair of the Australian Anglican and Roman Catholic Conversations (AustARC) and the chair of the Advisory Council for Anglican Religious Life. He has been a regular visitor to Tarrawarra Abbey for over fifty years. He qualified as a Scholar in Theology with the Australian College of Theology and holds an MA in theology from Durham University, UK. He is the author of a number of books, including one in which he shares his love of Tarrawarra Abbey: *Watchers in the Morning: A Spirituality for Contemporary Christians* (Dublin: Gill and Macmillan, 1994). He has written two short biblical commentaries: *The Heart of Christianity: Romans 1 to 8*, and *The Uniqueness of Jesus: Hebrews 1 to 13. The Potter God* was written as a Lenten Study for the Australian Anglican Church. With his son Jonathan, he coauthored *Beloved Father, Beloved Son: A Conversation about Faith between a Bishop and his Atheist Son.* His most recent book is entitled *A Little Book about a Big Story: God's Grand Plan from Creation to New Creation* (Eugene, OR: Wipf and Stock, 2015).

Manuela Scheiba, OSB, has been a member of the Benedictine abbey at Alexanderdorf, Germany, since 1988. From 1996 to 1999 she studied theology and monastic studies at Sant'Anselmo, the Benedictine university in Rome, and completed her doctoral thesis, on twentieth-century commentaries on the Rule of Saint Benedict dealing with the topic of obedience to the superior in 2007, under the direction of Aquinata Böckmann, OSB. Manuela teaches monastic studies at Sant'Anselmo and gives workshops and lectures on the Rule of Saint Benedict throughout the Benedictine world. She is also presently undertaking postgraduate studies in Eastern Monasticism at the Pontifical Oriental Institute in Rome.

Columba Stewart, OSB, has been a monk of Saint John's Abbey, Collegeville, Minnesota, since 1981. He completed his doctoral studies at Oxford in 1989. He is currently teaching monastic studies at Saint John's School of Theology Seminary and is executive director of the Hill Museum and Manuscript Library. Fr. Columba's publications include *Cassian the Monk* (New York: Oxford University Press, 1998) and *Prayer and Community: The Benedictine Tradition* (London: Darton, Longman & Todd, 1998).

Brendan Thomas, OSB, is a monk of Belmont Abbey, England, where he is currently novice master. Since 2002, he has been the director of the Monastic Formators' Programme, a three-month international course for Benedictines and Cistercians held in Rome and Assisi. He regularly gives retreats in various places around the world.

David Tomlins, OCSO, was North Queensland born and bred. He was destined, or doomed, to be a Cistercian, as his parents married on the feast of Saint Benedict, and he received his early education in Ayr from the Sisters of the Good Samaritan of the Order of St. Benedict. He entered Tarrawarra Abbey an hour before Michael Casey, and so, according to the Rule, has always been his senior! David studied for his STL in spirituality at the Gregorian University, Rome (1969–1971), has taught in the Tarrawarra formation program for many years, and was abbot of his community (1988–2012). He has now adopted the title of "Feather Duster" and rejoices in caring for the community's infirm and elderly.

Select Bibliography
of Michael Casey

Books

Cistercians and Cluniacs: St Bernard's Apologia to Abbot William, translation and notes. CF 1. Kalamazoo, MI: Cistercian Publications, 1970; repr. 1985.

Athirst for God: Spiritual Desire in Bernard of Clairvaux's Sermons on the Song of Songs. CS 77. Kalamazoo, MI: Cistercian Publications, 1988.

Towards God: The Western Tradition of Contemplation. Melbourne: Collins Dove, 1989; repr. 1991; rev. ed. Blackburn: Dove, 1995.

Toward God: the Ancient Wisdom of Western Prayer (revision of previous item). Ligouri: Triumph Books, 1996.

How the Word Visits the Soul. Tarrawarra, Victoria: The Abbey Press, 1990; repr. 1992.

Bernard of Clairvaux: Man, Monk, Mystic. Kalamazoo, MI: Cistercian Publications, 1991.

The Undivided Heart: The Western Monastic Approach to Contemplation. Petersham, MA: St. Bede's Publications, 1994.

The Art of Sacred Reading. Melbourne: Dove, 1995. US ed.: *Sacred Reading: The Ancient Art of Lectio Divina*. Ligouri: Triumph Books, 1996.

A River of Love: Frederic Ozanam and the Society of St. Vincent de Paul. Dublin: Columba Press, 1997.

Bernard of Clairvaux. "The Parables." Translation in *The Parables and the Sentences*, edited by Maureen M. O'Brien, 9–102. CF 55. Kalamazoo, MI: Cistercian Publications, 2000.

Return to the Heart: Daily Reflections for Lent. Denton, MO: Creative Communications, 2000.

Truthful Living: St. Benedict's Teaching on Humility. Petersham, MA: St. Bede's Publications, 1999. Repr. as *Guide to Living in the Truth: St. Benedict's Teaching on Humility*. Liguori, MO: Liguori, 2001.

Fully Human, Fully Divine: An Interactive Christology. Liguori, MO: Liguori, 2004.

Strangers to the City: Reflections on the Beliefs and Values of the Rule of Saint Benedict. Brewster, MA: Paraclete Press, 2005.

An Unexciting Life: Reflections on Benedictine Spirituality. Petersham, MA: St. Bede's Publications, 2005.

Advent Today: Welcoming Christ Every Day. Fenton, MO: Creative Communications, 2005.

Introducing Benedict's Rule: A Program of Formation, and David Tomlins. Sankt Ottilien: Eos, 2006.

Tarrawarra Abbey: Cistercian Monastery, Yarra Glen. Yarra Glen: Tarrawarra Abbey, 2008.

Listening to God. St. Meinrad, IN: Abbey Press, 2010.

The Road to Eternal Life: Reflections on the Prologue of Benedict's Rule. Collegeville, MN: Liturgical Press, 2011.

The Art of Winning Souls: Pastoral Care of New Members. MW 35. Collegeville, MI: Cistercian Publications, 2012.

Seventy-Four Tools for Good Living: Reflections on the Fourth Chapter of Benedict's Rule. Collegeville, MN: Liturgical Press, 2014.

Book Chapters

"The 'Humanitas' of the Benedictine Tradition." In *A Man with an Idea: St Benedict of Narsia,* edited by John Stanley Martin, 27–35. Melbourne: University of Melbourne, 1981.

"Bernard the Observer." In *Goad and Nail: Studies in Medieval Cistercian History X,* edited by E. Rozanne Elder, 1–20. Kalamazoo, MI: Cistercian Publications, 1985.

"Is There Life after Collegiality?" In *Towards the Summit,* edited by Patrick Hart. Trappist, KY: Gethsemani Abbey, 1987.

"Le Spirituel: Les grands thèmes Bernardins." In *Bernard de Clairvaux: Histoire, Mentalités, Spiritualité,* 605–35. SCh 380. Paris: Les Éditions du Cerf, 1992. Japanese translation and adaptation: *S. Bernardi Opera IV.* Tokyo: Akashi Shobo, 1996.

"Bernard of Clairvaux: Forty Years of Scholarship." In *A Man with an Idea: St. Benedict of Nursia,* edited by John Stanley Martin, 31–45. Melbourne: University of Melbourne, 1992.

"Toward a Methodology for the *Vita Prima*: Translating the First Life into Biography." In *Bernardus Magister: Papers Presented at the Nonacentenary Celebration of the Birth of Saint Bernard of Clairvaux,* edited by John R. Sommerfeldt, 55–70. CS 135. Kalamazoo, MI: Cistercian Publications, 1992.

"*Acedia*." In *The New Dictionary of Catholic Spirituality*, edited by Michael Downey, 4–5. Collegeville, MN: Michael Glazier, 1993.

"*Apatheia*." In *The New Dictionary of Catholic Spirituality*, edited by Michael Downey, 50–51. Collegeville, MN: Michael Glazier, 1993.

"Cistercian Spirituality." In *The New Dictionary of Catholic Spirituality*, edited by Michael Downey, 173–82. Collegeville, MN: Michael Glazier, 1993.

"Western (Latin) Spirituality." In *The New Dictionary of Catholic Spirituality*, edited by Michael Downey, 1021–27. Collegeville, MN: Michael Glazier, 1993.

"The Benedictine Balances." In *Saint Benedict of Nursia: A Way of Wisdom for Today*, 24–25. Paris: Éditions du Signe, 1994.

"The Journey from Fear to Love: Cassian's Road Map." In *Prayer and Spirituality in the Early Church*, vol. 1, edited by Pauline Allen, 181–95. Everton Park, Queensland, Australia: Centre for Early Christian Studies, 1998.

"Saint Bernard of Clairvaux (1090–1153)." In *Encyclopedia of Monasticism*, 143–49. Chicago: Fitzroy Dearborn, 2000.

"Australian Benedictine Spirituality." In *Benedictine Pathways*, edited by The Benedictine Union of Australia and New Zealand, 5–6. 2000.

"The Art of *Lectio Divina*." In *The Benedictine Handbook*, edited by Anthony Marrett-Crosby, 106–9. Norwich, UK: Canterbury Press, 2003.

"Thoughts on Monasticism's Possible Futures." In *A Monastic Vision for the 21st Century: Where Do We Go From Here?*, edited by Patrick Hart, 23–24. MW 8. Collegeville, MN: Cistercian Publications, 2006.

"Moderation: The Key to Permanence." In *The Oblate Life*, edited by Gervase Holdaway, 177–86. Collegeville, MN: Liturgical Press, 2008.

"Reading Saint Bernard: The Man, the Medium, the Message." In *A Companion to Bernard of Clairvaux*, edited by Brian Patrick McGuire, 62–107. Leiden: Brill Academic Publishers, 2011.

"Creating Space for Meditation: Monastic Life and Spirituality as Models of Dedication." In *Askese versus Konsumgesellshaft: Aktualität und Spiritualität von Mönchtum und Ordensleben im 21. Jahrhundert*, edited by Jürgen Henkel and Nikolaus Wyrwoll, 141–47. Bonn: Schiller Verlag, 2013.

"The Cistercian Order since 1600." In *The Cambridge Companion to the Cistercian Order*, edited by Mette Birkedal Bruun, 50–62. Cambridge, UK: Cambridge University Press, 2013.

"The Monastic Art of *Lectio Divina*." In *The Cistercian Arts from the 12th to the 21st Century*, edited by Terryl Kinder and Roberto Cassanelli, 215–22. Montreal: McGill-Queens University Press, 2014.

"A Personal Trajectory." In *We Are Already One: Thomas Merton's Message of Hope*, edited by Henry Gray, 265–67. Louisville, KY: Fons Vitae, 2014.

"From Desert to Cloister." In *Monks Road*, 9–87. Trappist, KY: Gethsemani Abbey, 2015.

"Introduction" to Bernard of Clairvaux. *Monastic Sermons*. Translated by Daniel Griggs, xiii–xxxix. CF 68. Collegeville, MN: Cistercian Publications, 2016.

Articles

"Variations on a Theme." *Tjurunga: An Australasian Benedictine Review* 2 (1971): 5–11.

"The Hard Sayings of RB." *Tjurunga* 3 (1972): 133–43.

"Community and Tradition." *Tjurunga* 4 (1973): 45–58

"The Hermeneutics of Tradition." *Tjurunga* 5 (1973): 39–50

"Discerning the True Values of Monastic Life in a Time of Change." *Regulae Benedicti Studia* 3/4 (1974/1975): 75–88.

"'Balance' in Monastic Life." *Tjurunga* 9 (1975): 5–11.

"Seven Principles of *Lectio Divina*." *Tjurunga* 12 (1976): 69–74.

"Eleven Difficulties in Reading the Fathers." *Tjurunga* 12 (1976): 74–83.

"God's Work and Our Prayer Presence." *Presence* 8 (1976): 4–5.

"The Cloud of Unknowing." *Bread and Wine* 22 (1977): 6–7.

"The Pilgrim's Lament." *Tjurunga* 13 (1977): 297–398.

"Paul's Response to Corinthian Enthusiasm." *Bible Today* 88 (1977): 1075–81.

"The Formative Influence of the Benedictine Community." *Tjurunga* 14 (1977): 7–26.

"Principles of Interpretation and Application of the Rule of Benedict." *Tjurunga* 14 (1977): 33–38.

"The Cloud of Unknowing: A Background Briefing." *Hallel* 5, no. 2 (1977): 151–62.

"Intentio Cordis (RB 52.4)." *Regulae Benedicti Studia* 6/7 (1977/1978): 105–20.

"Thomas Merton within a Tradition of Prayer." CSQ 13, no. 4 (1979): 372–78.

"Merton within a Tradition of Prayer (II)." CSQ 14, no. 1 (1980): 81–92.

"Cardiomimesis." *Tjurunga* 20 (1980): 118–22.

"Saint Benedict's Approach to Prayer." CSQ 15, no. 4 (1980): 327–43.

"1500 Year Influence of St Benedict of Nursia." *Advocate* (10 July 1980): 10–11.

"The Cistercians." *The Tablet* (12 July 1980): 10–11.

"The Monk in the Modern World." *Tjurunga* 21 (1981): 5–24.

"Emotionally Hollow, Esthetically Meaningless and Spiritually Empty: An Inquiry into Theological Discourse." *Colloquium* 14, no. 1 (1981): 54–61.

"Spiritual Desire in St Gregory the Great." CSQ 16, no. 4 (1981): 297–314.

"Leadership in a Benedictine Context." *Tjurunga* 22 (1982): 5–103.

"Nature & Grace in St Bernard of Clairvaux." *Tjurunga* 23 (1982): 39–49.

"Mindfulness of God in the Monastic Tradition." CSQ 17, no. 2 (1982): 111–26.

"Community in the Benedictine Rule." *Regulae Benedicti Studia* 8/9 (1982): 59–65.

"Hymn to St Benedict" [text]. *Tjurunga* 23 (1982): 60.

"The Benedictine Promises." *Tjurunga* 24 (1983): 17–34.

"Saint Bernard of Clairvaux: The Story of the King's Son." CSQ 18, no. 1 (1983): 16–23.

"The Virtue of Friendship in Monastic Tradition." *Tjurunga* 25 (1983): 21–35.

"The Prayer of Psalmody." CSQ 18, no. 2 (1983): 106–20.

"The Story of the Feud between Two Kings" [introduction, translation, and notes]. CSQ 18, no. 3 (1983): 192–200.

"The Prayer of Psalmody." CSQ 18, no. 2 (1983): 106–20.

"The Story of the King's Son Sitting on His Horse" [introduction, translation, and notes]. CSQ 18, no. 3 (1983): 192–200.

"Making Use of RB 1980." CSQ 18, no. 3 (1983): 240–49.

"RB 1980: A Tribute." ABR 34, no. 4 (1983): 331–36.

"The Story of Ecclesia Held Captive in Egypt [introduction]," [translation and notes]. CSQ 19, no. 3 (1984): 248–54.

"The Story of the Three Daughters of the King" [introduction, translation, and notes]. CSQ 20, no. 1 (1985): 21–31.

"Ascetic and Ecclesial: Reflections on RB 73.5." *Tjurunga* 28 (1985): 14–23.

"Strangers to Worldly Ways: RB 4.20." *Tjurunga* 29 (1985): 37–46.

"In Pursuit of Ecstasy: Reflections on Bernard of Clairvaux's *De Diligendo Deo.*" *Monastic Studies* 16 (1985): 139–56.

"Orthopraxy and Interpretation." *Regulae Benedicti Studia* 14/15 (1985/1986): 165–72.

"The Story of the Ethiopian Woman Whom the King's Son Took as His Wife" [introduction, translation, and notes]. CSQ 21, no. 2 (1986): 96–108.

"The Virtue of Patience in the Western Tradition." CSQ 21, no. 1 (1986): 3–23.

"Introduction and Translation of the Sixth Parable of Bernard of Clairvaux." CSQ 21, no. 2 (1986): 96–108.

"Consecrated Chastity: Gertrude the Great." *Tjurunga* 31 (1986): 3–14.

"Introduction and Translation of the Seventh and Eighth Parables of Bernard of Clairvaux." CSQ 22, no. 1 (1987): 37–54.

"Solitariness." *Tjurunga* 33 (1987): 3–21.

"Adding Death to Our Response to Local Culture: An Address to the National Assembly of Major Superiors." *Compass* 21 (1987): 7–11.

"The Dialectic of Solitude and Communion in Cistercian Communities." CSQ 23, no. 4 (1988): 273–309.

"Gertrude of Helfta & Bernard of Clairvaux: A Reappraisal." *Tjurunga* 35 (1988): 3–21; *Cistercienser Chronik* 97, nos. 3–4 (1990): 46–69.

"'How to Pray to God': A Sermon of St Bernard." *Tjurunga* 34 (1988): 21–24.

"Taking Counsel: Reflections on RB 3." *Tjurunga* 37 (1989): 12–19.

"Compassion: Mainspring of Ministry." *Tjurunga* 38 (1990): 3–12.

"Herbert of Clairvaux's Book of Wonderful Happenings." CSQ 25, no. 1 (1990): 37–64.

"Bernard of Clairvaux: The Man behind the Image." *Pacifica* 3, no. 3 (1990): 269–87; repr. as "Saint Bernard: A Man for Our Times." CSQ 25, no. 4 (1990): 257–66.

"Bernard of Clairvaux and the Assumption." *Word and Spirit* 12 (1990): 21–42.

"*In communi vita fratrum*: St Bernard's Teaching on Cenobitic Solitude." *Analecta Cisterciensia* 46 (1990): 243–61.

"El Patrimonio Cisterciense y el nuevo monasticismo: Reflexiones sobre la I parte de las Constituciones." *Cistercium* 186 (1991): 521–38.

"From the Silence of God to the God of Silence." *Tjurunga* 43 (1992): 3–24.

"Merton's Notes on Inner Experience." *Tjurunga* 44 (1993): 30–55.

"Models of Monastic Formation." *Tjurunga* 45 (1993): 3–31.

"Bernard's Biblical Mysticism: Approaching SC 74." *Studies in Spirituality* 4 (1994): 12–30.

"*Quod Experimento Didicimus*: Heuristic Wisdom of St Benedict." *Tjurunga* 48 (1995): 3–22.

"Beatrice of Nazareth (1200–1268): Cistercian Mystic." *Tjurunga* 50 (1996): 44–70.

"Beatrice of Nazareth: The Seven Modes of Love" [trans]. *Tjurunga* 50 (1996): 71–82.

"The Value of Stability." CSQ 31, no. 3 (1996): 278–301.

"The Practice of *Lectio Divina*." CSQ 31, no. 4 (1996): 456–76.

"The Deconstruction of Prayer." *Tjurunga* 51 (1996): 91–102.

"Mystical Experiences: The Cistercian Tradition." *Tjurunga* 52 (1997): 64–87.

"Sacramentality and Monastic Consecration." *Word and Spirit* 18 (1998): 27–48.

"Towards the Cistercian Millennium." *Tjurunga* 54 (1998): 57–67; *Collectanea Cisterciensia* 60, no. 1 (1998): 20–30.

"The Meaning of Poverty for Bernard of Clairvaux." CSQ 33, no. 4 (1998): 427–38.

"Merton's Teaching on the 'Common Will' and What the Journals Tell Us." *The Merton Annual* 12 (1999): 62–84.

"*Supensa Expectatio*: The Condition of the Spiritual Seeker in the Sermons of Guerric of Igny." *Studies in Spirituality* 9 (1999): 78–92.

"Gyrovague's Delight: A Benedictine CD-ROM." *Tjurunga* 57 (1999): 22.

"Thomas Merton's Journals: Condensed Version." *Tjurunga* 57 (1999): 40.

"A Lover of Letters, a Desirer of God, an Educator." *Tjurunga* 58 (2000): 5–10.

"Desire and Desires in Western Tradition." In *Desire: To Have or not to Have*. Canberra, The Humanita Foundation: Occasional Papers No. 2 (2000): 3–31.

"The Dynamic Unfolding of the Benedictine Charism." ABR 51, no. 2 (2000): 149–68.

"Marketing Monastic Tradition within Monasteries." *Tjurunga* 60 (2001): 27–52.

"Hildegard of Bingen: Biographical Sources." *Tjurunga* 60 (2001): 95–96.

"The RB and Inculturation: A Formation Perspective." *Tjurunga* 62 (2002): 15–46.

"Abbot Francis Acharya." *Tjurunga* 62 (2002): 93–97.

"Laws, Values & Practices for Early Cistercians." *Tjurunga* 63 (2002): 99–104.

"Bernard and the Crisis at Morimond: Did the Order Exist in 1124?" CSQ 38, no. 2 (2003): 119–75.

"De tien woorden van Benedictus." *Benedictijns Tijdschrift* 65, no. 1 (2004): 2–19.

"A Benedictine Decalogue: Ten Words from St Benedict." *Tjurunga* 66 (2004): 34–47.

"The Discipline of Psalmody: RB 19." *Tjurunga* 68 (2005): 57–79.

"Monastic Tonsure: The Western Tradition." *Tjurunga* 69 (2005): 75–91.

"Kommunitas Benediktini." *Samadi* 10 (2005): 21–24.

"The Western Monastic Art of *Lectio Divina*." *The Eye of the Heart* 2 (2006): 5–32.

"Salmodiai Sabiamente: A disciplina da Salmodia—RB 19." *Revista Benedictina* 3, no. 18 (2006): 3–31.

"Homily on the Occasion of the Sesquicentenary." *Tjurunga* 71 (2006): 26–30.

"Desire and Desires in Western Tradition." *Tjurunga* 71 (2006): 62–92.

"A Visit to the Monastery of La Trappe in 1817." *Tjurunga* 73 (2007): 26–40.

"*Suspensa expectatio*: Guerric d'Igny et l'attente de Dieu." *Collectanea Cisterciensia* 69 (2007): 41–59.

"La développement dynamique du charisme bénédictin." *Collectanea Cisterciensia* 69 (2007): 249–67.

"Ein benediktinishere Dekalog: Zehn Worte aus der RB für das 21. Jahrhudert." *Cistercienser Chronik* 114 (2007): 223–51.

"Disgnosis and Discernment: *Ut Sapiens Medicus.*" *Tjurunga* 74 (2008): 91–96.

"Modelling: A Challenge for Formators." *Tjurunga* 75 (2008): 18–30.

"The Failings of Monks in Guerric's Sermons." CSQ 43, no. 4 (2008): 439–64.

"Lo sviluppo dinamico del carisma benedettino." *Vita Nostra* 37, no. 1 (2008): 16–30.

"El deseo y los deseos en la tración occidental." *Cistercium* 60, no. 250 (2008): 103–38.

"An Early Teacher of Christian Mysticism: Evagrius of Pontus (345–399)." *Tjurunga* 76 (2009): 24–44.

"Manual Work in the Rule and Beyond." *Tjurunga* 78 (2010): 38–63.

"An Introduction to Ælred's Chapter Discourses." CSQ 45, no. 3 (2010): 279–314.

"In Anticipation of an Abbatial Election." *Tjurunga* 78 (2010): 72–100.

"From Being to Consciousness: The Journey to Spirit." *Tjurunga* 80 (2011): 5–25.

"In Praise of Murmuring." *Tjurunga* 80 (2011): 61–75.

"Sermon of Aelred of Rievaulx" [trans.]. *Tjurunga* 80 (2011): 84–92.

"The Book of Experience: The Western Monastic Art of *Lectio Divina*." *Tjurunga* 81 (2011): 35–58.

"Writing for Publication in Tjurunga." *Tjurunga* 83 (2012): 25–47.

"Die Autonomie der Klöster." *Erbe und Auftrag: Monastiche Welt* 89, no. 1 (2013): 7–21.

"Réflexion sur le Prologue de la Règle de saint Benoît." *Liens cisterciens* 25 (2013): 35–42.

"Autonomy." *Tjurunga* 84 (2014): 5–10.

"Conversatio e Riforma." *Inter Fratres* 64, no. 2 (2014): 113–27.

"The Contemplative Life: On Slowing Down Production by Elongating Wear." *Vestoj: The Journal of Sartorial Matters* 5 (2014): 21–27.

"Monasticism: Past and Future." ABR 65 (2014): 176–93, 296–311.

"The Word Became Text and Dwelt Among Us." *Tjurunga* 86 (2014): 27–39.

"Thomas Merton: Nomad of the Spirit." *Tjurunga* 87 (2015): 6–10.

"Un décalogue bénédictin." *Collectanea Cisterciensia* 73 (2011): 305–20, 386–403.

"Verkünde das Wort: Die geistliche Konferenz des Abtes." *Erbe und Auftrag* 88 (2012): 64–67.

"A Bernardine Plan for Monastic Formation in the Twenty–First Century." CSQ 51, no. 1 (2016): 519.

Hymns

"As Evening Spreads the Earth Grows Still." In *Nunc Dimittis: Night Prayer of the Church as Celebrated at Gort Muire*, edited by Margaret Daly, 41. Dublin: Veritas, 1991.

"O Lord of Light and Endless Day." In *Nunc Dimittis: Night Prayer of the Church as Celebrated at Gort Muire*, edited by Margaret Daly, 47. Dublin: Veritas, 1991.

"Who Can Scale the Lord's High Mountain?" In *Hymns for Prayer and Praise*, edited by John Harper, 195, no. 205. Norwich, UK: Canterbury Press, 1996.

"Word out of Silence." In *Hymns for Prayer and Praise*, edited by John Harper, 244, no. 230. Norwich, UK: Canterbury Press, 1996.